Signals, Systems, and Signal Processing

WOLFRAM ✦ eTEXTBOOK SERIES

Signals, Systems, and Signal Processing

A COMPUTATIONAL APPROACH

Mariusz Jankowski

Signals, Systems, and Signal Processing: A Computational Approach
by Mariusz Jankowski
Copyright © 2025 by Wolfram Media, Inc.

Wolfram Media, Inc. | wolfram-media.com

ISBN 978-0-9650532-9-7 (paperback)
ISBN 978-1-57955-093-6 (digital online)
ISBN 978-1-57955-094-3 (Kindle)

Library of Congress Control Number: 2024944759

This book is based on the Wolfram U interactive course Signals, Systems
and Signal Processing: wolfr.am/WolframU-SSSP

For information about permission to reproduce selections from this book, write to
permissions@wolfram.com.

Typeset with Wolfram Notebooks: wolfram.com/notebooks

Access the interactive Wolfram
Notebook edition of this textbook:

wolfr.am/eTextbook-SSSP

Opening these notebooks will require
Mathematica, Wolfram|One, or Wolfram Player.

Most organizations have a site license for Mathematica.
To find out if you have access, visit wolfr.am/siteinfo.

If you don't have access through your organization,
visit wolfr.am/downloads.

Contents

Fourier Analysis (Discrete)

Laplace Transform

z-Transform

Sampling and Filter Design

Preface

The topics discussed in this text are a mainstay of almost every electrical, computer, and biomedical engineering program in the United States and the world. In the US, they are typically taught in the second or third year of a four-year undergraduate program and provide a crucial gateway to more advanced engineering topics, such as control, communications, digital signal processing, image processing, machine learning, and more. They lie at the core of many applications: telecommunications, audio signal processing, speech recognition, computer vision, financial and genomic data analysis, sonar and radar, Internet-of-Things services, and AI-enabled systems. However, as I have observed and which I believe is widely shared by many engineering educators, a course on signals and systems, as it is commonly called, is one of the more difficult courses in a student's undergraduate experience. Many struggle with the mathematical skills required to deal with the multitude of concepts and methods introduced in the course.

To help students overcome some of the barriers they face in mastering its content, from my earliest teaching days, I have incorporated Wolfram Language into my pedagogy. First and foremost, it is a symbolic language with state-of-the-art algebraic capabilities essential to performing calculations of the type that are fundamental to a course on signals and systems and many other engineering fields, often using familiar mathematical notation. Its vast and excellent graphical and interactive functionality makes it easy to illustrate, visualize and actively explore difficult mathematical concepts. Finally, its advanced and efficient numeric algorithms and data handling capabilities allow for rapid prototyping of computations and solutions to practical problems otherwise inaccessible to a more traditional learning environment. This textbook is a culmination of many years of continued experimentation with Wolfram Language in developing lecture notes, examples, illustrations, exams, and laboratory experiments, all greatly assisted by the feedback that I have received from hundreds of my students. The book's concise but comprehensive content and its many fully worked-out, step-by-step examples and exercises should be of great value to current and future engineering students, but also to any engineer, researcher, or self-learner wishing to review or master the basic concepts and methods of signals, linear time-invariant (LTI) systems, and signal processing.

I hope you will enjoy reading and interacting with this text and the associated notebooks as much as I have enjoyed developing them. With over one hundred examples and over two hundred fully solved exercises, I hope it will help you understand and master this difficult but incredibly important and exciting subject.

Acknowledgments

I would like to thank my students and colleagues at the University of Southern Maine as well as all at Wolfram Research who have encouraged me and helped in bringing this project to its successful conclusion. Lastly, Judyta, Malinka and Leshka, thank you for all your love.

Signals and Systems

1 | Introduction to Signals and Systems

Signals, whether analog or digital, can be represented mathematically as functions of one or more independent variables. For example, a speech signal could be represented by acoustic pressure as a function of time, while a picture could be represented as a brightness function of two spatial variables.

A system is any circuit, algorithm, mechanism, or process that transforms some input signal into an output signal. In this book, the focus will be on an important category of systems known as linear time-invariant (LTI), or, equivalently, linear shift-invariant (LSI), systems with the goal of building a thorough understanding of how signals passing through such systems are modified by them.

Continuous Time and Analog Signals

Analog signals originate from all kinds of natural physical phenomena or are created by instruments and equipment built by people. They are typically represented by continuous functions of one or more independent variables. The dependent variable, the value of the function, can be any real number.

The human voice, other sounds either natural or produced by musical instruments, and electrical waves in an electrocardiogram or the recording of ground motion in a seismograph are all common examples of analog signals that can be captured, played back, and analyzed

Discrete Time and Digital Signals

A discrete-time signal is in its simplest form just a list of real or complex values. Signals, as sequences of numbers, arise naturally in many areas of human activity since many phenomena you might be interested in measuring and recording are countably finite:

- Daily amount of funds in a bank account
- Daily value of a publicly traded company

In[•]:=**DateListPlot [FinancialData ["AAPL", "Jan. 1, 2000"] , PlotRange → All]**

Out[•]=

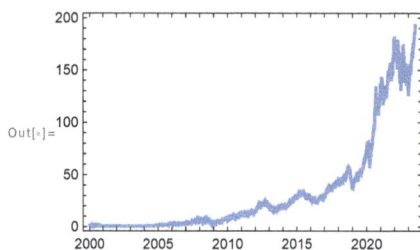

- The number of items produced in a manufacturing plant over some period of time
- Yield per acre of any harvested plant or crop on a farm
- Pixels in an image captured with a digital camera

In[•]:=**ExampleData [{ "TestImage", "Apples" }]**

Out[•]=

- Samples in a digital audio recording

In[•]:=**ExampleData [{ "Audio", "Apollo11SmallStep" }] / / AudioPlot**

Out[•]=

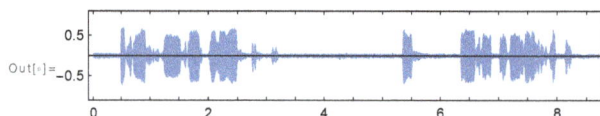

In a digital signal, the data range is also discretized, encoded using a finite number of bits. For example, voice or image data is typically encode using 8 bits per sample, while high-fidelity audio uses 16, 20, or even 24 bits per sample.

Sampling

Discrete-time signals also arise from a process called sampling. Given a continuous-time signal $x(t)$, a discrete-time signal $y[n]$ is typically obtained by evaluating $x(t)$ at uniformly spaced intervals

$$y[n] = x(n\,T)$$

where variable n is an integer and T is a real value known as the sampling step or period. The following shows a continuous-time signal $x(t)$ and its samples $x(n\,T)$ using the sampling step $T = 0.1$

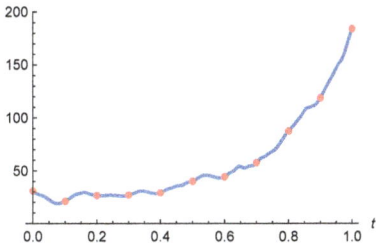

Here is the resulting discrete-time signal $y[n]$

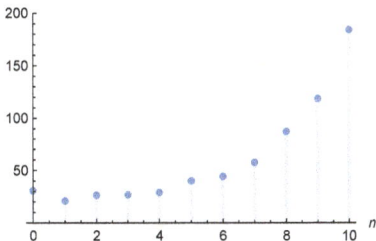

In digital audio, some typical values of sampling periods T are:

- $\frac{1}{8000}$ second (voice data)

- $\frac{1}{44\,100}$ second (CD-quality audio)

- $\frac{1}{192\,000}$ second (DVD audio)

In a digital signal, the data range is also discretized, typically encoded using 8 bits for voice data and low-quality audio or 16, 20, or 24 bits for high-fidelity audio data.

A detailed discussion of sampling will follow later in the book.

Continuous-Time Systems—RC Circuit

For the purposes of this book, a continuous-time system S is any electrical circuit, mechanism, or process that transforms an input signal into an output signal.

Electrical circuits, such as the series interconnection of a resistor and capacitor shown here, are examples of LTI systems familiar to practically all engineering students

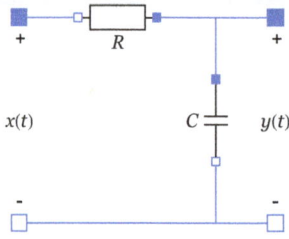

It is well known that the input-output relation in this circuit can be modeled with the following differential equation

$$RC\, y'(t) + y(t) = x(t)$$

This shows the response of the RC circuit (capacitor voltage) to three common inputs:

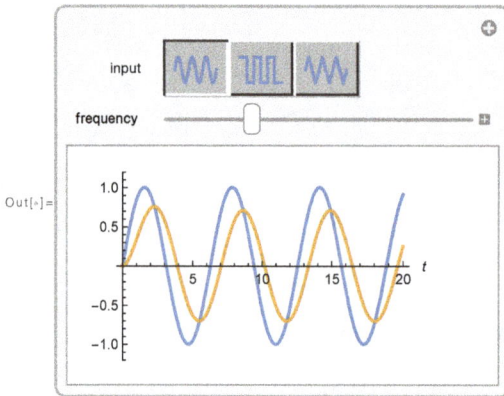

Observe that the RC circuit attenuates high-frequency sinusoids more than low-frequency ones. For this reason, it is known as a lowpass filter (more on this topic later).

Discrete-Time Systems—Bank Account

Turning to another familiar example, consider a bank account (or investment) with an r % annual rate of return. The relationship between the monthly output (balance) $y[n]$ and input (deposits) $x[n]$ with r as the percent annual average return is defined by the following first-order linear difference equation with constant coefficients

$$y[n] - \left(1 + \frac{r}{1200}\right) y[n-1] = x[n]$$

It is similar in many ways to the differential equation representing the RC circuit described earlier.

For example, assume you deposit $333 on a monthly basis into some investment account with an average annual return of 5.5%. Additionally, assume you opened the account with a $1000 initial deposit.

This results in the following difference equation

$$y[n] - \left(1 + \frac{5.5}{1200}\right) y[n-1] = 333, \qquad y[-1] = 1000$$

Here is a plot of the accumulation over a 20-year period as compared to a non-compounding or zero interest investment strategy

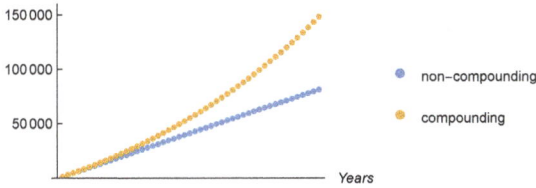

Signal Processing

The study of LTI systems is essential to developing the design skills needed to create systems that process signals in an intended way, meeting specific design requirements.

For example, the following returns a discrete-time filter that can be used to approximate the operation of taking a derivative of a signal:

```
In[•]:= fir = LeastSquaresFilterKernel [ { "Differentiator", π / 2 } , 13 ]
```

```
Out[•]= { 0.0833333, 0.0127324, −0.125, −0.0353678, 0.25, 0.31831,
        0, −0.31831, −0.25, 0.0353678, 0.125, −0.0127324, −0.0833333 }
```

The processing of an image using this differentiating filter results in an image with enhanced vertical edges as shown here:

```
In[•]:= 10 Abs [ ImageConvolve [ ExampleData [ { "TestImage", "Apples" } ] , { fir } ] ]
```

Out[•]=

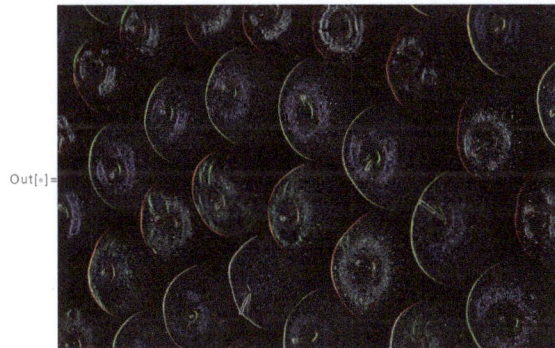

Such an operation is typically used to detect edges in digital images, which is a common preprocessing step in more advanced tasks such as shape description and object recognition.

Spectral Content of Signals and Systems

Fourier analysis gives us information about the frequency content of a signal. For instance, the pitch and timbre of a musical instrument are immediately determined from such an analysis. For example, here is a dual-tone multi-frequency (DTMF) audio signal used for phone dialing purposes:

In[•]:=**Periodogram [** ▶ 00:00 ⊙————00:00 ◀) ≡ , ⋯ ✦ **]**

Data in Notebook ⤴

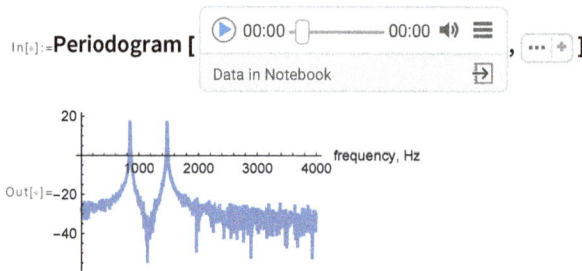

Out[•]=

Fourier analysis plays a critical role in developing a comprehensive understanding of signal processing in LTI systems. For example, from Fourier analysis, we learn that the frequency spectrum of the simple RC circuit (with RC = 1) takes the form of a complex function with frequency ω as the independent variable

$$H(j\,\omega) = \frac{1}{1+j\,\omega}$$

As explained later in the book, the magnitude, also known as gain, reveals that the filter's response to a sinusoidal input signal will diminish in amplitude with increasing frequency:

In[•]:=**Plot [Abs [** $\dfrac{1}{1 + i\,\omega}$ **] ,** ⋯ ✦ **]**

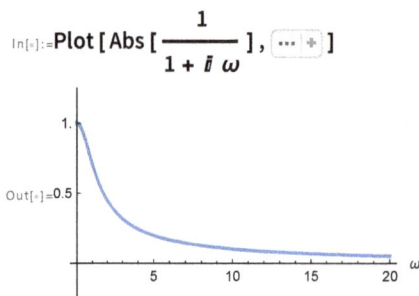

Out[•]=0.5

Summary

A short introduction to signals and systems was given.

Examples of select signals and systems were shown, including the differential and difference equation models of LTI systems.

Examples of signal and system analysis, including Fourier analysis, were given.

A filter was created and applied to an image as an example of discrete-time signal processing.

2 | Signal Classification

A small number of signal properties are used to classify all signals into useful, practical, and distinct categories. Typical signal properties that lead to distinct categories include:

- Continuity (continuous, discrete)
- Duration (finite length, infinite length)
- Symmetry (odd, even)
- Periodicity (periodic, aperiodic)
- Strength (bounded, unbounded, energy, power)

System properties and categories will be discussed at a later time.

Continuity

As evident from the Introduction, continuity is one of the main dividing lines in any presentation of signals, systems, and signal processing. Signals (and systems) are commonly referred to as either continuous time or discrete time depending on if they are defined over a continuous domain or only at a distinct set of points in its domain.

While there is much similarity in terms of concepts and methods, the differences between continuous-time and discrete-time signals and systems are sufficiently important that it is better to present them in two separate but parallel tracks.

A continuous-time function is defined at every point in its domain

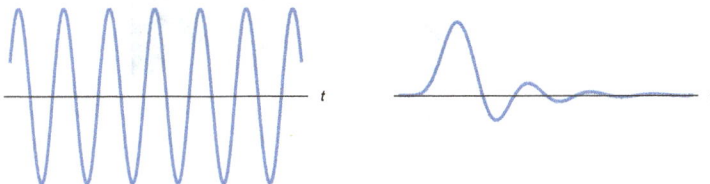

A piecewise continuous-time function is one that is continuous in each of a finite number of subintervals

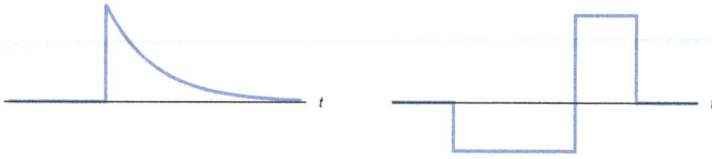

A discrete-time signal is defined only at a finite or infinite set of distinct points in its domain. These points are usually evenly spaced over the domain. For convenience, an interval of 1 is commonly used, giving a signal that is defined solely on the integers.

Here are two examples of discrete-time signals

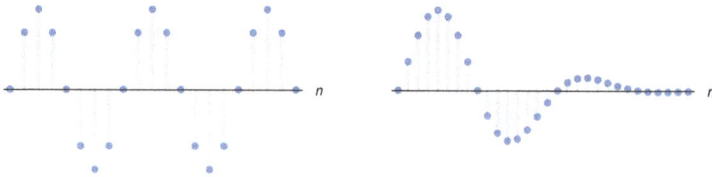

Duration

The duration of a signal can be either infinite (including semi-infinite) or finite. Continuous-time signals are typically defined over an infinite $(-\infty, +\infty)$ or semi-infinite $[0, +\infty)$ domain of the real line.

Infinite-duration signals and sequences

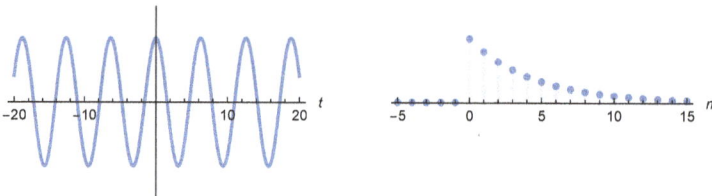

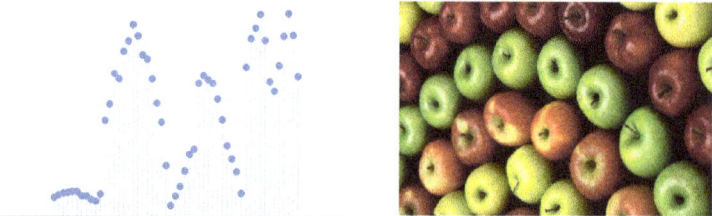

Finite-duration signals and sequence

Symmetry

Signals are categorized as either symmetric or asymmetric. Symmetric signals can be either even or odd. A continuous-time, infinite-duration signal $x(t)$ is said to have even symmetry if and only if

$x(t) = x(-t)$

Similarly, even symmetry for a discrete-time signal is defined as follows

$x[n] = x[-n]$

Here are two examples

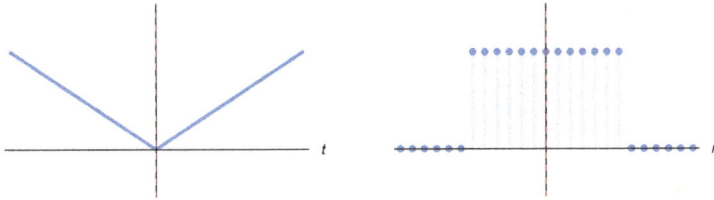

A continuous-time, infinite-duration signal $x(t)$ is said to have odd symmetry if and only if

$x(t) = -x(-t)$

In the case of a discrete-time signal, we have

$x[n] = -x[-n]$

This shows two signals with odd symmetry

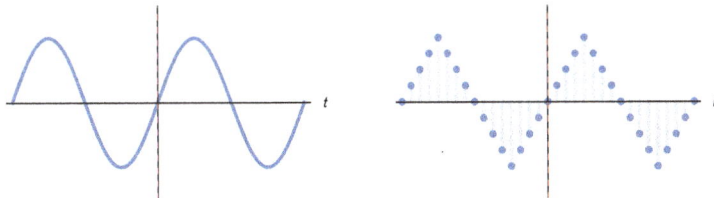

Finite-duration signals and sequences may also exhibit even or odd symmetry across the center point of their region of support

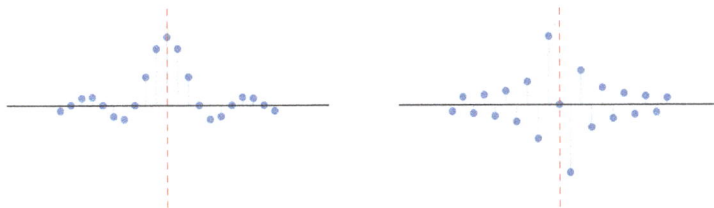

Periodicity

A signal is said to be periodic if a value T, called the period, can be found such that

$$x(t) = x(t - T)$$

Only infinite-duration signals have this property. Here are some common examples

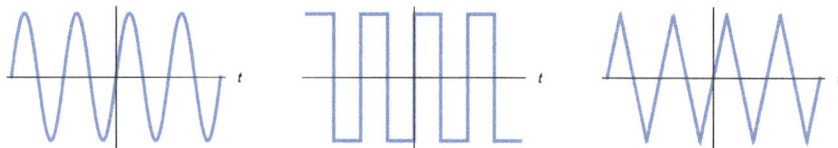

Similarly, in the case of discrete-time signals, periodicity means that an integer N exists such that

$$x[n] = x[n - N]$$

Common examples include

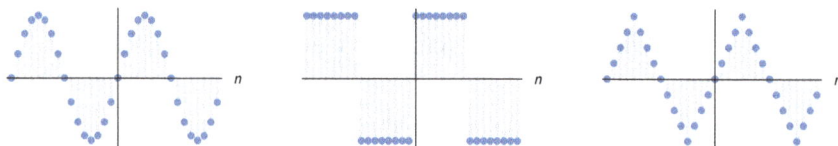

Boundedness

A signal is said to be bounded if its values at any and all times are finite

$$|x(t)| < \infty \qquad \text{for} \quad \forall\, t \in \mathbb{R}$$

$$|x[n]| < \infty \qquad \text{for} \quad \forall\, n \in \mathbb{Z}$$

Conversely, if a signal's value is infinite at any time, it is said to be unbounded.

Energy Signals

It is common practice to compare signals based on some measure of their strength. A frequently used measure of the strength of a signal is its energy. Signals with finite energy are categorized as energy signals.

The energy of a continuous-time signal $x(t)$ is defined

$$\mathcal{E} = \lim_{T \to \infty} \int_{-T}^{T} |x(t)|^2 \, dt = \int_{-\infty}^{\infty} |x(t)|^2 \, dt$$

Similarly, the energy of a sequence $x[n]$ is defined

$$\mathcal{E} = \lim_{N \to \infty} \sum_{n=-N}^{N} |x[n]|^2 = \sum_{n=-\infty}^{\infty} |x[n]|^2$$

Some useful observations:

- All bounded finite-duration signals and sequences have finite energy.
- Infinite-length signals and sequences may or may not have finite energy.
- All periodic signals and sequences have infinite energy.

Example 1

Calculate the energy of the function $x(t)$ defined as follows

$$x(t) = \begin{cases} -1, & -1 \leq t < 0 \\ 1, & 0 \leq t \leq 1 \end{cases}$$

Solution

This defines the function:

In[•]:=**x[t_] := Piecewise[{{-1, -1 ≤ t < 0}, {1, 0 ≤ t ≤ 1}}];**

This shows the function:

In[•]:=**Plot[x[t], ⋯ +]**

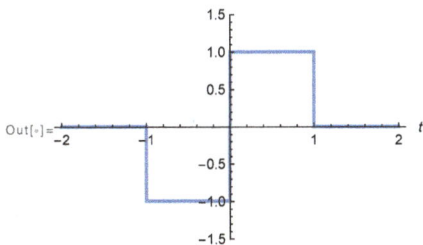

To calculate the energy, substitute the signal $x(t)$ into the definition of energy and evaluate:

In[•]:=**Integrate[Abs[x[t]]^2, {t, -∞, ∞}]**

Out[•]=**2**

Step-by-step

The energy of a continuous-time signal is defined

$$\mathcal{E} = \int_{-\infty}^{\infty} | x(t) |^2 \, dt$$

Substitute the signal into the definition

$$= \int_{-1}^{0} (-1)^2 \, dt + \int_{0}^{1} (1)^2 \, dt$$

$$= \int_{-1}^{0} dt + \int_{0}^{1} dt$$

Finally

$$= t \, |_{-1}^{0} + t \, |_{0}^{1}$$

$$= 2$$

Example 2

Calculate the energy of the following discrete-time signal

$$x[n] = \left(\frac{1}{3}\right)^n, \qquad n \geq 0$$

Solution

Define the signal:

In[•]:= **x [n_] := Piecewise [{ { $\left(\dfrac{1}{3}\right)^n$, n ≥ 0 } }];**

Use the definition of energy:

In[•]:= **Sum [Abs [x [n]]^2, { n, −∞, ∞ }]**

Out[•]= $\dfrac{9}{8}$

Step-by-step

Start with the definition of energy $\mathcal{E}$

$$\mathcal{E} = \sum_{n=-\infty}^{\infty} | x[n] |^2$$

Substitute the given signal, noting that it is equal to zero for $n < 0$

$$= \sum_{n=0}^{\infty} \left| \left(\frac{1}{3}\right)^n \right|^2$$

$$= \sum_{n=0}^{\infty} \left(\frac{1}{9}\right)^n$$

Using the formula $\sum_{n=0}^{\infty} \alpha^n = \frac{1}{1-\alpha}$, the final result is

$$= \frac{1}{1-\frac{1}{9}} = \frac{9}{8}$$

Power Signals

Power is a time average of energy. Power is another useful measure of signal strength, in particular with respect to periodic signals.

The power of a continuous-time signal $x(t)$ is defined

$$P = \lim_{T \to \infty} \frac{1}{2T} \int_{-T}^{T} (\mid x(t) \mid)^2 \, dt$$

The power of a sequence $x[n]$ is defined

$$P = \lim_{N \to \infty} \frac{1}{2N+1} \sum_{n=-N}^{N} (\mid x[n] \mid)^2$$

Signals with finite, nonzero power are called power signals. Observe that finite-duration signals and sequences have zero power.

The average power of a periodic signal with period T or a sequence with period N is measured over one period

$$P = \frac{1}{T} \int_{T} (\mid x(t) \mid)^2$$

$$P = \frac{1}{N} \sum_{n=0}^{N-1} (\mid x[n] \mid)^2$$

Example 3

Determine the average power of the following signal

$$x(t) = \begin{cases} 1, & t \geq 0 \\ 0, & \text{else} \end{cases}$$

Solution

Substitute the signal into the formula for average power:

```
In[•]:= x[t_] := Piecewise[ { {1, t ≥ 0} } ];
       Limit[
          1
          ── Integrate[Abs[x[t]]^2, {t, -T, T}, Assumptions → T ∈ Reals], T → ∞]
          2 T
            1
Out[•]= ──
            2
```

Step-by-step

Start with the definition

$$P = \lim_{T \to \infty} \frac{1}{2T} \int_{-T}^{T} (\mid x(t) \mid)^2 \, dt$$

Substitution of the signal into the definition reduces the integral to the following

$$= \lim_{T \to \infty} \frac{1}{2T} \int_{0}^{T} (1) \, dt$$

Integration results in the following

$$= \lim_{T \to \infty} \frac{1}{2T} \, T$$

Application of the limit operation gives the following result

$$= \frac{1}{2}$$

Example 4

Determine the average power of the periodic signal shown here:

In[•]:=**Plot [SquareWave [{ 0, 1 }, t] , ⋯ +]**

Out[•]=

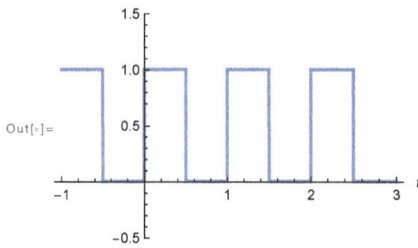

Solution

The given signal is a square wave with period $T = 1$ defined as follows:

In[•]:=**x [t_] := SquareWave [{ 0, 1 }, t] ;**

Use the formula for average power of a periodic signal:

In[•]:=**Integrate [Abs [x [t]] ^{2}, { t, 0, 1 }]**

Out[•]=$\dfrac{1}{2}$

Step-by-step

The definition of average power of a periodic continuous-time signal is

$$\mathcal{P} = \frac{1}{T} \int_T (| \, x(t) \, |)^2 \, dt$$

Recognize that the given signal is positive and has period $T = 1$

$$= \int_0^1 x(t)^2 \, dt$$

Since $x(t) = 1$ for $0 \le t \le \frac{1}{2}$ and $x(t) = 0$ for $\frac{1}{2} \le t < 1$, the integral reduces to the following

$$= \int_0^{1/2} dt$$

$$= \frac{1}{2}$$

Example 5

Determine the average power of the periodic signal shown here:

In[•]:=**DiscretePlot [SquareWave [n / 10] , $\cdots$ $+$]**

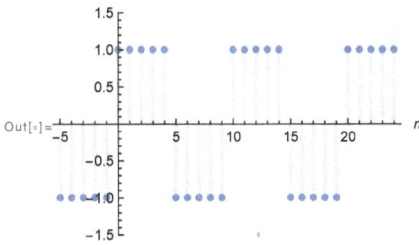

Out[•]=

Solution

The given signal is a square wave with period $\mathcal{N} = 10$. Use the formula for average power of a periodic signal:

In[•]:=$\dfrac{1}{10}$ **Sum [SquareWave [n / 10]^2 , { n, 0, 9 }]**

Out[•]=1

Step-by-step

Start with the definition and simplify

$$\mathcal{P} = \frac{1}{\mathcal{N}} \sum_{n=0}^{\mathcal{N}-1} \left(\, | \, x[n] \, | \, \right)^2$$

$$= \frac{1}{10} \sum_{n=0}^{9} \left(\, | \, x[n] \, | \, \right)^2$$

$$= \frac{1}{10} \sum_{n=0}^{9} (1)^2$$

$$= 1$$

Signal Energy and Image Classification

This application first demonstrates how signal energy can be used to organize a set of night and day images into two different classes. Next, a more sophisticated classification method is used.

Here is an example dataset containing labeled images of day and night:

In[·]:=**examples = <| "Night" → {** 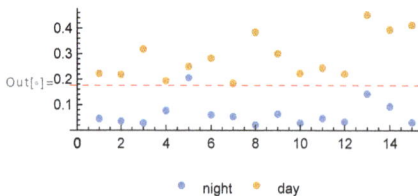 **},**

"Day" → { ... **} |>;**

Create a simple classifier by using signal energy as the distinguishing image feature between the two groups of images. As the images are not uniform in size, normalize the signal energy by dividing by the number of image pixels, thus, strictly speaking, this returns the power:

In[·]:=**powerNight = Total [Flatten [ImageData [ColorConvert [#, "Grayscale"]]]^2] /**
   Times @@ ImageDimensions [#] & / @ examples ["Night"]

Out[·]= { 0.0444728, 0.0349989, 0.0271933, 0.0758635, 0.204888,
   0.0590162, 0.0526043, 0.0199675, 0.0625401, 0.027756,
   0.0467196, 0.0324243, 0.141417, 0.0919702, 0.0302831 }

In[·]:=**powerDay = Total [Flatten [ImageData [ColorConvert [#, "Grayscale"]]]^2] /**
   Times @@ ImageDimensions [#] & / @ examples ["Day"]

Out[·]= { 0.222088, 0.218223, 0.31774, 0.192792, 0.249809, 0.282016, 0.182786, 0.383228,
   0.299851, 0.222646, 0.243953, 0.220565, 0.450966, 0.393167, 0.411159 }

Select a threshold that is the average of the mean energy of the night and day images, respectively. This returns the threshold value:

In[·]:=**thresh = Mean [{ Mean [powerNight] , Mean [powerDay] }]**

Out[·]=0.17477

Signal energy or power is a very simple image feature to use as a classifier but does a decent job of separating the example images into their respective classes:

In[·]:=**ListPlot [⋯ ✦]**

This applies the computed threshold to a number of unclassified images:

```
In[·]:=If [ Total [ Flatten [ ImageData [ ColorConvert [ #, "Grayscale" ] ] ]² ] /
        Times @@ ImageDimensions [ # ] ≥ thresh,
    "Day", "Night" ] & / @ {  }
```

Out[·]= { Day, Day, Day, Night, Day, Night }

It should not surprise you that this simple method failed to correctly classify one of the night scenes. With larger datasets and more sophisticated classification methods, including machine learning, much better results should be expected.

Summary

Several properties of signals were presented, including continuity, duration, symmetry, and periodicity.

Methods for calculating the energy and average power of both continuous-time and discrete-time signals were discussed, with several specific examples given

$$\mathcal{E}_{CT} = \lim_{T\to\infty} \int_{-T}^{T} |x(t)|^2 dt \qquad \mathcal{E}_{DT} = \lim_{N\to\infty} \sum_{n=-N}^{N} |x[n]|^2$$

$$\mathcal{P}_{CT} = \lim_{T\to\infty} \frac{1}{2T} \int_{-T}^{T} (|x(t)|)^2 dt \qquad \mathcal{P}_{DT} = \lim_{K\to\infty} \frac{1}{2K+1} \sum_{n=-K}^{K} (|x[n]|)^2$$

An application showing how signal energy may be used to classify images was discussed

{ } ⟶ { "Day", "Day", "Day", "Night", "Day", "Night" }

Exercises

Download the solutions manual at wolfr.am/eTextbook-SSSP

2.1 Select which are true about the following signal.

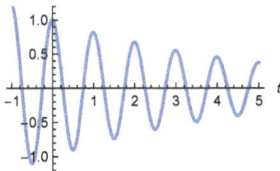

A. Periodic

B. Even symmetric

C. Discrete time

D. None of the above

2.2 Determine if the sequence $x[n] = (-1)^n$ is periodic.

2.3 Which signal or signals have finite energy?

A.

B.
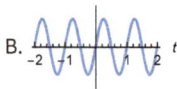

C.
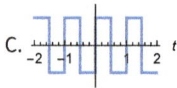

D. None of the above

2.4 Which signals have finite power?

A.
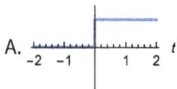

B.
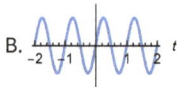

C.
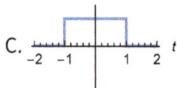

D. All of the above

2.5 Calculate the energy of the following signal.

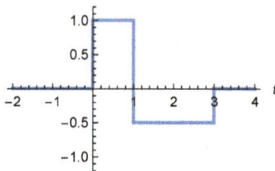

2.6 Calculate the energy of the following finite-length sequence.

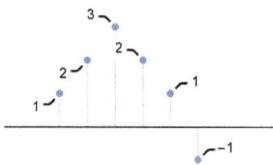

2.7 Calculate the energy of the following signal.

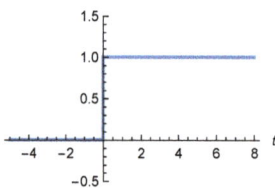

2.8 Determine the average power of the following sequence.

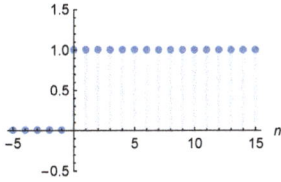

2.9 Determine the average power of the signal $x(t) = t$ for $t \geq 0$.

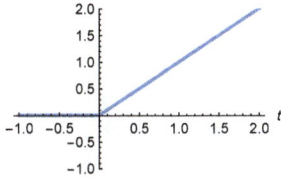

2.10 Determine the average power of the following sawtooth signal.

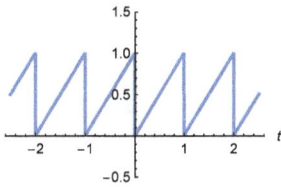

2.11 Determine the average power of the following periodic sequence.

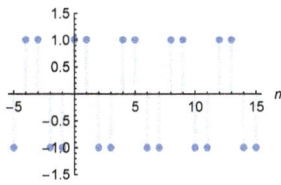

3 | Elementary Signals and Sequences

There is a small number of basic signals and sequences that are important in the study of linear systems. These include the families of sinusoidal and exponential signals and sequences, the discrete-time and continuous-time unit step, and, finally, the somewhat special unit impulse, also known as the Dirac delta function.

Real-Valued Sinusoidal Signals

The sine function in its most general form can be written as follows

$$x(t) = a \sin(\omega t + \theta)$$

The definition includes three parameters, amplitude (a), frequency (ω), and phase (θ), and this shows how each of the three parameters affects the shape of the function $x(t)$:

In[•]:=**Manipulate [** ⋯ + **]**

Out[•]=

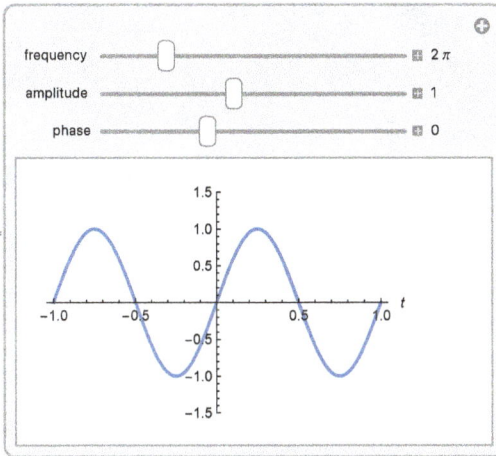

It is well known that sinusoids are periodic; namely, there exists a value T such that

$$\sin(\omega t) = \sin(\omega (t + T)) = \sin(\omega t + \omega T)$$

Also, it is well known that the sine function is 2π periodic in time

$$\sin(\omega t) = \sin(\omega t + 2\pi)$$

Therefore

$$\sin(\omega t + \omega T) = \sin(\omega t + 2\pi)$$

and

$$\omega T = 2\pi$$

Thus, period T and angular frequency ω (in radians per second) are scaled multiplicative inverses of each other

$$\omega = \frac{2\pi}{T}$$

Period T and frequency f (in hertz, Hz) are related as follows

$$f = \frac{1}{T}$$

The two frequency quantities are scalar multiples of each other

$$\omega = 2\pi f$$

Real-Valued Sinusoidal Sequences

Similarly, the general form of a sine sequence, defined in terms of the same three parameters, amplitude (a), angular frequency (ω), and phase (θ), is

$$x[n] = a\sin(\omega n + \theta)$$

This shows the sequence:

In[•]:=**Manipulate [⋯ ✛]**

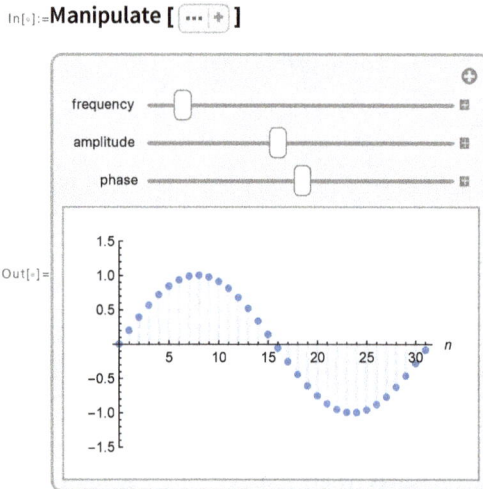

Note, however, that as the frequency is increased, the sequence may not look sinusoidal at all. Also, while a casual inspection may not make it apparent, the sequence may not be periodic at all. This is described next.

The period of a sequence $x[n]$ is a value N, such that $x[n] = x[n + N]$ for integers n and N. A sine sequence of period N can therefore be written as follows

$$\sin(\omega\, n) = \sin(\omega\, (n + N)) = \sin(\omega\, n + \omega\, N)$$

It is also well known that the following relation holds

$$\sin(\omega\, n) = \sin(\omega\, n + 2\,\pi\, k)$$

which leads to the following equality between the right-hand sides

$$\sin(\omega\, n + \omega\, N) = \sin(\omega\, n + 2\,\pi\, k)$$

As a result, the frequency ω and period N are related as follows

$$\omega\, N = 2\,\pi\, k$$

This effectively restricts the frequency of a periodic sine sequence to the following rational integer multiple of 2π

$$\omega = 2\,\pi\, \frac{k}{N}$$

Alternatively, any sine sequence whose angular frequency cannot be expressed as shown is not periodic.

This defines the period N in terms of the angular frequency

$$N = \frac{2\pi}{\omega}\, k$$

Example 1

Determine if the following sequence is periodic

$$x[n] = \cos\!\left(\frac{n}{2}\right)$$

If it is, determine the fundamental period and angular frequency.

Solution

The frequency $\omega = \frac{1}{2}$ radians/second is not a rational multiple of $2\,\pi$, so the period is not an integer and the sequence is <u>not</u> periodic.

This shows the sequence $x[n]$ with the vertical lines corresponding to integer multiples of the period T of a continuous-time cosine function with angular frequency $\omega = \frac{1}{2}$ radians/second, that is, $T = \frac{2\pi}{\omega} = 4\pi \approx 12.566$:

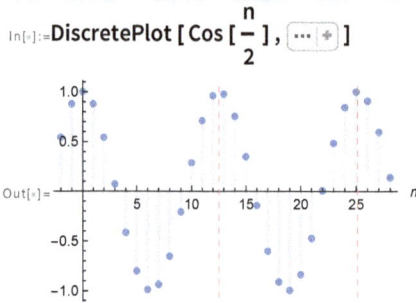

In[ ]:= **DiscretePlot [Cos [$\frac{n}{2}$], ⋯ +]**

Out[ ]=

Note the non-periodic nature of the sequence.

Harmonically Related Sinusoidal Signals and Sequences

Two signals or sequences are said to be harmonically related if their frequencies are positive integer multiples of some base frequency, called the fundamental frequency. Thus given the frequency ω, the following defines its harmonics

$$\omega_k = k \cdot \omega, \qquad k = 1, 2, 3, \; ...$$

With $\omega = 2\pi$ radians/second, this shows the fundamental and the 5th and 15th harmonics of a sine wave:

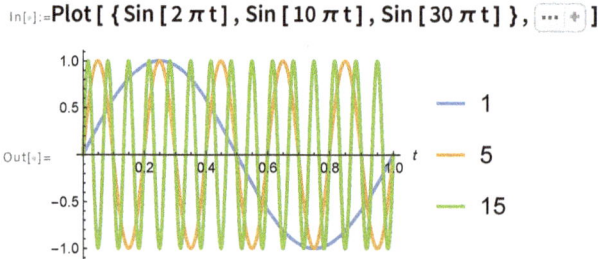

In[ ]:= **Plot [{ Sin [2 π t] , Sin [10 π t] , Sin [30 π t] } , ⋯ +]**

Out[ ]=

— 1
— 5
— 15

As previously discussed, the frequency of a periodic sinusoidal sequence with period N is $\omega = \frac{2\pi}{N}$. Thus the following defines the harmonic frequencies

$$\omega_k = \left(\frac{2\pi}{N}\right) k, \qquad k = 1, 2, 3, \; ...$$

And the following represents harmonically related cosine sequences with period N

$$x_k[n] = \cos(\omega_k n) = \cos\left(\frac{2\pi}{N} k n\right), \; k = 1, 2, 3, \; ...$$

This shows one period of the cosine sequences $x_k[n]$ with period $\mathcal{N} = 8$ for $k = 0,\ 1,\ ...,\ 11$:

In[·]:=**GraphicsGrid [** Partition[···] ⊞ **]**

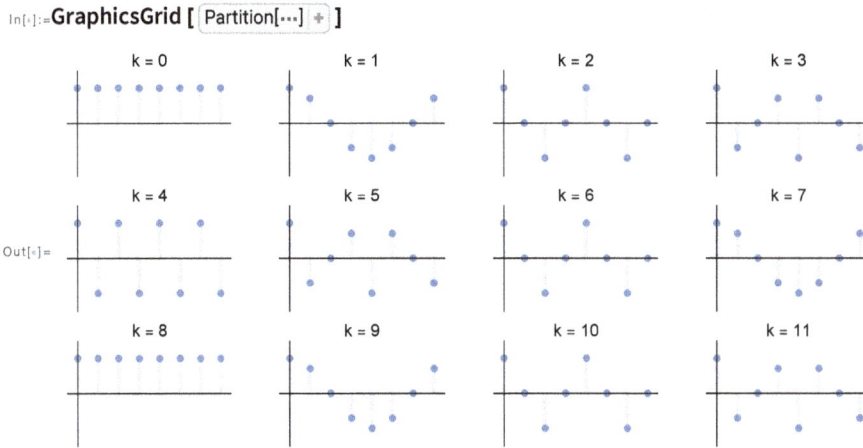

Note that starting with $k = \mathcal{N} = 8$, the sequences repeat. The number of distinct harmonically related sequences is therefore finite and equal to $\mathcal{N}$. This is in stark contrast with continuous-time sinusoidal signals, which have no bound on the number of harmonics.

This demonstrates that sinusoidal sequences with frequencies $\frac{2\pi}{\mathcal{N}} k$ and $\frac{2\pi}{\mathcal{N}} (k + \mathcal{N})$ are identical. To prove this using algebra, proceed as follows

$$\cos\!\left(\frac{2\pi}{\mathcal{N}} (k + \mathcal{N})\, n\right) = \cos\!\left(\frac{2\pi}{\mathcal{N}} k\, n + 2\pi n\right)$$

Use the sum of angles formula

$$= \cos\!\left(\frac{2\pi}{\mathcal{N}} k\, n\right) \cos(2\pi n) - \sin\!\left(\frac{2\pi}{\mathcal{N}} k\, n\right) \sin(2\pi n)$$

and simplify to complete the proof

$$= \cos\!\left(\frac{2\pi}{\mathcal{N}} k\, n\right) (1) - \sin\!\left(\frac{2\pi}{\mathcal{N}} k\, n\right) (0)$$

$$= \cos\!\left(\frac{2\pi}{\mathcal{N}} k\, n\right)$$

Real Exponential Signals

Another basic and important signal is the continuous-time exponential, which occurs naturally in the analysis and response of electric circuits and, more generally, any linear system. The general form of the exponential signal is r^t. However, the following formulation is frequently used instead

$$x(t) = e^{-a\,t}, a \in \mathbb{R}$$

This plots $x(t)$ for $t > 0$ as the value of the parameter a is varied in the range $-0.5 \leq a \leq 3.0$:

In[•]:=**Manipulate [$\cdots$ $+$]**

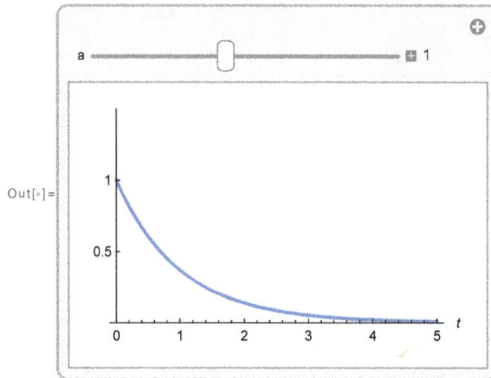

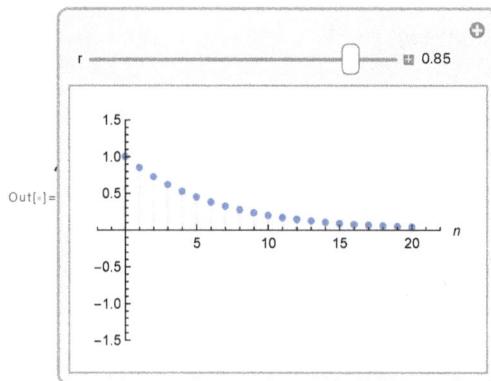

Out[•]=

Real Exponential Sequences

Similarly, a real discrete-time exponential signal is of the form

$$x[n] = r^n \ , r \in \mathbb{R}$$

A real exponential sequence is commonly known as a geometric sequence. This plots the real exponential sequence for $n \geq 0$ as the value of r varies in the range $-1.1 \leq r \leq 1.1$:

In[•]:=**Manipulate [$\cdots$ $+$]**

Out[•]=

This shows that the sequence $x[n]$ decays to zero for $|r| < 1$ and grows without bounds for $|r| > 1$.

Complex Exponential Signals

Now, with $r = e^{-(\sigma+j\,\omega)}$, where j is the imaginary number and σ and ω are real positive scalars, you get the following common definition of a complex exponential signal

$$x(t) = e^{-(\sigma+j\,\omega)\,t} = e^{-\sigma\,t}\,e^{-j\,\omega\,t}$$

It is a complex-valued function, which via Euler's identity ($e^{\pm j\,\omega} = \cos(\omega) \pm j\sin(\omega)$) has sinusoidal real and imaginary parts

$$x(t) = e^{-\sigma\,t}\,e^{-j\,\omega\,t}$$

$$= e^{-\sigma\,t}(\cos(\omega\,t) - j\sin(\omega\,t))$$

$$= e^{-\sigma\,t}\cos(\omega\,t) - j\,e^{-\sigma\,t}\sin(\omega\,t)$$

This shows the real and imaginary parts of $x(t)$ for varying values of σ and ω:

In[-]:=**Manipulate [** ⋯ + **]**

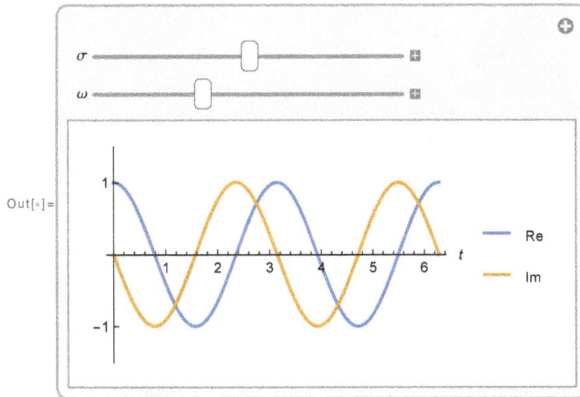

Complex Exponential Sequences

For complex values of r, for example, $r = e^{-(\sigma+j\,\omega)}$, you have

$$x[n] = e^{-(\sigma+j\,\omega)\,n} = e^{-\sigma\,n}\,e^{-j\,\omega\,n}$$

Then via Euler's identity $e^{\pm j\,\omega} = \cos(\omega) \pm j\sin(\omega)$, sequence $x[n]$ becomes

$$x[n] = e^{-\sigma\,n}(\cos(\omega\,n) - j\sin(\omega\,n)) = e^{-\sigma\,n}\cos(\omega\,n) + j\,e^{-\sigma\,n}\sin(\omega\,n))$$

Therefore the real and imaginary parts of the complex exponential sequence are scaled cosine and sine sequences.

Here are the real and imaginary parts of an example sequence for a range of values of σ and ω:

In[•]:=**Manipulate [** ⋯ ✦ **]**

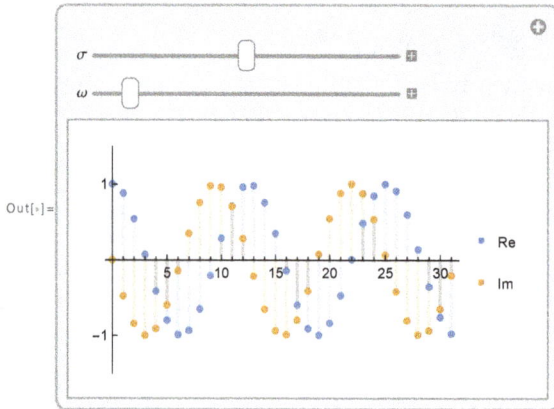

Unit Step Signal

The unit step function is useful in modeling a sudden application of a constant forcing function to a system.

The unit step function is commonly defined

$$u(t) = \begin{cases} 0, & t < 0 \\ 1, & t \geq 0 \end{cases}$$

Here is a plot of the function:

In[•]:=**Plot [UnitStep [t] ,** ⋯ ✦ **]**

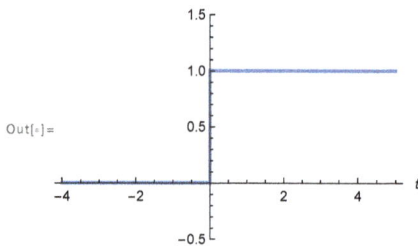

In Wolfram Language, it is occasionally preferable to use the HeavisideTheta function, which is defined

$$\theta(t) = \begin{cases} 0, & t < 0 \\ 1, & t > 0 \end{cases}$$

The HeavisideTheta and UnitStep functions look the same when plotted:

In[•]:=**Plot [HeavisideTheta [t] , ⋯ +]**

Out[•]=

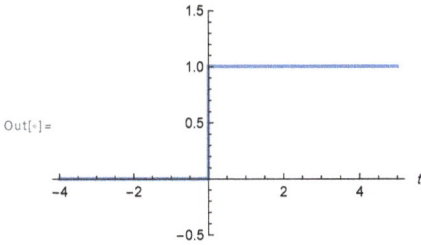

Unit Impulse Signal

The unit impulse function, also known as the Dirac delta function, is commonly used to model the operation of sampling (to be discussed later) and physical signals that act over very short periods of time, such as a hammer blow, a bat hitting a ball, or the burst of light from a flash lamp.

A simple model of the impulse function is a pulse of width ϵ and height $1/\epsilon$:

In[•]:=**Manipulate [⋯ +]**

Out[•]=

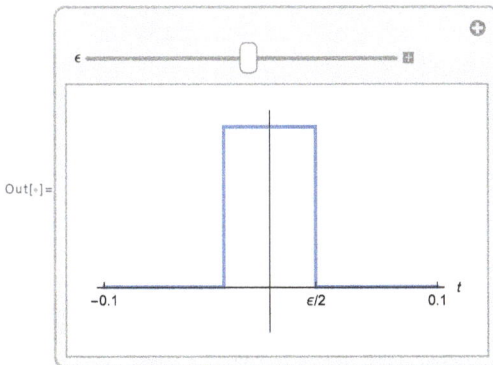

This conforms with the following property of the Dirac delta function

$$\int_{-\infty}^{\infty} \delta(t)\, dt = 1$$

The Dirac delta function $\delta(t)$ is the function such that

$$\int_{-\infty}^{\infty} \delta(t)\, f(t)\, dt = f(0)$$

This fundamental property of the delta function is also known as the sampling property. Similarly, for an impulse concentrated at the point t_0, you have

$$\int_{-\infty}^{\infty} \delta(t - t_0)\, f(t)\, dt = f(t_0)$$

Example 2

Determine the value of the following integral

$$\int_0^\infty e^{-t} \delta(t-3)\, dt$$

Solution

Direct evaluation gives:

In[•]:=**Integrate [e^{-t} DiracDelta [t – 3] , { t, 0, ∞ }]**

Out[•]=$\dfrac{1}{e^3}$

Step-by-step

With $f(t) = e^{-t}$ and $t_0 = 3$, according to the sampling property, the integral must equal $f(t_0) = f(3) = e^{-3}$.

Plotting the Unit Impulse

The commonly accepted graphical representation of a unit impulse function is an arrow of unit height. For example, given the following function $x(t)$

$$x(t) = \delta(t+1) - \delta(t) + 2\,\delta(t-2)$$

A plot of the function would then look as the one shown here:

In[•]:=**Graphics [⋯ ✦]**

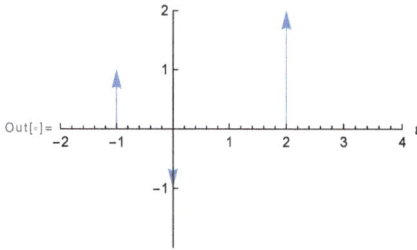

Relations between Unit Step and Unit Impulse Signals

The unit step and impulse are closely related. For example, the unit step is an integral of the unit impulse

$$u(t) = \int_{-\infty}^{t} \delta(\tau)\, d\tau$$

Therefore, in Wolfram Language you get:

In[•]:=**Integrate [DiracDelta [t] , t]**

Out[•]=HeavisideTheta [t]

Conversely, the unit impulse can be viewed as a derivative of the unit step

$$\delta(t) = \frac{d}{dt} \, u(t)$$

Indeed, using Wolfram Language you get:

In[•]:=**D [HeavisideTheta [t] , t]**

Out[•]=DiracDelta [t]

In contrast, a derivative of the unit step function evaluates as follows:

In[•]:=**D [UnitStep [t] , t]**

$$\text{Out[•]=}\begin{cases} \text{Indeterminate} & t == 0 \\ 0 & \text{True} \end{cases}$$

The HeavisideTheta function definition of the unit step is more convenient for symbolic computations, while the function UnitStep is more suitable for numerical calculations.

Unit Step Sequence

The discrete-time unit step signal $u[n]$ is defined

$$u[n] = \begin{cases} 1, & n \geq 0 \\ 0, & \text{else} \end{cases}$$

This shows the unit step sequence:

In[•]:=**DiscretePlot [UnitStep [n] , ⋯ +]**

Out[•]=

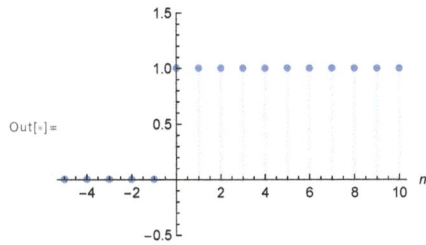

Unit Sample Sequence

The unit sample sequence typically denoted $\delta[n]$ or δ_n (**KroneckerDelta** in Wolfram Language), is defined

$$\delta[n] = \begin{cases} 1, & n = 0 \\ 0, & \text{else} \end{cases}$$

This shows the unit sample sequence:

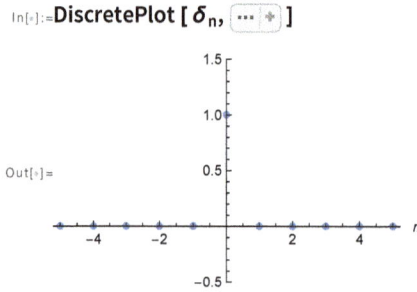

In[ ]:=**DiscretePlot [δ_n, ⋯ ◆]**

Out[ ]=

A unit sample located at $n = n_0$ is defined

$$\delta[n - n_0] = \begin{cases} 1, & n = n_0 \\ 0, & \text{else} \end{cases}$$

which for the value $n_0 = 2$ displays as follows

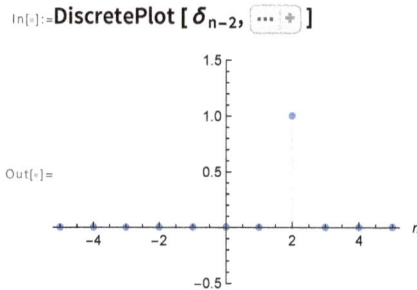

In[ ]:=**DiscretePlot [δ_{n-2}, ⋯ ◆]**

Out[ ]=

Sequences as Sums of Unit Samples

Any sequence can be represented as a weighted sum of unit samples. For example, consider the following finite-length sequence

$$x[n] = \begin{cases} 1, & n = 0 \\ 2, & n = 1 \ \& \ n = 2 \\ -1, & n = 3 \\ 0, & \text{else} \end{cases}$$

This sequence may be written in the form of shifted and scaled unit samples as follows:

In[•]:= **x[n_] := (1) δ_n + (2) δ_{n-1} + (2) δ_{n-2} + (−1) δ_{n-3}**

This plots the sequence:

In[•]:= **DiscretePlot[x[n], ⋯ ✦]**

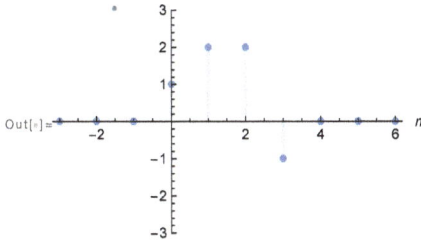

Relations between Unit Step and Unit Sample

The unit sample is a first difference of the discrete-time unit step

$$\delta[n] = u[n] - u[n - 1]$$

The unit step is a running sum of the unit sample

$$u[n] = \sum_{m=-\infty}^{n} \delta[m]$$

Summary

Elementary signals and sequences:

- Sine and cosine

- Exponential

- Complex exponential

- Unit step

- Unit impulse (sample)

Exercises

Download the solutions manual at wolfr.am/eTextbook-SSSP

3.1 What is the angular frequency of the following signal?

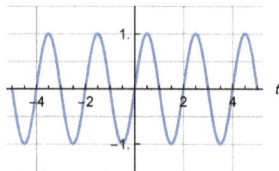

3.2 Which of the following states Euler's formula?

A. $e^{jx} = \cos(x) + j\sin(x)$

B. $\sin(x)^2 + \cos(x)^2 = 1$

C. $e^x = \cosh(x) + \sinh(x)$

D. None of the above

3.3 Determine the period of the following sequence.

$x[n] = \cos[n]$

3.4 Which of the given sequences are harmonically related?

$$\left\{ \sin\left(\frac{2\pi}{8} n\right),\ \sin\left(\frac{3\pi}{4} n\right),\ \sin\left(\frac{2\pi}{16} n\right),\ \sin\left(\frac{26\pi}{8} n\right) \right\}$$

A. None of the sequences

B. All four sequences

C. Only $\sin\left(\frac{2\pi}{8} n\right)$ and $\sin\left(\frac{3\pi}{4} n\right)$

D. Only $\sin\left(\frac{2\pi}{8} n\right)$, $\sin\left(\frac{3\pi}{4} n\right)$ and $\sin\left(\frac{2\pi}{16} n\right)$

3.5 Which, if any, of the given sequences are identical?

$$\left\{ \cos\left(\frac{2\pi}{8} n\right),\ \cos\left(\frac{2\pi}{8} 7n\right),\ \cos\left(-\frac{2\pi}{8} n\right),\ \cos\left(\frac{2\pi}{8} 25n\right) \right\}$$

3.6 Which of the following is a correct statement about the unit impulse signal $\delta(t)$?

A. The unit impulse signal has a height of 1

B. The unit impulse signal is undefined everywhere except at $t = 0$

C. The unit impulse signal has finite area

D. None of the above

3.7 According to the time-translation property of a unit impulse signal, what is the value of the following integral?

$$\int_{-\infty}^{\infty} e^t \, \delta(t-2) \, dt$$

3.8 Which of the following is a correct statement about the unit sample sequence $\delta[n]$?

A. The unit sample sequence has a height of 1

B. The unit sample sequence has an area of 1

C. The unit sample sequence is well defined for all values of n

D. None of the above

3.9 For a discrete sequence represented by the following function, what is the value at $n = 1$?

$$x[n] = \delta[n] + 3\,\delta[n-1] + 2\,\delta[n-2] - 2\,\delta[n-3]$$

3.10 Which sequence is commonly known as a geometric sequence?

A. Complex exponential sequence

B. Unit step sequence

C. Sinusoidal sequence

D. Real exponential sequence

4 | Elementary Operations

The elementary operations of interest at this time may be classified into two categories, those that affect either the dependent or the independent variables. Each of the variables may be scaled (using scalar multiplication) or shifted (via scalar addition). The independent variable is typically assumed to denote time and therefore is commonly represented by the variable t in the case of continuous-time signals or n for sequences, while the dependent variable is the value $x(t)$ or $x[n]$ of the signal or sequence, respectively.

Dependent variable operations:

- Amplitude scaling $x(t) \rightarrow a\,x(t)$ $x[n] \rightarrow a\,x[n]$
- Level shifting $x(t) \rightarrow x(t) + a$ $x[n] \rightarrow x[n] + a$

Independent variable operations:

- Time shifting $x(t) \rightarrow x(t + a)$ $x[n] \rightarrow x[n + k]$

                                                              $x[n] \rightarrow x[k\,n]$

                                                              or

- Time scaling $x(t) \rightarrow x(a\,t)$ $x[n] \rightarrow x\left[\dfrac{1}{k}\,n\right]$

where $a \in \mathbb{R}$ and $k \in \mathbb{Z}$.

Amplitude Scaling

Amplitude scaling transformation takes the form

$$x(t) \rightarrow a\,x(t), \qquad x[n] \rightarrow a\,x[n]$$

Scaling parameter values such that $|a| > 1$ result in signal magnification and values $|a| < 1$ result in signal reduction. Scaling by $a = -1$ negates the signal.

This demonstrates amplitude scaling:

In[•]:=**DynamicModule [** ··· + ▲ **]**

Out[•]=

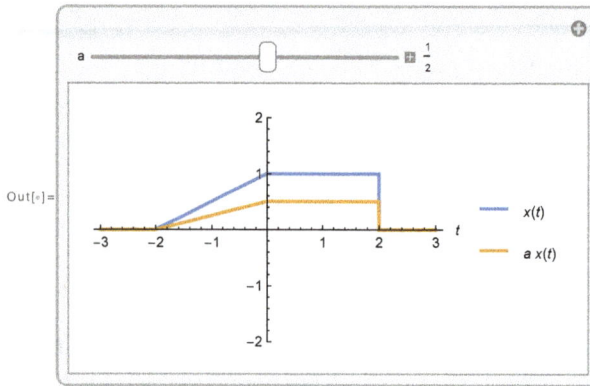

Level Shifting

The level shift transformation is defined

$$x(t) \rightarrow x(t) + a, \qquad x[n] \rightarrow x[n] + a$$

Positive values of the parameter a shift the signal up, while negative values shift it down:

In[•]:=**DynamicModule [** ··· + ▲ **]**

Out[•]=

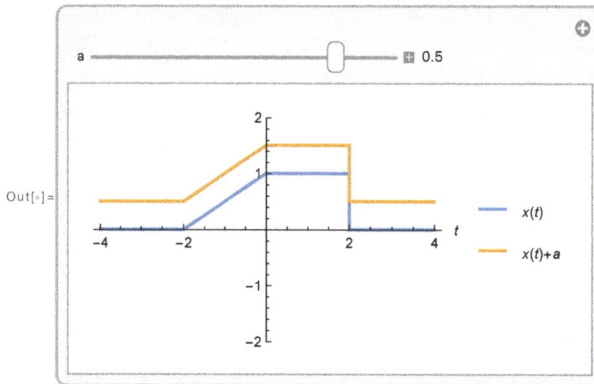

Example 1

Obtain the signal resulting from the transformation $x(t) \rightarrow 2\,x(t) - \frac{3}{2}$ given the following signal $x(t)$:

```
In[•]:= x[t_] := Piecewise[{{t, 0 ≤ t ≤ 1}, {1, 1 ≤ t ≤ 3}}];
       Plot[x[t], ⋯ + ]
```

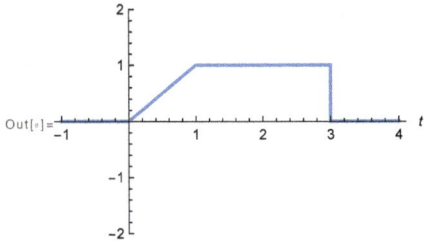

Out[•]=

Solution

Applying the transformation gives the following result:

```
In[•]:= 2 x[t] - 3/2 // PiecewiseExpand
```

$$
Out[•]= \begin{cases} -\frac{3}{2} & t > 3 \mid\mid t < 0 \\ \frac{1}{2} & 1 < t \le 3 \\ \frac{1}{2}\,(-3 + 4\,t) & \text{True} \end{cases}
$$

This shows the result:

```
In[•]:= Plot[{x[t], 2 x[t] - 3/2}, ⋯ + ]
```

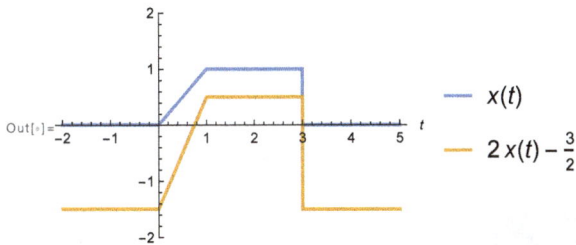

Out[•]=

— $x(t)$

— $2\,x(t) - \frac{3}{2}$

Step-by-step

Evaluating the transformation, you get

$$y(t) = 2\,x(t) - \frac{3}{2}$$

$$= 2\left(\left\{\begin{array}{ll} t, & 0 \le t \le 1 \\ 1, & 1 \le t \le 3 \\ 0, & \text{else} \end{array}\right\}\right) - \frac{3}{3}$$

$$= \left\{\begin{array}{ll} 2\,(t) - \frac{3}{2}, & 0 \le t \le 1 \\ 2\,(1) - \frac{3}{2}, & 1 \le t \le 3 \\ 2\,(0) - \frac{3}{2}, & \text{else} \end{array}\right.$$

$$= \left\{\begin{array}{ll} 2\,t - \frac{3}{2}, & 0 \le t \le 1 \\ \frac{1}{2}, & 1 \le t \le 3 \\ -\frac{3}{2}, & \text{else} \end{array}\right.$$

Example 2

Images are possibly the most common examples of discrete-time signals that one encounters on a daily basis. Given the image shown here:

In[•]:=**i =**  **;**

A. Scale the image by the factor $a = 0.2$.

B. Level shift the image by the value $b = 0.5$.

Solution

A. This shows the result of scaling the image pixels:

In[•]:=**0.2 i**

Out[•]=

B. This shows the result of adding 0.5 to each image pixel:

In[ ]:= **i + 0.5**

Out[ ]=

This shows the effect of the operations of amplitude scaling ($0 \le a \le 2$) and level shifting ($-1 \le b \le 1$) on an example image:

In[ ]:= **Manipulate [⋯ +]**

Out[ ]=

Independent Variable Operations

Elementary independent variable operations of interest in the study of signal processing include the following:

- Time shift $\qquad y(t) = x(t + a) \qquad\qquad y[n] = x[n + k]$

- Time reversal $\qquad y(t) = x(-t) \qquad\qquad y[n] = x[-n]$

- Compression $\qquad y(t) = x(a\,t) \qquad\qquad y[n] = x[k\,n]$

- Expansion $\qquad y(t) = x\left(\dfrac{t}{a}\right) \qquad\qquad y[n] = \begin{cases} x\left[\dfrac{n}{k}\right], & n = 0, \pm k, \ldots \\ 0, & \text{otherwise} \end{cases}$

where $a \in \mathbb{R}$ and $|a| > 1$ and $k \in \mathbb{Z}$.

Time Shift

The operation of addition applied to the independent variable has the effect of a time shift

$$x(t) \rightarrow x(t + a), \qquad x[n] \rightarrow x[n + k]$$

Negative values of the shift parameters, a and k, cause a shift right or time delay, while positive values cause a shift left or time advance.

This demonstrates time shift for different values of the parameter a:

In[·]:=**Manipulate [** ··· + **]**

Out[·]=

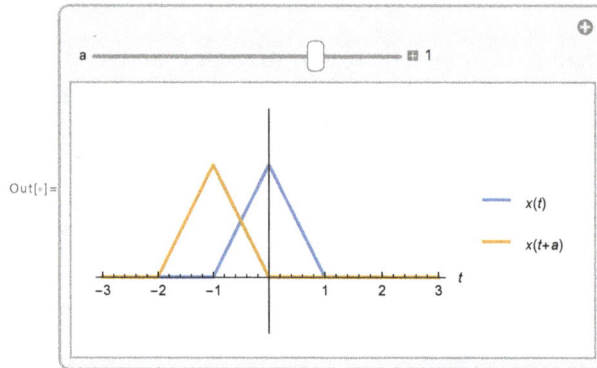

Time Scaling

The operation of multiplication, when applied to the independent variable, has the effect of time scaling the signal

$$x(t) \rightarrow x(a\,t), \qquad \text{with } a \in \mathbb{R}$$

Time scaling is also known as compression and expansion.

The operation of multiplying the independent variable by -1 has the effect of time reversing the signal or sequence. Time reversal is therefore a special case of time scaling.

Values $|a| > 1$ result in time compression, while values $|a| < 1$ cause time expansion:

In[•]:=**Manipulate [$\cdots$ $+$]**

Out[•]=

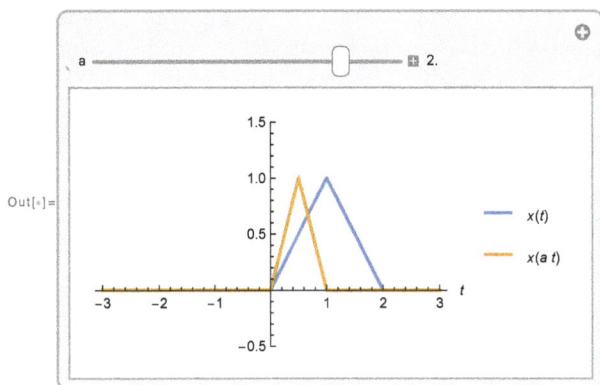

Example 3

Obtain $y[n] = x[n + 3]$ given the following sequence $x[n]$

$$x[n] = \delta[n] + 2\,\delta[n - 1] + 3\,\delta[n - 2] + 4\,\delta[n - 3]$$

Solution

Directly using Wolfram Language:

In[•]:=**x [n_] := δ_n + 2 δ_{n-1} + 3 δ_{n-2} + 4 δ_{n-3};**
y [n_] = x [n + 3] / / PiecewiseExpand

Out[•]= $\begin{cases} 1 & n == -3 \\ 2 & n == -2 \\ 3 & n == -1 \\ 4 & n == 0 \\ 0 & \text{True} \end{cases}$

This shows the sequences $x[n]$ and $y[n]$:

In[•]:=**DiscretePlot [{ x [n] , y [n] } , $\cdots$ $+$]**

Out[•]=

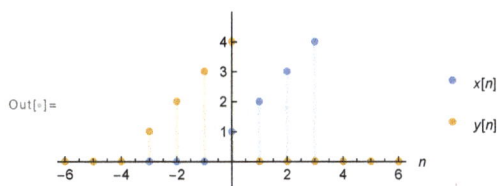

Step-by-step

Proceed as follows

$$y[n] = x[n + 3]$$

Substitute $n \to n + 3$ in the expression for $x[n]$

$$y[n] = \delta[n + 3] + 2\,\delta[(n + 3) - 1] + 3\,\delta[(n + 3) - 2] + 4\,\delta[(n + 3) - 3]$$

Simplify

$$= \delta[n + 3] + 2\,\delta[n + 2] + 3\,\delta[n + 1] + 4\,\delta[n]$$

$$= \begin{cases} 1, & n = -3 \\ 2, & n = -2 \\ 3, & n = -1 \\ 4, & n = 0 \\ 0 & \text{True} \end{cases}$$

Example 4

Obtain the signal resulting from the transformation $x(t) \to x\left(\frac{t-1}{2}\right)$ given the following signal $x(t)$:

```
In[•]:= x[t_] := Piecewise[{ { {t + 1, -1 < t < 0}, {1 - t, 0 < t < 1} } }];
        Plot[x[t], ⋯ ➕ ]
```

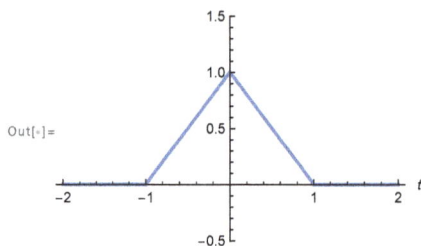

```
Out[•]=
```

Solution

The substitution $t \to \frac{t-1}{2}$ gives:

```
In[•]:= x[ (t - 1)/2 ] // PiecewiseExpand
```

$$\text{Out[•]} = \begin{cases} \frac{3-t}{2} & 1 < t < 3 \\ \frac{1+t}{2} & -1 < t < 1 \\ 0 & \text{True} \end{cases}$$

This shows the two signals:

In[•]:=**Plot [{ x [t] , x [** $\frac{t-1}{2}$ **] } ,** ⎡•••|+⎤ **]**

Out[•]=

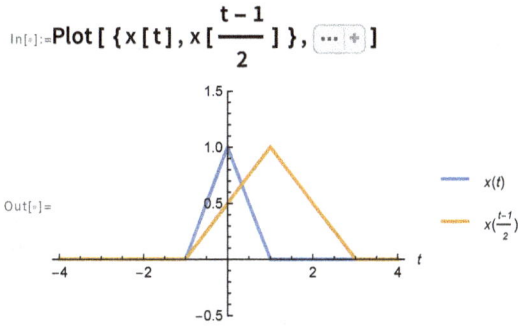

Step-by-step

Substitute $t \to \frac{t-1}{2}$ into the piecewise definition of the signal $x(t)$

$$y(t) = x\!\left(\frac{t-1}{2}\right) = \begin{cases} 1 + \frac{t-1}{2}, & -1 < \frac{t-1}{2} < 0 \\ 1 - \frac{t-1}{2}, & 0 < \frac{t-1}{2} < 1 \\ 0, & \text{else} \end{cases} = \begin{cases} \frac{1}{2} + \frac{t}{2}, & -1 < t < 1 \\ \frac{3}{2} - \frac{t}{2}, & 1 < t < 3 \\ 0, & \text{else} \end{cases}$$

Example 5

Given the signals $x(t)$ and $y(t)$ shown here, determine the transformation $x(t) \to y(t)$:

In[•]:=**x [t_] := Piecewise [{ {** $\frac{1}{2}$ **, −2 ≤ t ≤ 1} , {1 , 1 ≤ t ≤ 2} }];**

GraphicsRow [⎡•••|+⎤ **]**

Out[•]=

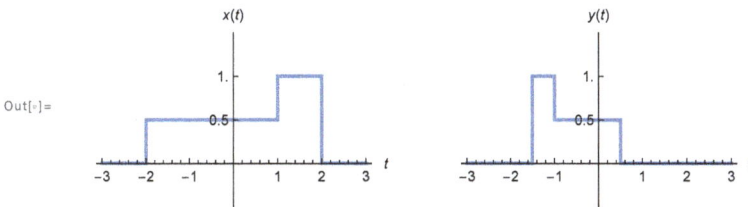

Solution

The shown transformation relates the two signals by a time translation and a time reversal. Therefore, it takes the following form

$$y(t) = x(a\,t + b)$$

The transformation is defined by two unknown parameters, a and b. These two parameters can be obtained from two equations that relate the positions of two corresponding points in the left and right figures, for example, $-2 \to \frac{1}{2}$ and $2 \to -\frac{3}{2}$:

In[•]:=**x [t_] := Piecewise [{ { $\frac{1}{2}$, $-2 \le t \le 1$}, {1, $1 \le t \le 2$} }];**

    GraphicsRow [⋯ ➕]

Out[•]=

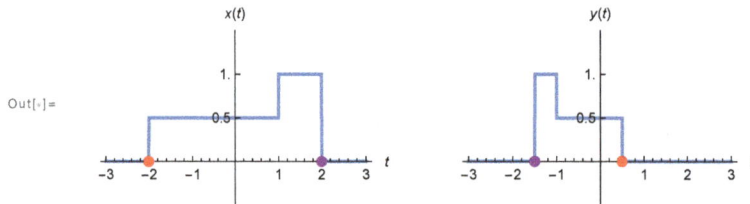

The selected points result in the following system of two equations and two unknowns:

In[•]:=**eqns = { $-2 ==$ ($\frac{1}{2}$) a + b, $2 ==$ ($-\frac{3}{2}$) a + b };**

Solving the system gives the desired parameter values:

In[•]:=**Solve [eqns]**

Out[•]= **{ { a → −2, b → −1 } }**

The transformation takes the form $y(t) = x(-2\,t - 1)$, which results in the following piecewise definition for the function $y(t)$:

In[•]:=**x [t_] := Piecewise [{ { $\frac{1}{2}$, $-2 \le t \le 1$}, {1, $1 \le t \le 2$} }];**

    PiecewiseExpand [x [−2 t − 1]]

Out[•]=
$$
\begin{cases}
\frac{1}{2} & -1 \le t \le \frac{1}{2} \\
1 & -\frac{3}{2} \le t < -1 \\
0 & \text{True}
\end{cases}
$$

A plot of the function confirms that you have the correct solution:

In[•]:=**Plot [x [−2 t − 1], ⋯ ➕]**

Out[•]=

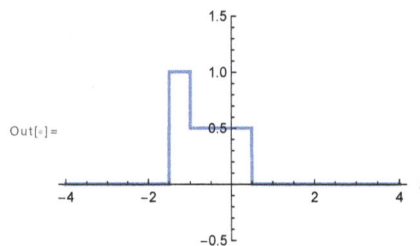

Downsampling

Given a sequence $x[n]$, it is frequently of interest to generate a new sequence by keeping every k^{th} sample only. This is known as downsampling by integer factor k and is defined by the following relation

$$y[n] = x[k\,n], \quad n = 0, 1, 2, \ldots$$

For example

$$y[0] = x[0]$$

$$y[1] = x[k]$$

$$y[2] = x[2\,k]$$

$$y[3] = x[3\,k]$$

This demonstrates downsampling of a finite-length sequence for a range of values of the downsampling factor k:

In[·]:=**DynamicModule [** ⋯ **+** **]**

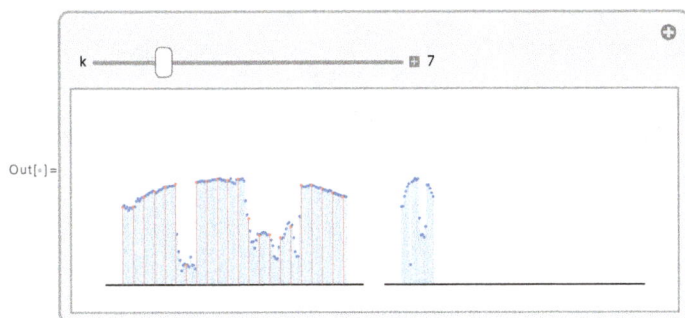

Downsampling is a form of time compression.

Example 6

Downsampling is a common image processing operation. It is frequently employed when transmitting images or when conserving storage space, whether inside a camera, personal computer, or phone.

Use the function **Downsample** with downsampling factor $k = 4$ to diminish the size of the following image:

In[·]:=**i =** **;**

Solution

This returns the downsampled image:

In[•]:=**Downsample [i, 4]**

Out[•]=

This compares the image dimensions before and after downsampling:

In[•]:=**ImageDimensions / @ { i, Downsample [i, 4] }**

Out[•]= { { 300, 200 }, { 75, 50 } }

This shows the effect of downsampling for $1 \leq k \leq 10$:

In[•]:=**Manipulate [··· +]**

Out[•]=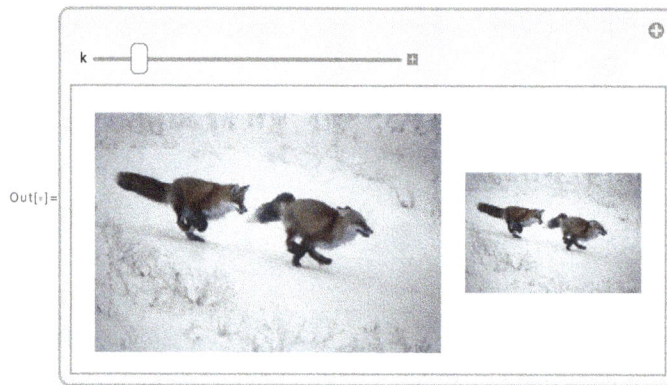

Upsampling

Upsampling is a time-scaling operation defined by the following input-output relationship

$$y[n] = \begin{cases} x\left[\dfrac{n}{k}\right], & n = 0,\ \pm k,\ \pm 2\,k,\ \ldots \\ 0 & \text{otherwise} \end{cases}$$

where k, called the upsampling factor, is a positive integer. Upsampling inserts $k - 1$ zeros between samples of the original signal.

For example, for $k = 2$

$$y[0] = x[0]$$

$$y[1] = 0$$

$$y[2] = x[1]$$

$$y[3] = 0$$

$$y[4] = x[2]$$

$$\vdots$$

This demonstrates upsampling for a range of values of the upsampling factor k:

In[•]:=**DynamicModule [[⋯ +]ᴬ]**

Out[•]=

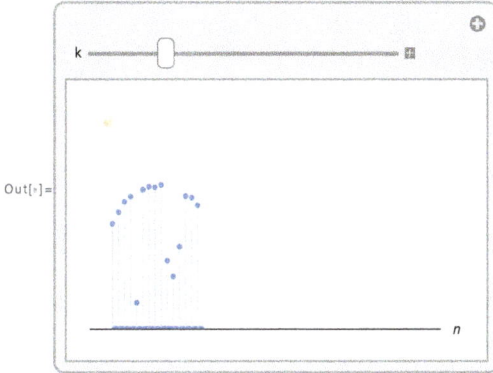

Upsampling is a form of time expansion. Upsampling is usually followed by some kind of averaging to replace the zeros with sample values that better match the original sequence.

Time Compression and Expansion of Audio

To conclude the discussion of elementary operations on signals and sequences, consider the effect of downsampling and upsampling an audio signal.

Here is a clip of Neil Armstrong's famous first words on the moon:

In[•]:=**audio = ExampleData [{ "Audio", "Apollo11SmallStep" }]**

Out[•]=

Time compression of the audio file:

In[•]:=**Downsample [audio, 2]**

Out[•]=

Time expansion of the audio file:

In[•]:=**Upsample [audio, 2]**

Out[•]=

The following sequence of operations returns the original:

In[◦]:=**Downsample [Upsample [audio, 2] , 2]**

Out[◦]=
> ▶ 00:00 ◦——————— 00:09 ◀) ≡
>
> Data in Notebook   ⇥

But reversing the order of the two operations distorts the result since the dropped samples are subsequently replaced by zeros:

In[◦]:=**Upsample [Downsample [audio, 8] , 8]**

Out[◦]=
> ▶ 00:00 ◦——————— 00:09 ◀) ≡
>
> Data in Notebook   ⇥

Summary

Elementary signal processing operations:

- Amplitude scaling
- Level shifting
- Time shifting
- Compression/downsampling
- Expansion/upsampling

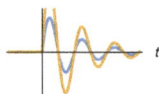

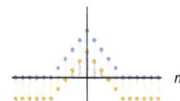

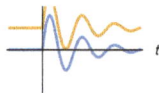

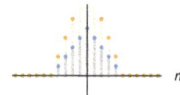

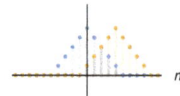

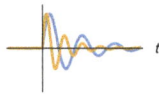

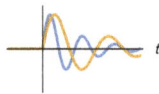

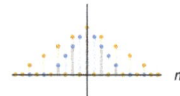

Exercises

Download the solutions manual at wolfr.am/eTextbook-SSSP

4.1 Given the signal $x(t)$ shown here, determine and plot the signal that represents $y(t) = 1 - \frac{3}{2}\, x(t)$.

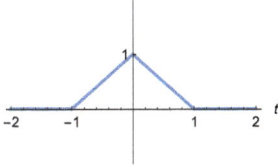

4.2 Obtain $y[n] = 1 - x[n]$ given the following sequence $x[n]$.

$x[n] = 2\,\delta[n] + \delta[n-1] - \delta[n-2] + \delta[n-3]$

4.3 Given the signal $x(t) = e^{-t}\, u(t)$, determine and plot the signal that represents $y(t) = x(1-t)$.

4.4 Obtain $y[n] = x[-1-n]$ given the following sequence $x[n]$.

$x[n] = 2\,\delta[n+1] + \delta[n] - \delta[n-2] + 3\,\delta[n-3]$

4.5 Given the signals $x(t)$ and $y(t)$ shown here, obtain the transformation $x(t) \rightarrow y(\tau) = x(a\,\tau + b)$.

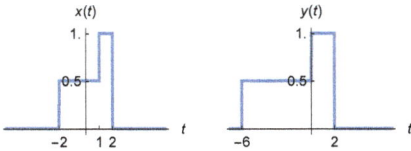

4.6 Given the sequence $x[n] = \cos(\pi\, n)$, determine the sequence that represents $y[n] = x[2\,n]$.

4.7 Given $x(t) = \begin{cases} 1, & -1 \le t \le 1 \\ 0, & \text{else} \end{cases}$, obtain the signal $y(t) = x(t) \cdot x(t-1)$.

4.8 Determine the signal $h(t)$ resulting from the product of the following two signals.

$f(t) = \frac{1}{2} + \frac{1}{2}\cos(2\,\pi\, t)\big)$

$g(t) = u\left(t + \frac{1}{2}\right) - u\left(t - \frac{1}{2}\right)$

4.9 Given the unit step sequence $x[n] = u[n]$, obtain the sequence $y[n] = x[n+2] - x[n-2]$.

4.10 Determine the product of the following two sequences.

$x[n] = \delta[n+1] + \delta[n-1]$

$y[n] = u[n]$

5 | System Properties

For the purposes of this text, a continuous-time system is any circuit, process, or mechanism that transforms an input signal $x(t)$ into an output signal $y(t)$, and in the case of discrete-time systems, any algorithm that transforms an input sequence $x[n]$ into an output sequence $y[n]$.

This chapter begins with a couple of examples. First, a circuit familiar to practically all engineers, a series interconnection of a resistor and capacitor, serves as a simple stand-in for all continuous-time systems. Next, a moving average and an exponentially weighted moving-average system are presented as examples of discrete-time systems.

Signal processing systems are categorized according to the following short list of properties: linearity, time invariance, causality, stability, and memory. Each of the properties will be defined and examples of how to determine if a particular system satisfies a specific property will be shown.

Featured System—RC Circuit

The mathematical model of a passive electrical circuit consisting of a series interconnection of a resistor and capacitor with input $x(t)$ and output $y(t)$, as shown here, is a first-order ordinary differential equation with constant coefficients

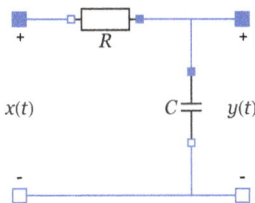

Application of standard circuit analysis techniques (Kirchhoff's current law and Ohm's law, for example) results in the following differential equation, where R and C are the values of the resistor and capacitor circuit components, respectively

$$R\,C\,\frac{d\,y(t)}{d\,t} + y(t) = x(t)$$

Moving-Average System

The moving-average system is commonly used to smooth data. Here is the definition of a moving-average system that averages over N consecutive input sample values

$$y[n] = \frac{1}{N}\,(x[n] + x[n-1] + \dots + x[n-N-1])$$

This shows the result of averaging over N neighboring samples for a row of an image and an entire image:

In[•]:=**Manipulate [$\cdots$ +]**

Out[•]=

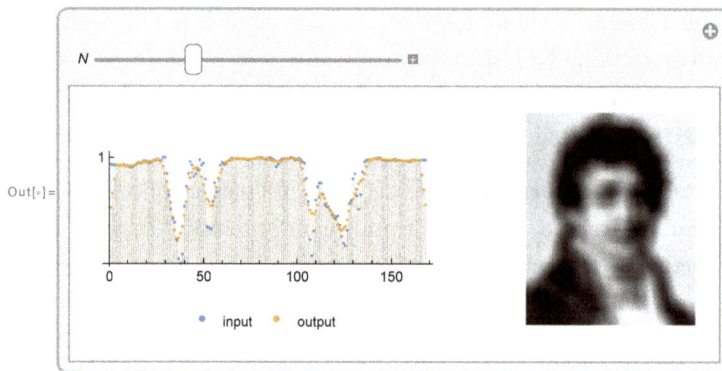

Note how increasing the number of samples N being averaged increases the degree of smoothing.

Exponentially Weighted Moving-Average Filter

The moving-average filter applies the same weight to all input samples. In some applications, it may be beneficial to place more emphasis on data samples near the time instant n and less emphasis on data samples that are further away in determining the average.

Such an average can be computed using an exponentially weighted moving-average filter

$$y[n] - \alpha\,y[n-1] = x[n], \qquad 0 < \alpha < 1$$

The following derivation illustrates the exponential weighting of the system inputs

$$y[n] = \alpha\ y[n-1] + x[n]$$

$$= \alpha\ (\alpha\ y[n-2] + x[n-1]) + x[n]$$

$$= \alpha^2\ y[n-2] + \alpha\ x[n-1] + x[n]$$

$$= \alpha\ (\alpha^2\ y[n-3] + x[n-2]) + \alpha\ x[n-1] + x[n]$$

$$= \alpha^3\ y[n-3] + \alpha^2\ x[n-2] + \alpha\ x[n-1] + x[n]$$

For $0 < \alpha < 1$, it can be seen that the weights of the past inputs get progressively smaller at an exponential rate.

This shows the output of a similar system for values of α in the range $0 \le \alpha \le 1$ when applied to the sample values of an image row and the entire image:

In[∘]:=**Manipulate [** ⎡ ⋯ + ⎤ **]**

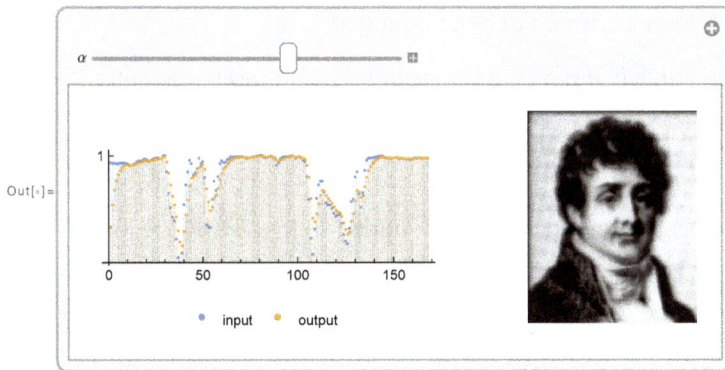

System Properties—Memory

A system is said to be memoryless if its output at a given time is dependent only on the input at that same time. For example, the systems specified by the relations shown here are memoryless

$$y(t) = a\ x(t)$$

$$y[n] = 2\ x[n] - \frac{1}{2}\ x[n]^2$$

$$y(t) = (t-1)\ x(t)$$

Conversely, in so-called memory systems, the output is a function of present and past outputs. The following are examples of memory systems

$$y(t) = x(t - 1)$$

$$y(t) = \frac{1}{C} \int_{-\infty}^{t} x(\tau) \, d\tau$$

$$y[n] = \frac{1}{3} \left(x[n] + x[n - 1] + x[n - 2] \right)$$

Stability

A signal $x(t)$ (or sequence $x[n]$) defined on some interval with real or complex values is called bounded if its values are bounded. There exists a real number such that for all t (or n) on the interval of interest

$$|x(t)| < A_x \qquad (\text{or } |x[n]| < B_x)$$

A function that is not bounded is said to be unbounded.

A system is defined as stable if and only if for every bounded input, the output $y(t)$ (or $y[n]$) is bounded

$$|y(t)| < A_y \qquad (\text{or } |y[n]| < B_y)$$

This type of stability is called bounded-input, bounded-output (BIBO) stability.

Example 1

Determine the stability of the following system

$$y(t) = t \, x(t)$$

Solution

Consider the bounded input $x(t) = \sin(t) \, u(t)$. Evaluating for $t \geq 0$, you get $y(t) = t \sin(t)$, which grows without bounds for increasing values of t. The system is unstable.

Here is a plot of the input and output:

In[•]:=**Plot [{ Sin [t] , t Sin [t] } , ⋯ +]**

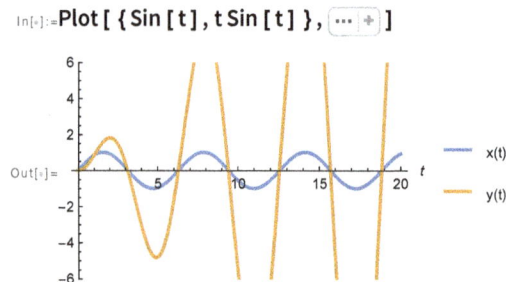

Example 2

Determine the stability of the following averaging system if the sequence $x[n]$ is bounded

$$y[n] = \frac{1}{N} \sum_{k=0}^{N-1} x[n-k]$$

Solution

The magnitude of the output is

$$|y[n]| = \left| \frac{1}{N} \sum_{k=0}^{N-1} x[n-k] \right| \leq \frac{1}{N} \sum_{k=0}^{N-1} |x[n-k]| \leq \frac{1}{N} N B_x \leq B_x$$

This shows that the averaging system is BIBO stable.

System Properties—Causality

In a causal system, the output signal at time t_0, namely $y(t_0)$, depends on only values of the input signal $x(t)$ for $t \leq t_0$. Equivalently, using discrete-time notation, if $x[n] = 0$ for $n < n_0$, then the output must be such that $y[n] = 0$ for $n < n_0$. In other words, the output may never precede the input or anticipate future values of the input. Causal systems are therefore also known as non-anticipative.

Given an input that starts at $t_0 = 0$, the following outputs represent causal responses (i.e. outputs)

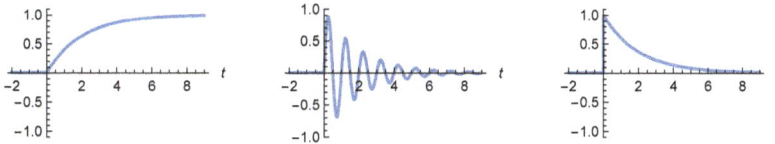

Conversely, the following are examples of non-causal system responses

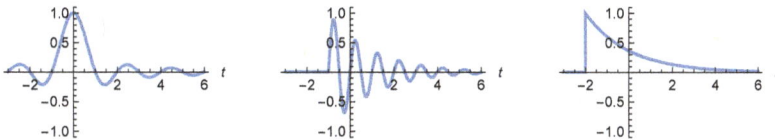

Example 3

In a system with a unit pulse input and a unit triangle output as shown here

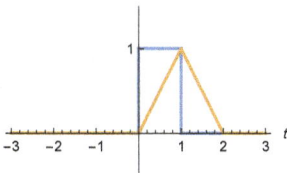

which of the following responses characterizes a causal and which a non-causal system?

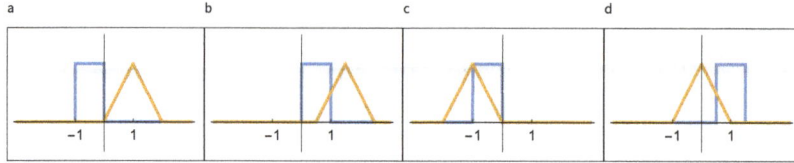

Solution

A. Causal since the output does not precede the input.

B. Causal since the output does not precede the input.

C. Non-causal since the output precedes the input.

D. Non-causal since the output precedes the input.

Example 4

Determine the causality of the following system

$$y[n] = x[n + 1] + x[n] + x[n - 1]$$

Solution

Use the unit sample as the input, $x[n] = \delta[n]$, and evaluate

$$y[n] = \delta[n + 1] + \delta[n] + \delta[n - 1]$$

Now determine if the system returns a nonzero output value prior to the onset of the input sequence at $n = 0$. Starting at $n = -2$, you get

$$y[-2] = \delta[-1] + \delta[-2] + \delta[-3] = 0$$

$$y[-1] = \delta[0] + \delta[-1] + \delta[-2] = 1$$

$$y[0] = \delta[1] + \delta[0] + \delta[-1] = 1$$

$$y[1] = \delta[2] + \delta[1] + \delta[0] = 1$$

$$y[2] = 0, \text{ etc.}$$

Note that $y[-1] = 1$; therefore, since $y[n] \neq 0$ prior to the onset of the input at $n = 0$, the system is non-causal. Also, directly from the defining equation, note that in order to determine the output value at time n, the system needs to "know" the value of the input at time $n + 1$, namely a future value. This again leads to the conclusion that the system is non-causal.

System Properties—Time Invariance

For a time-invariant system, if the response to an input $x(t)$ (or $x[n]$) is the output $y(t)$ (or $y[n]$)

$$x(t) \rightarrow y(t), \qquad x[n] \rightarrow y[n]$$

then the response to a delayed input must be delayed by the same amount

$$x(t - t_0) \rightarrow y(t - t_0), \qquad x[n - n_0] \rightarrow y[n - n_0]$$

Time invariance is also frequently called shift invariance.

Example 5

In a system in which a unit pulse input results in a unit triangle output as shown here

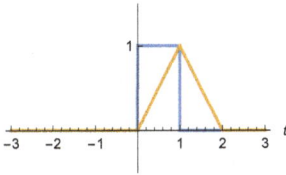

which of the input-output examples shown here represent time-invariant and which time-variant systems?

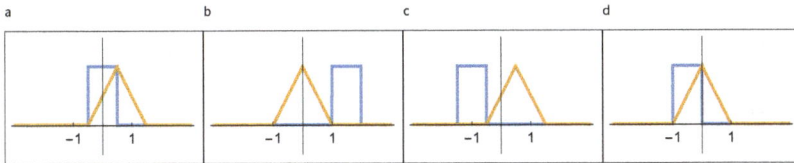

Solution

A. The input is $x(t + 1/2)$ and the output is $y(t + 1/2)$; therefore, the system is time invariant.

B. The shown input is $x(t - 1)$, but the output is $y(t + 1)$; therefore, the system is NOT time invariant.

C. The shown input is $x(t + 3/2)$, but the output is $y(t + 1/2)$; therefore, the system is NOT time invariant.

D. The shown input is $x(t + 1)$ and the output is $y(t + 1)$; therefore, the system is time invariant.

Example 6

Determine if the downsampling system defined here is time invariant

$$y[n] = x[2\,n], \qquad n = \ldots, -1, 0, 1, 2, \ldots$$

Solution

Time invariance requires that a shifted input sequence results in an equally shifted output. However, as shown here, a shift in the output sequence does not correspond to an equal shift in the input sequence

$$y[n - n_0] = x[2\,(n - n_0)] = x[2\,n - 2\,n_0] \neq x[2\,n - n_0]$$

Therefore, the downsampling system is not time invariant.

For example, consider the following sequence

$$x[n] = (-1)^n$$

The sequence is shown here:

```
In[•]:= x[n_] := (-1)^n;
        DiscretePlot[x[n], ··· + ]
```

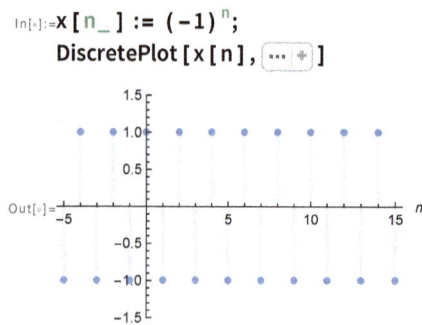

Downsampling by a factor of 2 results in the following

$$x[2\,n] = (-1)^{2\,n} = 1$$

Shown here:

```
In[•]:= DiscretePlot[x[2n], ··· + ]
```

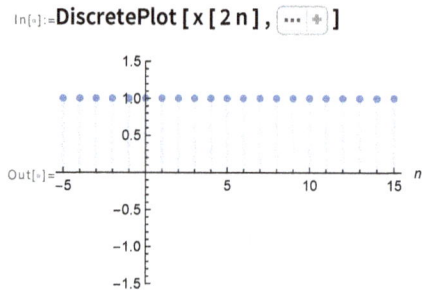

However, the time-shifted sequence $y[n] = x[n-1]$ is

$$y[n] = (-1)^{n-1} = -(-1)^n$$

Downsampling this sequence, you get

$$y[2\,n] = -(-1)^{2\,n} = -1$$

Shown here:

```
In[•]:= y[n_] := x[n-1];
        DiscretePlot[y[2n], ··· + ]
```

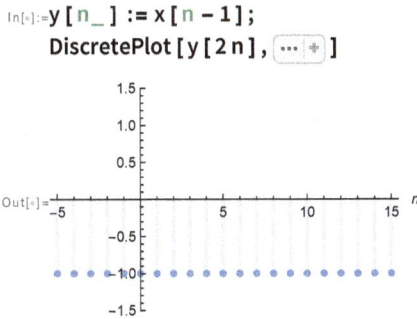

Clearly, the second result is not a shifted version of the first. This confirms that the downsampling operation is not time invariant.

System Properties—Linearity

Given that a response to input $x_1(t)$ is $y_1(t)$, denoted $x_1(t) \rightarrow y_1(t)$ and the response to $x_2(t)$ is $x_2(t) \rightarrow y_2(t)$, the response of a linear system to the following linear superposition of $x_1(t)$ and $x_2(t)$

$$x(t) = a\,x_1(t) + b\,x_2(t)$$

must take the following form, a superposition of the individual responses $y_1(t)$ and $y_2(t)$

$$y(t) = a\,y_1(t) + b\,y_2(t)$$

Otherwise, the system is said to be nonlinear.

A system that is both linear and time invariant (shift invariant) is known as a linear time-invariant (LTI) or linear shift-invariant (LSI) system.

Example 7

Consider a system S whose input $x(t)$ and output $y(t)$ are related by

$$y(t) = x^2(t)$$

Determine if the system is linear.

Solution

Let $x(t)$ be a linear combination of $x_1(t)$ and $x_2(t)$

$$x(t) = a\, x_1(t) + b\, x_2(t)$$

If $x(t)$ is an input into system $\mathcal{S}$, then the output is

$$
\begin{aligned}
y(t) &= x^2(t) \\
&= (a\, x_1(t) + b\, x_2(t))^2 \\
&= a^2\, x_1{}^2(t) + b^2\, x_2{}^2(t) + 2\, a\, b\, x_1(t)\, x_2(t) \\
&\neq a\, y_1(t) + b\, y_2(t)
\end{aligned}
$$

The system is not linear.

Example 8

Determine if the system described by the equation shown here is linear

$$y(t) = x(t)\cos(\omega_0\, t)$$

Solution

Let

$$x(t) = a_1\, x_1(t) + a_2\, x_2(t)$$

Then

$$y(t) = (a_1\, x_1(t) + a_2\, x_2(t))\cos(\omega_0\, t)$$

$$= a_1\, x_1(t)\cos(\omega_0\, t) + a_2\, x_2(t)\cos(\omega_0\, t)$$

$$= a_1\, y_1(t) + a_2\, y_2(t)$$

The system is linear, because the superposition property is satisfied.

Example 9

In an LTI system, the pulse input $x(t)$ results in a unit triangle output $y(t)$ as shown here

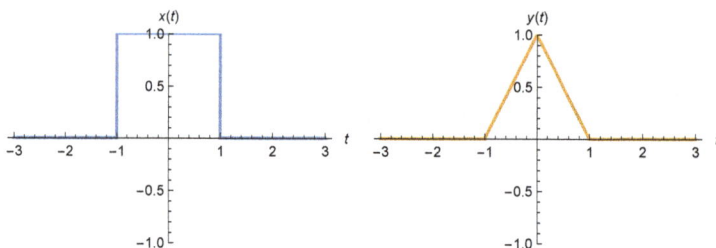

Given the input $w(t)$ shown here, use the principles of linearity and time invariance to determine the output

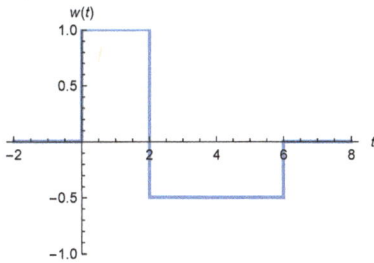

Solution

This defines signals $x(t)$ and $y(t)$, respectively:

```
In[•]:= x [ t_ ] := UnitBox [ t / 2 ];
        y [ t_ ] := UnitTriangle [ t ];
```

Observe that the signal $w(t)$ can be obtained from a superposition of the following scaled and shifted copies of $x(t)$:

```
In[•]:= GraphicsRow [ ⋯ + ]
```

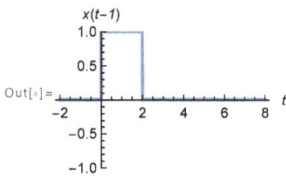 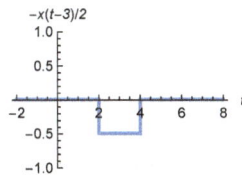 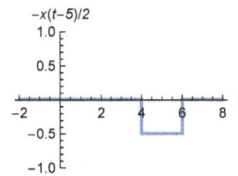

Resulting in the following formula for $w(t)$:

```
In[•]:= w [ t_ ] := x [ t − 1 ] − ½ x [ t − 3 ] − ½ x [ t − 5 ];
```

Now, due to linearity and time invariance, the output must have the following form:

```
In[•]:= z [ t_ ] := y [ t − 1 ] − ½ y [ t − 3 ] − ½ y [ t − 5 ];
```

This shows the input $w(t)$ and the output $z(t)$:

```
In[•]:= Plot [ { w [ t ], z [ t ] }, ⋯ + ]
```

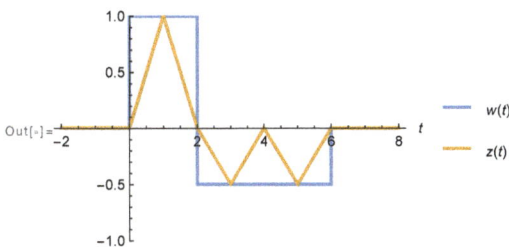

Example 10

In a discrete-time LSI system, a unit sample input $x_1[n] = \delta[n]$ results in the output $y_1[n] = \delta[n] + \frac{1}{2}\,\delta[n-1]$ as shown here

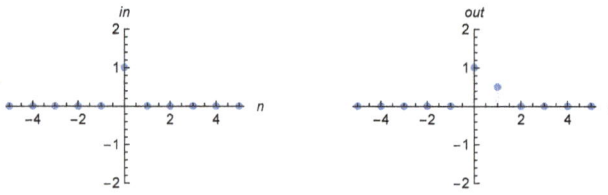

Given the input $x[n] = -\delta[n+1] + \delta[n] - 2\,\delta[n-2]$ shown here, use the principles of linearity and shift invariance to determine the output

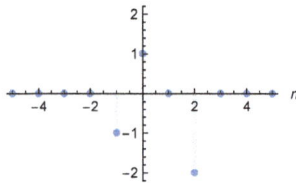

Solution

Express $x[n]$ in terms of input $x_1[n]$. This gives

$$x[n] = -\delta[n+1] + \delta[n] - 2\,\delta[n-2] = -x_1[n+1] + x_1[n] - 2\,x_1[n-2]$$

Now in an LSI system, the output must be a superposition of system responses due to each of the scaled and shifted inputs. Therefore

$$y[n] = -y_1[n+1] + y_1[n] - 2\,y_1[n-2]$$

Use time invariance to express each output in terms of unit samples

$$= -\left(\delta[n+1] + \frac{1}{2}\,\delta[n]\right) + \left(\delta[n] + \frac{1}{2}\,\delta[n-1]\right) - 2\left(\delta[n-2] + \frac{1}{2}\,\delta[n-3]\right)$$

Simplify

$$= -\delta[n+1] + \frac{3}{2}\,\delta[n] + \frac{1}{2}\,\delta[n-1] - 2\,\delta[n-2] - \delta[n-3]$$

This shows the output:

$$\mathrm{In[\bullet]:=}\ \mathbf{DiscretePlot}\left[-\boldsymbol{\delta}_{n+1} + \frac{\boldsymbol{\delta}_n}{2} + \frac{\boldsymbol{\delta}_{n-1}}{2} - 2\,\boldsymbol{\delta}_{n-2} - \boldsymbol{\delta}_{n-3}, \boxed{\cdots +} \right]$$

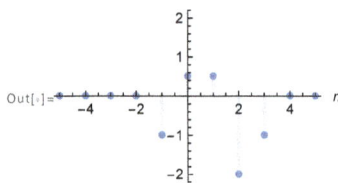

Summary

This chapter presented several fundamental properties of linear time-invariant, continuous-time, and discrete-time systems.

Continuous-time systems:

- Linearity $\qquad\qquad$ $a\, x_1(t) + b\, x_2(t) \;\longrightarrow\;$ $\qquad$ $a\, y_1(t) + b\, y_2(t)$

- Time invariance $\qquad$ $x(t - t_0)$ $\qquad\qquad\longrightarrow\;$ $\qquad$ $y(t - t_0)$

- Causality $\qquad\qquad$ $x(t) = 0,\; t < t_0 \;\longrightarrow\;$ $\qquad$ $y(t) = 0,\; t < t_0$

- Stability $\qquad\qquad$ $|x(t)|_{\max} < A \;\longrightarrow\;$ $\qquad$ $|y(t)|_{\max} < B$

Discrete-time systems:

- Linearity $\qquad\qquad$ $a\, x_1[n] + b\, x_2[n] \;\longrightarrow\;$ $\qquad$ $a\, y_1[n] + b\, y_2[n]$

- Time invariance $\qquad$ $x[n - n_0]$ $\qquad\qquad\longrightarrow\;$ $\qquad$ $y[n - n_0]$

- Causality $\qquad\qquad$ $x[n] = 0,\; n < n_0 \;\longrightarrow\;$ $\qquad$ $y[n] = 0,\; n < n_0$

- Stability $\qquad\qquad$ $|x[n]|_{\max} < A \;\longrightarrow\;$ $\qquad$ $|y[n]|_{\max} < B$

Examples of determining and verifying the properties of a system were also given.

Exercises

Download the solutions manual at wolfr.am/eTextbook-SSSP

5.1 Various output responses are shown for a unit pulse input (shown in blue). Which case represents a non-causal response?

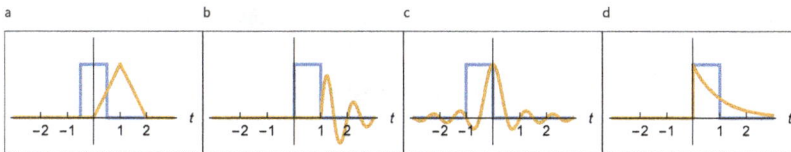

5.2 Which of the following discrete-time systems represents a memory system?

A. $y[n] = (n - 1)\, x[n]$

B. $y[n] = x[n - 1]$

C. $y[n] = 2\, x[n] - x[n]^2$

D. None of the above

5.3 The response $y(t)$ of an LTI system to an input $x(t)$ is shown here.

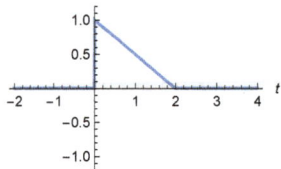

Obtain the response to the input $x(t-1)$.

5.4 In an LTI system, the following input-output pair is observed.

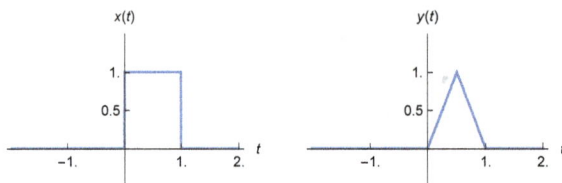

Determine the response of the system to the following input.

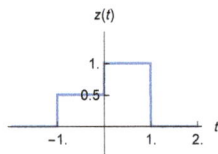

5.5 In an LTI system, the input $x(t) = \delta(t)$ results in a response $h(t)$ of the following form.

$$h(t) = e^{-3t}\, u(t)$$

Use principles of linearity and time invariance to determine the output $y(t)$ given the following input.

$$x(t) = -\delta(t) + 2\,\delta(t-2) + \frac{1}{2}\,\delta(t-5)$$

5.6 In an LTI system, the input $\delta[n]$ results in the response $h[n] = \delta[n+1] - \delta[n] + \delta[n-1]$. Use time invariance to determine the response of the system to the input signal $\delta[n-2]$.

5.7 In an LTI system, the input $\delta[n]$ results in the following response.

$$h[n] = \delta[n] + \delta[n-1] + \delta[n-2]$$

Use linearity and time invariance to determine the response of the system to the following input sequence.

$$x[n] = -\delta[n] + 2\,\delta[n-1] + \delta[n-2]$$

5.8 Determine the (A) linearity and (B) time invariance of the following system.

$$y(t) = x(\alpha t)$$

5.9 Given the system $y[n] = x[n] + \alpha$, where α is a nonzero constant, determine whether or not it is linear.

5.10 Determine the (A) linearity and (B) time invariance of the following discrete-time system.

$$y[n] = \frac{1}{2}\,(x[n] + x[n+1])$$

Time-Domain Analysis (Continuous)

6 | Continuous-Time Systems as Differential Equations

Linear time-invariant (LTI) systems naturally lead to mathematical models in terms of ordinary constant coefficient differential equations. Constant coefficient differential equations are a particularly simple category of differential equations for which solution methods are well known and computationally simple. Such equations, or systems of such equations, are encountered in the study and practice of almost any area of engineering.

In electrical engineering, such systems take the form of interconnected networks of electrical components, such as resistors, capacitors, and operational amplifiers (op-amps) to name just a select few. The voltages and currents in these networks (also known as circuits) are governed by fundamental laws, such as Ohm's and Kirchhoff's, and systematic methods of analysis have been developed to derive their mathematical models.

Two popular circuits, the series RC circuit and a unity gain Sallen–Key lowpass filter, will be introduced next, and standard circuit analysis will be used to derive their mathematical models.

The RC Circuit

The simple series interconnection of a resistor and a capacitor is the most common circuit encountered in the study of electrical engineering

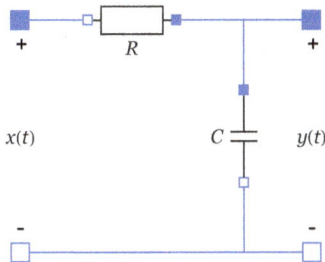

Recall that the current and voltage in a resistor and a capacitor are related, respectively, by the following two equations

$$i_R(t) = \frac{1}{R}\, v_R(t), \qquad i_C(t) = C\, \frac{d\,v_C(t)}{d\,t}$$

This identifies the resistor and capacitor currents and voltages in the circuit

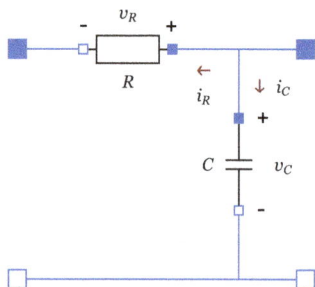

Applying Kirchhoff's current law to the node between the resistor and capacitor yields the following relation between the resistor and capacitor currents

$$i_R(t) + i_C(t) = 0$$

Substitution of the current-voltage relations for each of the two circuit components results in the following differential equation in terms of the voltage drops across the two components

$$\frac{1}{R}\, v_R(t) + C\, \frac{d\,v_C(t)}{d\,t} = 0$$

Recognizing that $v_C(t) = y(t)$ and $v_R(t) = y(t) - x(t)$ gives an equation in terms of the input and output signals, respectively, $x(t)$ and $y(t)$, as shown here

$$\frac{1}{R}\, (y(t) - x(t)) + C\, \frac{d\,y(t)}{d\,t} = 0$$

Next, a simple reordering of the terms gives the differential equation in a common form that leads with the highest derivative of the output signal $y(t)$

$$R\,C\, \frac{d\,y(t)}{d\,t} + y(t) = x(t)$$

The product $R\,C$ is commonly called the time constant of the circuit. The equation belongs to a class of equations known as ordinary linear constant coefficient differential equations.

The typical goal in circuit analysis is to obtain the output signal $y(t)$, in this case the voltage across the capacitor, in response to some given input voltage $x(t)$. Given the differential equation model of the circuit, the output $y(t)$ can be readily obtained by solving the differential equation. The method for solving such an equation will be presented in a later chapter.

This shows the response of the RC circuit to three common input signals:

In[•]:=**DynamicModule [⋯ ➕ ▲]**

Out[•]=

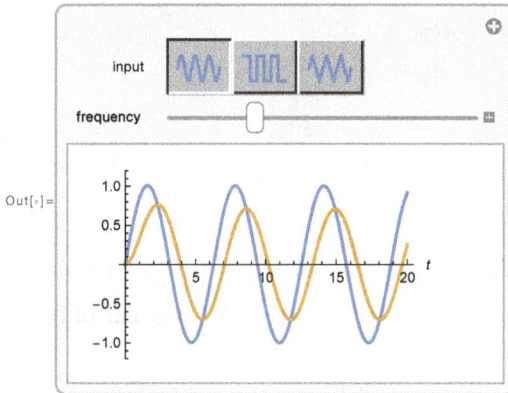

The Unity Gain Sallen–Key Circuit

The Sallen–Key active filters are a well-known and popular family of op-amp–based circuit structures for implementing common forms of analog filters typically needed in continuous-time signal processing applications.

This shows a model of the so-called unity gain lowpass Sallen–Key filter

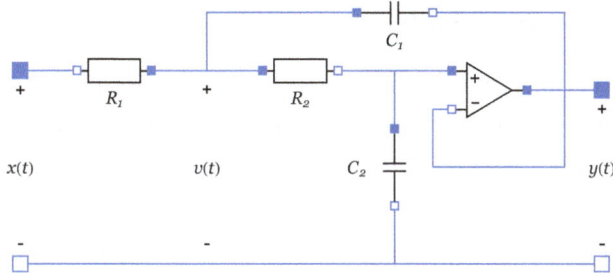

As shown here, the unity gain lowpass Sallen–Key filter can be modeled by a second-order differential equation or a system of two first-order equations. Applying basic circuit laws and assuming an ideal op-amp gives the following two current equations

$$\begin{cases} i_{R_1} + i_{C_1} + i_{R_2} = 0 \\ -i_{R_2} + i_{C_2} = 0 \end{cases}$$

This shows all the relevant branch currents

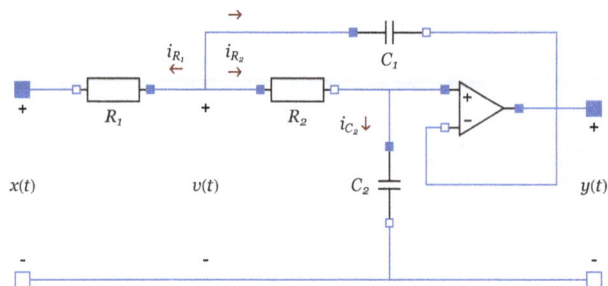

With the substitutions $i_{R_1} = \frac{1}{R_1}(v(t) - x(t))$, $i_{R_2} = \frac{1}{R_2}(v(t) - y(t))$, $i_{C_1} = C_1 \frac{d}{dt}(v(t) - y(t))$, and $i_{C_2} = C_2 \frac{d}{dt} y(t)$, the pair of current equations becomes the following pair of first-order differential equations

$$\begin{cases} \frac{1}{R_1}(v(t) - x(t)) + C_1 \frac{d}{dt}(v(t) - y(t)) + \frac{1}{R_2}(v(t) - y(t)) = 0 \\ -\frac{1}{R_2}(v(t) - y(t)) + C_2 \frac{d}{dt} y(t) = 0 \end{cases}$$

Given an input signal $x(t)$, this system of first-order differential equations can be solved to obtain explicit solutions for the node voltage $v(t)$ and output voltage $y(t)$. Alternatively, the two equations can be combined into one second-order differential equation by solving for $v(t)$ in the second equation and substituting it into the first. The resulting equation implicitly relates the input and output signals

$$R_1 R_2 C_1 C_2 \frac{d^2}{dt^2} y(t) + (R_1 + R_2) C_2 \frac{d}{dt} y(t) + y(t) = x(t)$$

As was the case with the RC circuit, the mathematical model is in the form of an ordinary linear constant coefficient differential equation. Also, as in the case of the RC circuit, this differential equation can be solved for the output signal $y(t)$ using a well-known solution method.

This shows the response of a Sallen–Key lowpass filter to sine, square, and triangle waves across a range of frequencies of the input signals:

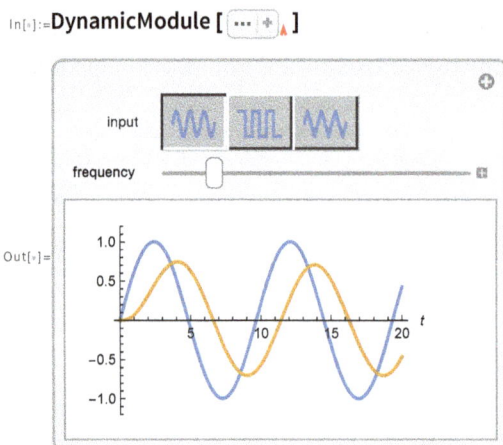

As can be observed, the amplitude of the output signal diminishes as the frequency of the input signal is increased. This type of response characterizes so-called low-pass filters. The analysis and design of filters will be a major topic in subsequent chapters of this book.

Time-Domain Representation of LTI Systems

As demonstrated, passive and active electronic circuits are modeled by linear constant coefficient differential equations.

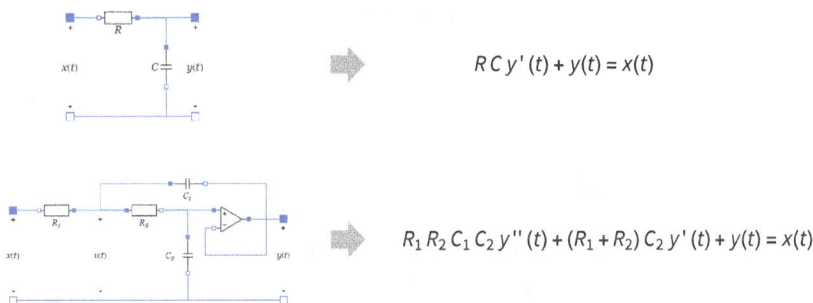

In general, such equations take the following general form

$$a_n \, y^{(n)}(t) + a_{n-1} \, y^{(n-1)}(t) + \ldots + a_0 \, y(t) = b_m \, x^{(m)}(t) + b_{m-1} \, x^{(m-1)}(t) + \ldots + b_0 \, x(t)$$

where $y^{(n)} = \frac{d^n}{dt^n} \, y(t)$, $x^{(m)} = \frac{d^m}{dt^m} \, x(t)$, and n is known as the order of the equation.

Frequently, the following simplified form is used

$$a_n \, y^{(n)}(t) + a_{n-1} \, y^{(n-1)}(t) + \ldots + a_0 \, y(t) = x(t)$$

The differential equation describes how the input $x(t)$, output $y(t)$, and their derivatives interrelate, and the goal is to find the output signal $y(t)$, the so-called response, given knowledge of the input signal $x(t)$, namely, to find an explicit expression for $y(t)$.

Both analytical and numerical methods are readily available.

Summary

Mathematical modeling of passive and active electrical circuits was described.

Such models take the form of linear constant coefficient differential equations

$$R\,C\,y'(t) + y(t) = x(t)$$

$$R_1 \, R_2 \, C_1 \, C_2 \, y''(t) + (R_1 + R_2) \, C_2 \, y'(t) + y(t) = x(t)$$

Typical responses to sine waves and square waves were demonstrated and their dependence on the frequency of the input signal was illustrated.

Exercises

6.1 Obtain the differential equation model for the voltage across the resistor in the series RC circuit shown here.

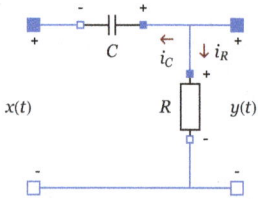

Recall that the current and voltage in the resistor and capacitor are related by the equations $i_R(t) = \frac{1}{R} v_R(t)$ and $i_C(t) = C \frac{d v_C(t)}{dt}$, respectively. Use Kirchhoff's current law that states that the sum of directed currents at a node must be zero.

6.2 Obtain the differential equation model for the loop current $i(t)$ in the following series RL circuit. The signal labeled $x(t)$ is the source voltage.

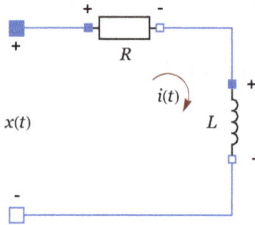

Recall that the current and voltage in the resistor and inductor are related by the equations $v_R(t) = R\, i_R(t)$ and $v_L(t) = L \frac{d i_L(t)}{dt}$, respectively. Use Kirchhoff's voltage law that states that the directed sum of the voltages around a circuit loop must be zero.

6.3 Obtain the differential equation model for the voltage $y(t)$ across the capacitor in the following RLC circuit. The signal labeled $x(t)$ is the source voltage.

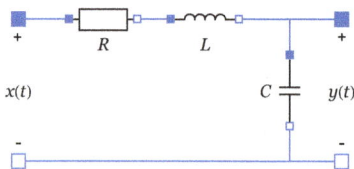

6.4 Obtain the differential equation model for the voltage $y(t)$ in the following circuit. Assume $R_1 = R_2 = 1\,\Omega$ and $C_1 = C_2 = 1$ F.

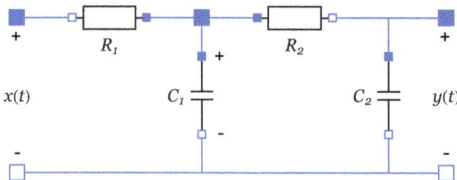

6.5 Obtain the differential equation model for the voltage $y(t)$ in the following circuit.

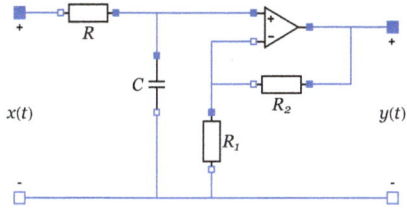

6.6 Obtain the differential equation model for the voltage $y(t)$ in the following circuit.

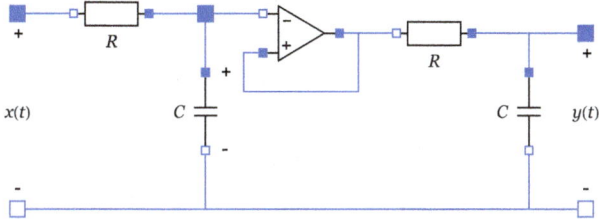

7 | Differential Equation Solution Methods

In this chapter, a classic approach to solving ordinary constant coefficient differential equations is presented. Algebraic solutions of constant coefficient differential equations are well known, mostly a sequence of well-defined but tedious and time-consuming steps if done by hand. Of course, it is still important to learn and understand these algebraic solution methods even if modern computer software can be used to obtain these results for us.

The solution method consists of the following two steps. First, one finds a general solution of the differential equation with the input set to zero. This is commonly referred to as the complementary, homogeneous, or null solution. Next, a solution commonly called a particular solution, one that matches the form of the input signal, is found. One method for finding the particular solution is the method of undetermined coefficients. Its main limitation, that it can be used to solve for only a limited number of input signals, is of no great concern in the case of linear time-invariant (LTI) systems since the signals for which this method works includes all that are of interest, namely the unit step, a sine or cosine, and a real or complex exponential. In the end, a sum of the two solutions gives the total solution of the differential equation. The two steps are described in more detail next.

Complementary Solution

The complementary (also homogeneous or null) solution is a solution of the following differential equation

$$a_n \, y^{(n)}(t) + a_{n-1} \, y^{(n-1)}(t) + \ldots + a_0 \, y(t) = 0$$

This equation implies that $y^{(n)}(t)$ is a linear combination of all the lower derivatives. This in turn suggests that the solution must be of the form $y(t) = e^{st}$ since derivatives of e^{st} are just constants times e^{st}. Substitution of $y(t) = e^{st}$ into the homogeneous differential equation gives

$$a_n s^n e^{st} + a_{n-1} s^{n-1} e^{st} + \ldots + e^{st} = 0$$

$$\left(a_n s^n + a_{n-1} s^{n-1} + \ldots + a_0\right) e^{st} = 0$$

Since e^{st} can never be zero, it can be eliminated, resulting in the following polynomial equation, commonly called the characteristic equation

$$a_n s^n + a_{n-1} s^{n-1} + \ldots + a_0 = 0$$

The n roots of this equation are called the characteristic roots. There are now two possible cases to explore. All the roots may be distinct or some of them may repeat.

If the roots are distinct, the complementary solution is then a linear combination of n exponentials

$$y_c(t) = c_1 e^{s_1 t} + c_2 e^{s_2 t} + \ldots + c_n e^{s_n t}$$

However, if a root s_i is repeated k times (also known as multiplicity k), then it can be shown that the form of the solution is

$$y_c(t) = c_1 e^{s_1 t} + \ldots + c_{i1} e^{s_i t} + c_{i2} t e^{s_i t} + \ldots + c_{ik} t^{k-1} e^{s_i t} + \ldots + c_{n-k} e^{s_{n-k} t}$$

Here each exponential term, due to the repeated root s_i, is multiplied by a different power of t. This is necessary so no two terms are scalar multiples of each other, namely linearly dependent of each other.

The coefficients c_i can be determined if n initial conditions are given.

Example 1

Find the complementary solution $y_c(t)$ for $t > 0$ of the following homogeneous differential equation

$$y'(t) + y(t) = 0$$

Solution

The general form of the homogeneous solution has the shape of a scaled exponential:

In[•]:= `DSolveValue [ y'[t] + y[t] == 0, y[t], t]`

Out[•]= $e^{-t} c_1$

This shows a family of solutions for several values of the coefficient c_1:

In[•]:= **Plot [** $\boxed{\cdots \,\, +}$ **]**

Out[•]=

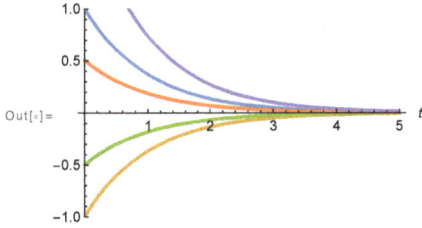

Step-by-step

Substitution of $y(t) = e^{st}$ and $y'(t) = s\,e^{st}$ into the homogeneous differential equation and the subsequent elimination of the e^{st} term results in the following characteristic equation

$$s\,e^{st} + e^{st} = (s + 1)\,e^{st} = 0$$

Therefore

$$s + 1 = 0$$

and the characteristic root is

$$s = -1$$

Therefore, the complementary solution for $t \geq 0$ takes the form

$$y(t) = c_1\,e^{-t}$$

Example 2

Find the complementary solution $y_c(t)$ for $t > 0$ of the following homogeneous differential equation

$$y''(t) + 2\,y'(t) + y(t) = 0$$

Solution

The general form of the complementary solution of the given differential equation is:

In[•]:= **DSolveValue [y''[t] + 2 y'[t] + y[t] == 0, y[t], t]**

Out[•]= $e^{-t}\,c_1 + e^{-t}\,t\,c_2$

This plots the solutions for a few values of the coefficients c_1 and c_2:

In[•]:=**Plot [** ⋯ **+** **]**

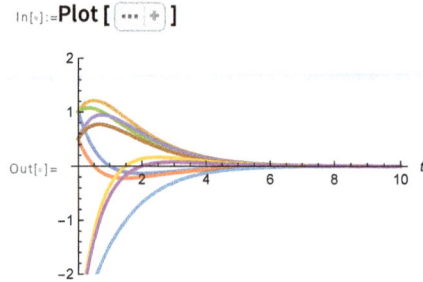

Out[•]=

Step-by-step

Substitution of $y(t) = e^{st}$ into the homogeneous differential equation yields the following equation

$$s^2 \, e^{st} + 2 \, s \, e^{st} + e^{st} = e^{st}(s^2 + 2 \, s + 1) = 0$$

The characteristic equation is

$$s^2 + 2 \, s + 1 = 0$$

which gives the following repeated characteristic root (multiplicity of 2)

$$s_1 = s_2 = -1$$

and the following single exponential term $e^{s_1 t} = e^{s_2 t} = e^{-t}$. Multiplication by t gives the second linearly independent term of the solution. The general solution then takes the form

$$y_c(t) = c_1 \, e^{-t} + c_2 \, t \, e^{-t}$$

Particular Solution—Method of Undetermined Coefficients

The method of undetermined coefficients is an approach to finding a particular solution $y_p(t)$ to certain nonhomogeneous ordinary linear constant coefficient differential equations.

The method may only be used to find a solution for a limited set of forcing functions (and their additive and multiplicative combinations): polynomials, exponentials, and trigonometric functions.

forcing function	particular solution
$t^n \ (n = 0, 1, \ldots)$	$\sum_{k=0}^{n} C_k \, t^n$
$e^{\alpha t}$	$C \, e^{\alpha t}$
$\cos(\alpha \, t)$ or $\sin(\alpha \, t)$	$C \cos(\alpha \, t) + D \sin(\alpha \, t)$

The solution is obtained by matching the forcing function to an appropriate trial solution $y_p(t)$ with undetermined coefficients, plugging into the differential equation, and solving for the unknown coefficients.

Note, however, that if any term in the complementary solution duplicates any term of the trial solution $y_p(t)$, then it is multiplied by the lowest power of t that eliminates duplication.

Example 3

Find a particular solution $y_p(t)$ of the following nonhomogeneous differential equation

$$y'(t) + \frac{1}{2}\, y(t) = u(t)$$

Solution

Since the input is a unit step function, constant for $t \geq 0$, the particular solution must be in the form of a constant signal:

In[•]:=**yp [t_] := c**

To find the value of the constant c, substitute $y_p(t)$ and its derivatives into the differential equation and solve for the constant, which yields:

In[•]:=**Solve [yp' [t] + $\frac{1}{2}$ yp [t] == 1, c]**

Out[•]=**{ { c → 2 } }**

Therefore, the particular solution for $t \geq 0$ is:

In[•]:=**yp [t_] := 2**

Example 4

Find a particular solution $y_p(t)$ of the following nonhomogeneous differential equation

$$y'(t) + y(t) = \sin(t)$$

Solution

Since the input is a sine function, the particular solution must be of the form:

In[•]:=**yp [t_] := c_1 Cos [t] + c_2 Sin [t]**

To find the values of the constants c_1 and c_2, substitute $y_p(t)$ and its derivative into the differential equation:

In[•]:=**yp' [t] + yp [t] == Sin [t]**

Out[•]=**Cos [t] c_1 – Sin [t] c_1 + Cos [t] c_2 + Sin [t] c_2 == Sin [t]**

This yields two equations for the coefficients c_1 and c_2:

In[•]:= `eqns = {c₁ + c₂ == 0, -c₁ + c₂ == 1};`

Solving for the undetermined coefficients, you get:

In[•]:= `Solve[eqns, {c₁, c₂}] // First`

Out[•]= $\left\{c_1 \to -\dfrac{1}{2}, c_2 \to \dfrac{1}{2}\right\}$

The particular solution is:

In[•]:= `yp[t_] := -`$\dfrac{1}{2}$` Cos[t] +`$\dfrac{1}{2}$` Sin[t]`

Example 5

Find a particular solution $y_p(t)$ of the following nonhomogeneous differential equation

$$y'(t) + y(t) = e^{-t}$$

Solution

The complementary solution is of the form:

In[•]:= `DSolveValue[y'[t] + y[t] == 0, y[t], t]`

Out[•]= $e^{-t} c_1$

Note that the complementary solution matches the forcing function, thus the complementary and particular solutions are no longer linearly independent from each other. The standard corrective measure is to multiply the particular solution by the smallest power of t to make it linearly independent from the complementary solution.

The particular solution must be of the following form:

In[•]:= `yp[t_] := c₂ t`e^{-t}

The value of the undetermined coefficient c_2 is found by substituting $y_p(t)$ and its derivatives into the differential equation and solving for the coefficient:

In[•]:= `Solve[yp'[t] + yp[t] ==`e^{-t}`, c₂]`

Out[•]= $\{\{c_2 \to 1\}\}$

The particular solution takes the form:

In[•]:= `yp[t_] := t`e^{-t}

Total Solution

A solution of a nonhomogeneous linear constant coefficient differential equation is the sum of the complementary and particular solutions

$$y(t) = y_c(t) + y_p(t)$$

For example, consider the following nonhomogeneous differential equation

$$y'(t) + y(t) = u(t)$$

From prior examples:

In[•]:=`yc [t_] := c₁ ℯ⁻ᵗ;`

In[•]:=`yp [t_] := 1;`

Which results in the following family of solutions:

In[•]:=`yc [t] + yp [t]`

Out[•]=$1 + e^{-t} c_1$

Given an initial value for the output $y(t)$, the coefficient c_1 can be determined and a single unique solution that satisfies both the differential equation and the initial state of the system can be found.

Here is the solution with the initial condition set to zero, $y(0) = 0$:

In[•]:=`DSolveValue [ {y'[t] + y[t] == 1, y[0] == 0}, y[t], t] // Simplify`

Out[•]=$1 - e^{-t}$

This shows the three solutions:

In[•]:=`Plot [ { - ℯ⁻ᵗ, 1, 1 - ℯ⁻ᵗ}, ⋯ + ]`

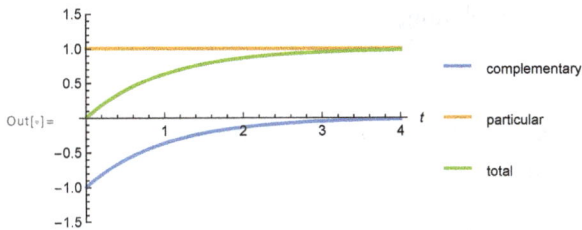

Example 6

Find the solution of the following nonhomogeneous differential equation

$$y''(t) + \sqrt{2} \; y'(t) + y(t) = \left(1 - e^{-t}\right) u(t)$$

with initial conditions $y(0) = 0$, $y'(0) = 0$.

Solution

Directly from the function `DSolveValue`, one gets the following solution:

In[•]:=**sol = DSolveValue [{y" [t] + √2 y' [t] + y [t] == (1 − e⁻ᵗ),**
y [0] == 0, y' [0] == 0}, y [t], t] // Simplify // Expand

Out[•]=$1 - e^{-t} - \dfrac{e^{-t}}{\sqrt{2}} + \dfrac{e^{-\frac{t}{\sqrt{2}}}\cos\left[\frac{t}{\sqrt{2}}\right]}{\sqrt{2}} - e^{-\frac{t}{\sqrt{2}}}\sin\left[\dfrac{t}{\sqrt{2}}\right] - \dfrac{e^{-\frac{t}{\sqrt{2}}}\sin\left[\frac{t}{\sqrt{2}}\right]}{\sqrt{2}}$

This shows the solution:

In[•]:=**Plot [sol, ⋯ +]**

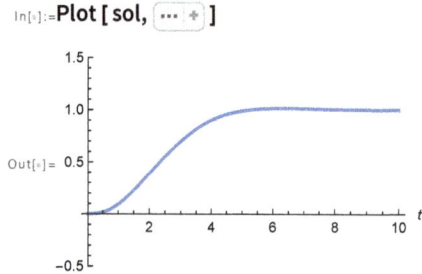

Step-by-step

As discussed earlier, begin with the complementary solution. The characteristic equation is

$$s^2 + \sqrt{2}\, s + 1 = 0$$

The roots are

$$s_1 = -\dfrac{1+j}{\sqrt{2}}, \qquad s_2 = -\dfrac{1-j}{\sqrt{2}}$$

This gives the following complementary solution:

In[•]:=**yc [t_] := c₁ e^{-\frac{1+I}{\sqrt{2}} t} + c₂ e^{-\frac{1-I}{\sqrt{2}} t};**

The input is a sum of constant and exponential signals; therefore, the particular solution must have the following form:

In[•]:=**yp [t_] := c₃ + c₄ e⁻ᵗ;**

Substitution into the left-hand side of the differential equation gives:

In[•]:=**yp" [t] + √2 yp' [t] + yp [t] // Simplify**

Out[•]=$c_3 - \left(-2 + \sqrt{2}\right) e^{-t} c_4$

Equating this with the right-hand side in the form of $1 - e^{-t}$ results in two equations for the undetermined coefficients c_3 and c_4. This returns the two coefficients:

In[•]:= **Solve [{ c_3 == 1, ($-2 + \sqrt{2}$) c_4 == 1}] // First**

Out[•]= $\left\{ c_3 \rightarrow 1, c_4 \rightarrow \dfrac{1}{-2 + \sqrt{2}} \right\}$

Therefore:

In[•]:= **yp [t_] := 1 + $\dfrac{1}{-2 + \sqrt{2}}$ e^{-t};**

The total solution is:

In[•]:= **y [t_] = yc [t] + yp [t]**

Out[•]= $1 + \dfrac{e^{-t}}{-2 + \sqrt{2}} + e^{-\frac{(1+i)t}{\sqrt{2}}} c_1 + e^{-\frac{(1-i)t}{\sqrt{2}}} c_2$

The coefficients c_1 and c_2 can be determined from the initial conditions by solving the following system of two equations:

In[•]:= **coefs = Solve [{ y [0] == 0, y' [0] == 0}, { c_1, c_2 }] // First // Simplify**

Out[•]= $\left\{ c_1 \rightarrow \dfrac{(1+i) - \sqrt{2}}{2 \left(-2 + \sqrt{2} \right)}, c_2 \rightarrow -\dfrac{(-1+i) + \sqrt{2}}{2 \left(-2 + \sqrt{2} \right)} \right\}$

Substitution of the two coefficients into the complementary solution, using the Wolfram Language ReplaceAll function, denoted by /., gives the final result:

In[•]:= **ytotal [t_] = (yc [t] /. coefs) + yp [t] // Expand**

Out[•]= $1 + \dfrac{e^{-t}}{-2 + \sqrt{2}} + \dfrac{\left(\frac{1}{2} + \frac{i}{2} \right) e^{-\frac{(1+i)t}{\sqrt{2}}}}{-2 + \sqrt{2}} - $

$\dfrac{e^{-\frac{(1+i)t}{\sqrt{2}}}}{\sqrt{2} \left(-2 + \sqrt{2} \right)} + \dfrac{\left(\frac{1}{2} - \frac{i}{2} \right) e^{-\frac{(1-i)t}{\sqrt{2}}}}{-2 + \sqrt{2}} - \dfrac{e^{-\frac{(1-i)t}{\sqrt{2}}}}{\sqrt{2} \left(-2 + \sqrt{2} \right)}$

This shows the total solution and its two components:

In[•]:= **Plot [{ yc [t] /. coefs, yp [t] , ytotal [t] } , ··· +]**

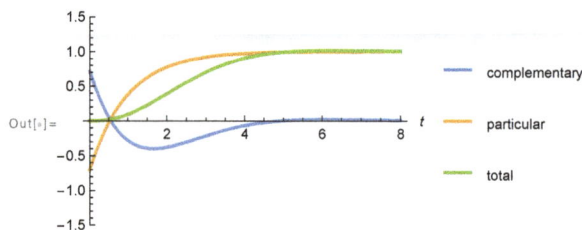

In[•]:= **Clear [y, yc, yp, ytotal] ;**

Summary

The classical method for finding solutions of homogeneous and nonhomogeneous ordinary constant coefficient differential equations was presented

$$a_n \, y^{(n)}(t) + a_{n-1} \, y^{(n-1)}(t) + \dots + a_0 \, y(t) = x(t)$$

The homogeneous solution is typically of the form

$$y_c(t) = c_1 \, e^{s_1 t} + c_2 \, e^{s_2 t} + \dots + c_n \, e^{s_n t}$$

The method of undetermined coefficients was used to find the particular solution. For select input signals, the general forms of the particular solutions are known and shown in the following table.

input : $x(t)$	particular solution : $y_p(t)$
$t^n \ (n = 0, 1, \dots)$	$\sum_{k=0}^{n} c_k \, t^n$
e^{at}	$c \, e^{at}$
$\cos(\alpha t)$ or $\sin(\alpha t)$	$c_1 \cos(\alpha t) + c_2 \sin(\alpha t)$

The total solution of a nonhomogeneous ordinary differential equation is a sum of a complementary and a particular solution

$$y(t) = y_c(t) + y_p(t)$$

Exercises

Download the solutions manual at wolfr.am/eTextbook-SSSP

7.1 Find the solution of the following homogeneous differential equation with given initial condition.

$$\frac{1}{5} \, y'(t) + y(t) = 0, \qquad y(0) = -1$$

7.2 Find the solution of the following homogeneous differential equation with given initial conditions.

$$y''(t) + 3 \, y'(t) + 2 \, y(t) = 0, \qquad y'(0) = 1, \ y(0) = 1$$

7.3 Find the solution $y(t)$ of the following homogeneous differential equation with given initial conditions.

$$y''(t) + 2\,y'(t) + y(t) = 0, \qquad y'(0) = 1,\, y(0) = 1$$

7.4 Find the solution of the following nonhomogeneous differential equation with given initial condition.

$$\tfrac{1}{5}\,y'(t) + y(t) = u(t), \qquad y(0) = 0$$

7.5 Find the solution of the following nonhomogeneous differential equation with given initial condition.

$$\tfrac{1}{5}\,y'(t) + y(t) = \cos(\pi t)\,u(t), \qquad y(0) = 0$$

7.6 Find the solution of the following nonhomogeneous differential equation with given initial conditions.

$$y''(t) + \sqrt{2}\,y'(t) + y(t) = \sin(t)\,u(t), \qquad y'(0) = 0,\, y(0) = 0$$

8 | Continuous-Time System Response

A system response is simply the signal observed at the output of the system in response to some nonzero input signal. The three classic signals used to characterize a linear time-invariant (LTI) system based on its response are impulse, step, and sinusoid. These inputs are typically applied to systems at rest, namely with initial conditions set to zero. Each of the three responses will be discussed in greater detail in the sections that follow.

In addition to the full system response, it is also of interest to be able to determine and analyze constituent parts of the response. The following are commonly of interest: zero-state and zero-input responses and transient and steady-state responses.

Impulse Response

The impulse response is possibly the most desirable of the three responses to be discussed here. It completely characterizes an LTI system at rest. Most importantly, given an LTI system's impulse response, its response to any input can be obtained by means of a convolution.

To determine the impulse response of a continuous-time system at rest, solve the system's n^{th}-order homogeneous differential equation with a modified set of initial conditions by setting the highest order initial condition to 1, $y^{(n-1)}(0) = 1$. This effectively captures the full effect of the unit impulse in the initial condition and removes it from the system's input.

For example, to find the impulse response of the following (initially at rest) system

$$y''(t) + \frac{1}{3} y'(t) + y(t) = x(t), \qquad y(0) = 0, \ y'(0) = 0$$

first, one has to change the initial conditions to

$$y(0) = 0, \ y'(0) = 1$$

and set the input $x(t)$ to zero, resulting in the following differential equation and initial conditions

$$y''(t) + \frac{1}{3} y'(t) + y(t) = 0, \qquad y(0) = 0, \ y'(0) = 1$$

The solution gives the impulse response:

In[·]:=**impulse = DSolveValue [{y" [t] + $\frac{1}{3}$ y' [t] + y [t] == 0, y [0] == 0, y' [0] == 1},**

   y [t] , t] / / Simplify

Out[·]=$\dfrac{6\, e^{-t/6}\, \mathrm{Sin}\left[\frac{\sqrt{35}\,t}{6}\right]}{\sqrt{35}}$

This plots the response:

In[·]:=**Plot [impulse, ⋯ +]**

Out[·]=

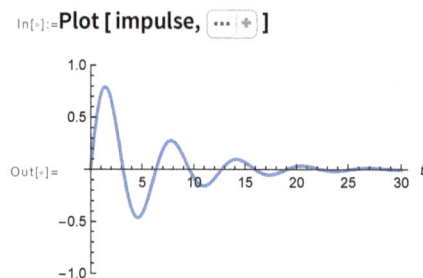

Step Response

The step response provides invaluable insights into the time domain characteristics of the system, such as rise time, settling time, steady-state behavior, and more.

For example, here is the step response of a second-order system represented by the following differential equation and initial conditions:

In[·]:=**eqns = {y" [t] + $\frac{1}{3}$ y' [t] + y [t] == UnitStep [t] , y [0] == 0, y' [0] == 0};**

The step response is:

In[·]:=**step = DSolveValue [eqns, y [t] , t] / / Simplify**

Out[·]=$\left(1 - e^{-t/6}\, \mathrm{Cos}\left[\frac{\sqrt{35}\,t}{6}\right] - \dfrac{e^{-t/6}\, \mathrm{Sin}\left[\frac{\sqrt{35}\,t}{6}\right]}{\sqrt{35}}\right)$ UnitStep [t]

This shows the step response:

In[·]:=**Plot [step, ⋯ +]**

Out[·]=

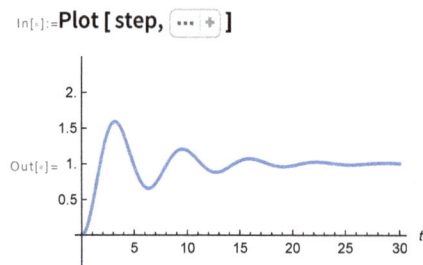

Note the oscillations evident in the response signal, a characteristic feature of a so-called underdamped system. The transient and steady-state responses of a system similar to this will be shown later in this chapter.

Sinusoidal Response

Sinusoidal signals are eigenfunctions of LTI systems, meaning that a system's response to a sinusoidal signal is a sinusoid of the same frequency, differing from the input only in amplitude and phase. Responses to sinusoidal input signals characterize the frequency-dependent properties of an LTI system.

For example, the following returns the response of a first-order system to the input $x(t) = \sin(\omega t)\, u(t)$:

In[∘]:= **DSolveValue [{y'[t] + y[t] == Sin[ωt], y[0] == 0}, y[t], t] // Expand**

Out[∘]= $\dfrac{e^{-t}\,\omega}{1+\omega^2} - \dfrac{\omega\,\mathrm{Cos}[t\,\omega]}{1+\omega^2} + \dfrac{\mathrm{Sin}[t\,\omega]}{1+\omega^2}$

This shows the input and the response as a function of frequency ω:

In[∘]:= **DynamicModule [⋯ ➕ ◣]**

Out[∘]=

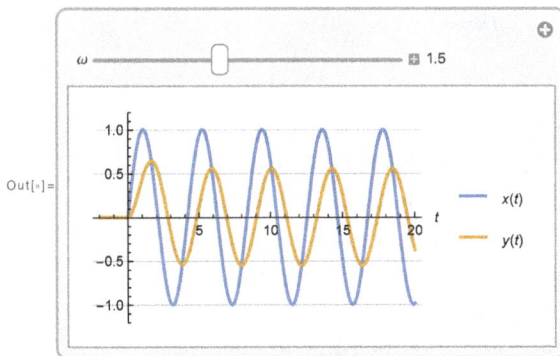

The change in amplitude and phase as a function of frequency ω directly measures how the system will alter that specific frequency component of some arbitrary input signal. Frequency domain analysis of LTI systems is an important topic that will be discussed a little later in the book.

The Gain Function

A common laboratory experiment encountered in an introductory circuits course is to obtain the ratio of the amplitudes of the input and output sinusoidal signals over a range of frequencies. Typically, a simple RC circuit, a function generator, and an oscilloscope are used to conduct the experiment. These measurements give an estimate of the so-called gain function, a function of frequency that captures how a circuit will attenuate (or amplify) a signal over its operating range.

In this example, actual laboratory measurements will be compared with solutions of a differential equation model of the following circuit

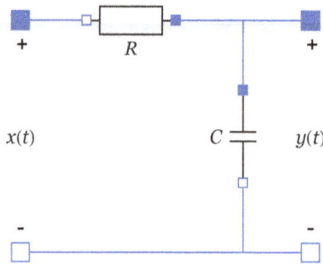

As derived earlier, the differential equation model for the output voltage $y(t)$ given the input voltage $x(t)$ is

$$R\,C\,\frac{d\,y(t)}{d\,t} + y(t) = x(t)$$

With resistor and capacitor values $R = 820\ \Omega$ and $C = 33$ nF, one gets the following relationship between the input and output signals

$$2.7\ 10^{-5}\ y'\,(t) + y(t) = x(t)$$

This shows the solutions for sinusoidal inputs of the form $x(t) = \sin(\omega\,t)$ evaluated at frequencies $\omega = 6000\,\pi,\ 10\,000\,\pi$, and $20\,000\,\pi$:

```
In[·]:= r = 820; c = 33. 10⁻⁹;
     ( in = Sin [2 π #1 t];
          out = FullSimplify [ DSolveValue [ {r c y'[t] + y[t] == Sin [2 π #1 t],
                    y[0] == 0}, y[t], t]]) & / @ {3000., 5000., 10000.}

Out[·]= {0.404762 e⁻³⁶⁹⁵⁴·⁹ᵗ − 0.404762 Cos [18849.6 t] + 0.793543 Sin [18849.6 t],
     0.49348 e⁻³⁶⁹⁵⁴·⁹ᵗ − 0.49348 Cos [31415.9 t] + 0.580486 Sin [31415.9 t],
     0.436989 e⁻³⁶⁹⁵⁴·⁹ᵗ − 0.436989 Cos [62831.9 t] + 0.257018 Sin [62831.9 t] }
```

This compares the input to the output at each of the three frequencies

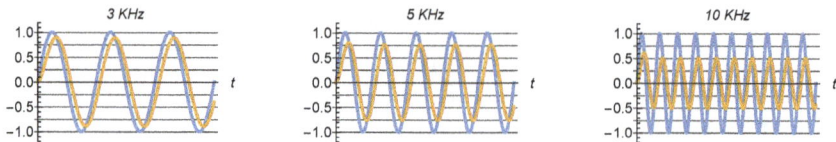

Here is a list of measurements obtained from the actual physical circuit, shown in the format {frequency in KHz, gain value}:

```
In[·]:= data = { {1., 1.}, {2.5, 0.94}, {3., 0.92}, {4., 0.85},
          {5., 0.79}, {5.5, 0.75}, {6., 0.72}, {6.5, 0.68}, {7., 0.65},
          {8., 0.60}, {9., 0.55}, {10., 0.51}, {12.5, 0.43}, {24.5, 0.26} };
```

This plots the measurements and compares them to the circuit's ideal gain function:

In[·]:=**Show [{ Plot [** ··· + **] , ListPlot [data,** ··· → ··· + **] }]**

Out[·]=

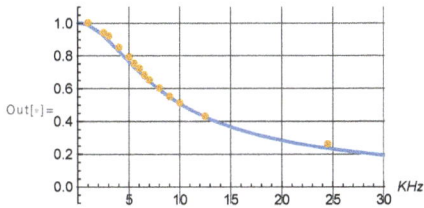

Zero-State and Zero-Input Responses

It should be fairly clear from the discussions leading up to this point that the response of an LTI system depends both on its input and its initial conditions. Therefore, it should not be a surprise that the two components of the total response, the zero-state and zero-input responses, are of practical interest.

The zero-state response (ZSR) assumes nonzero input and zero initial conditions. This returns the ZSR to a step input:

In[·]:=**yzsr [t_] = DSolveValue [{ y' [t] + y [t] == 1, y [0] == 0 }, y [t], t] / / Simplify**

Out[·]=$1 - e^{-t}$

The zero-input response (ZIR) assumes a zero input and nonzero values for the initial conditions:

In[·]:=**yzir [t_] = DSolveValue [{ y' [t] + y [t] == 0, y [0] == -1 }, y [t], t]**

Out[·]=$-e^{-t}$

The total response of the given LTI system is the sum of the two responses:

In[·]:=**yzsr [t] + yzir [t]**

Out[·]=$1 - 2 e^{-t}$

To confirm, solve the differential equation:

In[·]:=**DSolveValue [{ y' [t] + y [t] == 1, y [0] == -1 }, y [t], t] / / Simplify**

Out[·]=$1 - 2 e^{-t}$

This shows the total response and its two components:

In[•]:=**Plot [{ yzsr [t] , yzir [t] , yzsr [t] + yzir [t] } , ⋯ +]**

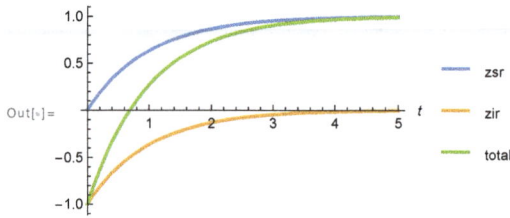

Out[•]=

Example 1

Determine the ZIR and ZSR of the following system with given initial conditions

$$y''(t) + \sqrt{2}\ y'(t) + y(t) = u(t), \quad y(0) = 0, \quad y'(0) = -1$$

Solution

The ZIR is the solution of the following homogeneous differential equation:

In[•]:=**y$_{ZIR}$ [t_] = DSolveValue [**
{y''[t] + $\sqrt{2}$ y'[t] + y[t] == 0, y[0] == 0, y'[0] == -1}, y[t], t]

Out[•]=$-\sqrt{2}\ e^{-\frac{t}{\sqrt{2}}} \sin\left[\dfrac{t}{\sqrt{2}}\right]$

The ZSR is the solution of the following differential equation:

In[•]:=**y$_{ZSR}$ [t_] = DSolveValue [**
{y''[t] + $\sqrt{2}$ y'[t] + y[t] == 1, y[0] == 0, y'[0] == 0}, y[t], t]

Out[•]=$e^{-\frac{t}{\sqrt{2}}}\left(e^{\frac{t}{\sqrt{2}}} - \cos\left[\dfrac{t}{\sqrt{2}}\right] - \sin\left[\dfrac{t}{\sqrt{2}}\right]\right)$

The two components and the total solution are:

In[•]:=**Plot [{ y$_{ZIR}$ [t] , y$_{ZSR}$ [t] , y$_{ZIR}$ [t] + y$_{ZSR}$ [t] } , ⋯ +]**

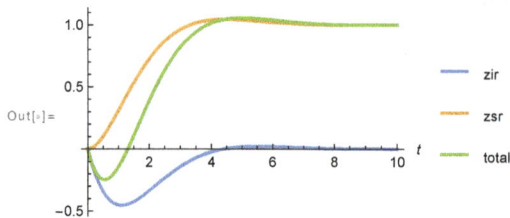

Out[•]=

Transient and Steady-State Responses

The response of any LTI system to an input starting at time t_0 has two components called the transient and steady-state responses.

The transient response provides useful information about an LTI system, such as rise time, overshoot, and settling time. If the system is stable, the transient response denoted $y_{tr}(t)$ is guaranteed to disappear

$$\lim_{t \to \infty} y_{tr}(t) = 0$$

If the system is unstable, then the transient response grows without bounds.

In stable LTI systems, the long-term system response is determined by its steady-state component only. With the transient response vanishing to zero, the steady-state response is

$$y_{ss}(t) = \lim_{t \to \infty} y(t)$$

Example 2

Determine the rise time in a first-order LTI system defined by the following differential equation and excited by a unit step input (assume the system is at rest)

$$y'(t) + y(t) = u(t)$$

Solution

The step response is:

In[•]:=**DSolveValue [{y'[t] + y[t] == 1, y[0] == 0}, y[t], t] // Expand**

Out[•]=$1 - e^{-t}$

The rise time is usually measured as the time it takes the system output to rise from 10% to 90% of its steady-state value.

This determines the time values t_1 and t_2 at which the signal reaches 10% and 90% of a steady-state value of 1, respectively:

In[•]:=**{ t1 = −Log [0.9] , t2 = −Log [0.1] }**

Out[•]=**{ 0.105361, 2.30259 }**

The following difference gives the rise time:

In[•]:=**t2 − t1**

Out[•]=**2.19722**

This illustrates the rise time interval:

In[•]:=**Plot [1 − e^{-t}, [··· +]]**

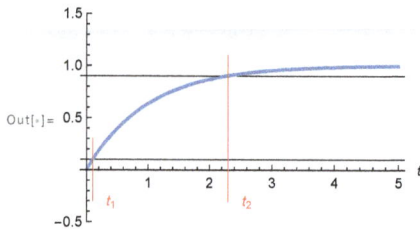

Example 3

Determine the steady-state and transient responses of the following second-order system

$$y''(t) + \sqrt{2}\, y'(t) + y(t) = \sin(t)\, u(t), \quad y(0) = 0, \quad y'(0) = 0$$

Solution

Consider the response of the following second-order differential equation to a sine input and given initial conditions:

In[•]:=**sol = DSolveValue [{ y'' [t] + $\dfrac{1}{\sqrt{2}}$ y' [t] + 2 y [t] == Sin [t] ,**

y [0] == 0, y' [0] == 0 } , y [t] , t] // Simplify

Out[•]=$\dfrac{1}{15}$ $\left(-5\sqrt{2}\, \text{Cos} [t] + 5\sqrt{2}\, e^{-\frac{t}{2\sqrt{2}}}\, \text{Cos} \left[\dfrac{1}{2} \sqrt{\dfrac{15}{2}}\, t \right] + \right.$

$\left. 10\, \text{Sin} [t] - \sqrt{30}\, e^{-\frac{t}{2\sqrt{2}}}\, \text{Sin} \left[\dfrac{1}{2} \sqrt{\dfrac{15}{2}}\, t \right] \right)$

The steady-state component of the response is:

In[•]:=**yss [t_] := $\dfrac{1}{15}$ (−5 $\sqrt{2}$ Cos [t] + 10 Sin [t])**

While the transient response is:

In[•]:=**ytr [t_] := $\dfrac{1}{15}$ (5 $\sqrt{2}$ $e^{-\frac{t}{2\sqrt{2}}}$ Cos [$\dfrac{1}{2}$ $\sqrt{\dfrac{15}{2}}$ t] − $\sqrt{30}$ $e^{-\frac{t}{2\sqrt{2}}}$ Sin [$\dfrac{1}{2}$ $\sqrt{\dfrac{15}{2}}$ t])**

This shows all three signals:

In[•]:=**Plot [{ sol, yss [t] , ytr [t] } ,** ⋯ ✦ **]**

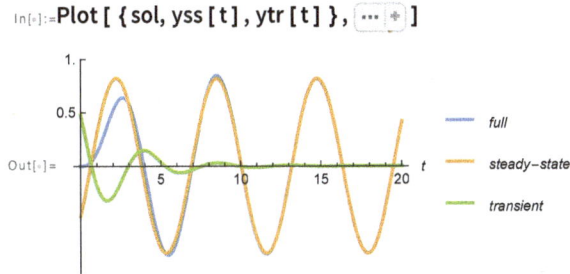

Second-Order Canonical Systems

First- and second-order systems play a prominent role in the study of LTI systems. This is especially true of second-order systems due to the fact that they exhibit the full range of time-domain and frequency-domain behavior that characterizes LTI systems. Therefore, to conclude the discussion of continuous-time system responses, it is of interest to consider a second-order system defined using the following parametrized form

$$y''(t) + 2\,\xi\,\omega_n\,y'(t) + \omega_n^2\,y(t) = 0$$

The parameters ξ and ω_n are known as the damping ratio and natural frequency, respectively. The natural frequency ω_n determines the time scale of the response ($\omega_n > 0$). The damping ratio ξ determines much of the character of the natural response. The parametrization introduced here permits an investigation of all common forms of LTI system responses.

These can be summarized as follows:

- If $\xi < 0$, then the system is unstable and the natural response grows in time without bound.

- If $\xi = 0$, then the system is marginally stable and the response is oscillatory in nature with a constant amplitude.

- If $\xi > 0$, then the system is stable and the natural response decays exponentially to zero.

This stable case is further subdivided into three possibilities:

- If $0 < \xi < 1$, then the system is underdamped, the poles have imaginary components, and the natural response contains some amount of oscillatory behavior. Lower values of ξ correspond with relatively more oscillatory responses, i.e. less damped.

- If $\xi = 1$, then the system is critically damped and the poles are coincident on the negative real axis at location $-\omega_n$.

- If $\xi > 1$, then the system is overdamped and the poles are at distinct locations on the negative real axis. This case can also be thought of as two independent first-order systems.

This shows the root locations (left) and the impulse response (right) as the natural frequency and damping ratio are varied:

In[∘]:=**DynamicModule [** ⋯ ➕ ▲ **]**

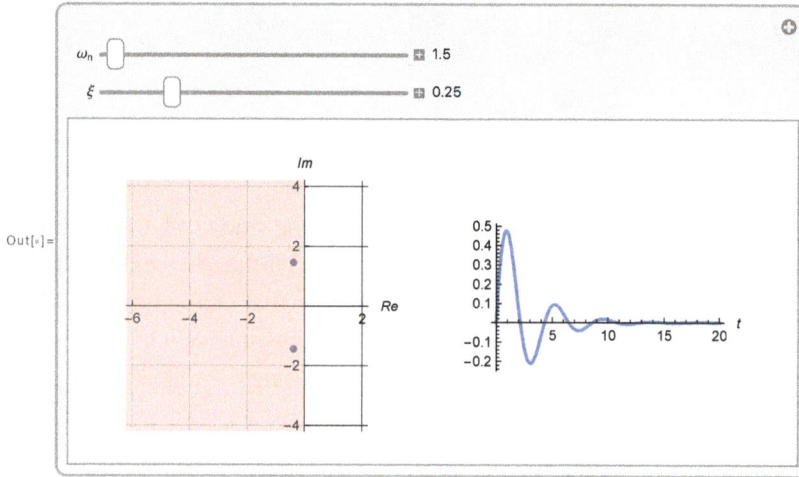

Out[∘]=

Summary

In this chapter, select continuous-time system response types were investigated.

System responses based on type of input:

- Impulse response

- Step response

- Sinusoidal response

System responses based on time duration (persistency):

- Transient response

- Steady-state response

LTI system responses based on system parameters:

- Zero-state response (ZSR) $\qquad$ $x(t) \neq 0, y(0) = y'(0) = y''(0) = \ldots = 0$

- Zero-input response (ZIR) $\qquad$ $x(t) = 0, \exists \{y(0), y'(0), y''(0), \ldots\} \neq 0$

Exercises

Download the solutions manual at wolfr.am/eTextbook-SSSP

8.1 Find the impulse response of the following initially at rest system.

$$y'(t) + 2y(t) = x(t)$$

8.2 Find the impulse response of the following initially at rest system.

$$y''(t) + 2y'(t) + y(t) = x(t)$$

8.3 Find the impulse response of the following initially at rest system.

$$y''(t) + y(t) = x(t)$$

8.4 Determine the step response of a system defined by the following differential equation with given initial conditions.

$$y''(t) + 2y'(t) + y(t) = x(t), \qquad y'(0) = y(0) = 0$$

8.5 Determine the step response of a system defined by the following differential equation with given initial conditions.

$$y''(t) + 2y'(t) + y(t) = x(t), \qquad y''(0) = y'(0) = y(0) = 0$$

8.6 Find the ZIR and ZSR responses of the following differential equation with given initial conditions.

$$y''(t) + 4y'(t) + 3y(t) = u(t), \qquad y'(0) = -1, y(0) = 1$$

8.7 Determine the ZIR and ZSR of the following system with given initial conditions.

$$y''(t) + \sqrt{2}\,y'(t) + y(t) = u(t), \qquad y(0) = 0, y'(0) = -1$$

8.8 Determine if a series RC circuit is a linear system if the initial conditions are nonzero. Use inputs $x_1(t) = u(t)$ and $x_2(t) = e^{-2t}u(t), RC = 1$, and any nonzero initial condition, for example, $y(0) = -1$.

9 | Continuous-Time Convolution

Convolution is a mathematical operation of fundamental importance in the theory of linear systems. It relates a linear time-invariant (LTI) system's input to its output; specifically, given the system's impulse response and input, it returns the output. The operation is defined by an integral that is derived next using the properties of linearity and time invariance.

Convolution as a Superposition

Given an LTI system S, the impulse response of the system denoted by $h(t)$ is the response to a unit impulse

$$h(t) = S\{\delta(t)\}$$

Using the sampling property of the impulse function, an arbitrary continuous-time signal $x(t)$ can be expressed in terms of a superposition of scaled and shifted impulses as follows

$$x(t) = \int_{-\infty}^{\infty} x(\tau)\,\delta(t-\tau)\,d\tau$$

Now, the output of an LTI system S to input $x(t)$ will be

$$y(t) = S\{x(t)\}$$
$$= S\left\{\int_{-\infty}^{\infty} x(\tau)\,\delta(t-\tau)\,d\tau\right\}$$
$$= \int_{-\infty}^{\infty} x(\tau)\,S\{\delta(t-\tau)\}\,d\tau$$

Due to time invariance, $S\{\delta(t-\tau)\} = h(t-\tau)$, so finally

$$y(t) = \int_{-\infty}^{\infty} x(\tau)\,h(t-\tau)\,d\tau$$

The resulting integral is known as the convolution integral. Convolution of signals $x(t)$ and $h(t)$ is usually denoted as $x(t) * h(t)$ and satisfies the commutative, associative, and distributive laws of algebra

$$x(t) * h(t) = h(t) * x(t)$$

$$(x(t) * h_1(t)) * h_2(t) = x(t) * (h_1(t) * h_2(t)) = x(t) * h_1(t) * h_2(t)$$

$$x(t) * (h_1(t) + h_2(t)) = x(t) * h_1(t) + x(t) * h_2(t)$$

The impulse function $\delta(t)$ is the identity element of convolution

$$x(t) * \delta(t) = x(t)$$

"Flip-and-Slide" Convolution

Consider the following convolution integral

$$y(t) = \int_{-\infty}^{\infty} h(\tau)\, x(t - \tau)\, d\tau$$

Observe that the function $x(t - \tau)$ can be viewed as a function of τ instead of t. Therefore, it represents a time-reversed and time-shifted version of the function $x(\tau)$. This leads to an effective divide-and-conquer method for evaluating the integral.

This gives a demonstration of a signal $x(\tau)$ and its reversed and shifted version, $x(t - \tau)$:

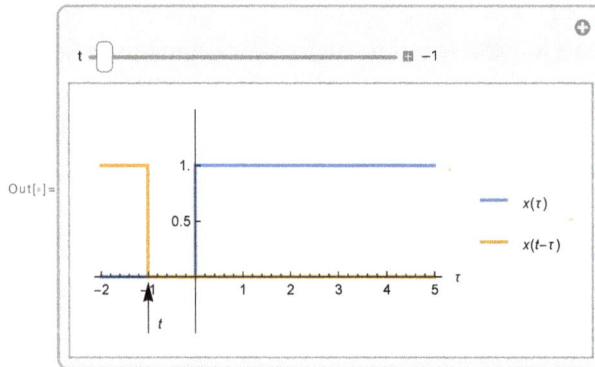

A Demonstration

The convolution integral returns the area of the product of two signals as one signal slides across the other. Here is a demonstration of convolution in action for the following two signals

$$x(t) = u(t)$$

$$h(t) = e^{-t}\, u(t)$$

This shows the two signals $h(\tau)$ and $x(t - \tau)$, their product $h(\tau)\,x(t - \tau)$, and the resulting area $y(t)$:

In[•]:=**DynamicModule [** ⋯ + ⬚ **]**

Out[•]=

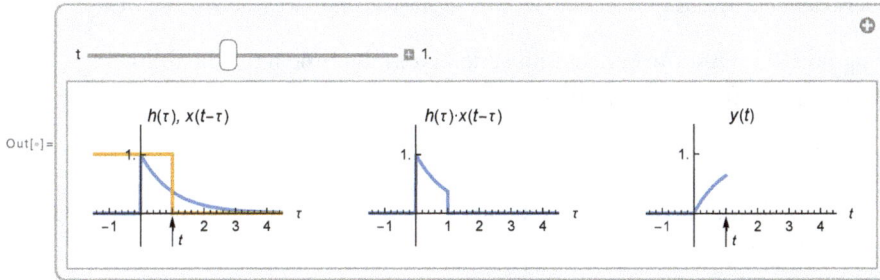

Example 1

Convolve the following two signals:

In[•]:=**x [t_] := UnitStep [t] ;**
    h [t_] := e^{-t} UnitStep [t] ;

Solution

This shows the two signals:

In[•]:=**GraphicsRow [{⋯} +]**

Out[•]=

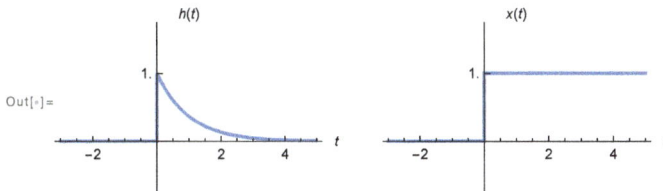

Substituting the two signals into the **Convolve** function and evaluating gives the following result:

In[•]:=**y [t_] = Convolve [h [τ] , x [τ] , τ , t] // TrigToExp // Simplify**

Out[•]=$(1 - e^{-t})$ UnitStep [t]

This shows the result:

In[•]:=**Plot [y [t] , ⋯ +]**

Out[•]=

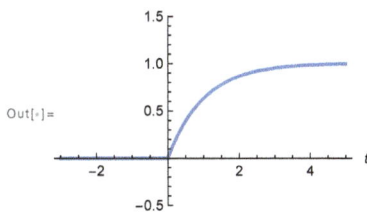

Step-by-step

The convolution integral is typically solved using a divide-and-conquer approach by splitting the region of integration into non-overlapping subregions. Each distinct region is uniquely defined by the product of the two signals as one slides across the other.

As the signal $x(t)$ is easier to reflect and slide across the time axis, the following convolution integral will be evaluated

$$y(t) = \int_{-\infty}^{\infty} h(\tau) \, x(t - \tau) \, d\tau$$

There are two distinct regions that need to be considered in evaluating this integral: $t < 0$ and $t \geq 0$.

For $t < 0$, there is no overlap between $h(\tau)$ and $x(t - \tau)$, as shown here for $t = -1.5$:

In[•]:=**Plot [{ h [τ] , x [−1.5 − τ] } , ⋯ +]**

Out[•]=

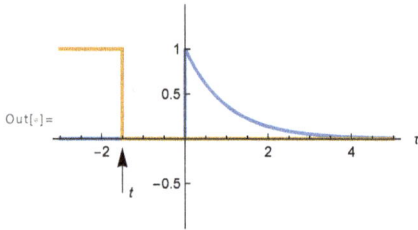

The product of the two signals is zero, and therefore $y(t)$ is

$$y(t) = 0, \; t < 0$$

For $t \geq 0$, there is a partial overlap between $h(\tau)$ and $x(t - \tau)$, as shown here for $t = 1.5$:

In[•]:=**Plot [{ h [τ] , x [1.5 − τ] } , ⋯ +]**

Out[•]=

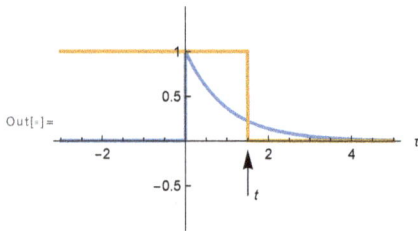

The area of the product of the two signals is given by the following integral

$$y(t) = \int_0^t e^{-\tau} \, d\tau = -e^{-\tau} \big|_0^t = -\left(e^{-t} - 1\right) = 1 - e^{-t}$$

Example 2

Convolve the following two signals:

In[•]:=**x [t_] := UnitStep [t] − UnitStep [t − 3] ;**
  h [t_] := *e*$^{-t}$ UnitStep [t] ;

Solution

This shows the two signals:

In[•]:=**GraphicsRow [⋯ +]**

Out[•]=
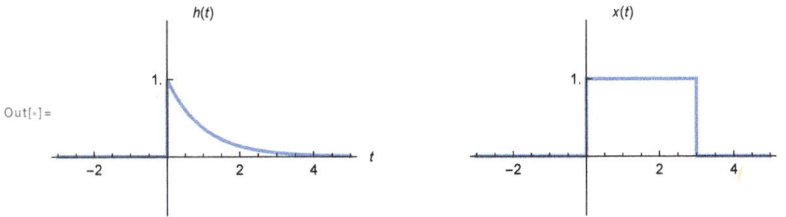

Convolution of the two signals gives:

In[•]:=**y [t_] = Convolve [h [τ] , x [τ] , τ , t] / / Simplify**

Out[•]=$e^{-t} \left(\left(e^3 - e^t \right) \text{UnitStep} [-3 + t] + \left(-1 + e^t \right) \text{UnitStep} [t] \right)$

This plots the result:

In[•]:=**Plot [y [t] , ⋯ +]**

Out[•]=
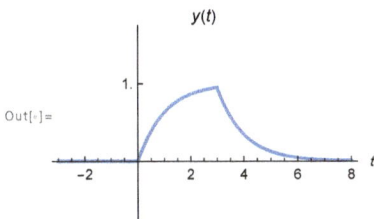

Step-by-step

Since the pulse signal is easier to reverse and shift across the time domain, use the following formulation of the convolution integral

$$y(t) = \int_{-\infty}^{\infty} h(\tau)\, x(t - \tau)\, d\tau$$

This plots $h(\tau)$ and the shifted and time-reversed signal $x(t - \tau)$:

In[•]:=**DynamicModule [⋯ +]**

Out[•]=
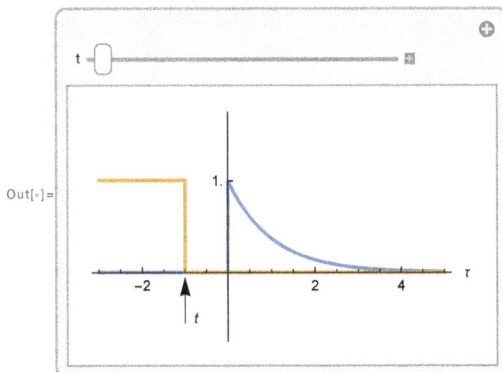

Three distinct regions can be identified by observing the domain while shifting $x(t - \tau)$. The region $t < 0$ is the no-overlap region, the signals partially overlap for $0 \le t < 3$, and, finally, the pulse completely overlaps the decaying exponential for $t \ge 3$.

For $t < 0$, the two signals do not overlap; therefore, the function $y(t)$ evaluates to zero

$$y(t) = 0$$

On the interval $0 \le t < 3$, the convolution integral evaluates to the following:

In[·]:=**Integrate [$e^{-\tau}$, { τ, 0, t}] / / TrigToExp**

Out[·]=$1 - e^{-t}$

On the interval $t \ge 3$, the result is:

In[·]:=**Integrate [$e^{-\tau}$, { τ, t − 3, t}] / / TrigToExp**

Out[·]=$e^{3-t} - e^{-t}$

Putting the three results together in a single piecewise definition yields

$$y(t) = \begin{cases} 1 - e^{-t}, & 0 \le t < 3 \\ \left(e^3 - 1\right) e^{-t}, & t \ge 3 \\ 0, & \text{else} \end{cases}$$

Convolution and the Step Response

It is of interest to obtain a direct formula for the step response of a system given a known impulse response

$$y(t) = \int_{-\infty}^{\infty} h(\tau)\, u(t - \tau)\, d\tau$$

Now, since $u(t - \tau) = 0$ for $\tau > t$, the upper limit of integration changes from ∞ to t, resulting in the following well-known relationship between the step response and impulse response of an LTI system

$$y(t) = \int_{-\infty}^{\infty} h(\tau)\, u(t - \tau)\, d\tau \ = \ \int_{-\infty}^{t} h(\tau)\, d\tau$$

Example 3

Obtain the step response of a system with the following impulse response:

In[·]:=**h [t_] := e^{-t} UnitStep [t]**

Solution

Substituting the given signal into the integral relation between the step and impulse responses and evaluating gives the following result:

In[•]:=**Integrate [h [τ] , { τ , 0 , t } , Assumptions → Element [t, Reals]]**

Out[•]=$1 - e^{-t}$

Summary

Convolution is defined by the following two integrals

$$y(t) = \int_{-\infty}^{\infty} x(\tau)\, h(t - \tau)\, d\tau = \int_{-\infty}^{\infty} h(\tau)\, x(t - \tau)\, d\tau$$

Convolution returns the output $y(t)$ of a system given its impulse response $h(t)$ and input $x(t)$

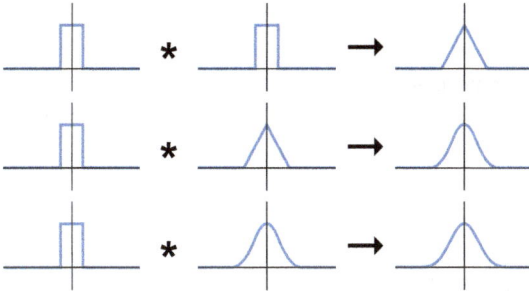

Details of a divide-and-conquer method of evaluating the convolution integral were shown.

Exercises

Download the solutions manual at wolfr.am/eTextbook-SSSP

9.1 Determine the area of the product of the two signals shown here.

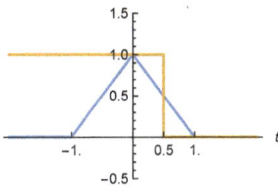

9.2 Given $h(t) = e^{-t}\, u(t)$ and $x(t) = u(t)$, determine $\int_{-\infty}^{\infty} h(\tau)\, x(3 - \tau)\, d\tau$.

9.3 Convolve the following two signals and plot the result.

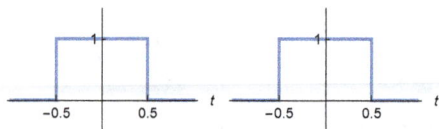

9.4 Convolve the following two signals and plot the result.

$$x(t) = \begin{cases} 1, & -2 \le t \le 1 \\ 0, & \text{else} \end{cases}$$

$$h(t) = \begin{cases} 1, & 0 \le t \le 1 \\ 0, & \text{else} \end{cases}$$

9.5 Convolve the following two signals and plot the result.

$$x(t) = \begin{cases} 1, & -0.5 \le t \le 0.5 \\ 0, & \text{else} \end{cases}$$

$$h(t) = \begin{cases} 1+t, & -1 \le t \le 0 \\ 1-t, & 0 \le t \le 1 \\ 0, & \text{else} \end{cases}$$

9.6 Convolve the following two signals and plot the result.

$$x(t) = \begin{cases} 1+t, & -1 \le t \le 0 \\ 1-t, & 0 \le t \le 1 \\ 0, & \text{else} \end{cases}$$

$$h(t) = \delta(t+1/2) + \delta(t-1/2)$$

9.7 Convolve the following two signals and plot the result.

$$x(t) = \begin{cases} 1, & -0.5 \le t \le 0.5 \\ 0, & \text{else} \end{cases}$$

$$h(t) = \begin{cases} \cos(\pi t), & -0.5 \le t \le 0.5 \\ 0, & \text{else} \end{cases}$$

9.8 Obtain the step response of a system with impulse response given by

$$h(t) = \begin{cases} \sin\left(\frac{\pi}{2} t\right), & 0 \le t \le 2 \\ 0, & \text{else} \end{cases}$$

Time-Domain Analysis
(Discrete)

10 | Discrete-Time Systems as Difference Equations

Discrete-time systems are mathematical algorithms that operate on numerical data or sampled versions of analog signals. This section begins with examples of three common discrete-time linear shift-invariant (LSI) systems and some practical applications. Also, a method of obtaining the output of any of these systems using a simple recursive numerical calculation is presented.

Time-Domain Representation of Discrete-Time LSI Systems

An important class of LSI systems is characterized by a linear constant coefficient difference equation of the form

$$y[n] + a_1 \, y[n-1] + \ldots + a_N \, y[n-N] = b_0 \, x[n] + b_1 \, x[n-1] + \ldots + b_M \, x[n-M]$$

where $y[n]$ and $x[n]$ are the output and input of the system, respectively.

The difference equation is also known as a recursive difference equation and systems characterized by such equations are known as recursive systems. Equations of this type can be solved analytically in a manner analogous to that for differential equations, giving an explicit solution for the output $y[n]$, but they can also be solved numerically by recursion for any value $y[n]$ if the N preceding values $y[n-1]$, $y[n-2]$, ..., $y[n-N]$ are known.

Another important class of systems modeled by difference equations is independent of past outputs

$$y[n] = b_0 \, x[n] + b_1 \, x[n-1] + \ldots + b_M \, x[n-M]$$

Such systems are called non-recursive. In such systems, the output $y[n]$ is simply a weighted average of the $M + 1$ values of the input $x[n]$.

Moving-Average System

A simple averaging system, commonly known as the moving-average system, is probably the most frequently encountered discrete-time system in practice. It is an example of a non-recursive system. Such a system is typically used to smooth an input sequence (i.e. data) by reducing the local variations in sample values.

It is usually defined by the following non-recursive difference formula

$$y[n] = \frac{1}{N} \left(x[n] + x[n-1] + \dots + x[n-N+1] \right)$$

Therefore, the output value at time n is simply the mean of N present and past values of the input. Such an operation has a smoothing, also called blurring, effect on the processed data, as shown here:

In[•]:=**Manipulate [⋯ +]**

Out[•]=

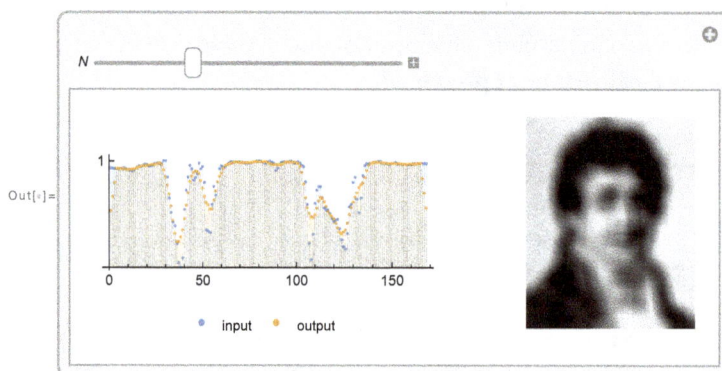

Compound Interest and Exponential Growth

Compound interest is the addition of interest to the principal sum of a loan or deposit. It is used in most transactions in the banking and finance sectors. For example, in a savings account, the principal $y[n]$ at time n is equal to the principal at time $n-1$ plus the accumulated interest using interest rate r and any deposits or deductions $x[n]$

$$y[n] = y[n-1] + r\, y[n-1] + x[n] = (1+r)\, y[n-1] + x[n]$$

In standard form

$$y[n] - (1+r)\, y[n-1] = x[n]$$

This shows the effect of compounding interest on the amount of principal $y[n]$ over a range of interest rates with an initial deposit of $x[0] = 1000$ and no further deposits or deductions ($x[n] = 0$ for $n > 0$):

In[ ]:=**DynamicModule [[⋯ ✦]▲]**

Out[ ]=

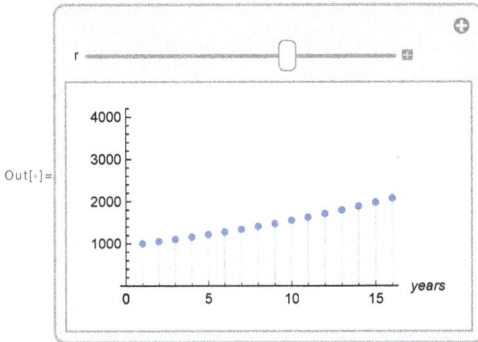

Such first-order difference equations also model other phenomena, such as increase or decrease in population, growth of bacteria, rise or depreciation in the value of an item, and more.

Equalization

Equalization, commonly used in audio recording and reproduction, is the process of adjusting the balance between frequency components in an audio signal. The effect is achieved by increasing or decreasing the signal magnitude within specific frequency bands. The following recursive difference equation models an equalizer that amplifies a band of mid-range frequencies in a signal

$$y[n] - 1.7\ y[n - 1] + 0.9\ y[n - 2] = 1.2\ x[n] - 1.7\ x[n - 1] + 0.7\ x[n - 2]$$

Such an equalizer is known as a peaking equalizer. Observe how as the frequency of the input sequence $x[n]$ increases, the amplitude of the output sequence, $y[n]$, also increases but only for a limited range of frequencies:

In[ ]:=**Manipulate [[⋯ ✦]]**

Out[ ]=

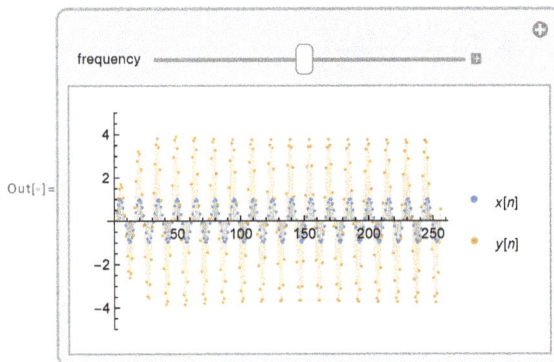

Numerical Solutions

Consider the following general form of an Nth-order difference equation

$$y[n] + a_1\, y[n-1] + \dots + a_N\, y[n-N] = b_0\, x[n] + b_1\, x[n-1] + \dots + b_M\, x[n-M]$$

Assuming, as is common, that you want to obtain the output for $n \geq 0$, this equation can be solved numerically by iteration given an input $x[n]$ and N so-called initial conditions: $y[-1], y[-2], .., y[-N]$.

The output value $y[n]$ is given by the following equation

$$y[n] = b_0\, x[n] + b_1\, x[n-1]\ \dots + b_M\, x[n-M] - a_1\, y[n-1] \dots - a_N\, y[n-N]$$

Starting at $n = 0$

$$y[0] = b_0\, x[0] + b_1\, x[-1] \dots + b_M\, x[-M] - a_1\, y[-1] - a_2\, y[-2] \dots - a_N\, y[-N]$$

Continuing for $n = 1$

$$y[1] = b_0\, x[1] + b_1\, x[0] \dots + b_M\, x[1-M] - a_1\, y[0] - a_2\, y[-1] \dots - a_N\, y[1-N]$$

Finally, in general, for any value $n = k$

$$y[k] = b_0\, x[k] + b_1\, x[k-1] \dots + b_M\, x[k-M] - a_1\, y[k-1] - a_2\, y[k-2] \dots$$
$$-a_N\, y[k-N]$$

This process can be continued until all desired output values are obtained. A numerical solution may therefore be easily obtained with nothing more than a simple calculator.

Example 1

Obtain the output $y[n]$ for $n = 0, 1, 2$ given input $x[n] = \cos(\pi n) = (-1)^n$ and the following first-order difference equation and initial condition

$$y[n] - \tfrac{2}{3}\, y[n-1] = x[n], \qquad y[-1] = 0$$

Solution

The function RecurrenceTable returns the desired values:

```
In[•]:= RecurrenceTable [
          {y[n] - 2/3 y[n-1] == (-1)^n, y[-1] == 0}, y[n], {n, 0, 2}]

Out[•]= {1, -1/3, 7/9}
```

This plots the output for $0 \le n \le 31$:

In[◦]:=**ListPlot [** ⋯ ⊕ **]**

Out[◦]=

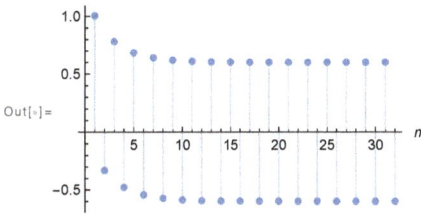

Step-by-step

First, rewrite the equation so that the only term on the left is the desired output at time n

$$y[n] = (-1)^n + \frac{2}{3} y[n-1], \qquad y[-1] = 0$$

Then recursively, for values of $n = 0, 1, 2, \ldots$, you get

$$y[0] = 1 + \frac{2}{3} y[-1] = 1 + \frac{2}{3} 0 = 1$$

$$y[1] = -1 + \frac{2}{3} y[0] = -1 + \frac{2}{3} 1 = -\frac{1}{3}$$

$$y[2] = 1 + \frac{2}{3} y[1] = 1 + \frac{2}{3} \left(-\frac{1}{3}\right) = \frac{7}{9}$$

$\vdots$

Example 2

Obtain the output $y[n]$ for $n = 0, 1, 2, 3, \ldots$ given input $x[n] = u[n]$ and the following third-order difference equation and initial conditions

$$y[n] - \frac{2}{3} y[n-3] = x[n], \qquad y[-3] = y[-2] = y[-1] = 0$$

Solution

Using RecurrenceTable:

In[◦]:=**RecurrenceTable [{y [n] $-\dfrac{2}{3}$ y [n − 3] == UnitStep [n],**

y [−3] == 0, y [−2] == 0, y [−1] == 0}, y [n] , {n, 0, 9}]

Out[◦]=$\left\{1, 1, 1, \dfrac{5}{3}, \dfrac{5}{3}, \dfrac{5}{3}, \dfrac{19}{9}, \dfrac{19}{9}, \dfrac{19}{9}, \dfrac{65}{27}\right\}$

This plots the output for $0 \le n \le 31$:

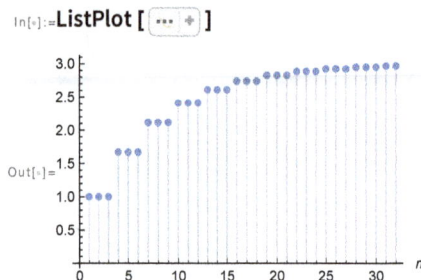

In[ ]:= **ListPlot [⋯ +]**

Out[ ]=

Step-by-step

First, rewrite the equation so that the only term on the left is the desired output at time n

$$y[n] = 1 + \frac{2}{3}\, y[n-3]$$

Then for values of $n = 0,\ 1,\ ...,$ you get

$$y[0] = 1 + \frac{2}{3}\, y[-3] = 1$$

$$y[1] = 1 + \frac{2}{3}\, y[-2] = 1$$

$$y[2] = 1 + \frac{2}{3}\, y[-1] = 1$$

$$y[3] = 1 + \frac{2}{3}\, y[0] = \frac{5}{3}$$

$$\vdots$$

Summary

Select LSI systems were presented along with their common practical applications.

Such systems are modeled by ordinary constant coefficient difference equations

$$y[n] = \frac{1}{3}\, (x[n] + x[n-1] + x[n-2])$$

$$y[n] - \frac{3}{4}\, y[n-1] = \frac{1}{4}\, x[n]$$

It was shown that the output of any LSI system can be easily obtained numerically given the input and the requisite number of initial conditions by simply recursively evaluating the difference equation for each desired output value.

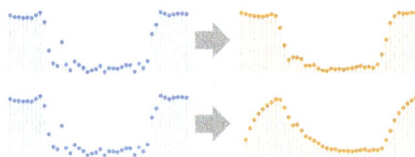

Exercises

Download the solutions manual at wolfr.am/eTextbook-SSSP

10.1 The input into a moving average system of order $M = 2$ is the sequence $x[n] = \cos\left(\frac{\pi}{2} n\right)$. Obtain the output $y[n]$ for $n = 0, 1, 2, 3$.

10.2 A non-recursive system is defined

$$y[n] = x[n] + x[n - 2]$$

Obtain the output $y[n]$ for $n = 0, 1, 2, 3$ given the input $x[n] = \sin\left(\frac{\pi}{2} n\right)$.

10.3 A moving average system is defined

$$y[n] = \frac{1}{3}\,(x[n] + x[n - 1] + x[n - 2])$$

Obtain the output $y[n]$ for $n = -3, -2, -1, 0, 1, 2, 3$ given the input sequence $x[n] = \delta[n]$.

10.4 Given the input sequence $x[n] = \delta[n]$, use recursion to solve the following difference equation for $n = -1, 0, 1, 2, 3$.

$$y[n] = 0, \qquad n < 0$$

$$y[n] - y[n - 1] = \frac{1}{3} x[n] - \frac{1}{3} x[n - 3], \qquad n \geq 0$$

10.5 Use recursion to solve the following difference equation for $n = 2, 3, \ldots, 7$.

$$y[n] - y[n - 1] - y[n - 2] = 0, \qquad y[1] = 1, y[0] = 0$$

10.6 Use recursion to obtain the output $y[n]$ for $n = 0, 1, 2, 3$ given input $x[n] = \delta[n]$ and the following first-order difference equation and initial condition.

$$y[n] - \frac{1}{2} y[n - 1] = x[n], \quad y[-1] = 0$$

10.7 Use recursion to obtain the output $y[n]$ for $n = 0, 1, 2, 3$ given the input $x[n] = (-1)^n$ and the following difference equation and initial conditions.

$$8\,y[n] - 6\,y[n - 1] + 3\,y[n - 2] = x[n] + 2\,x[n - 1] + x[n - 2], \quad y[-1] = 1, y[-2] = 0$$

10.8 Given an input of the form $x[n] = \alpha\,u[n]$ and an initial condition of $y[-1] = 1$, use recursion to show that the following difference equation returns a sequence that converges on the value of $\sqrt{\alpha}$ as $n \to \infty$.

$$y[n] = \frac{1}{2}\,(y[n - 1] + x[n]\,/\,y[n - 1])$$

Obtain the value of $\sqrt{2}$.

11 | Difference Equation Solution Methods

The classical solution method is analogous to Euler's method used for solving linear constant coefficient ordinary differential equations. Examination of the homogeneous form of a difference equation reveals that the solution must be of the form r^n, as this is the only sequence that does not change its form under the delay operation, i.e. the exponential r^n is an eigenfunction of discrete-time linear time-invariant (LTI) systems.

The classical method of solving constant coefficient ordinary difference equations is as follows:

- Find the solution to the homogeneous equation, called the homogeneous, complementary, or null solution.

- Find any solution to the nonhomogeneous equation, called the particular solution, using the method of undetermined coefficients.

The general solution is then the sum of the complementary and particular solutions.

Complementary Solution

Examination of the homogeneous equation

$$\sum_{k=0}^{N} a_k \, y[n-k] = 0$$

shows that the complementary solution $y_c[n]$ must be of the form

$$y_c[n] = r^n$$

Substituting into the homogeneous equation, you get

$$\sum_{k=0}^{N} a_k \, r^{n-k} = 0$$

Expand the sum

$$\left(a_0 \, r^n + a_1 \, r^{n-1} + \dots + a_N \, r^{n-N}\right) = 0$$

Factor out the common term r^{n-N}

$$r^{n-N}\left(a_0 \, r^N + a_1 \, r^{N-1} + \dots + a_N\right) = 0$$

The polynomial $\mathcal{P} = \left(a_0\, r^N + a_1\, r^{N-1} + ... + a_N\right)$ is called the characteristic polynomial and the equation $\mathcal{P} = 0$ is called the characteristic equation.

Assuming that all N roots of the equation, $r_1, r_2, ..., r_N$, are distinct, you get the following general form of the complementary solution

$$y_c[n] = c_1\, r_1{}^n + c_2\, r_2{}^n + ... + c_N\, r_N{}^n$$

The roots of the characteristic equation can be complex. If so, they will occur in complex conjugate pairs.

For repeated roots, the form of the homogeneous solution must be modified. If root i repeats k times, the homogeneous solution takes the form

$$y_c[n] = c_1\, r_1{}^n + ... + \left(c_{i_1} + c_{i_2}\, n + c_{i_3}\, n^2 + ... + c_{i_k}\, n^{k-1}\right) r_i{}^n + ... + c_{N-k}\, r_{N-k}{}^n$$

Example 1

Find the homogeneous solution of the following first-order difference equation

$$y[n] - \tfrac{2}{3}\, y[n-1] = 0$$

Solution

Use the function RSolve to obtain the solution of the given difference equation:

$$\text{In[\cdot]:=}\; \textbf{RSolveValue}\left[\, \textbf{y[n]} - \frac{2}{3}\, \textbf{y[n-1]} == \textbf{0}, \textbf{y[n]}, \textbf{n}\,\right]\; \textbf{//}\; \textbf{Simplify}$$

$$\text{Out[\cdot]=}\; \left(\frac{3}{2}\right)^{1-n}\; \mathbb{C}_1$$

Step-by-step

Substitution of the eigenfunction $y_c[n] = r^n$ into the homogeneous difference equation returns the following polynomial equation

$$r^n - \tfrac{2}{3}\, r^{n-1} = r^{n-1}\left(r - \tfrac{2}{3}\right) = 0$$

The characteristic polynomial is $\mathcal{P} = r - \tfrac{2}{3}$, and solving the characteristic equation gives the desired root, $r = \tfrac{2}{3}$. Substitution of the root, $r = \tfrac{2}{3}$, into the expression for the complementary solution gives the following sequence

$$y_c[n] = c_1\, r_1{}^n = c_1\left(\frac{2}{3}\right)^n$$

Distinct Real Roots

The following second-order homogeneous difference equation has two distinct roots

$$y[n] + 3\,y[n-1] + 2\,y[n-2] = 0$$

Substitution of the eigenfunction $y[n] = r^n$ into the homogeneous difference equation gives

$$r^n + 3\,r^{n-1} + 2\,r^{n-2} = 0$$

Extracting the lowest power of r

$$r^{n-2}(r^2 + 3\,r + 2) = 0$$

The characteristic equation is $r^2 + 3\,r + 2 = 0$. The real and distinct roots are:

In[•]:= **Roots [r^2 + 3 r + 2 == 0, r]**

Out[•]= r == −2 | | r == −1

Thus the complementary solution takes the form

$$y_c[n] = c_1(-1)^n + c_2(-2)^n$$

The following returns the complementary solution:

In[•]:= **RSolveValue [y [n] + 3 y [n − 1] + 2 y [n − 2] == 0, y [n], n]**

Out[•]= $(-2)^n\,c_1 + (-1)^n\,c_2$

Distinct Complex Roots

The following second-order homogeneous difference equation has distinct complex roots

$$y[n] - \sqrt{2}\,y[n-1] + y[n-2] = 0$$

The characteristic equation is

$$r^2 - \sqrt{2}\,r + 1 = 0$$

The two roots are:

In[•]:= **Roots [r^2 − $\sqrt{2}$ r + 1 == 0, r]**

Out[•]= r == $\dfrac{1-i}{\sqrt{2}}$ | | r == $\dfrac{1+i}{\sqrt{2}}$

The solution that satisfies the difference equation is:

In[•]:= **RSolveValue [y [n] − $\sqrt{2}$ y [n − 1] + y [n − 2] == 0, y [n], n]**

Out[•]= $(1-i)^n\,2^{-n/2}\,c_1 + (1+i)^n\,2^{-n/2}\,c_2$

Here are the three possible forms of the solution of a second-order LTI system with complex roots

$$y_c[n] = c_1\left(\frac{1+i}{\sqrt{2}}\right)^n + c_1{}^*\left(\frac{1-i}{\sqrt{2}}\right)^n$$

$$= 2\,|c_1|\cdot\cos\left(\frac{\pi}{4}\,n + \angle c_1\right)$$

$$= 2\left(\mathrm{Re}(c_1)\cdot\cos\left(\frac{\pi}{4}\,n\right) - \mathrm{Im}(c_1)\cdot\sin\left(\frac{\pi}{4}\,n\right)\right)$$

Given two initial conditions, the complex coefficient c_1 can be determined.

Repeated Roots

The characteristic polynomial may have repeated roots. For example, consider the following second-order difference equation

$$y[n] + 2\,y[n-1] + y[n-2] = 0$$

The characteristic equation is

$$r^2 + 2\,r + 1 = 0$$

The two roots are:

In[·]:=**Roots [r^2 + 2 r + 1 == 0, r]**

Out[·]=r == −1 || r == −1

Note that by substituting the repeated root into the formula for distinct roots, one gets only one of the two required solutions for a second-order system

$$y_c[n] = c_1(-1)^n + c_2(-1)^n = (c_1 + c_2)(-1)^n$$

The two additive terms are linearly dependent. The standard corrective step is to multiply each repeated term by successive powers of the independent variable n. This results in the following

$$y_c[n] = c_1(-1)^n + c_2\,n(-1)^n$$

This returns the complementary solution:

In[·]:=**RSolveValue [y [n] + 2 y [n − 1] + y [n − 2] == 0, y [n], n]**

Out[·]= $(-1)^n\,c_1 + (-1)^n\,n\,c_2$

Example 2

Find a complementary solution of the following homogeneous difference equation

$$y[n] - \frac{2}{3}\,y[n-2] = 0$$

Solution

This gives the complementary solution:

In[•]:= **RSolveValue** $[\, y \, [\, n \,] \, - \dfrac{2}{3} \, y \, [\, n - 2 \,] \, == 0, \, y \, [\, n \,] \, , \, n \,]$

Out[•]= $\left(\dfrac{2}{3}\right)^{n/2} c_1 + (-1)^n \left(\dfrac{2}{3}\right)^{n/2} c_2$

Solution plots for several combinations of values of the coefficients c_1 and c_2:

In[•]:= **GraphicsGrid** $[\, \boxed{\text{Table}[\cdots] \; +} \,]$

Out[•]=

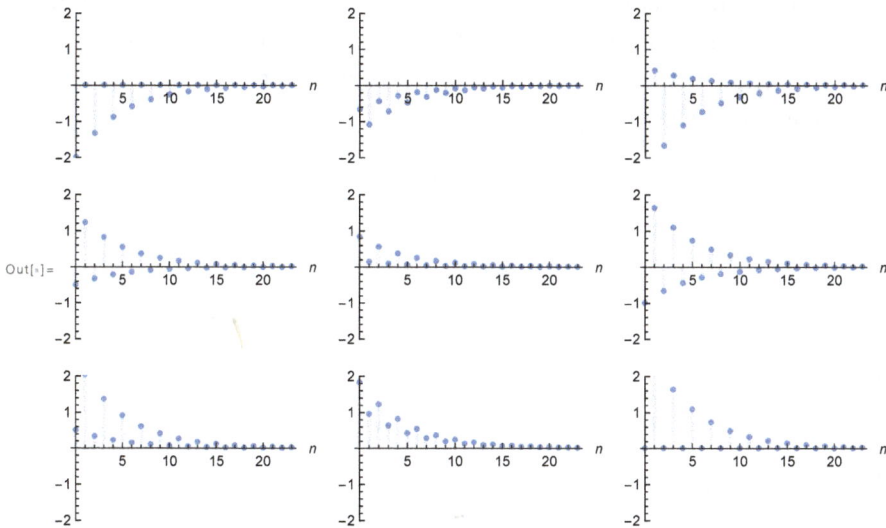

Step-by-step

Substitution of the eigenfunction $y[n] = r^n$ into the homogeneous difference equation returns the following polynomial equation

$$r^n - \frac{2}{3} r^{n-2} = r^{n-2}\left(r^2 - \frac{2}{3}\right) = 0$$

The characteristic equation is

$$r^2 - \frac{2}{3} = 0$$

The characteristic roots are:

In[•]:= **Roots** $[\, r^2 - \dfrac{2}{3} \, == 0, \, r \,]$

Out[•]= $r == \sqrt{\dfrac{2}{3}} \; || \; r == -\sqrt{\dfrac{2}{3}}$

Which yields the following complementary solution

$$y_c[n] = c_1\left(\frac{2}{3}\right)^{n/2} + c_2\left(-\frac{2}{3}\right)^{n/2}$$

Particular Solution

The method of undetermined coefficients is an approach to finding a particular solution $y_p[n]$ to certain nonhomogeneous ordinary difference equations of the form

$$a_0\, y[n] + a_1\, y[n-1] + \ldots + a_N\, y[n-N] = b_0\, x[n] + b_1\, x[n-1] + \ldots + b_M\, x[n-M]$$

The particular solution that solves the nonhomogeneous equation often relates to the nonhomogeneous term, also known as the input or forcing function. The method may only be used to solve nonhomogeneous difference equations for a limited set of forcing functions.

Here is a list of common forcing functions and the corresponding forms of particular solutions.

Input	Particular solution
A (constant)	K_0 (constant)
$A\, r^n$	$K_0\, r^n$
$A\, n^k$	$K_0 + K_1\, n + K_2\, n^2 + \ldots + K_k\, n^k$
$\sin(\omega n)$ or $\cos(\omega n)$	$K_1 \sin(\omega n) + K_2 \cos(\omega n)$
$n^k\, r^n$	$r^n\left(K_0 + K_1\, n + K_2\, n^2 + \ldots + K_k\, n^k\right)$
$r^n \sin(\omega n)$ or $r^n \cos(\omega n)$	$r^n(K_1 \sin(\omega n) + K_2 \cos(\omega n))$

The solution is obtained by matching the forcing function to an appropriate trial solution, substituting into the equation, and solving for the undetermined coefficients K_i.

The terms of a trial solution $y_p[n]$ must be linearly independent from the terms of the complementary solution. If any term in the complementary solution duplicates any term of the trial solution, then multiply $y_p[n]$ by the lowest power of n that eliminates duplication.

The examples that follow illustrate the technique.

Example 3

Find the particular solution of the following first-order difference equation

$$y[n] - \frac{2}{3}\, y[n-1] = u[n]$$

Solution

The particular solution is determined solely by the input. If the input is constant, the output must also be constant, yielding:

In[•]:= **yp [n_] := K**

To find the value of the undetermined coefficient K, substitute $y_p[n]$ into the difference equation and solve for the constant:

In[•]:= **Solve [yp [n]** $-\dfrac{2}{3}$ **yp [n − 1] == 1, K]**

Out[•]= **{ { K → 3 } }**

This gives $K = 3$, and therefore the particular solution is

$$y_p[n] = 3$$

Example 4

Find the particular solution of the following first-order difference equation

$$y[n] - \frac{2}{3}\, y[n-1] = 2 \left(\frac{2}{3}\right)^n$$

Solution

The particular solution is determined solely by the input. If the input is exponential, the trial solution should have the form

$$y_p[n] = K \left(\frac{2}{3}\right)^n$$

However, since the trial solution matches the form of the complementary solution $y_c[n] = c_1\left(\frac{2}{3}\right)^n$ as obtained earlier in Example 1, the particular solution must be modified as follows:

In[•]:= **yp [n_] := K n** $\left(\dfrac{2}{3}\right)^n$ **;**

Substitution into the difference equation returns:

In[•]:= **yp [n]** $-\dfrac{2}{3}$ **yp [n − 1] == 2** $\left(\dfrac{2}{3}\right)^n$ **/ / FullSimplify**

Out[•]= $\left(\dfrac{2}{3}\right)^n$ **(−2 + K) == 0**

Solving for the undetermined coefficient:

In[•]:= **Solve [%, K]**

Out[•]= **{ { K → 2 } }**

This results in the following particular solution:

In[•]:= $\mathsf{yp\,[\,n\_\,]\,:=\,2\,n\,\left(\dfrac{2}{3}\right)^{n}}$;

Total Solution

As in the case of differential equations, the total solution is a superposition of the complementary and particular solutions

$$y[n] = y_c[n] + y_p[n]$$

Given a sufficient number of initial conditions, the constants in the general solution can be resolved, resulting in a unique solution to the initial value problem.

The following two examples illustrate the process.

Example 5

Obtain the total solution of the following initial value problem

$$y[n] - \tfrac{2}{3}\,y[n-1] = u[n], \qquad y[-1] = 0$$

Solution

Here is the solution of the first-order difference equation with the given initial condition:

In[•]:= $\mathsf{sol\,=\,RSolveValue\,[\,\{\,y\,[\,n\,]\,-\dfrac{2}{3}\,y\,[\,n-1\,]\,==\,UnitStep\,[\,n\,]\,,\,y\,[\,-1\,]\,==\,0\,\}}$,

$\mathsf{y\,[\,n\,]\,,\,n\,]\,/\,/\,FullSimplify}$

Out[•]= $\begin{cases} 3 - 2^{1+n}\,3^{-n} & n \geq 0 \\ 0 & \text{True} \end{cases}$

This shows the result:

In[•]:= $\mathsf{DiscretePlot\,[\,sol,\,\boxed{\cdots\,\ast}\,]}$

Out[•]=

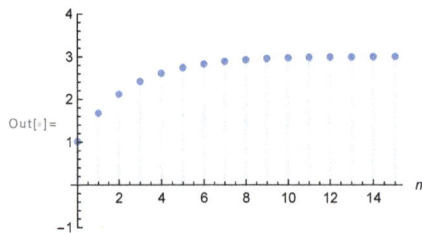

Step-by-step

The total solution is the sum of the homogeneous and particular solutions (see Examples 1 and 3), resulting in the following

$$y[n] = y_h[n] + y_p[n] = c_1 \left(\frac{2}{3}\right)^n + 3$$

The constant c_1 is resolved using the given auxiliary condition

$$y[-1] = c_1 \left(\frac{2}{3}\right)^{-1} + 3 = 0$$

Solving for the constant c_1, you get $c_1 = -2$.

Therefore the total solution is

$$y[n] = (-2)\left(\frac{2}{3}\right)^n + 3, \ n \geq 0$$

Example 6

Find the solution of the following second-order difference equation with nonzero initial conditions

$$y[n] + \frac{3}{10}\, y[n-1] - \frac{1}{10}\, y[n-2] = u[n], \quad y[-2] = 0, \ y[-1] = 1$$

Solution

This returns the solution of the given difference equation:

In[•]:= **sol = RSolveValue [{y [n] +** $\dfrac{3}{10}$ **y [n − 1] −** $\dfrac{1}{10}$ **y [n − 2] == 1,**

y [−2] == 0, y [−1] == 1}, y [n], n] / / FullSimplify / / Expand

Out[•]= $\dfrac{5}{6} - \dfrac{5}{21}\,(-1)^n\, 2^{-1-n} - \dfrac{5^{-1-n}}{14}$

Here are the values of the output sequence for $n = 0, \ ..., 5$:

In[•]:= **Table [sol, {n, 0, 5}]**

Out[•]= $\left\{ \dfrac{7}{10}, \dfrac{89}{100}, \dfrac{803}{1000}, \dfrac{8481}{10\,000}, \dfrac{82\,587}{100\,000}, \dfrac{837\,049}{1\,000\,000} \right\}$

This shows the solution:

In[•]:= **DiscretePlot [sol ,** ⋯ ✦ **]**

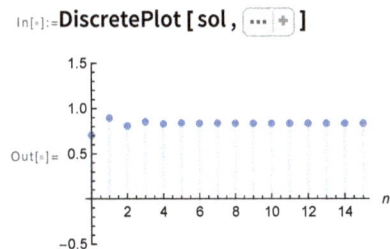

Step-by-step

Begin by finding the solution of the following homogeneous equation

$$y[n] + \frac{3}{10} y[n-1] - \frac{1}{10} y[n-2] = 0$$

The characteristic roots are:

In[·]:= **Roots** $[r^2 + \frac{3}{10} r - \frac{1}{10} == 0, r]$

Out[·]= $r == \frac{1}{5} \, || \, r == -\frac{1}{2}$

The homogeneous (or complementary) solution has the form:

In[·]:= **yc** $[n\_] := c_1 \left(-\frac{1}{2} \right)^n + c_2 \left(\frac{1}{5} \right)^n$

For a constant input, the particular solution must also be constant, so the particular solution has the form:

In[·]:= **yp** $[n\_] := K$

Substitute it into the difference equation and solve for the value of the constant K:

In[·]:= **Solve** $[yp[n] + \frac{3}{10} yp[n-1] - \frac{1}{10} yp[n-2] == 1, K]$

Out[·]= $\left\{ \left\{ K \to \frac{5}{6} \right\} \right\}$

This gives $K = \frac{5}{6}$, and therefore the following particular solution:

In[·]:= **yp** $[n\_] := \frac{5}{6}$

The total solution is the sum of the homogeneous and particular solutions:

In[·]:= **ytotal** $[n\_] = yc[n] + yp[n]$

Out[·]= $\frac{5}{6} + \left(-\frac{1}{2} \right)^n c_1 + 5^{-n} c_2$

Resolve the undetermined coefficients using the given auxiliary conditions $y[-2] = 0$ and $y[-1] = 1$:

In[·]:= **eqns** $= \{ ytotal[-2] == 0, ytotal[-1] == 1 \}$

Out[·]= $\left\{ \frac{5}{6} + 4 c_1 + 25 c_2 == 0, \frac{5}{6} - 2 c_1 + 5 c_2 == 1 \right\}$

Solve for the coefficients c_1 and c_2:

In[*]:=**Solve [eqns]**

$\text{Out[*]=}\left\{\left\{c_1 \to -\dfrac{5}{42}, c_2 \to -\dfrac{1}{70}\right\}\right\}$

Therefore, the total solution is:

In[*]:=**ytotal [n]** $/. \left\{c_1 \to -\dfrac{5}{42}, c_2 \to -\dfrac{1}{70}\right\}$

$\text{Out[*]=}\dfrac{5}{6} - \dfrac{5}{21}(-1)^n 2^{-1-n} - \dfrac{5^{-1-n}}{14}$

Summary

The classical methods for finding solutions of homogeneous and nonhomogeneous ordinary constant coefficient difference equations were presented.

The homogeneous solution of a difference equation of the form

$$y[n] + a_1\, y[n-1] + \ldots + a_N\, y[n-N] = x[n]$$

is typically of the following form

$$y_c[n] = c_1\, r_1{}^n + c_2\, r_2{}^n + \ldots + c_N\, r_N{}^n$$

where the r_i's are the roots of the characteristic equation.

The method of undetermined coefficients is used to find the particular solution $y_p[n]$.

Input	Particular solution
A (constant)	c_0 (constant)
$A\, r^n$	$c_0\, r^n$
$\sin(\omega n)$ or $\cos(\omega n)$	$c_1 \sin(\omega n) + c_2 \cos(\omega n)$

The total solution of a nonhomogeneous ordinary constant coefficient difference equation is a sum of the complementary and particular solutions

$$y[n] = y_c[n] + y_p[n]$$

Constant coefficient difference equations can be solved numerically using a simple iterative process.

Exercises

Download the solutions manual at wolfr.am/eTextbook-SSSP

11.1 Find the complementary solution of the following first-order difference equation.

$$y[n] - \alpha\, y[n-1] = 0$$

11.2 Find the solution of the following first-order difference equation and initial condition.

$$y[n] - \alpha\, y[n-1] = 0, \qquad y[-1] = \beta$$

11.3 Solve the following initial value problem.

$$y[n] + y[n-2] = 0, \qquad y[-1] = 1,\, y[-2] = 0$$

11.4 Solve the following initial value problem.

$$y[n] + 2\, y[n-1] + y[n-2] = 0, \qquad y[-1] = 1,\, y[-2] = 0$$

11.5 Solve the following initial value problem.

$$y[n] - y[n-1] - y[n-2] = 0, \qquad y[0] = 0,\, y[1] = 1$$

11.6 Find the particular solution of the following difference equation.

$$y[n] + y[n-2] = \alpha\, u[n]$$

11.7 Find the particular solution of the following first-order difference equation.

$$y[n] - \frac{2}{3}\, y[n-1] = \cos\!\left(\frac{\pi}{2}\, n\right)$$

11.8 Solve the following initial value problem.

$$y[n] - \frac{2}{3}\, y[n-1] = \cos\!\left(\frac{\pi}{2}\, n\right), \qquad y[-1] = 1$$

11.9 Solve the following initial value problem.

$$y[n] - y[n-1] + y[n-2] = u[n], \qquad y[-1] = 1,\, y[-2] = 0$$

12 | Discrete-Time System Response

A system response is the sequence observed at the output of a system in response to some nonzero input sequence. In this chapter, the time-domain input-output relations in discrete-time linear shift-invariant (LSI) systems are summarized.

The input sequences that are of particular interest in the study of LSI systems are:

- Unit sample
- Unit step
- Sinusoidal

Depending on the length of the response to a unit sample, all discrete-time LSI systems belong to one of the following two categories:

- Infinite-impulse response (IIR)
- Finite-impulse response (FIR)

A system's response depends on the form of the defining difference equation. The two forms are:

- Recursive
- Non-recursive

Unit Sample Response of a Recursive System

The classical method of solving a constant coefficient ordinary difference equation can be simplified if the forcing function on the right-hand side of the equation is a unit sample.

Consider the difference equation

$$y[n] + a_1\, y[n-1] + ... + a_N\, y[n-N] = x[n]$$

with initial conditions $y[-1]$, $y[-2]$, ..., $y[-N]$.

The objective is to obtain the unit sample response, namely the response of the system to the input $x[n] = \delta[n]$. This problem can be simplified to one of finding the homogeneous solution of the difference equation with a time-shifted set of initial conditions that now contains $y[0]$.

The value for $y[0]$ is readily obtained from the difference equation and initial conditions

$$y[0] = \delta[0] - a_1 \ y[-1] - \ldots - a_N \ y[-N]$$

$$= 1 - a_1 \ y[-1] - \ldots - a_N \ y[-N]$$

The unit sample response now reduces to solving the following homogeneous difference equation

$$y[n] + a_1 \ y[n-1] + \ldots + a_N \ y[n-N] = 0$$

with initial conditions $y[0]$, $y[1]$, ..., $y[N-1]$.

Recursive systems usually have unit sample responses of infinite duration. For this reason, they are frequently called infinite-impulse response (IIR) systems.

Example 1

Obtain the unit sample response of the following system and given initial condition

$$y[n] - \tfrac{2}{3} \ y[n-1] = x[n], \quad y[-1] = \tfrac{1}{2}$$

Solution

Use recursion to find the response $y[0]$

$$y[0] = x[0] + \tfrac{2}{3} \ y[-1] = \delta[0] + \tfrac{2}{3} \ y[-1] = 1 + \tfrac{2}{3} \left(\tfrac{1}{2}\right) = \tfrac{4}{3}$$

The unit sample response is now obtained from the following initial value problem:

In[•]:= **sol = RSolveValue [{y[n] $-\dfrac{2}{3}$ y[n − 1] == 0, y[0] == $\dfrac{4}{3}$ }, y[n], n]**

Out[•]= $2^{2+n} \ 3^{-1-n}$

This shows the result:

In[•]:= **DiscretePlot [sol, ⋯ ✦]**

Out[•]=

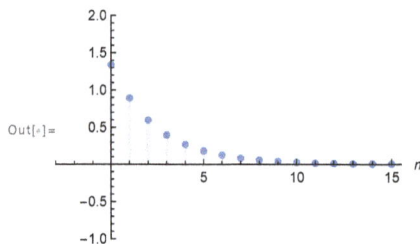

This returns the solution as initially formulated:

In[•]:= **RSolveValue [{ y [n]** $- \dfrac{2}{3}$ **y [n − 1] == KroneckerDelta [n] , y [−1] == 1 / 2 },**

y [n] , n] / / Simplify / / Expand

$\text{Out[•]=} 2^{n} \, 3^{-1-n} + \left(\dfrac{3}{2}\right)^{1-n} \left(\begin{cases} \dfrac{2}{3} & n \geq 0 \\ 0 & \text{True} \end{cases} \right)$

Unit Sample Response of a Non-recursive System

The unit sample responses of non-recursive systems are always finite in length, thus they are known as finite-impulse response (FIR) systems.

For example, the following non-recursive system

$$y[n] = \tfrac{1}{3} \, (x[n] + x[n-1] + x[n-2])$$

has a unit sample response of length 3. Evaluating for $-1 \leq n \leq 3$, you get

$$y[-1] = \tfrac{1}{3} \, (x[-1] + x[-2] + x[-3]) = \tfrac{1}{3} \, (\delta[-1] + \delta[-2] + \delta[-3]) = 0$$

$$y[0] = \tfrac{1}{3} \, (x[0] + x[-1] + x[-2]) = \tfrac{1}{3} \, (\delta[0] + \delta[-1] + \delta[-2]) = \tfrac{1}{3}$$

$$y[1] = \tfrac{1}{3} \, (x[1] + x[0] + x[-1]) = \tfrac{1}{3} \, (\delta[1] + \delta[0] + \delta[-1]) = \tfrac{1}{3}$$

$$y[2] = \tfrac{1}{3} \, (x[2] + x[1] + x[0]) = \tfrac{1}{3} \, (\delta[2] + \delta[1] + \delta[0]) = \tfrac{1}{3}$$

$$y[3] = \tfrac{1}{3} \, (x[3] + x[2] + x[1]) = \tfrac{1}{3} \, (\delta[3] + \delta[2] + \delta[1]) = 0$$

In general, an FIR system defined as follows

$$y[n] = \sum_{k=0}^{M-1} b_k \, x[n-k]$$

will have a unit sample response of the form

$$y[n] = \sum_{k=0}^{M-1} b_k \, \delta[n-k]$$

Step Response

The step response is another important system response that characterizes a linear time-invariant (LTI) system. Much like the unit sample response, it provides information about the system's transient behavior, stability, and causality. The step response shows a system's output due to a constant forcing function.

For example, consider the step response of the following second-order system

$$y[n] - y[n-1] + 0.6 \, y[n-2] = x[n], \; y[-1] = 0, \; y[-2] = 0$$

The step response is:

In[•]:=**step =**
    RSolveValue [{ y [n] − y [n − 1] + 0.6 y [n − 2] == 1, y [−1] == 0, y [−2] == 0 },
       y [n] , n] / / Simplify

Out[•]=$1.66667 - (0.333333 - 0.563436\,i)\,(0.5 - 0.591608\,i)^n -$
    $(0.333333 + 0.563436\,i)\,(0.5 + 0.591608\,i)^n$

This shows the step response revealing the characteristic oscillatory behavior of an underdamped system:

In[•]:=**DiscretePlot [step , ⋯ +]**

Out[•]=

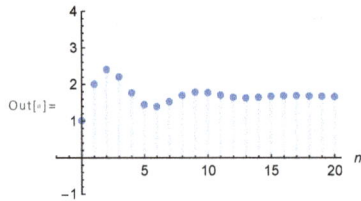

Sinusoidal Response

Recall that one of the main properties of LSI systems is that a sinusoidal input results in a sinusoidal output. By capturing the response at different frequencies of the input signal, the analysis of sinusoidal responses gives insight into the behavior of a system as a function of frequency. Here is a simple example.

This returns the response of a first-order discrete-time system at rest $(y[-1] = 0)$ to a sinusoidal input with frequency $\omega = 0.1\,\pi$:

In[•]:=**sol = RSolveValue [{ y [n] − 0.5 y [n − 1] == 0.5 Cos [0.1 π n] , y [−1] == 0.,**
      y [−1] == 0. } , y [n] , n, ⋯ → ⋯ +] / / Simplify / / Chop

Out[•]=$-0.377209\,e^{-0.693147\,n} + (0.438604 + 0.129212\,i)\,e^{(0.-0.314159\,i)\,n} +$
    $(0.438604 - 0.129212\,i)\,e^{(0.+0.314159\,i)\,n}$

This shows the input and the response:

In[•]:=**DiscretePlot [{ Cos [(0.1 π) n] , sol } , ⋯ +]**

Out[•]=

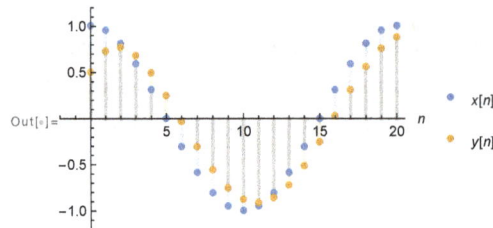

As expected, the output is simply a scaled and shifted copy of the input. Now observe the response to an input at frequency $\omega = 0.3\,\pi$:

In[•]:= **sol = RSolveValue [{ y [n] − 0.5 y [n − 1] == 0.5 Cos [0.3 π n] , y [−1] == 0.,**
$\qquad$ **y [−1] == 0.} , y [n] , n, $\boxed{\cdots \rightarrow \cdots \; +}$] // Simplify // Chop**

Out[•]= $-0.0331408\, e^{-0.693147\, n} + (0.26657 + 0.15271\, i)\, e^{(0.-0.942478\, i)\, n} +$
$\qquad (0.26657 - 0.15271\, i)\, e^{(0.+0.942478\, i)\, n}$

This shows the input and the response:

In[•]:= **DiscretePlot [{ Cos [(0.3 π) n] , sol } , $\boxed{\cdots \; +}$]**

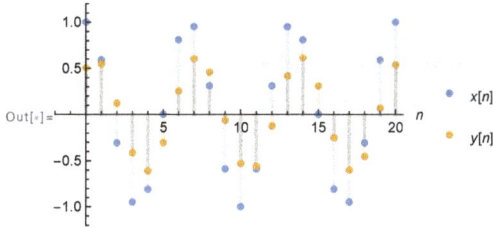

Note how the amplitude of the output sequence decreased.

Zero-Input Response

The complementary and particular solutions are two classic components of the total solution of a difference equation that arise naturally from the typically used solution method. However, here two alternative components of the solution, the so-called zero-input and zero-state responses, are considered.

The zero-input response (ZIR) assumes a zero input (i.e. $x[n] = 0$) and nonzero values for the initial conditions, which is simply the homogeneous initial value problem.

For example, take the following first-order system (see Example 1)

$$y[n] - \tfrac{2}{3}\, y[n-1] = 0, \qquad y[-1] = \tfrac{1}{2}$$

This returns the ZIR of the system:

In[•]:= **yzir [n_] = RSolveValue [{ y [n] $-\dfrac{2}{3}$ y [n − 1] == 0, y [−1] == $\dfrac{1}{2}$ } , y [n] , n]**
$\qquad$ **UnitStep [n] // Simplify**

Out[•]= $2^{n}\, 3^{-1-n}$ UnitStep [n]

This shows the result:

In[•]:=**DiscretePlot [yzir [n] , ⸱⸱⸱ ✦]**

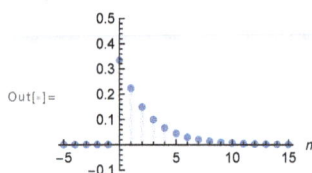

Out[•]=

This shows the result:

Zero-State Response

The zero-state response (ZSR) assumes a nonzero input and zero initial conditions. This returns the ZSR of a first-order system to a unit step input:

In[•]:=**yzsr [n_] = RSolveValue [**

$$\{ y [n] - \frac{2}{3} y [n - 1] == UnitStep [n] , y [-1] == 0 \} , y [n] , n] \ // \ Simplify$$

Out[•]=$\begin{cases} 3 - 2^{1+n} \, 3^{-n} & n \geq 0 \\ 0 & True \end{cases}$

This shows the result:

In[•]:=**DiscretePlot [yzsr [n] , ⸱⸱⸱ ✦]**

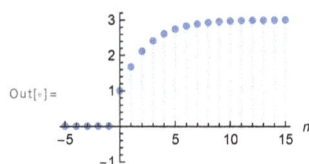

Out[•]=

Total Response

The total response is the sum of the ZSR and ZIR:

In[•]:=**ytotal [n_] = yzir [n] + yzsr [n] \ // \ Simplify**

Out[•]=$\begin{cases} \frac{1}{3} \left(9 - 5 \left(\frac{2}{3} \right)^n \right) & n \geq 0 \\ 0 & True \end{cases}$

This shows the three responses:

In[•]:=**DiscretePlot [{ yzir [n] , yzsr [n] , ytotal [n] } , ⸱⸱⸱ ✦]**

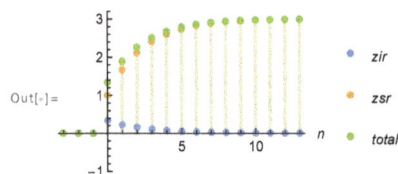

Out[•]=

Second-Order Canonical Systems

As was the case with continuous-time LTI systems, second-order discrete-time systems exhibit the full range of time-domain and frequency-domain behavior of higher-order systems. Therefore, again it is of interest to consider the responses of a canonical second-order system defined by the pair of parameters, namely damping ratio ξ and natural frequency ω_n, as used in the continuous-time case. The following canonical representation can be used for this purpose. It was obtained by using a common continuous-to-discrete transformation to be discussed later in the book

$$a_0 \, y[n] + a_1 \, y[n-1] + a_2 \, y[n-2] = b_0 \, x[n] + b_1 \, x[n-1] + b_2 \, x[n-2]$$

with

$$a_0 = 1 + \xi \sin(\omega_n)$$

$$a_1 = -2 \cos(\omega_n)$$

$$a_2 = 1 - \xi \sin(\omega_n)$$

$$b_1 = 1 - \cos(\omega_n)$$

$$b_0 = b_2 = \frac{1}{2} \, b_1$$

This shows the location of the characteristic roots of the canonical difference equation and its unit sample response as the two parameters are varied:

In[•]:= **DynamicModule [** ⋯ ➕ ▲ **]**

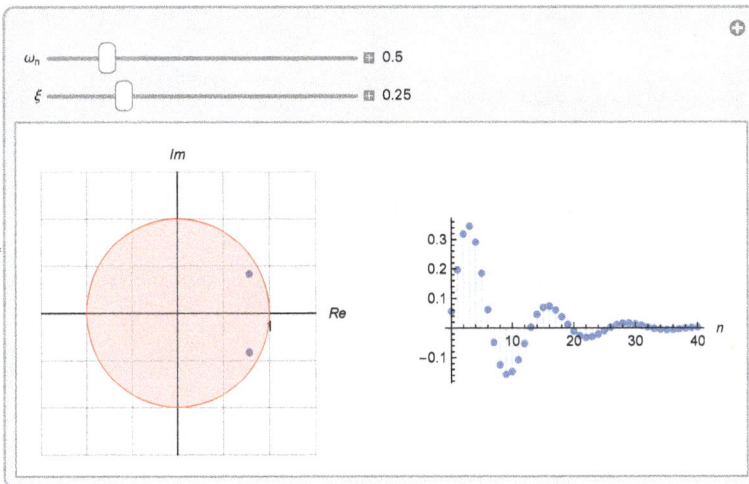

Summary

Three important system responses:

- Unit sample response

- Step response

- Sinusoidal response

Important discrete-time LTI system categories:

- Recursive vs. non-recursive

- FIR vs. IIR

Two important response components:

- ZIR

- ZSR

Exercises

Download the solutions manual at wolfr.am/eTextbook-SSSP

12.1 Use recursion to obtain the unit sample response for $n = -2, -1, 0, 1, 2$ of a system defined by the following difference equation.

$$y[n] = \frac{1}{3}\left(x[n+1] + x[n] + x[n-1]\right)$$

12.2 Obtain the unit step response of a moving average filter of order $N = 5$ defined by the following non-recursive difference equation.

$$y[n] = \frac{1}{5}\left(x[n] + x[n-1] + x[n-2] + x[n-3] + x[n-4]\right)$$

12.3 Use recursion to obtain the step response for $n = 0, 1, 2, 3$ of a system defined by the following difference equation.

$$y[n] - \frac{1}{2}y[n-1] = \frac{1}{3}\left(x[n] + x[n-1] + x[n-2]\right)$$

Assume zero initial conditions.

12.4 Consider a discrete-time system described by the following difference equation and initial condition.

$$y[n] - a\,y[n-1] = x[n] - a^3\,x[n-3], \qquad y[-1] = 0$$

Use recursion to obtain the unit sample response.

12.5 Obtain the unit sample response of the following LSI system.

$$y[n] - y[n-1] = x[n], \qquad y[-1] = 0$$

12.6 Obtain the unit step response of the following LSI system.

$$y[n] + y[n-1] = x[n], \qquad y[0] = 0$$

12.7 Determine the unit step response of the following discrete-time system.

$$y[n] + y[n-1] - \frac{1}{2} y[n-2] = x[n], \qquad y[-2] = 0, \ y[-1] = -1$$

12.8 Obtain the unit step response of the following LSI system.

$$y[n] - y[n-2] = x[n], \qquad y[-1] = 0, y[-2] = 0$$

13 | Discrete-Time Convolution

Discrete-time convolution is one of the more important and frequently used signal processing operations. Convolution is so important because in the case of linear shift-invariant (LSI) systems, it returns the response to any input, given the system's unit sample response. Furthermore, even more importantly, for finite-length sequences, it can be evaluated using a fast numerical algorithm (to be discussed later). First, the convolution sum is derived from first principles using the properties of linearity and time invariance.

Convolution Sum

An arbitrary discrete-time signal can be represented as a linear combination of scaled and shifted unit samples $\delta[n - k]$, where the weights in this linear combination are simply the values of the sequence, $x[k]$

$$x[n] = \sum_{k=-\infty}^{\infty} x[k]\, \delta[n - k]$$

You are interested in the response of an LSI system to such an input. So, let $h[n]$ denote the LSI system's response to a unit sample

$$h[n] = \mathcal{S}\, \{\delta[n]\}$$

Due to time invariance, a delayed unit sample input results in a delayed unit sample response

$$h[n - k] = \mathcal{S}\, \{\delta[n - k]\}$$

Now, due to linearity, a sum of scaled and shifted unit sample inputs results in a sum of responses

$$y\,[n] = \mathcal{S}\, \{\, \sum_{k=-\infty}^{\infty} x[k]\, \delta[n - k]\}$$

$$= \sum_{k=-\infty}^{\infty} x[k]\, \mathcal{S}\, \{\delta[n - k]\}$$

The resulting formula

$$y[n] = \sum_{k=-\infty}^{\infty} x[k]\, h[n - k]$$

is known as the convolution sum representation of an LSI system. Convolution of two sequences $x[n]$ and $h[n]$ is typically denoted as $x[n] * h[n]$.

Convolution is commutative, namely, $x[n] * h[n] = h[n] * x[n]$. Therefore, the convolution sum may also be written

$$y[n] = \sum_{k=-\infty}^{\infty} h[k]\, x[n-k]$$

Convolution is also associative and distributive. Given three sequences $x[n]$, $y[n]$, and $z[n]$, associativity implies

$$(x[n] * y[n]) * z[n] = x[n] * (y[n] * z[n]) = x[n] * y[n] * z[n]$$

While the distributive property implies

$$(x[n] + y[n]) * z[n] = x[n] * z[n] + y[n] * z[n]$$

The unit sample $\delta[n]$ is the identity element of convolution, namely $h[n] * \delta[n] = h[n]$.

Convolution as Superposition

A useful interpretation of the convolution sum is as a superposition of scaled translations of a sequence. For example, consider the convolution of the following two finite-duration sequences

$$x[n] = \delta[n] + 2\,\delta[n-1] + 2\,\delta[n-2] - \delta[n-3]$$

$$h[n] = \delta[n] - \delta[n-1]$$

Recognizing that the sequence $x[k]$ is only nonzero for $0 \le k \le 3$, the convolution sum reduces to

$$y[n] = \sum_{k=0}^{3} x[k]\, h[n-k]$$

Expansion of the sum and substitution of the known values of $x[k]$ results in the following superposition of the scaled and shifted unit sample responses

$$y[n] = x[0]\, h[n] + x[1]\, h[n-1] + x[2]\, h[n-2] + x[3]\, h[n-3]$$

$$= (1)\, h[n] + (2)\, h[n-1] + (2)\, h[n-2] + (-1)\, h[n-3]$$

This shows each of the four terms in the preceding sum

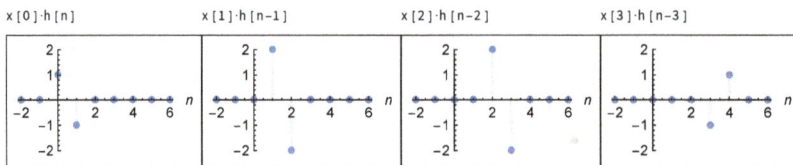

Substitution of $h[n]$ and simplification gives the following final result

$$y[n] = (1)\,(\delta[n] - \delta[n-1]) + (2)\,(\delta[n-1] - \delta[n-2]) +$$
$$(2)\,(\delta[n-2] - \delta[n-3]) + (-1)\,(\delta[n-3] - \delta[n-4])$$
$$= \delta[n] + \delta[n-1] - 3\,\delta[n-3] + \delta[n-4]$$

Direct application of the DiscreteConvolve function confirms the result:

```
In[•]:= x[n_] := δ_n + 2 δ_{n-1} + 2 δ_{n-2} − δ_{n-3};
       h[n_] := δ_n − δ_{n-1};
       y[n_] = DiscreteConvolve[x[k], h[k], k, n] // Simplify
```

$$\text{Out[•]} = \begin{cases} -3 & n == 3 \\ 1 & n == 0 \mid\mid n == 1 \mid\mid n == 4 \\ 0 & \text{True} \end{cases}$$

This displays the result:

```
In[•]:= DiscretePlot[y[n], ⋯ + ]
```

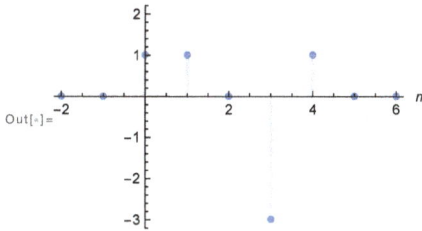

Out[•]=

"Flip-and-Slide" Convolution

An alternative interpretation of convolution is as an operation of "sliding" a reversed version of one signal past the other. In this interpretation, $h[n-k]$ is a sequence of time k that is time reversed and shifted to the position n on the time axis.

Here is an interactive demonstration of the flip-and-slide evaluation showing for each value of n the two sequences, the sample-by-sample products, and the resulting sum:

```
In[•]:= DynamicModule[ ⋯ + ]
```

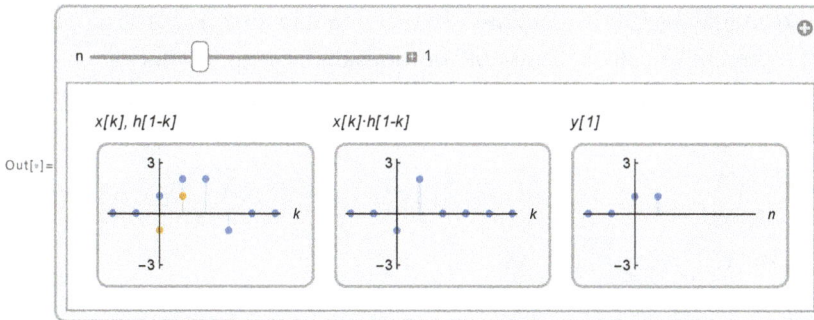

Out[•]=

Summation of the sample-by-sample products of the two sequences for each value of n gives the desired result. For example, for $n = 0$, convolution reduces to

$$y[0] = \sum_{k=0}^{3} x[k]\,h[-k]$$

$$= x[0]\,h[0] + x[1]\,h[-1] + x[2]\,h[-2] + x[3]\,h[-3]$$

Substitution of the known values for $x[n]$ and $h[n]$ and summation of the products gives

$$= (1)\,(1) + (2)\,(0) + (2)\,(0) + (-1)\,(0) = 1$$

Repeating for $n = 1$ gives

$$y[1] = \sum_{k=0}^{3} x[k]\,h[1-k]$$

$$= x[0]\,h[1] + x[1]\,h[0] = (1)\,(-1) + (2)\,(1) = 1$$

The remaining values are

$$y[2] = 0,$$

$$y[3] = -3,$$

$$y[4] = 1,$$

and

$$y[n] = 0,\ n > 4.$$

Steady-State and Transient Samples

It is instructive to once again return to the linear equations representing the convolution of sequences $x[n]$ and $h[n]$

$$y[0] = x[0]\,h[0]$$
$$y[1] = x[0]\,h[1] + x[1]\,h[0]$$
$$y[2] = x[1]\,h[1] + x[2]\,h[0]$$
$$y[3] = x[2]\,h[1] + x[3]\,h[0]$$
$$y[4] = x[3]\,h[1]$$

The output shown may be subdivided into two sections. The first and last samples $y[0]$ and $y[4]$ represent so-called "transient" portions of the output sequence resulting from a partial overlap of nonzero values of $x[n]$ with the reversed and shifted sequence $h[n]$

$$y[0] = x[0]\,h[0]$$
$$\vdots \qquad \vdots$$
$$y[4] = x[3]\,h[1]$$

The middle samples $y[1]$, $y[2]$, and $y[3]$ represent the so-called "steady-state" portion of the output sequence resulting from a full overlap of the $x[n]$ and $h[n]$ sequences

$$\vdots \qquad \vdots$$
$$y[1] = x[0]\,h[1] + x[1]\,h[0]$$
$$y[2] = x[1]\,h[1] + x[2]\,h[0]$$
$$y[3] = x[2]\,h[1] + x[3]\,h[0]$$
$$\vdots \qquad \vdots$$

In general, for two finite-length sequences of lengths L_x and L_h, respectively, the number of steady-state values is always $L_x - L_h + 1$, the number of transient samples is $L_h - 1$ at the beginning and the end, and therefore the total number of nonzero samples is $L_x + L_h - 1$.

Convolution Sum—Efficient Evaluation

Convolution is such an important mathematical operator that most advanced computational systems available today have built-in functions for computing the convolution of two finite-length numerical sequences. For example, the sequences $x[n]$ and $h[n]$ shown earlier can be represented by the following two lists of numbers:

```
In[•]:= Clear [ x, h ] ;
        x = {1, 2, 2, −1}; h = {1, −1};
```

The result can be obtained using the built-in convolution operator ListConvolve. By default, only the steady-state values are returned:

```
In[•]:= ListConvolve [ h, x ]
```

```
Out[•]= {1, 0, −3}
```

In order to return all the desired values, steady state and transient, ListConvolve needs two more arguments. The third argument in the form **{1,−1}** indicates that all the transient samples are to be returned, while the fourth argument defines how the list **x** is to be padded, which, in this case is with zeros.

This returns the expected result:

```
In[•]:= ListConvolve [ h, x, {1, −1}, 0 ]
```

```
Out[•]= {1, 1, 0, −3, 1}
```

Example 1

Convolve the two sequences given here using ListConvolve. Return the steady-state values only:

In[•]:=**Clear [x, h] ;**

$$x = \{0, 0, 0, 1, 1, 1, 1, 1, 0, 0, 0\}; h = \frac{1}{3} \{1, 1, 1\};$$

Solution

This returns the steady-state values only:

In[•]:=**ListConvolve [h, x]**

Out[•]=$\left\{0, \frac{1}{3}, \frac{2}{3}, 1, 1, 1, \frac{2}{3}, \frac{1}{3}, 0\right\}$

Convolution of Infinite (or Long) Sequences

Convolution of sequences defined as discrete-time functions over infinite or semi-infinite intervals requires an algebraic approach. Sometimes, this may require not much more than substitution into the defining convolution sum. For example, given the following two sequences

$$x[n] = u[n]$$

$$h[n] = \left(\frac{3}{4}\right)^n u[n]$$

one proceeds as follows

$$y[n] = \sum_{k=-\infty}^{\infty} h[k]\, x[n-k]$$

Now, since $h[k]$ is nonzero for $k \geq 0$, the sum reduces to

$$y[n] = \sum_{k=0}^{\infty} \left(\frac{3}{4}\right)^n \cdot x[n-k]$$

Next, $x[n-k] = u[n-k] = 0$ for $k > n$ and has the value of 1 for $0 \leq k \leq n$, resulting in

$$y[n] = \sum_{k=0}^{n} \left(\frac{3}{4}\right)^n$$

which, recalling a well-known sum formula, evaluates to

$$y[n] = \frac{\left(\frac{3}{4}\right)^{n+1} - 1}{\frac{3}{4} - 1} = 4 - 4\left(\frac{3}{4}\right)^n, \; n \geq 0$$

Or more directly:

In[•]:=**Sum [($\frac{3}{4}$)^k, { k, 0, n }] / / Simplify**

Out[•]=$4 - 3^{1+n}\, 4^{-n}$

Alternatively, using the function DiscreteConvolve:

$$\text{In[\cdot]:=}\ \text{DiscreteConvolve} \left[\text{UnitStep} [\, k \,], \left(\frac{3}{4} \right)^k \text{UnitStep} [\, k \,], k, n \right]$$

$$\text{Out[\cdot]=} \begin{cases} 4 - 3^{1+n}\, 4^{-n} & n \geq 0 \\ 0 & \text{True} \end{cases}$$

Here is a graphical demonstration:

$$\text{In[\cdot]:=}\ \text{DynamicModule} \left[\ \cdots\ + \ \right]$$

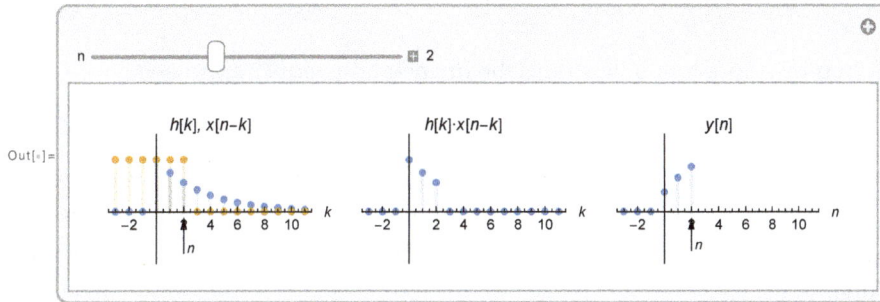

However, in most cases, the convolution sum is evaluated using a "divide-and-conquer" approach, with the region of summation broken up into non-overlapping subregions.

For example, the following two sequences are to be convolved:

```
In[·]:= Clear [ x, h ] ;
       x [ n_ ] := UnitStep [ n + 3 ] - UnitStep [ n - 4 ] ;
       h [ n_ ] := ( 3/4 )^n UnitStep [ n ] ;
```

The two sequences are shown here:

$$\text{In[\cdot]:=}\ \text{GraphicsRow} \left[\ \cdots\ + \ \right]$$

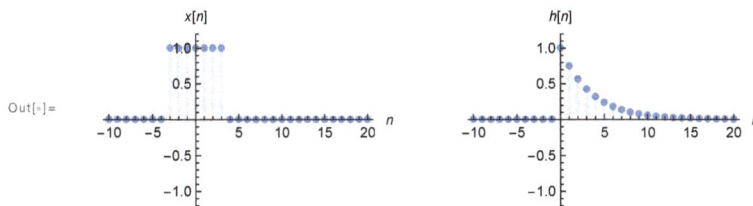

Evaluation using the function DiscreteConvolve returns the following result:

$$\text{In[\cdot]:=}\ \text{sol} = \text{DiscreteConvolve} [\, h\,[\, k \,], x\,[\, k \,], k, n \,] \ // \ \text{Simplify}$$

$$\text{Out[\cdot]=} \begin{cases} 14\,197 \cdot 3^{-3+n}\, 4^{-3-n} & n \geq 4 \\ 4 - 3^{4+n}\, 4^{-3-n} & -3 \leq n < 4 \\ 0 & \text{True} \end{cases}$$

This shows the result:

In[ ]:=**DiscretePlot [sol, ⋯ +]**

Out[ ]=

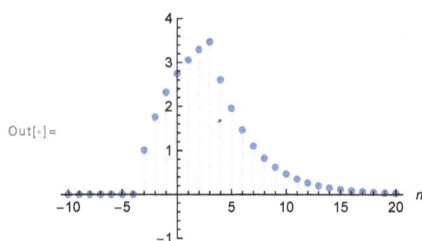

Next, a step-by-step solution illustrates the divide-and-conquer approach.

Step-by-step

Inspection of the two sequences indicates that it is easier to flip and slide sequence $x[n]$. Also, an examination of the regions of support of the two sequences reveals that there are three distinct regions that need to be considered when evaluating the convolution sum.

For $n + 3 < 0$, there is no overlap between $h[k]$ and $x[n - k]$:

In[ ]:=**DynamicModule [⋯ +]**

Out[ ]=

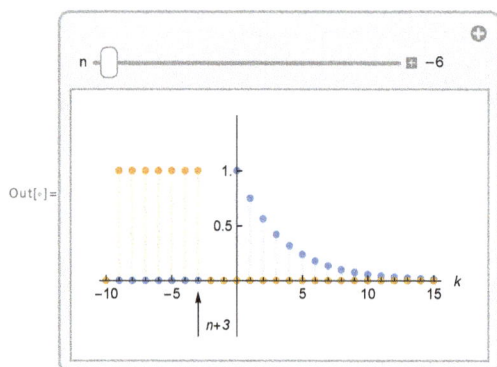

Therefore, the product of the two sequences is zero and the result for $n < -3$ is:

In[ ]:=**y [n_ /; n < -3] = 0;**

Next, for $n + 3 \geq 0$ and $n - 3 < 0$, or, equivalently, $-3 \leq n < 3$, there exists a partial overlap between $h[k]$ and $x[n - k]$:

In[•]:=**DynamicModule [** ⎡ ⋯ ⎢ + ⎤ ⎦ **]**

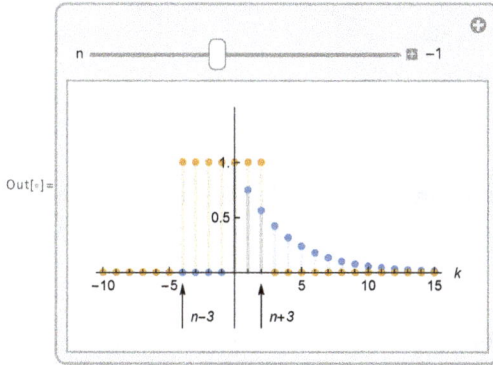

The limits of summation are $k = 0$ (leftmost sample of sequence $h[k]$) and $k = n + 3$ (rightmost sample of sequence $x[n - k]$); therefore, for $-3 \leq n < 3$, the convolution formula reduces to the following sum and result:

In[•]:=**y [n_ /; -3 ≤ n < 3] = Sum [$\left(\dfrac{3}{4}\right)^k$, { k, 0, n + 3 }] / / Simplify**

Out[•]=$4 - 3^{4+n}\, 4^{-3-n}$

Finally, for $n - 3 \geq 0$, there is full overlap between $h[k]$ and $x[n - k]$:

In[•]:=**DynamicModule [** ⎡ ⋯ ⎢ + ⎤ ⎦ **]**

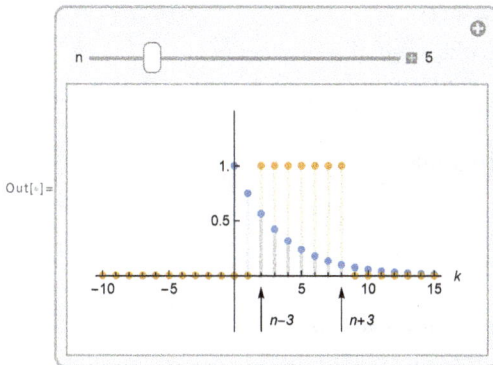

Now the limits of summation are $n - 3$ and $n + 3$, and on the interval $n \geq 3$, the result is:

In[•]:=**y [n_ /; n ≥ 3] = Sum [$\left(\dfrac{3}{4}\right)^k$, { k, n - 3, n + 3 }]**

Out[•]=$\left(\dfrac{3}{4}\right)^{-3+n} + \left(\dfrac{3}{4}\right)^{-2+n} + \left(\dfrac{3}{4}\right)^{-1+n} + \left(\dfrac{3}{4}\right)^{n} + \left(\dfrac{3}{4}\right)^{1+n} + \left(\dfrac{3}{4}\right)^{2+n} + \left(\dfrac{3}{4}\right)^{3+n}$

Putting it all together

$$y[n] = \begin{cases} 4 - \frac{81}{256}\left(\frac{3}{4}\right)^n, & -3 \le n < 3 \\ \left(\frac{3}{4}\right)^{-3+n} + \left(\frac{3}{4}\right)^{-2+n} + \left(\frac{3}{4}\right)^{-1+n} + \left(\frac{3}{4}\right)^{n} + \left(\frac{3}{4}\right)^{1+n} + \left(\frac{3}{4}\right)^{2+n} + \left(\frac{3}{4}\right)^{3+n}, & n \ge 3 \\ 0, & \text{else} \end{cases}$$

Convolution and the Unit Sample Response

The unit sample response $h[n]$ of a linear time-invariant (LTI) system is the system output when the input is a unit sample

$$y[n] = \sum_{k=-\infty}^{\infty} h[k]\, \delta[n-k] = h[n]$$

The causality and stability of an LTI system may be determined directly from its unit sample response. A discrete-time LTI system is said to be causal if $h[n] = 0$ for $n < 0$. A sufficient and necessary condition for the stability of an LTI system is that the unit sample response be absolutely summable, that is

$$\sum_{k=-\infty}^{\infty} |h[k]| \le \infty$$

Convolution and the Unit Step Response

It is also of interest to obtain the formula for the step response of a system given a known unit sample response

$$y[n] = \sum_{k=-\infty}^{\infty} h[k]\, u[n-k]$$

Now, since $u[n-k] = 1$ for $k \le n$ and zero otherwise, the sum reduces to

$$y[n] = \sum_{k=-\infty}^{n} h[k]$$

which gives the step response from a unit sample response.

Example 2

Obtain the step response of a system with the following unit sample response:

```
In[•]:= Clear [ h ] ;

h [ n_ ] := ( 2/3 )^n UnitStep [ n ]
```

Solution

Substitution into the step response formula immediately yields the following result:

In[•]:=**Sum [h [k] , { k , −∞, n } , Assumptions → Element [n , Integers]] // Simplify**

Out[•]=$\begin{cases} 3 - 2^{1+n}\, 3^{-n} & n \geq 0 \\ 0 & \text{True} \end{cases}$

Step-by-step

Since $h[n] = 0$ for $n < 0$, you can define

$$y[n] = 0,\ n < 0$$

Then for $n \geq 0$, sum over the values of the unit sample response starting from $k = 0$ and ending on $k = n$

$$y[n] = \sum_{k=0}^{n} h[k]$$

$$= \sum_{k=0}^{n} \left(\frac{2}{3}\right)^{k}$$

$$= \frac{\left(\frac{2}{3}\right)^{n+1} - 1}{\frac{2}{3} - 1}$$

$$= 3 - 2\left(\frac{2}{3}\right)^{n},\ n \geq 0$$

This shows the step response:

In[•]:=**y [n_] := (3 − 2 ($\frac{2}{3}$)^{n}) UnitStep [n] ;**

DiscretePlot [y [n] , ⋯ +]

Out[•]=

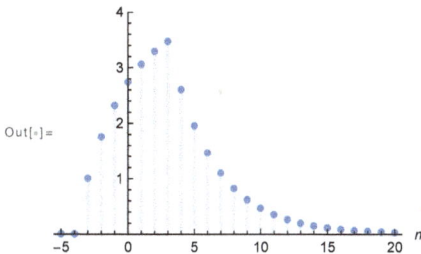

Convolution of $h[n]$ with the unit step gives the same result:

In[•]:=**DiscreteConvolve [h [k] , UnitStep [k] , k , n] // Simplify**

Out[•]=$\begin{cases} 3 - 2^{1+n}\, 3^{-n} & n \geq 0 \\ 0 & \text{True} \end{cases}$

Summary

Convolution returns the output $y[n]$ of an LTI system given its unit sample response $h[n]$ and input $x[n]$

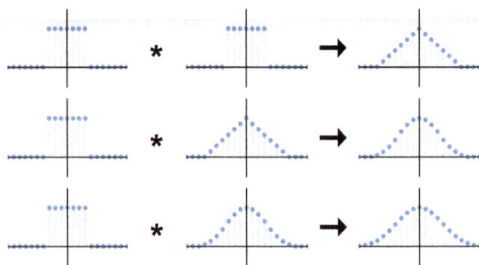

Discrete-time convolution is defined by the following sums

$$y[n] = \sum_{k=-\infty}^{\infty} x[k]\, h[n-k] = \sum_{k=-\infty}^{\infty} h[k]\, x[n-k]$$

Given finite-length sequences, the convolution sum can be evaluated numerically in finite time.

A divide-and-conquer technique for evaluating the convolution sum analytically was shown.

Exercises

Download the solutions manual at wolfr.am/eTextbook-SSSP

13.1 Let

$$h[n] = \begin{cases} 1, & n = -1 \\ -1, & n = 1 \\ 0, & \text{otherwise} \end{cases} \quad \text{and} \quad x[n] = \begin{cases} 2, & n = 0 \\ 1, & n = 1, 2 \\ -1, & n = 3 \\ 0, & \text{otherwise} \end{cases}$$

Determine the value of the following sum.

$$\sum_{k=-\infty}^{\infty} x[k]\, h[1-k]$$

13.2 Given the following two sequences

$$x[n] = u[n]$$

$$h[n] = \left(\frac{2}{3}\right)^n u[n]$$

determine the value of the following sum.

$$\sum_{k=-\infty}^{\infty} h[k]\, x[10-k]$$

13.3 Let

$$h[n] = \begin{cases} \frac{1}{2}, & n = -1 \\ \frac{1}{2}, & n = 1 \\ 0, & \text{otherwise} \end{cases} \quad \text{and} \quad x[n] = \begin{cases} 2, & n = 0 \\ 1, & n = 1, 2 \\ -1, & n = 3 \\ 0, & \text{otherwise} \end{cases}$$

Convolve the two sequences and plot the result.

13.4 Let

$$h[n] = \begin{cases} \frac{1}{2}, & n = -1 \\ \frac{1}{2}, & n = 1 \\ 0, & \text{otherwise} \end{cases} \quad \text{and} \quad x[n] = \begin{cases} 2, & n = 0 \\ 1, & n = 1, 2 \\ -1, & n = 3 \\ 0, & \text{otherwise} \end{cases}$$

Convolve the two sequences using the function ListConvolve. First return the steady-state values only, then the full result.

13.5 Convolve the following two sequences and plot the result.

$$x[n] = u[n] - u[n - 10]$$

$$h[n] = \left(\frac{2}{3}\right)^n u[n]$$

13.6 Convolve the following two sequences.

$$x[n] = \left(\frac{1}{2}\right)^n u[n]$$

$$h[n] = \left(\frac{2}{3}\right)^n u[n]$$

13.7 Convolve the following two sequences and plot the result.

$$x[n] = u[n + 2]$$

$$h[n] = \left(\frac{1}{2}\right)^{n-2} u[n - 2]$$

13.8 Obtain the step response of a system with the following unit sample response.

$$h[n] = \frac{n}{5} \left(u[n] - u[n - 6]\right)$$

Fourier Analysis
(Continuous)

14 | Continuous-Time Fourier Series

The relevance of the Fourier series in the study of linear time-invariant (LTI) systems stems from one particularly important property of such systems—the response to a sinusoidal input is also sinusoidal and of the same frequency

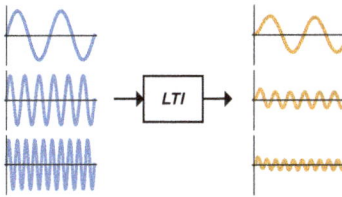

Furthermore, a large class of periodic functions can be represented by linear superpositions of sinusoids

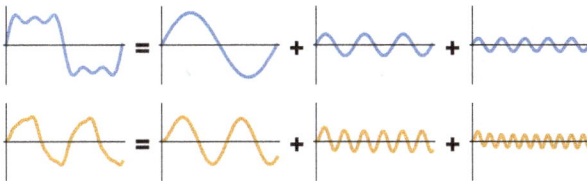

Therefore, the response of an LTI system to a periodic signal can be obtained as a superposition of the individual responses to each of the input sinusoids

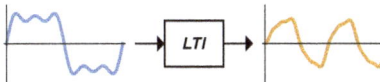

Sinusoidal Response of LTI Systems

Consider an LTI system with impulse response $h(t)$ and sinusoidal input of the form $x(t) = e^{j\omega t}$. To obtain the output $y(t)$, convolve the signals $h(t)$ and $x(t)$

$$y(t) = \int_{-\infty}^{\infty} h(\tau)\, x(t-\tau)\, d\tau$$

$$= \int_{-\infty}^{\infty} h(\tau)\, e^{j\omega(t-\tau)}\, d\tau$$

$$= e^{j\omega t} \int_{-\infty}^{\infty} h(\tau)\, e^{-j\omega\tau}\, d\tau$$

Assuming that the last integral exists and returns $H(\omega)$, namely

$$H(\omega) = \int_{-\infty}^{\infty} h(\tau)\, e^{-j\omega\tau}\, d\tau$$

the output of the LTI system may be written as

$$y(t) = H(\omega)\, e^{j\omega t}$$

where $H(\omega)$, for any specific frequency value ω, is a complex constant. This demonstrates that the output will have the form $e^{j\omega t}$; thus, the response of an LTI system to a sinusoidal input is itself sinusoidal.

Superposition of Sine Waves

A Fourier series is a way to represent a periodic signal as a sum of simple sinusoidal waves. The sinusoidal waves in a Fourier series are harmonically related, meaning their frequencies are integer multiples of a single frequency known as the fundamental frequency.

For example, this defines an infinite family of simple sine waves $s_k(t)$ with a fundamental frequency of $\omega_0 = 2\pi$ radians/second:

In[•]:=**s [k_] := Sin [2 π k t]**

Here are three members of this family of sine functions with frequencies $\omega_k = 2\pi k$ with $k = 1, 3, 5$:

In[•]:=**Plot [{ s [1], s [3], s [5] }, ⋯ ⊕]**

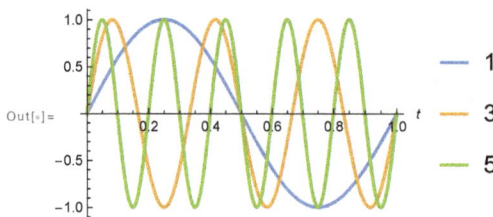

This shows three sine waves scaled by 1, $1/3$, and $1/5$, respectively:

In[•]:=**Plot [{ s [1], $\frac{1}{3}$ s [3], $\frac{1}{5}$ s [5] }, ⋯ ⊕]**

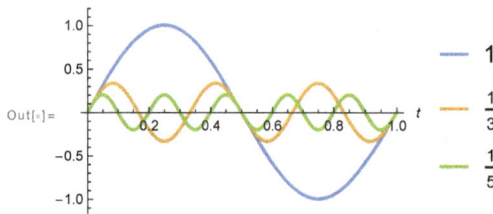

A linear combination of these sine waves gives a new periodic signal:

In[•]:= **Plot [s [1] + $\frac{1}{3}$ s [3] + $\frac{1}{5}$ s [5] , $\cdots$ $+$]**

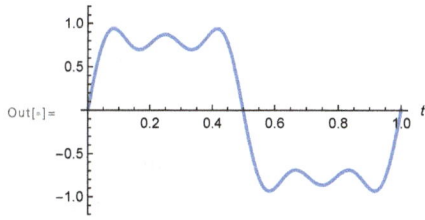

Out[•]=

The Sound of a Piano Key

The fundamental frequency f of a theoretically ideal piano key n is given by the following formula:

In[•]:= **f [n_] := 440. $2^{\frac{n-49}{12}}$**

For example, the frequency of key 52 (note C_5) on a modern 88-key piano is:

In[•]:= **f [52]**

Out[•]= 523.251

The family of harmonically related sines with a frequency given by $f(52)$ is:

In[•]:= **s [k_] := Sin [2 π f [52.] k t]**

Here is a linear combination of the fundamental and its three lowest-order harmonics:

In[•]:= **s [1] + 0.7 s [2] + 0.4 s [3] + 0.1 s [4]**

Out[•]= Sin [3287.68 t] + 0.7 Sin [6575.37 t] + 0.4 Sin [9863.05 t] + 0.1 Sin [13 150.7 t]

Here is what this synthesized piano key sounds like:

In[•]:= **Audio [$\cdots$ $+$]**

Out[•]=

> 00:00 ○———— 00:02 ◀) ≡
> Data in Notebook   ⇥

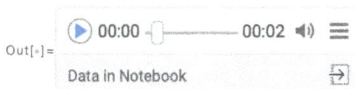

For comparison, here is an actual recording of the C_5 key:

In[•]:= **AudioChannelMix [ExampleData [{ "Audio", "Piano" }] , "Mono"]**

Out[•]=

> 00:00 ○———— 00:04 ◀) ≡
> Data in Notebook   ⇥

Definition

The complex Fourier series is a representation of periodic signals in terms of linear combinations of harmonically related complex exponentials.

The so-called synthesis formula takes the following form

$$x(t) = \sum_{k=-\infty}^{\infty} c_k \, e^{j\frac{2\pi}{T}kt}$$

Here T denotes the period of the signal $x(t)$ and the quantity $\frac{2\pi}{T}$ is the fundamental frequency of the signal. The coefficients c_k are known as the complex Fourier series coefficients of the signal $x(t)$.

The analysis formula shows how to obtain these coefficients for any periodic function $x(t)$

$$c_k = \frac{1}{T} \int_{-\frac{T}{2}}^{\frac{T}{2}} x(t) \, e^{-j\frac{2\pi}{T}kt} \, dt$$

Existence

For the Fourier series to exist, the Fourier coefficients c_k must be finite. This is guaranteed if the periodic signal $x(t)$ has finite energy over a single period

$$\int_T |x(t)|^2 \, dt < \infty$$

Examples of signals for which the Fourier series exists

Fourier series may not exist for signals such as the following

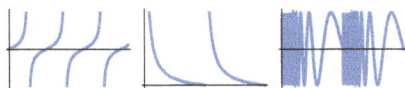

An alternative set of conditions, known as the Dirichlet conditions, states that in any single period, three conditions must be satisfied.

Condition 1: Signal $x(t)$ must be absolutely integrable

$$\int_T |x(t)| \, dt < \infty$$

Condition 2: There are a finite number of maxima and minima

Condition 3: There are a finite number of discontinuities

Example 1

Obtain the Fourier coefficients of the square wave shown:

In[•]:=**Plot [SquareWave [{0, 1}, t], ⋯ +]**

Out[•]=

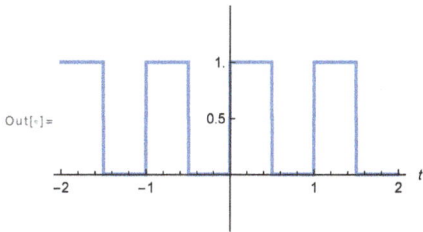

Solution

Specific Fourier coefficients or a general formula for all the coefficients may be obtained using the FourierCoefficient function. The FourierParameters must be set to match the analysis formula and the frequency of the time signal. Thus, for example, given some periodic signal $x(t)$ with period T and fundamental frequency $\omega_0 = \frac{2\pi}{T}$, the FourierParameters option value in the FourierCoefficient function should be set as shown here

In[•]:=**FourierCoefficient [x [t] , t, k, FourierParameters → { 1, ω_0 }]**

So, given that the square wave has period $T = 1$, the fundamental frequency is $\omega_0 = \frac{2\pi}{T} = 2\pi$. Therefore, this gives the Fourier coefficients:

In[•]:=**c [k_] = FourierCoefficient [**
SquareWave [{0, 1}, t], t, k, FourierParameters → { 1, 2 π }]

Out[•]=
$$
\begin{cases}
\frac{1}{2} & k == 0 \\
-\frac{i\,(-1)^k\,(-1+(-1)^k)}{2k\pi} & \text{True}
\end{cases}
$$

Here are values of the coefficients c_k for $-5 \le k \le 5$:

In[•]:=**Table [c [k] , { k, −5, 5 }]**

Out[•]=$\left\{ \dfrac{i}{5\pi}, 0, \dfrac{i}{3\pi}, 0, \dfrac{i}{\pi}, \dfrac{1}{2}, -\dfrac{i}{\pi}, 0, -\dfrac{i}{3\pi}, 0, -\dfrac{i}{5\pi} \right\}$

Step-by-step

The Fourier series analysis formula

$$ c_k = \frac{1}{T} \int_T x(t)\, e^{-j\frac{2\pi}{T}kt}\, dt $$

Substitute $T = 1$ and $x(t) = 1$ for $0 \le t \le \frac{1}{2}$

$$ = \int_0^{\frac{1}{2}} (1)\, e^{-j2\pi kt}\, dt $$

Now integrate

$$= -\frac{1}{j2\pi k}\, e^{-j2\pi kt}\, \Big|_0^{1/2}$$

$$= -\frac{1}{j2\pi k}\left(e^{-j\pi k} - 1\right)$$

and replace $e^{-j\pi k}$ with $(-1)^k$

$$c_k = -\frac{1}{j2\pi k}\left((-1)^k - 1\right)$$

Simplify the last expression to get

$$c_0 = \frac{1}{2}$$

and

$$c_k = \begin{cases} -j\,\frac{1}{\pi k}, & \text{odd } k \\ 0 & \text{even } k \end{cases}, \; k \neq 0$$

Example 2

Obtain the Fourier coefficients of the signal $x(t) = \sin(2\pi t)$.

Solution

Substituting $x(t) = \sin(2\pi t)$ and $\omega_0 = 2\pi$ into the FourierCoefficient function gives the following result:

In[•]:=**FourierCoefficient [Sin [2 π t] , t, k, FourierParameters $\rightarrow$ { 1, 2 π }]**

Out[•]=$\begin{cases} -\frac{i}{2} & k == 1 \\ \frac{i}{2} & k == -1 \\ 0 & \text{True} \end{cases}$

Step-by-step

Instead of direct substitution into the analysis integral, expand $x(t)$ into a sum of complex exponentials using Euler's identity

$$x(t) = \sin(2\pi t) = \frac{1}{2j}\, e^{j2\pi t} - \frac{1}{2j}\, e^{-j2\pi t}$$

Compare with the Fourier series synthesis formula

$$x(t) = \sum_{k=-\infty}^{\infty} c_k\, e^{j2\pi kt} = \ldots + c_{-2}e^{-j4\pi t} + c_{-1}\, e^{-j2\pi t} + c_0 + c_1\, e^{j2\pi t} + c_2 e^{j4\pi t} + \ldots$$

Compare terms in the Euler's representation of $\sin(2\pi t)$ with the synthesis formula to get

$$c_{-1} = -\frac{1}{2j}, \; c_1 = \frac{1}{2j}, \text{ and } c_k = 0, \, k \neq \pm 1$$

Fourier Line Spectrum

The Fourier coefficients are typically complex, $c_k \in \mathbb{C}$, so it is common to plot the magnitude and phase or the real and imaginary parts of each coefficient.

This shows the magnitude $|c_k|$ and phase $\angle c_k$ of the coefficients obtained in the earlier example:

In[•]:=**GraphicsRow [** ⋯ **+** **]**

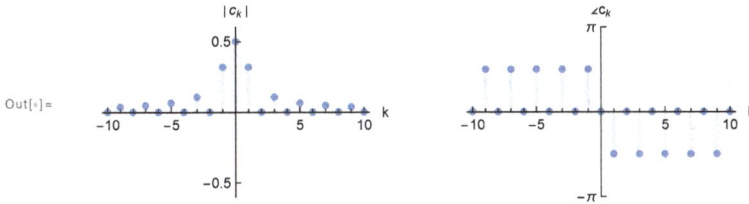

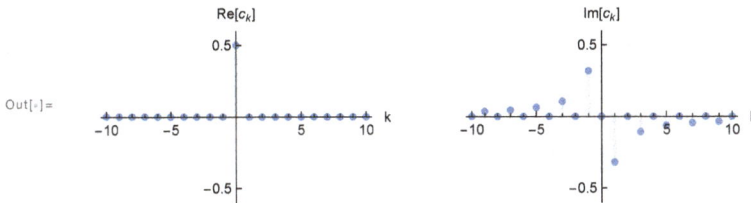

Out[•]=

Fourier Series Synthesis

Recall that the complex Fourier series is a representation of periodic signals in terms of linear combinations of harmonically related complex exponentials as defined with the following formula

$$x(t) = \sum_{k=-\infty}^{\infty} c_k \; e^{\; j\frac{2\pi}{T} kt}$$

Thus a real periodic signal $x(t)$ is simply a finite or infinite linear superposition of scaled harmonically related complex exponentials.

Earlier examples showed that:

- Coefficients $c_1 = \frac{1}{2j}$ and $c_{-1} = -\frac{1}{2j}$ return a sine wave.

- Coefficients $c_0 = \frac{1}{2}$ and $c_k = -\frac{1}{j2\pi k}\left((-1)^k - 1\right)$ for $k \neq 0$ return a square wave with period $T = 1$.

Approximating a Square Wave

A finite-length evaluation of the generally infinite-length synthesis formula results in an approximation to the original signal.

This represents a synthesis of the M lowest-order Fourier coefficients

$$x_M(t) = \sum_{k=-M}^{M} c_k \, e^{j\frac{2\pi}{T} kt}$$

Consider, for example, the Fourier coefficients of a centered square wave:

```
In[•]:= c [ k_ ] = FourierCoefficient [
            1                          1     1
            - SquareWave [ t + - ] + -, t, k, FourierParameters → { 1, -2 π } ]
            2                      4     2
```

$$\text{Out[•]=} \begin{cases} \dfrac{1}{2} & k == 0 \\[2ex] \dfrac{\operatorname{Sin}\left[\frac{k\pi}{2}\right]}{k\pi} & \text{True} \end{cases}$$

Here is a synthesis of the square wave for $M = 3$:

```
In[•]:=  1   3
         -  ∑   c [ k ] ℯ^{ⅈ 2 π k t}  // ExpToTrig
         2  k=-3
```

$$\text{Out[•]=} \frac{1}{4} + \frac{\operatorname{Cos}[2\pi t]}{\pi} - \frac{\operatorname{Cos}[6\pi t]}{3\pi}$$

This shows the result for values of M such that $1 \le M \le 17$:

```
In[•]:= DynamicModule [ ··· + ]
```

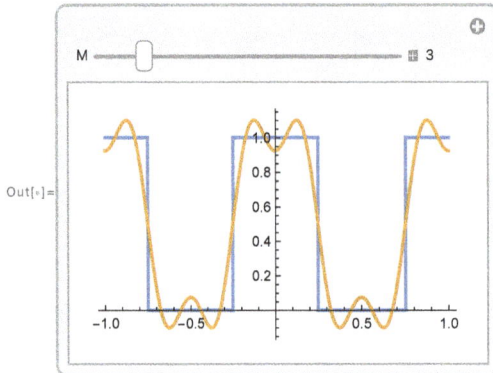

The approximations exhibit behavior commonly known as the Gibbs phenomenon—the maximum value of the ripple nearest to a discontinuity remains constant and independent of the order M of the approximation.

How to Measure the Quality of an Approximation

The approximation error in a Fourier series representation is usually measured in terms of the average power of the error signal, where the error signal is defined

$$e_M(t) = |x(t) - x_M(t)|$$

The average power of the signal is conveniently given by Parseval's relation for continuous-time Fourier series

$$\mathcal{P}_{\text{avg}} = \frac{1}{T} \int_T |x(t)|^2 \, dt = \sum_{k=-\infty}^{\infty} |c_k|^2$$

The average power of the ideal square wave with unit period is $\mathcal{P}_{\text{avg}} = \frac{1}{2}$. The following formula gives the power of the approximation signal as a function of the number of Fourier coefficients

$$\mathcal{P}_M = \sum_{k=-M}^{M} |c_k|^2$$

Therefore, the power in the approximation signal $e_M(t)$ is

$$\mathcal{P}_E = \mathcal{P}_{\text{avg}} - \mathcal{P}_M = \frac{1}{2} - \sum_{k=-M}^{M} |c_k|^2$$

This plots the average power of the approximation error for $1 \le M \le 51$:

In[•]:= **ListPlot [** ⋯ **+]**

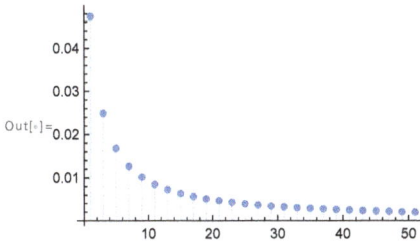

The average power of the approximation error signal is guaranteed to diminish as the number of coefficients is increased.

Summary

Sinusoids are eigenfunctions of LTI systems, so the response to a sinusoid is a scaled and time-shifted sinusoid of the same frequency

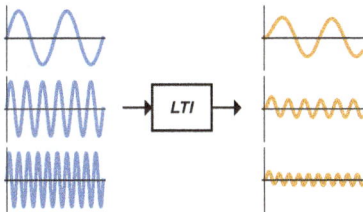

Periodic signals have finite or infinite Fourier series expansions

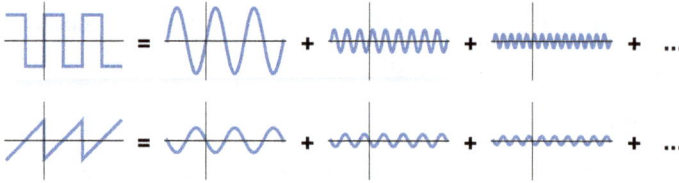

Examples of evaluating the analysis and synthesis Fourier series formulations were shown.

Exercises

Download the solutions manual at wolfr.am/eTextbook-SSSP

14.1 Obtain the c_0 coefficient of the following periodic signal.

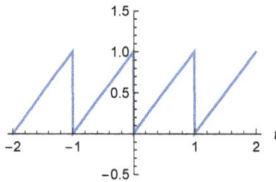

14.2 Obtain the c_1 coefficient of the following periodic signal.

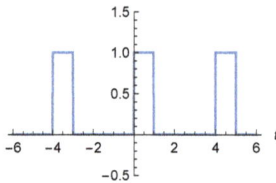

14.3 A continuous-time periodic signal $x(t)$ is given by the following sum.

$$x(t) = 2 + 3\sin(2\pi t)$$

Determine the complex Fourier series coefficients of $x(t)$.

14.4 Obtain the Fourier series coefficients of an impulse train. The impulse train, denoted $\delta_T(t)$, is defined as follows.

$$\delta_T(t) = \sum_{n=-\infty}^{\infty} \delta(t - nT)$$

This shows an impulse train with $T = 1$.

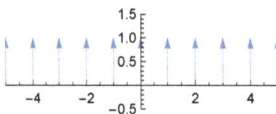

14.5 Calculate the Fourier series coefficients of the following sawtooth wave.

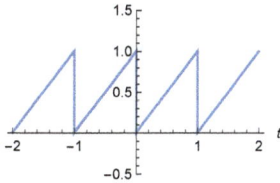

14.6 Obtain the Fourier series coefficients of a full-wave rectified sine function.

$x(t) = |\sin(\pi t)|$

The following shows $x(t)$.

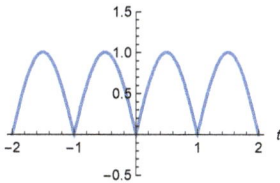

14.7 A continuous-time periodic signal $x(t)$ with fundamental frequency $\omega_0 = 2\pi$ has only three nonzero Fourier coefficients, $c_0 = 1$, $c_2 = -j$, and $c_{-2} = j$. Obtain and plot $x(t)$.

14.8 A sawtooth wave with period $T = 1$ has the following Fourier series coefficients.

$$c_0 = \frac{1}{2}$$

$$c_k = j\frac{1}{2\pi k}, \qquad k \neq 0$$

Reconstruct and plot an approximation of the sawtooth wave from the lowest order 2 nonzero Fourier series coefficients.

15 | Continuous-Time Fourier Transform

The Fourier transform may be viewed as a natural extension of the Fourier series by considering an aperiodic signal as periodic with the period extending to infinity. As an illustration, consider the following demonstration showing a Fourier series line spectrum of a square wave as its period is increased:

In[·]:=**Manipulate [⋯ +]**

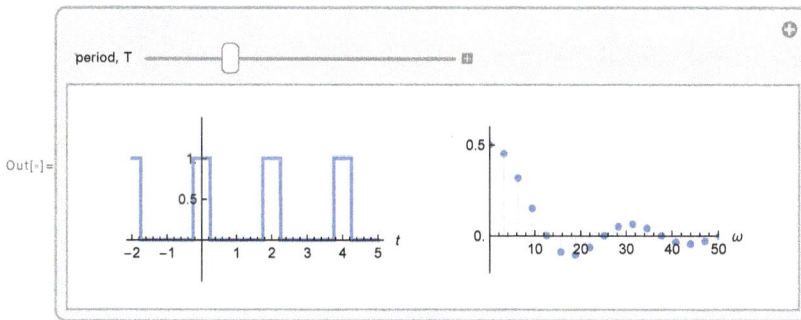

Observe that as the period increases, the frequency resolution of the Fourier series coefficients diminishes, and in the limit, it approaches a continuum.

Definition

The continuous-time Fourier transform (CTFT) is defined by the following pair of equations

$$\text{analysis:} \quad X(j\omega) = \int_{-\infty}^{\infty} x(t)\, e^{-j\omega t}\, dt$$

$$\text{synthesis:} \quad x(t) = \frac{1}{2\pi} \int_{-\infty}^{\infty} X(j\omega)\, e^{j\omega t}\, d\omega$$

The function $X(j\omega)$ is called the Fourier transform (or Fourier spectrum) of $x(t)$. $X(j\omega)$ is a continuous function of frequency ω and is generally complex.

The conditions for the existence of the Fourier transform are similar to those for the Fourier series. Signals with finite energy are guaranteed to have a Fourier transform

$$\int_{-\infty}^{\infty} |x(t)|^2 \, dt < \infty$$

Therefore, all bounded, finite-duration signals have a Fourier transform. Also, the following Dirichlet sufficiency conditions apply:

- On any finite interval, $x(t)$ is bounded, has a finite number of maxima and minima, and has a finite number of discontinuities

- Signal $x(t)$ is absolutely integrable

$$\int_{-\infty}^{\infty} |x(t)| \, dt < \infty$$

Example 1

Obtain the Fourier transform of the unit pulse signal

$$x(t) = \begin{cases} 1, & |t| \leq \frac{1}{2} \\ 0, & \text{else} \end{cases}$$

Solution

The Fourier transform exists because the given signal satisfies the absolute integrability condition:

In[·]:=**Integrate [UnitBox [t] , { t, −∞, ∞ }]**

Out[·]=**1**

This returns the result using the FourierTransform function with FourierParameters matching the definition given earlier:

In[·]:=**FourierTransform [UnitBox [t] , t, ω, FourierParameters → {1, −1}]**

Out[·]=**Sinc$\left[\dfrac{\omega}{2} \right]$**

Here are plots of the time function (left) and its Fourier transform (right):

In[·]:=**GraphicsRow [{⋯} +]**

Out[·]=

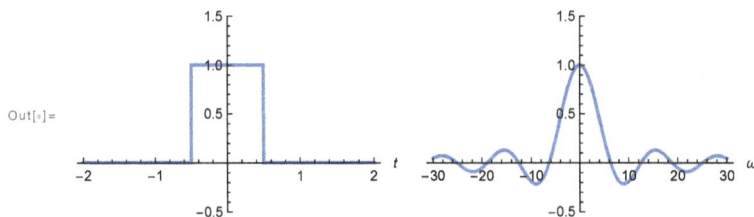

Step-by-step

The Fourier transform analysis formula is

$$X(j\omega) = \int_{-\infty}^{\infty} x(t)\, e^{-j\omega t}\, dt$$

Substitution of the signal into the Fourier transform integral reduces to the following definite integral

$$= \int_{-1/2}^{1/2} e^{-j\omega t}\, dt$$

Integration yields

$$= -\frac{1}{j\omega}\, e^{-j\omega t}\, \Big|_{-\frac{1}{2}}^{\frac{1}{2}}$$

$$= -\frac{1}{j\omega} \left(e^{-j\frac{\omega}{2}} - e^{j\frac{\omega}{2}} \right)$$

$$= \frac{2 \sin\left(\frac{\omega}{2}\right)}{\omega}$$

$$= \operatorname{sinc}\left(\frac{\omega}{2}\right)$$

Example 2

Obtain the Fourier transform of the signal $x(t) = e^{-t}\, u(t)$.

Solution

The signal is absolutely integrable and so it satisfies the existence condition:

In[•]:=**Integrate [e^{-t} UnitStep [t] , { t, −∞, ∞ }]**

Out[•]=**1**

The Fourier transform of the signal $x(t)$ is:

In[•]:=**FourierTransform [e^{-t} UnitStep [t] , t, ω, FourierParameters → { 1, −1 }]**

Out[•]=$-\dfrac{i}{-i + \omega}$

Step-by-step

The Fourier transform analysis formula is

$$X(j\omega) = \int_{-\infty}^{\infty} x(t)\, e^{-j\omega t}\, dt$$

Substitution of the signal into the Fourier transform integral reduces to the following improper definite integral

$$= \int_0^{\infty} e^{-t}\, e^{-j\omega t}\, dt = \int_0^{\infty} e^{-(j\omega+1)t}\, dt$$

Integration yields

$$= -\frac{1}{j\omega+1} \, e^{-(j\omega+1)t} \, \big|_0^\infty$$

$$= -\frac{1}{j\omega+1} \left(e^{-(j\omega+1)t} \, \big|_{t\to\infty} - 1 \right)$$

Since $e^{-t} \to 0$ as $t \to \infty$, the result reduces to

$$= -\frac{1}{j\omega+1} \, (0 - 1)$$

Finally

$$= \frac{1}{j\omega+1}$$

Visualizing Fourier Transforms

The Fourier transform is generally complex; therefore, plots of the magnitude and phase, or, less frequently, the real and imaginary parts, are used.

Use the following Fourier transform to illustrate all the visualization alternatives:

In[*]:= $\mathbf{X[\,\omega\_\,] := \dfrac{1}{1 + \textit{i}\ \omega}};$

This shows the magnitude and phase:

In[*]:= **GraphicsRow [{⋯} +]**

Out[*]=

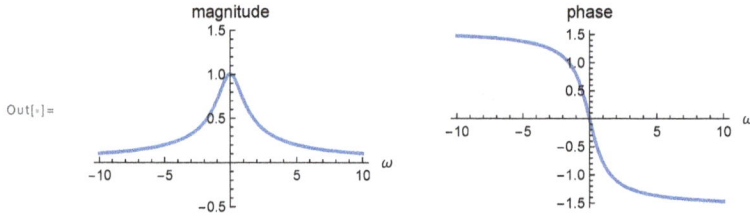

Here are the real and imaginary components:

In[*]:= **GraphicsRow [{⋯} +]**

Out[*]=

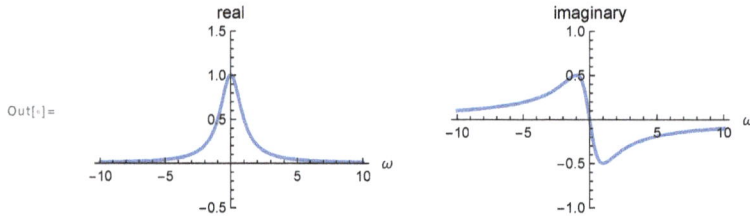

The plots reveal the following well-known symmetry properties of the Fourier transform of a real signal

$$|X(j\omega)| = |X(-j\omega)|$$

$$\angle X(j\omega) = -\angle X(-j\omega)$$

$$\mathrm{Re}\,[X(j\omega)] = \mathrm{Re}\,[X(-j\omega)]$$

$$\mathrm{Im}\,[X(j\omega)] = -\mathrm{Im}\,[X(-j\omega)]$$

Due to these symmetry properties, the Fourier transform is typically plotted over positive values of frequency only:

In[•]:= **GraphicsRow [** {⋯} ✦ **]**

Out[•]=

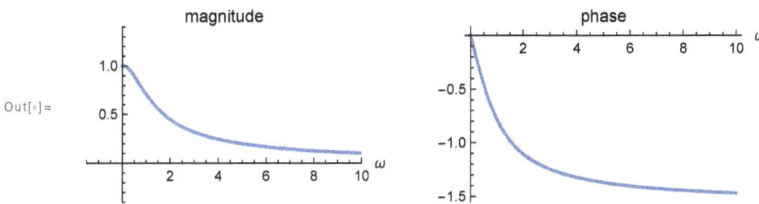

Frequently, a logarithmic scale, the so-called decibel scale, is used to plot the magnitude values:

In[•]:= **Plot [20 Log10 [Abs [X [ω]]],** ⋯ ✦ **]**

Out[•]=−20

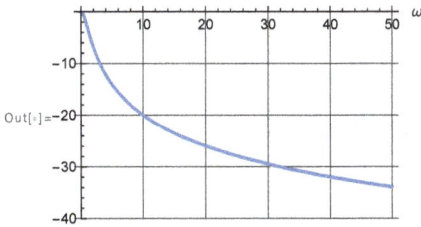

It is also very common to use logarithmic scaling of the frequency axis, which results in the so-called Bode plot:

In[•]:= **LogLinearPlot [20 Log10 [Abs [X [ω]]],** ⋯ ✦ **]**

Out[•]=−20

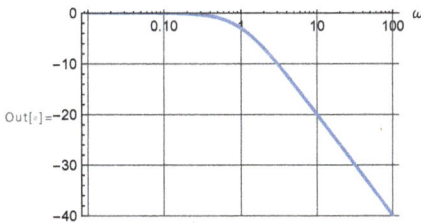

Inverse Fourier Transform

The inverse Fourier transform is defined

$$x(t) = \frac{1}{2\pi} \int_{-\infty}^{\infty} X(j\omega)\, e^{j\omega t}\, d\omega$$

The inverse transform allows the computation of a time signal $x(t)$ from its Fourier transform $X(j\omega)$. Recall from an earlier example the following transform pair

$$e^{-t}\, u(t) \xrightarrow{\;\mathcal{F}\;} \frac{1}{1+j\omega}$$

Now, with the following inverse calculation, the time signal can be recovered from its Fourier transform:

In[•]:=**InverseFourierTransform** $\left[\dfrac{1}{1 + i\,\omega}, \omega, t, \text{FourierParameters} \rightarrow \{1, -1\} \right]$

Out[•]= e^{-t} HeavisideTheta [t]

Example 3

Obtain the inverse Fourier transform of the following function of frequency:

In[•]:=**Plot** $\left[\text{UnitBox} \left[\dfrac{\omega}{2} \right], \boxed{\cdots\;+} \right]$

Out[•]=
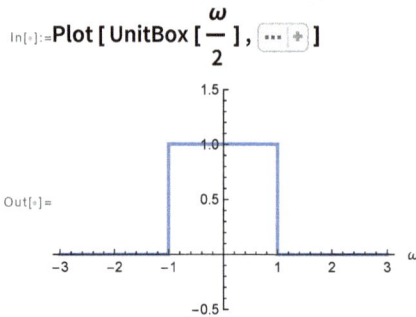

Solution

Using the InverseFourierTransform:

In[•]:=**InverseFourierTransform** [UnitBox [ω / 2] , ω, t, FourierParameters $\rightarrow$ {1, −1}]

Out[•]= $\dfrac{\text{Sinc [t]}}{\pi}$

Here are plots of the Fourier transform (left) and the time signal (right):

In[•]:=**GraphicsRow [** {⋯} **+]**

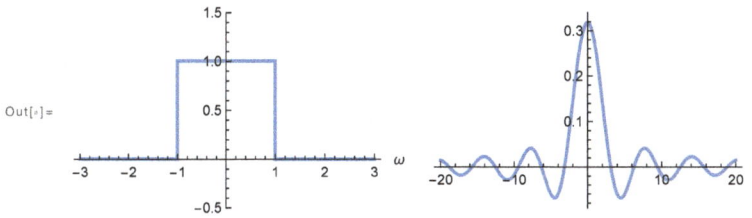

Out[•]=

Step-by-step

The inverse Fourier transform integral

$$x(t) = \frac{1}{2\pi} \int_{-\infty}^{\infty} X(j\omega)\, e^{\,j\omega t}\, d\omega$$

Substitution yields the following definite integral

$$= \frac{1}{2\pi} \int_{-1}^{1} e^{\,j\omega t}\, d\omega$$

Integration returns

$$= \frac{1}{2\pi} \frac{1}{jt}\, e^{\,j\omega t}\, \Big|_{-1}^{1}$$

$$= \frac{1}{2\pi} \frac{1}{jt}\, \left(e^{\,jt} - e^{-jt}\right)$$

Simplification gives the following result

$$= \frac{1}{2\pi} \frac{1}{jt}\, (2\,j \sin(t))$$

$$= \frac{1}{\pi t} \sin(t)$$

Bandwidth

The bandwidth of a signal may be defined as the range of frequencies where the signal magnitudes are relatively "large." To develop an intuitive understanding of bandwidth, compare the spectra of the following four pulse-shaped signals

The four signals and their Fourier transforms are:

In[•]:=**Grid [⋯ ✦]**

Out[•]=

$\text{UnitBox}[t]$	$\overset{\mathcal{F}}{\longleftrightarrow}$	$\text{Sinc}[\frac{\omega}{2}]$
$\text{UnitTriangle}[t]$	$\overset{\mathcal{F}}{\longleftrightarrow}$	$\text{Sinc}[\frac{\omega}{2}]^2$
$\frac{1}{2}(1+\text{Cos}[\pi t])\,\text{UnitBox}[\frac{t}{2}]$	$\overset{\mathcal{F}}{\longleftrightarrow}$	$\frac{1}{2}(\text{Sinc}[\pi-\omega] + 2\,\text{Sinc}[\omega] + \text{Sinc}[\pi+\omega])$
$e^{-2t^2}\sqrt{\frac{2}{\pi}}$	$\overset{\mathcal{F}}{\longleftrightarrow}$	$e^{-\frac{\omega^2}{8}}$

This shows and compares the magnitude spectra of the four signals:

In[•]:=**LogLinearPlot [⋯ ✦]**

Out[•]=

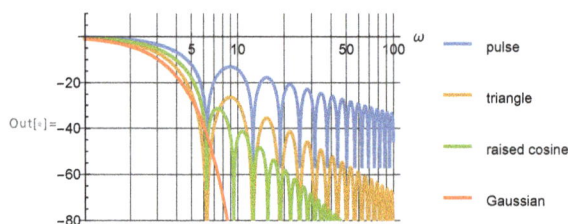

The spectrum of the square pulse, the "sharpest" of the signals, drops off the slowest as the frequency increases; it has the widest bandwidth.

Fourier Transform of Periodic Signals

Periodic signals do not satisfy the existence condition of the Fourier integral:

In[•]:=**Integrate [Abs [Sin [2 π t]]^2, { t, −∞, ∞ }]**

⋯ Integrate : Integral of Sin $[2\pi t]^2$ does not converge on $\{-\infty, \infty\}$.

Out[•]= $\int_{-\infty}^{\infty} \text{Abs}[\text{Sin}[2\pi t]]^2 \, dt$

However, periodic signals do have Fourier transforms, but they must be obtained indirectly using the Fourier series and are formulated using the Dirac delta function. To derive the formula for the Fourier transform of a periodic signal, consider first the case of a signal $x(t)$ with a Fourier transform given by the following formula

$$X(j\omega) = 2\pi\,\delta(\omega - \omega_0)$$

Now use the inverse Fourier transform to determine the signal $x(t)$:

In[•]:=**InverseFourierTransform [2 π DiracDelta [ω − ω0],**
    ω, t, FourierParameters → {1, −1}]

Out[•]= $e^{i\,t\,\omega 0}$

This establishes the following relationship between a complex exponential (in time) and an impulse function (in frequency)

$$e^{j\omega_0 t} \overset{\mathcal{F}}{\longleftrightarrow} 2\pi\,\delta(\omega - \omega_0)$$

The rest is relatively straightforward. Recall that a periodic signal $x(t)$ has the following Fourier series representation

$$x(t) = \sum_{k=-\infty}^{\infty} c_k\, e^{j\omega_0 k t}$$

Taking the Fourier transform on both sides and substituting the Fourier transform of the complex exponential gives the following result

$$X(j\omega) = 2\pi \sum_{k=-\infty}^{\infty} c_k\, \delta(\omega - k\omega_0)$$

This result states that the Fourier transform of a periodic signal is a superposition of impulses scaled by the coefficients of the Fourier series expansion of the signal.

Example 4

Obtain the Fourier transform of the square wave shown

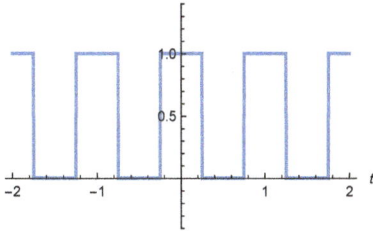

Solution

The given signal has a period of $T = 1$ and a fundamental frequency of $\omega_0 = 2\pi$. The Fourier series coefficients are:

In[•]:= **FourierCoefficient [UnitBox [t] , t, k, FourierParameters $\rightarrow$ {1, π}]**

$$\text{Out[•]=} \begin{cases} \dfrac{1}{2} & k == 0 \\[2mm] \dfrac{\operatorname{Sin}\left[\frac{k\pi}{2}\right]}{k\pi} & \text{True} \end{cases}$$

Equivalently

$$c_k = \frac{1}{2}\,\operatorname{sinc}\!\left(\tfrac{\pi}{2}\,k\right)$$

The transform follows immediately

$$X(j\omega) = 2\pi \sum_{k=-\infty}^{\infty} c_k\, \delta(\omega - k\omega_0)$$

$$= \pi \sum_{k=-\infty}^{\infty} \operatorname{sinc}\!\left(\tfrac{\pi}{2}\,k\right) \delta(\omega - k\,2\pi)$$

This shows the magnitude spectrum $|X(j\omega)|$ of the square wave:

In[•]:= **Graphics** [$\cdots$ ⊞]

Out[•]=

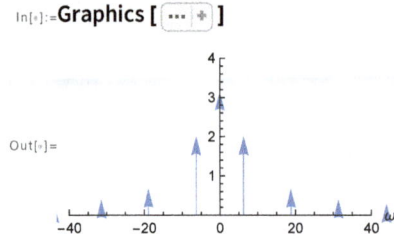

Summary

The Fourier transform was defined.

Several forward and inverse transforms were shown

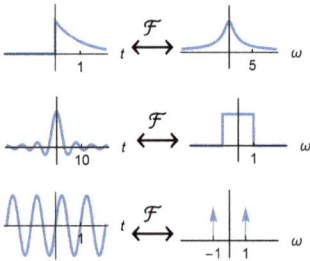

The bandwidths of several pulse-shaped signals were compared

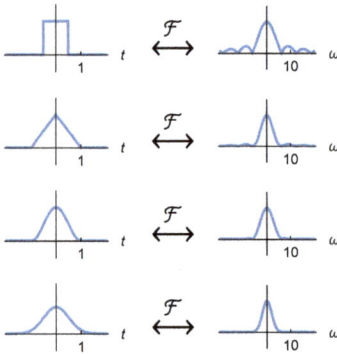

The Fourier transform of periodic signals was derived and was shown to be a sum of scaled and shifted Dirac delta functions.

Exercises

Download the solutions manual at wolfr.am/eTextbook-SSSP

15.1 Obtain the Fourier transform of the following signal.

$x(t) = \delta(t)$

15.2 Obtain the Fourier transform of the following signal.

$$x(t) = e^{-|t|}$$

15.3 Obtain the Fourier transform of the following signal.

$$x(t) = \begin{cases} t+1, & -1 \le t < 0 \\ 1-t, & 0 \le t \le 1 \\ 0, & \text{else} \end{cases}$$

15.4 Obtain the Fourier transform of the following signal.

$$x(t) = \begin{cases} \frac{1}{2}(1+\cos(\pi t)), & -1 \le t \le 1 \\ 0, & \text{else} \end{cases}$$

15.5 Obtain the inverse Fourier transform.

$$X(j\omega) = \begin{cases} -j, & -1 \le \omega \le 0 \\ j, & 0 \le \omega \le 1 \\ 0, & \text{else} \end{cases}$$

15.6 Obtain the inverse Fourier transform.

$$X(j\omega) = \begin{cases} j\omega, & -1 < \omega \le 1 \\ 0, & \text{else} \end{cases}$$

15.7 Obtain the Fourier transform of the periodic signal $x(t) = 1 - \frac{1}{2}\cos(2\pi t) + \frac{3}{2}\cos(8\pi t)$.

15.8 Obtain the Fourier transform of the following full-wave rectified sine wave.

$$x(t) = |\sin(\pi t)|$$

This shows the signal.

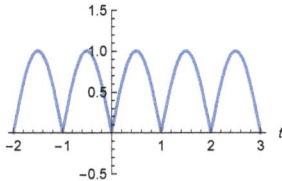

16 | Continuous-Time Fourier Transform Theorems

The Fourier transform is a fundamentally important mathematical tool used in the analysis and design of linear time-invariant (LTI) systems. It is therefore useful to be familiar with properties of the Fourier transform and with a select number of its theorems. Here are a few of the most important theorems that will be presented:

- Time shift
- Time scaling
- Time differentiation
- Convolution in time
- Multiplication in time
- Parseval's relation

Time Shift

Given a signal $x(t)$ and its Fourier transform $X(j\omega)$, the Fourier transform of the shifted signal $x(t - t_0)$ is

$$x(t - t_0) \overset{\mathcal{F}}{\longleftrightarrow} X(j\omega) \cdot e^{-j\omega t_0}$$

Proof

Begin with the signal $y(t) = x(t - t_0)$ and substitute it directly into the Fourier transform analysis formula

$$Y(j\omega) = \mathcal{F}\{y(t)\} = \int_{-\infty}^{\infty} x(t - t_0) e^{-j\omega t} \, dt$$

Follow with the substitution $\tau = t - t_0$

$$Y(j\omega) = \int_{-\infty}^{\infty} x(\tau) e^{-j\omega(\tau + t_0)} \, d\tau$$

Extract the exponential term $e^{-j\omega t_0}$ since it is independent of the variable of integration

$$= e^{-j\omega t_0} \int_{-\infty}^{\infty} x(\tau) e^{-j\omega\tau} \, d\tau$$

Finally, recognize that the integral is simply the Fourier transform of $x(t)$

$$= e^{-j\omega t_0} \cdot X(j\omega)$$

This completes the proof.

The time shift theorem implies that the magnitude spectrum of a time-shifted signal remains unchanged

$$|Y(j\omega)| = \left|e^{-j\omega t_0} X(j\omega)\right| = \left|e^{-j\omega t_0}\right| \cdot |X(j\omega)| = |X(j\omega)|$$

but the phase spectrum does change

$$\angle Y(j\omega) = \angle\left(e^{-j\omega t_0} \cdot X(j\omega)\right) = \angle e^{-j\omega t_0} + \angle X(j\omega) = \angle X(j\omega) - \omega t_0$$

Example 1

Verify the time shift theorem by comparing the Fourier transforms of the following two signals:

```
In[·]:= x[t_] := UnitBox[t - 1/2];
        y[t_] := UnitBox[t - 2];
```

This plots the two signals:

```
In[·]:= Plot[ {x[t], y[t]}, ···  +  ]
```

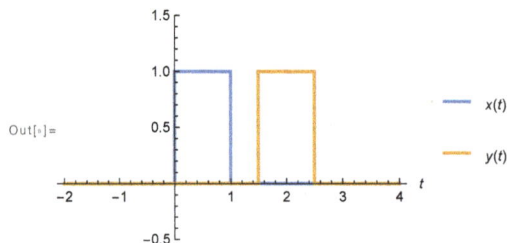

Out[·]=

Solution

The Fourier transforms of the two signals are:

```
In[·]:= X[ω_] = FourierTransform[x[t], t, ω, FourierParameters → {1, −1}]
```

$$\text{Out[·]}= \frac{-i + i \cos[\omega] + \sin[\omega]}{\omega}$$

```
In[·]:= Y[ω_] = FourierTransform[y[t], t, ω, FourierParameters → {1, −1}]
```

$$\text{Out[·]}= \frac{2 e^{-2 i \omega} \sin\left[\frac{\omega}{2}\right]}{\omega}$$

This shows that the magnitudes (left) are indeed equal and that the phases (right) are different:

In[•]:=**GraphicsRow [** ⬚ **+]**

Out[•]=

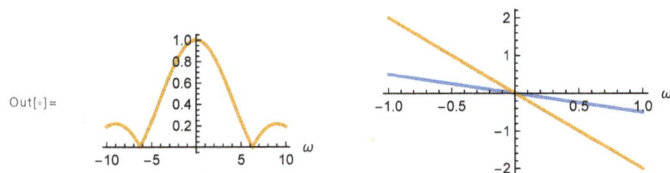

Time and Frequency Scaling

Given a signal $x(t)$ and its Fourier transform $X(j\omega)$, the Fourier transform of the scaled signal $x(at)$ where a is a real constant is given by the following formula

$$x(at) \overset{\mathcal{F}}{\longleftrightarrow} \frac{1}{|a|} X\left(j\frac{\omega}{a}\right)$$

Note the special case of time reversal

$$x(-t) \overset{\mathcal{F}}{\longleftrightarrow} X(-j\omega)$$

Proof

This property follows directly from the definition of the Fourier transform

$$\mathcal{F}\{x(at)\} = Y(j\omega) = \int_{-\infty}^{\infty} x(at) e^{-j\omega t}\, dt$$

Now, with the substitution $\tau = at$, you get

$$\mathcal{F}\{x(at)\} = \begin{cases} \frac{1}{a} \int_{-\infty}^{\infty} x(\tau) e^{-j\frac{\omega}{a}(\tau)}\, d\tau, & a > 0 \\ -\frac{1}{a} \int_{-\infty}^{\infty} x(\tau) e^{-j\frac{\omega}{a}(\tau)}\, d\tau, & a < 0 \end{cases}$$

Example 2

Verify the time scaling theorem for the following signal:

In[•]:=**x [t_] :=** $\dfrac{1}{\sqrt{\pi}}$ **Exp [-t^2]**

Solution

The Fourier transform of $x(t)$ is:

In[•]:= **X [ω_] = FourierTransform [x [t] , t, ω, FourierParameters → {1, −1}]**

Out[•]= $e^{-\frac{\omega^2}{4}}$

Direct application of the Fourier transform to the time-compressed signal $x(2\,t)$ gives the following result:

In[•]:= **FourierTransform [x [2 t] , t, ω, FourierParameters → {1, −1}]**

Out[•]= $\frac{1}{2}\,e^{-\frac{\omega^2}{16}}$

Which is the same result as:

In[•]:= $\frac{1}{2}$ **X [$\frac{\omega}{2}$]**

Out[•]= $\frac{1}{2}\,e^{-\frac{\omega^2}{16}}$

This example shows that time compression increases the signal's bandwidth.

Time Differentiation

Given a signal $x(t)$ and its Fourier transform $X(j\omega)$, the Fourier transform of the derivative of $x(t)$ is

$$\mathcal{F}\left\{\tfrac{dx(t)}{dt}\right\} = j\omega \cdot X(j\omega)$$

Proof

Differentiating both sides of the synthesis formula immediately gives the desired result

$$\frac{d}{dt}x(t) = \frac{d}{dt}\left(\frac{1}{2\pi}\int_{-\infty}^{\infty}X(j\omega)e^{j\omega t}\,d\omega\right) = \frac{1}{2\pi}\int_{-\infty}^{\infty}(j\omega X(j\omega))e^{j\omega t}\,d\omega$$

Example 3

Use the time differentiation theorem to obtain the Fourier transform of the following signal:

In[•]:=**x [t_] := − Sign [t] UnitBox [t / 2];**
   Plot [x [t], ⋯ +]

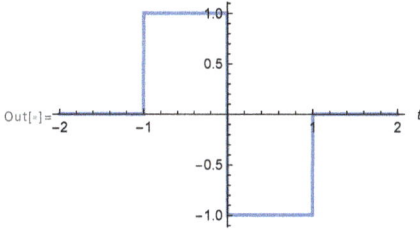

Solution

Observe that the signal $x(t)$ is a derivative of the unit triangle:

In[•]:=**D [UnitTriangle [t], t] // Simplify**

$$
\text{Out[•]=}\begin{cases} -1 & 0 < t < 1 \\ 1 & -1 < t < 0 \\ 0 & t > 1 \,||\, t < -1 \\ \text{Indeterminate} & \text{True} \end{cases}
$$

Therefore, according to the differentiation theorem, the Fourier transform of the signal $x(t)$ equals the following:

In[•]:=**ⅈ ω FourierTransform [UnitTriangle [t], t, ω, FourierParameters → {1, −1}]**

Out[•]= $ⅈ \, ω \, \text{Sinc}\left[\dfrac{ω}{2}\right]^2$

Comparison with a direct evaluation of the transform of $x(t)$ gives:

In[•]:=**FullSimplify [**
   % == FourierTransform [x [t], t, ω, FourierParameters → {1, −1}]]

Out[•]=**True**

Time Convolution

Given two signals and their respective Fourier transforms

$$x(t) \overset{\mathcal{F}}{\longleftrightarrow} X(j\omega) \text{ and } y(t) \overset{\mathcal{F}}{\longleftrightarrow} Y(j\omega)$$

the convolution property states that

$$x(t) * y(t) \overset{\mathcal{F}}{\longleftrightarrow} X(j\omega) \cdot Y(j\omega)$$

where $*$ denotes convolution.

Thus, the Fourier transform maps the convolution of two signals into a product of their Fourier transforms.

Proof

Proceed directly by calculating the Fourier transform of the convolution integral

$$\mathcal{F}\{x(t) * y(t)\} = \mathcal{F}\left\{\int_{-\infty}^{\infty} x(\tau)\, y(t-\tau)\, d\tau\right\}$$

$$= \int_{-\infty}^{\infty}\left(\int_{-\infty}^{\infty} x(\tau)\, y(t-\tau)\, d\tau\right)e^{-j\omega t}\, d\omega$$

Change the order of integration

$$= \int_{-\infty}^{\infty} x(\tau)\left(\int_{-\infty}^{\infty} y(t-\tau)e^{-j\omega t}\, d\omega\right)d\tau$$

Apply the shift theorem to the inner integral

$$= Y(j\omega)\int_{-\infty}^{\infty} x(\tau)e^{-j\omega\tau}\, d\tau$$

where $Y(j\omega) = \int_{-\infty}^{\infty} y(t)\, e^{-j\omega t}\, dt$ is the Fourier transform of signal $y(t)$ and the remaining integral is simply the Fourier transform of signal $x(t)$; therefore, finally you get

$$= Y(j\omega)\, X(j\omega)$$

which completes the proof.

Example 4

Use the convolution theorem to obtain $x(t) * y(t)$ with $x(t) = e^{-t}\, u(t)$ and $y(t) = \cos(t)$.

Solution

The Fourier transforms of the two signals are:

In[*]:= **X[ω_] =**
  FourierTransform [e^{-t} UnitStep [t] , t, ω, FourierParameters → {1, −1}]

Out[*]= $-\dfrac{i}{-i + \omega}$

In[*]:= **Y[ω_] = FourierTransform [Cos [t] , t, ω, FourierParameters → {1, −1}]**

Out[*]= π DiracDelta [−1 + ω] + π DiracDelta [1 + ω]

This shows the Fourier transform magnitudes of the two signals:

In[•]:=**Plot [⋯ +]**

Out[•]=

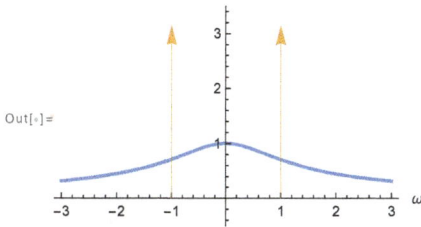

The inverse Fourier transform of the product $X(j\omega) \cdot Y(j\omega)$ gives the desired result:

In[•]:=**InverseFourierTransform [X [ω] Y [ω] ,**
        ω, t, FourierParameters → { 1, −1 }] // FullSimplify

Out[•]=$\frac{1}{2}$ (Cos [t] + Sin [t])

As expected, direct convolution of the signals $x(t)$ and $y(t)$ gives the same result:

In[•]:=**Convolve [e⁻ᵗ UnitStep [τ] , Cos [τ] , τ , t]**

Out[•]=$\frac{1}{2}$ (Cos [t] + Sin [t])

This plots the two signals and their convolution:

In[•]:=**Plot [{ e⁻ᵗ UnitStep [t] , Cos [t] , $\frac{1}{2}$ (Cos [t] + Sin [t]) } , ⋯ +]**

Out[•]=

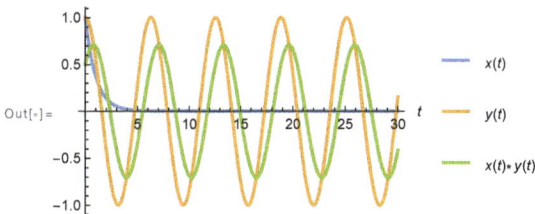

Time Multiplication

Given two signals and their respective Fourier transforms, $x(t) \overset{\mathcal{F}}{\longleftrightarrow} X(j\omega)$ and $y(t) \overset{\mathcal{F}}{\longleftrightarrow} Y(j\omega)$, the multiplication property states that

$$x(t) \cdot y(t) \overset{\mathcal{F}}{\longleftrightarrow} \frac{1}{2\pi} X(j\omega) * Y(j\omega)$$

where the symbol * denotes convolution.

This property relates time-domain multiplication to convolution in the frequency domain. This theorem is also known as the modulation theorem.

Example 5

Use the multiplication-in-time property to obtain the Fourier transform of the product of the following two signals

$$x(t) = e^{-t} u(t), \quad y(t) = \cos(10t)$$

Solution

Multiplication in time of a sinusoidal signal, called the carrier, with some other signal is known as modulation. Here the sinusoidal carrier signal is modulated by an exponential signal. This effectively centers the Fourier transform of the modulating signal on the frequency of the carrier.

The Fourier transforms of the two signals are:

In[·]:= $X [\omega\_] =$
  FourierTransform [e^{-t} **UnitStep** [t] , t, ω, **FourierParameters** $\rightarrow$ {1, −1}]

Out[·]= $-\dfrac{i}{-i + \omega}$

In[·]:= $Y [\omega\_] =$ **FourierTransform** [**Cos** [10 t] , t, ω, **FourierParameters** $\rightarrow$ {1, −1}]

Out[·]= π **DiracDelta** [−10 + ω] + π **DiracDelta** [10 + ω]

According to the modulation theorem, the Fourier transform of the modulated signal is:

In[·]:= $\dfrac{1}{2\,\pi}$ **Convolve** [X [w] , Y [w] , w, ω] // **Simplify**

Out[·]= $\dfrac{1 + i\,\omega}{101 + 2\,i\,\omega - \omega^2}$

This shows the magnitude spectrum of the resulting function:

In[·]:= **Plot** [**Abs** [$\dfrac{1 + i\,\omega}{101 + (2\,i)\,\omega - \omega^2}$] , [··· +]]

Out[·]=

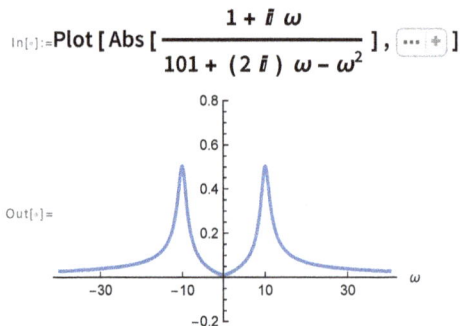

Step-by-step

The Fourier transforms of the two signals are

$$X(j\omega) = \frac{1}{1+j\omega}$$

$$Y(j\omega) = \pi(\delta(\omega + 10) + \delta(\omega - 10))$$

According to the multiplication-in-time property, the Fourier transform is given by a convolution of $X(j\omega)$ and $Y(j\omega)$. This yields

$$\frac{1}{2\pi} X(j\omega) * Y(j\omega) = \frac{1}{2} \left(\frac{1}{1+j\omega}\right) * (\delta(\omega + 10) + \delta(\omega - 10))$$

$$= \frac{1}{2} \left(\frac{1}{1+j(\omega+10)} + \frac{1}{1+j(\omega-10)}\right)$$

Parseval's Relation

Given a signal $x(t)$ and its Fourier transform $X(j\omega)$, the following relation establishes an equality between time- and frequency-domain evaluations of the energy of a signal

$$\mathcal{E} = \int_{-\infty}^{\infty} |x(t)|^2 \, dt = \frac{1}{2\pi} \int_{-\infty}^{\infty} |X(j\omega)|^2 \, d\omega$$

The energy of a signal can be found by integrating over the magnitude squared of the Fourier transform.

Example 6

Verify Parseval's relation for the unit pulse signal

$$x(t) = \begin{cases} 1, & -\frac{1}{2} \le t \le \frac{1}{2} \\ 0, & \text{else} \end{cases}$$

Solution

Evaluating in the time domain, the energy of the unit pulse is:

In[·]:=**Integrate [UnitBox [t]^2, { t, $-\infty$, ∞ }]**

Out[·]=**1**

The Fourier transform of the unit pulse is:

In[·]:=**FourierTransform [UnitBox [t], t, ω, FourierParameters $\rightarrow$ {1, -1}]**

Out[·]=$\text{Sinc}\left[\dfrac{\omega}{2}\right]$

According to Parseval's relation, the following frequency-domain evaluation also returns the energy of a signal:

In[•]:= $\dfrac{1}{2\pi}$ **Integrate [Abs [Sinc [ω / 2]]** ^{2}**, { ω, $-\infty$, ∞ }]**

Out[•]=1

This verifies the relation.

Summary

The following important Fourier transform theorems were presented:

- Time shift

- Time scaling

- Time differentiation

- Convolution in time

- Multiplication in time

- Parseval's relation

Examples showing applications of the theorems in solving several elementary signal processing problems were given.

Exercises

Download the solutions manual at wolfr.am/eTextbook-SSSP

16.1 Given that $x(t)$ has the Fourier transform $X(j\omega)$, express the transform of the following signal in terms of $X(j\omega)$.

$y(t) = x(t) - x(t-1)$

16.2 Given that $x(t)$ has the Fourier transform $X(j\omega)$, express the transform of the following signal in terms of $X(j\omega)$.

$y(t) = \dfrac{d^2}{dt^2} x(t)$

16.3 Given the signals $h(t) = u\left(t + \frac{1}{2}\right) - u\left(t - \frac{1}{2}\right)$ and $x(t) = \cos(2\pi t)$, use the convolution theorem to obtain $y(t) = x(t) * h(t)$.

16.4 The Fourier transform $X(j\omega)$ of a signal $x(t)$ is

$X(j\omega) = \begin{cases} 1 + \omega, & -1 \le \omega \le 0 \\ 1 - \omega, & 0 \le \omega \le 1 \\ 0, & \text{else} \end{cases}$

This shows $X(j\omega)$.

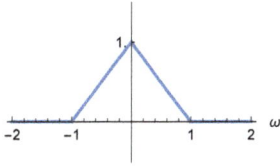

Obtain and plot the spectrum of the signal $x(t) \cdot \cos(2\,t)$.

16.5 Verify Parseval's relation for the signal $x(t) = e^t\,u(-t)$.

17 | Continuous-Time Filters

In continuous-time signal processing, a filter is a circuit, a network of interconnected electrical components such as resistors, capacitors, inductors, diodes, transistors, and operational amplifiers (op-amps). Filters are widely used in electronics and telecommunication, including in radio, television, audio recording, radar, control systems, music synthesis, image processing, and computer graphics.

Earlier discussions of the Fourier transform have now prepared you to apply this valuable mathematical tool to the analysis of filters from the frequency domain perspective

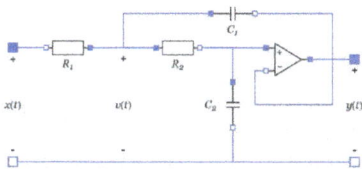

Two Views of Filtering

The convolution theorem leads to one of the more important results in the study of signal processing with linear time-invariant (LTI) systems. Recall from an earlier discussion that the response $y(t)$ of an LTI system with impulse response $h(t)$ to an input $x(t)$ is given by the following convolution integral

$$y(t) = \int_{-\infty}^{\infty} h(\tau)\, x(t - \tau)\, d\tau$$

Now, according to the Fourier transform convolution theorem, the following relation holds for the Fourier transforms of the three signals

$$Y(j\omega) = H(j\omega) \cdot X(j\omega)$$

Thus, in the frequency domain, the operation of filtering is effectively a multiplication operation involving the Fourier transforms of the impulse response $H(j\omega)$ and the input $X(j\omega)$, respectively. The function $H(j\omega)$ is known as the LTI system's frequency response. The impulse response $h(t)$ and the frequency response $H(j\omega)$ are a Fourier transform pair.

Ideal Filters

Ideal filters allow distortion-free transmission of a signal for a certain range of frequencies while completely suppressing the remaining frequencies. In a distortion-free system, the output must be a delayed copy of the input or zero

$$y(t) = x(t - t_0)$$

In the frequency domain, the input and output are related in the following way

$$Y(j\omega) = e^{-j\omega t_0} X(j\omega) = H(j\omega) \cdot X(j\omega)$$

which gives the frequency response of an ideal filter as

$$H(j\omega) = e^{-j\omega t_0}$$

An ideal filter has constant gain and linear phase over one or more frequency bands and zero gain otherwise. The frequency interval over which the gain is nonzero is called a passband, while the interval over which the gain is zero is called a stopband. Note, however, that ideal filters are not realizable in practice.

The following four filter types describe the four most common arrangements of passband and stopband intervals

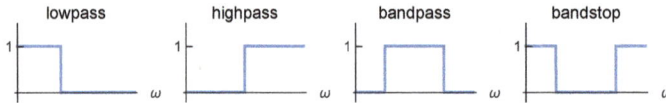

The frequency where a passband ends and a stopband begins is called a cutoff frequency. A filter that passes all frequencies is called an allpass filter.

The Impulse Response of an Ideal Filter

Consider the following ideal linear-phase lowpass filter

$$H(j\omega) = \begin{cases} e^{-j\omega t_0}, & |\omega| < 1 \\ 0, & \text{else} \end{cases}$$

This shows the magnitude and phase for $t_0 = 2$:

```
In[•]:= H[ω_] := UnitBox[ω / 2] e^(-i 2 ω);
        Plot[ {Abs[H[ω]], Arg[H[ω]] }, ⋯ + ]
```

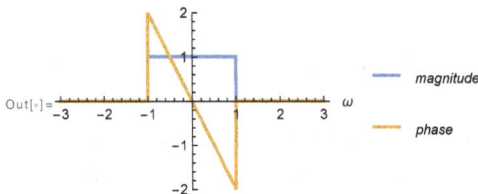

The impulse response is the inverse Fourier transform of $H(j\omega)$

$$h(t) = \frac{1}{2\pi} \int_{-\infty}^{\infty} H(j\omega)e^{j\omega t}\, d\omega$$

Therefore, for an arbitrary delay value t_0, the impulse response takes the form of a sinc function:

In[•]:= **InverseFourierTransform [UnitBox [ω / 2] $e^{-i\,\omega\,t0}$,**
    ω, t, FourierParameters → {1, −1}]

Out[•]= $\dfrac{\text{Sinc}\,[\,t - t0\,]}{\pi}$

This shows the impulse response for $0 \le t_0 \le 10$:

In[•]:= **Manipulate [⋯ +]**

Out[•]=

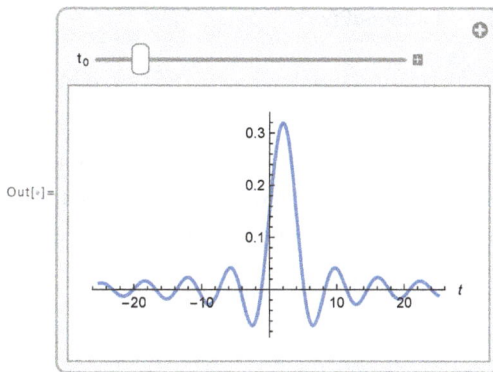

Signal Transmission in an Ideal Filter—Frequency Domain Analysis

First, consider a sinusoidal signal passing through an ideal lowpass filter defined as follows:

In[•]:= **H [ω_] := UnitBox [ω / 2] $e^{-i\,2\,\omega}$;**

As shown earlier, the magnitude and phase are:

In[•]:= **Plot [{ Abs [H [ω]] , Arg [H [ω]] } , ⋯ +]**

Out[•]=

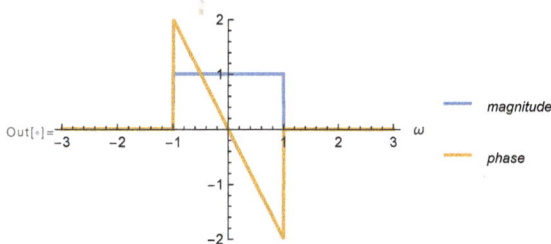

The input signal is:

In[•]:= **x [t_] := Sin [$\dfrac{1}{2}$ t];**

As stated earlier, the output signal is the inverse Fourier transform of the product of $X(j\omega)$ and $H(j\omega)$. The Fourier transform of the input is:

In[•]:=**X[ω_] = FourierTransform [x [t] , t, ω, FourierParameters → {1, −1}]**

Out[•]=**−2 i π DiracDelta [1 − 2 ω] + 2 i π DiracDelta [1 + 2 ω]**

The Fourier transform of the output is the product of $X(j\omega)$ and $H(j\omega)$:

In[•]:=**H [ω] X [ω] / / PiecewiseExpand**

Out[•]=$\begin{cases} -2\,i\,e^{-2\,i\,\omega}\,\pi\,(\text{DiracDelta}[1-2\,\omega] - \text{DiracDelta}[1+2\,\omega]) & -1 \leq \omega \leq 1 \\ 0 & \text{True} \end{cases}$

The inverse Fourier transform gives the time-domain output signal:

In[•]:=**InverseFourierTransform [H [ω] X [ω] ,
          ω, t, FourierParameters → {1, −1}] / / FullSimplify**

Out[•]=$-\text{Sin}\left[1 - \dfrac{t}{2}\right]$

For signal frequencies below the cutoff frequency $\omega < 1$, the input signal will pass through the filter undisturbed and the output will be a delayed version of the input. However, for frequencies exceeding the cutoff frequency $\omega > 1$, the output will be zero.

This demonstrates the response of an ideal lowpass filter to a pure sine function:

In[•]:=**DynamicModule [[⋯ ✛]▲]**

Out[•]=
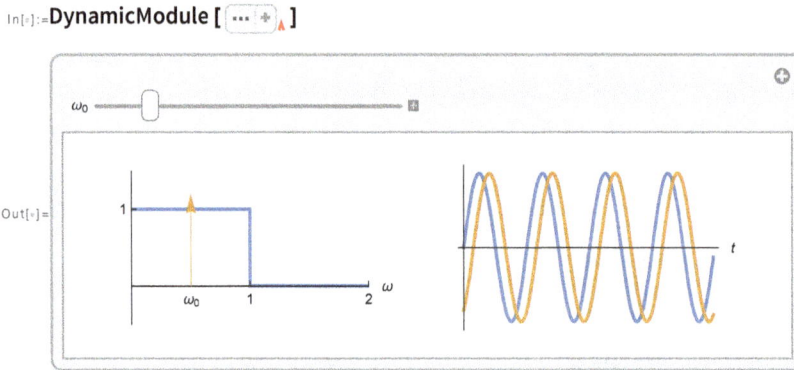

Response of an Ideal Lowpass Filter to a Periodic Signal

Building on the earlier example, now consider the response of an ideal lowpass filter to a square wave input.

The ideal lowpass filter is defined:

In[•]:= H [ω_] := UnitBox [ω / 20] $e^{-i \frac{\omega}{10}}$;
    Plot [{Abs [H [ω]] , Arg [H [ω]] }, ⋯ +]

Out[•]=

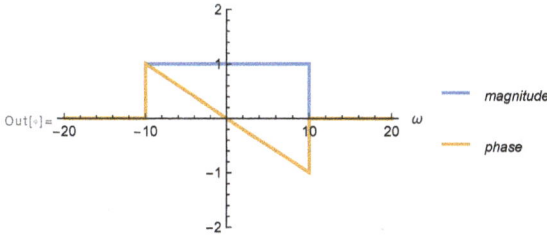

The input signal $x(t)$ is the following square wave:

In[•]:= x [t_] := SquareWave [{0, 1}, t + 1 / 4];
    Plot [x [t], ⋯ +]

Out[•]=

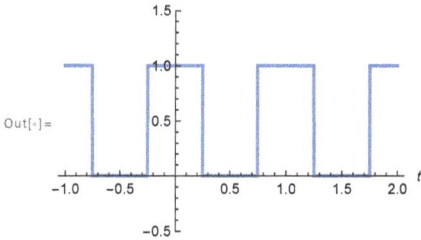

The Fourier transform of the input signal $x(t)$ is given by the following expression

$$X(j\omega) = 2\pi \sum_{k=-\infty}^{\infty} c_k \, \delta(\omega - k\omega_0)$$

where $\omega_0 = 2\pi$.

The Fourier coefficients of this square wave are:

In[•]:= FourierCoefficient [x [t] , t, k, FourierParameters → {1, 2π}]

Out[•]= $\begin{cases} \dfrac{1}{2} & k == 0 \\[2ex] \dfrac{\sin\left[\frac{k\pi}{2}\right]}{k\pi} & \text{True} \end{cases}$

Substituting into the formula for the Fourier transform of a periodic signal gives the following result

$$X(j\omega) = \pi \sum_{k=-\infty}^{\infty} \text{sinc}\left(\frac{\pi}{2} k\right) \delta(\omega - 2\pi k)$$

This shows the magnitude spectra of the ideal filter and the input signal:

In[•]:= **Plot [** ⋯ ✦ **]**

Out[•]=

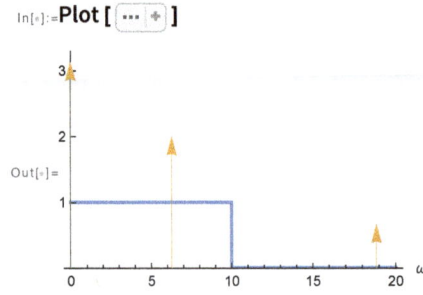

The Fourier transform of the output is given by a product of $X(j\omega)$ and $H(j\omega)$ and therefore is equal to

$$Y(j\omega) = 2\pi H(j\omega)\left(\sum_{k=-\infty}^{\infty} c_k \delta(\omega - 2\pi k)\right)$$

With the passband given as $|\omega| < 10$, the product reduces to

$$= 2\pi e^{-j\frac{\omega}{10}}\left(\sum_{k=-1}^{1} c_k\delta(\omega - 2\pi k)\right)$$

$$= 2\pi(c_{-1}\,\delta(\omega + 2\pi) + c_0\delta(\omega) + c_1\,\delta(\omega - 2\pi))e^{-j\frac{\omega}{10}}$$

$$= 2\pi\left(\frac{1}{\pi}\,\delta(\omega + 2\pi) + \frac{1}{2}\,\delta(\omega) + \frac{1}{\pi}\,\delta(\omega - 2\pi)\right)e^{-j\frac{\omega}{10}}$$

Finally, you arrive at the following expression for the Fourier transform of the output signal

$$Y(j\omega) = 2e^{-j\frac{2\pi}{10}}\,\delta(\omega + 2\pi) + \pi\delta(\omega) + 2e^{-j\frac{2\pi}{10}}\,\delta(\omega - 2\pi)$$

The inverse Fourier transform is easy to obtain, as each impulse in frequency corresponds to a decaying exponential in time, which gives

$$y(t) = \frac{1}{\pi}e^{-j2\pi\left(t-\frac{1}{10}\right)} + \frac{1}{2} + \frac{1}{\pi}e^{+j2\pi\left(t-\frac{1}{10}\right)}$$

and reduces to the following real signal

$$y(t) = \frac{1}{2} + \frac{2}{\pi}\cos\left(2\pi\left(t - \frac{1}{10}\right)\right)$$

This shows the input and output signals:

In[•]:= **Plot [{x[t] ,** $\dfrac{1}{2}$ **+** $\dfrac{2\,\text{Cos}\,[\,(2\,\pi)\,(t-\frac{1}{10})\,]}{\pi}$ **} ,** ⋯ ✦ **]**

Out[•]=

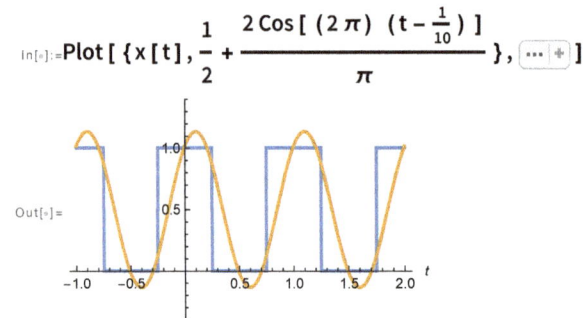

Note how the lowpass filter removes all the signal frequencies in the square wave beyond the cutoff frequency of $\omega = 10$ radians/second.

The following demonstration extends the example to include two other common inputs and shows how the output changes as the cutoff frequency of the ideal filter is varied over the range $5 \leq \omega \leq 65$ radians/second:

In[•]:=**DynamicModule [⋯ + ▲]**

Out[•]=
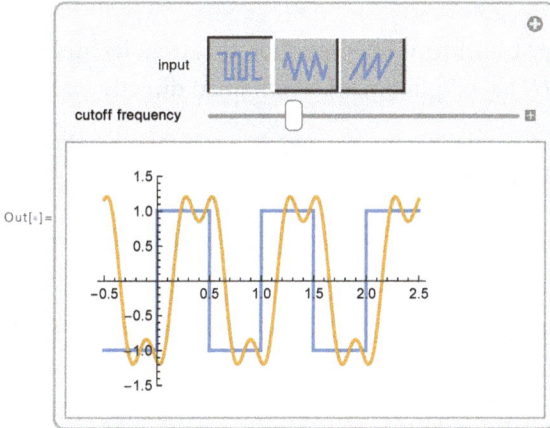

Non-ideal Filters

Non-ideal filters exhibit both magnitude and phase distortion. Magnitude distortion occurs when the magnitude response within the passband frequencies is not constant

$$|H(j\omega)| \neq 1$$

Phase distortion causes the phase of the filter to differ from a straight line

$$\llcorner H(j\omega) \neq \pm\, \alpha\omega$$

For example, the well-known RC filter exhibits both of these distortions:

In[•]:=**GraphicsRow [{⋯} +]**

Out[•]=
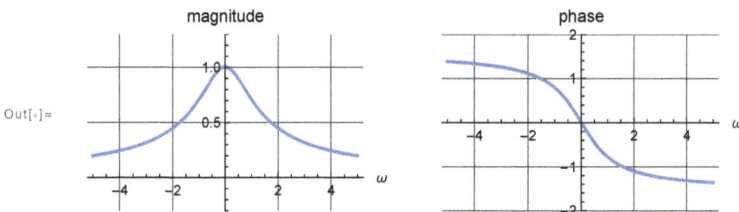

Frequency Response of an LTI System

As demonstrated earlier, filters are modeled by linear constant coefficient differential equations. Recall that, in general, such equations take the following general form

$$a_n \, y^{(n)}(t) + a_{n-1} \, y^{(n-1)}(t) + \ldots + a_0 \, y(t) = b_m \, x^{(m)}(t) + b_{m-1} x^{(m-1)}(t) + \ldots + b_0 x(t)$$

where $y(t)$ and $x(t)$ denote the filter's output and input signals, respectively, with $y^{(n)} = \frac{d^n}{dt^n} \, y(t)$ and $x^{(m)} = \frac{d^m}{dt^m} \, x(t)$.

Now, taking advantage of the Fourier transform differentiation theorem, it can be shown that the frequency response $H(j\omega)$ of a filter can be obtained directly from its differential equation model.

Using the differentiation property, proceed as follows

$$\mathcal{F}\left[a_n \, y^{(n)}(t)\right] + \mathcal{F}\left[a_{n-1} \, y^{(n-1)}(t)\right] + \ldots + \mathcal{F}[a_0 \, y(t)] =$$
$$\mathcal{F}\left[b_m \, x^{(m)}(t)\right] + \mathcal{F}\left[b_{m-1} x^{(m-1)}(t)\right] + \ldots + \mathcal{F}[b_0 x(t)]$$

With $\mathcal{F}[x(t)] = X(j\omega)$ and $\mathcal{F}[y(t)] = Y(j\omega)$, you get

$$a_n(j\omega)^n Y(j\omega) + a_{n-1}(j\omega)^{n-1} \, Y(j\omega) + \ldots + a_0 \, Y(j\omega) =$$
$$b_m(j\omega)^m X(j\omega) + b_{m-1}(j\omega)^{m-1} \, X(j\omega) + \ldots + b_0 \, X(j\omega)$$

$$\left(a_n(j\omega)^n + a_{n-1}(j\omega)^{n-1} + \ldots + a_0\right) Y(j\omega) = \left(b_m(j\omega)^m + b_{m-1}(j\omega)^{m-1} + \ldots + b_0\right) X(j\omega)$$

Finally, solving for the ratio $Y(j\omega)/X(j\omega)$, you get the following expression for the frequency response of the filter

$$H(j\omega) = \frac{Y(j\omega)}{X(j\omega)} = \frac{b_m(j\omega)^m + b_{m-1}(j\omega)^{m-1} + \ldots + b_0}{a_n(j\omega)^n + a_{n-1}(j\omega)^{n-1} + \ldots + a_0}$$

Example 1

Obtain the frequency response and plot the magnitude spectrum of the second-order system described by the following differential equation

$$y''(t) + \sqrt{2} \, y'(t) + y(t) = x(t)$$

Solution

Use the differentiation property of the Fourier transform

$$\mathcal{F}[y''(t)] + \sqrt{2} \, \mathcal{F}[y'(t)] + \mathcal{F}[y(t)] = \mathcal{F}[x(t)]$$
$$(j\omega)^2 Y(j\omega) + j \sqrt{2} \, \omega Y(j\omega) + Y(j\omega) = X(j\omega)$$

Collect terms

$$\left(-\omega^2 + j \sqrt{2} \, \omega + 1\right) Y(j\omega) = X(j\omega)$$

The frequency response is the ratio of the output to the input

$$H(j\omega) = \frac{Y(j\omega)}{X(j\omega)} = \frac{1}{-\omega^2 + j\sqrt{2}\,\omega + 1}$$

Here are plots of the magnitude and phase of the filter $H(j\omega)$:

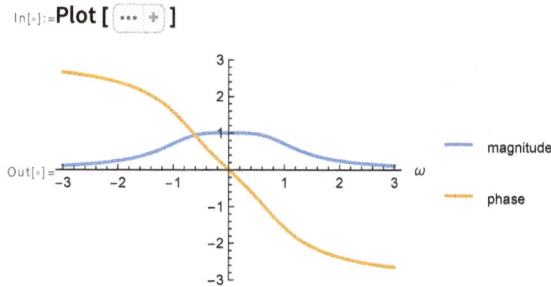

Sinusoidal Steady-State Response of an LTI Filter

Consider an LTI system with an input of the form $x(t) = e^{j\omega t}$. The output is given by the following convolution integral

$$y(t) = \int_{-\infty}^{\infty} h(\tau)\, x(t - \tau)\, d\tau$$

Substituting the exponential input and simplifying gives

$$= \int_{-\infty}^{\infty} h(\tau)\, e^{j\omega(t-\tau)}\, d\tau$$

$$= e^{j\omega t} \int_{-\infty}^{\infty} h(\tau)\, e^{-j\omega\tau}\, d\tau$$

Recognizing that the integral is simply the Fourier transform of $h(t)$ gives the final result

$$y(t) = H(j\omega) \cdot e^{j\omega t}$$

In conclusion, the output $y(t)$ of an LTI system is simply the input $x(t) = e^{j\omega t}$ scaled by the Fourier transform of the impulse response $H(j\omega)$ evaluated at the frequency ω. This is a fundamental property of LTI systems.

Example 2

Determine the response to the sinusoidal input $x(t) = \sin(t)$ of a filter with the following frequency response

$$H(j\omega) = \frac{1}{1 + j\omega}$$

Solution

Using the Fourier transform convolution theorem, proceed as follows.

The Fourier transform $X(j\omega)$ of the input $x(t) = \sin(t)$ is:

In[•]:= **x[t_] := Sin[t];**
X[ω_] = FourierTransform[x[t], t, ω, FourierParameters → {1, −1}]

Out[•]= **− i π DiracDelta[−1 + ω] + i π DiracDelta[1 + ω]**

The product of the functions $X(j\omega)$ and $H(j\omega)$ is the Fourier transform of the output $Y(j\omega)$:

In[•]:= **($\dfrac{1}{1 + i\,\omega}$) X[ω]**

Out[•]= $\dfrac{- i\,\pi\,\text{DiracDelta}[-1 + \omega] + i\,\pi\,\text{DiracDelta}[1 + \omega]}{1 + i\,\omega}$

The inverse Fourier transform returns the time-domain signal:

In[•]:= **InverseFourierTransform[($\dfrac{1}{1 + i\,\omega}$) X[ω], ω, t,**
FourierParameters → {1, −1}] // Expand // Simplify

Out[•]= $\dfrac{1}{2}$ **(−Cos[t] + Sin[t])**

Alternatively, the response of an LTI system to a sinusoidal input can be obtained as a scaled $(|H(j\omega)|_{\omega\to1} = \frac{1}{\sqrt{2}})$ and shifted $(\angle\, H(j\omega)_{\omega\to1} = -\frac{\pi}{4})$ version of the input:

In[•]:= **AbsArg[($\dfrac{1}{1 + i\,1}$)]**

Out[•]= $\left\{ \dfrac{1}{\sqrt{2}}, -\dfrac{\pi}{4} \right\}$

This gives the output signal:

In[•]:= **y[t_] := $\dfrac{1}{\sqrt{2}}$ Sin[t − $\dfrac{\pi}{4}$];**

This shows the input and output signals:

In[•]:= **Plot[{x[t], y[t]}, ⋯ +]**

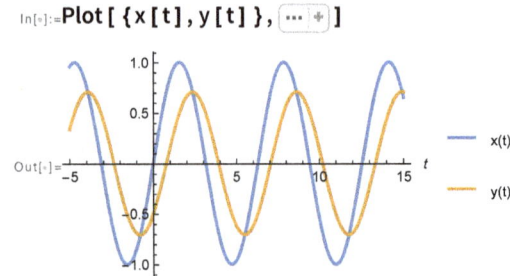

Response of a Lowpass RC Filter to Select Periodic Signals

You are now ready to derive the response of the RC filter to a periodic signal. Recall the following Fourier series representation of a periodic signal

$$x(t) = \sum_{k=-\infty}^{\infty} c_k e^{j\omega_0 k t}$$

If such a signal is applied to the input of an LTI system with frequency response $H(j\omega)$, it follows that the response will be

$$y(t) = \sum_{k=-\infty}^{\infty} c_k H(j\omega_0 k) e^{j\omega_0 k t}$$

This shows how the RC filter's frequency response $H(j\omega)$ scales the Fourier coefficients c_k of a square wave:

In[•]:=**Manipulate [** ⋯ + **]**

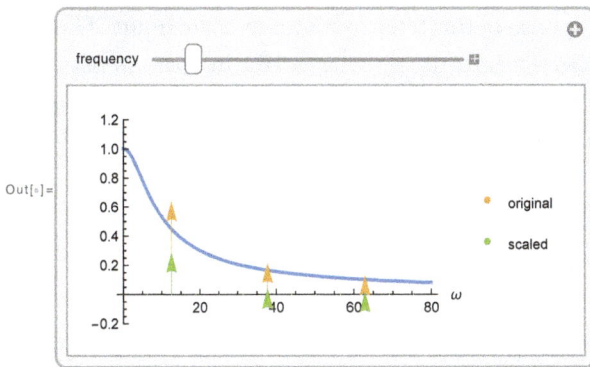

Out[•]=

Here is an example of a simple RC filter acting on one of three commonly used test signals. As the bandwidth of the filter is increased, the output signal looks increasingly like the input signal:

In[•]:=**DynamicModule [** ⋯ + **]**

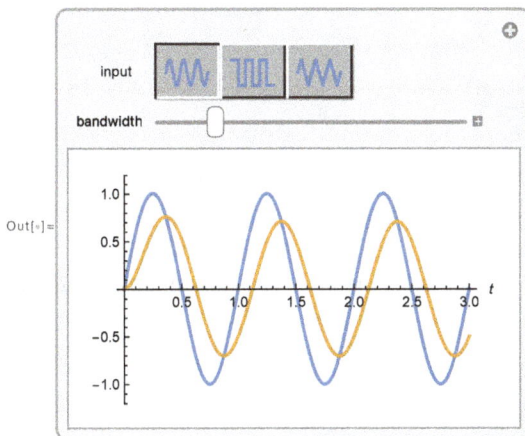

Out[•]=

Phase Distortion

An ideal filter has linear phase. But one can ask:

- What happens if the filter has some degree of phase distortion?
- How important is linear phase?
- How does nonlinear phase manifest itself in the output of a filter?

To answer these questions, consider the case of a square wave input into a filter with phase distortion. Here is one such filter

$$H(j\omega) = \begin{cases} e^{j\omega^{1+\epsilon}}, & -\omega_c < \omega < 0 \\ e^{-j\omega^{1+\epsilon}} & 0 < \omega < \omega_c \\ 0, & \text{else} \end{cases}$$

Now calculate and display the response of this filter to a square wave input. The cutoff frequency of the filter has been arbitrarily set to $\omega_c = 16\pi$ in order to pass the first several sinusoidal components of the square wave. As the factor ϵ is varied in the range $0 \leq \epsilon \leq 2$, the nonlinearity of the filter's phase increases, causing visible distortion in the square wave:

In[•]:= **DynamicModule [** ⋯ ✛ ▲ **]**

Out[•]=

Summary

The frequency response of an LTI system is the Fourier transform of its unit impulse response $h(t)$

$$h(t) \overset{\mathcal{F}}{\longleftrightarrow} H(j\omega)$$

The frequency response of a continuous-time LTI system is a rational polynomial in terms of powers of $j\omega$

$$H(j\omega) = \frac{b_0 + b_1(j\omega) + \ldots + b_m(j\omega)^m}{a_0 + a_1(j\omega) + \ldots + a_n(j\omega)^n}$$

Four types of ideal filters were shown

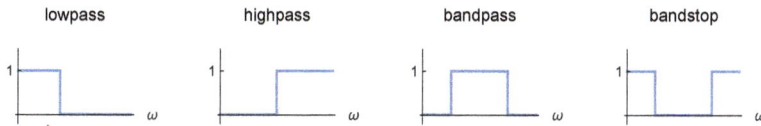

| lowpass | highpass | bandpass | bandstop |

The characteristics of ideal and non-ideal filters were described.

Several examples of signal processing with ideal and practical filters were given.

The effect of nonlinear phase on a periodic signal was demonstrated, showing the potential distortion it can impart on a signal.

Exercises

Download the solutions manual at wolfr.am/eTextbook-SSSP

17.1 Obtain the frequency response of an LTI system defined by the following differential equation.

$$y''(t) + y(t) = x(t)$$

17.2 Obtain the impulse response of the following ideal filter.

$$H(j\omega) = \begin{cases} j\omega, & |\omega| < 2 \\ 0, & \text{else} \end{cases}$$

17.3 Obtain the impulse response of the following ideal bandpass filter.

$$H(j\omega) = \begin{cases} e^{-j5\omega}, & 1 < |\omega| < 5 \\ 0, & \text{else} \end{cases}$$

17.4 The frequency response of an ideal lowpass filter is defined as follows.

$$H(j\omega) = \begin{cases} 1, & |\omega| < 1 \\ 0, & \text{else} \end{cases}$$

Determine the output signal $y(t)$ given the following input.

$$x(t) = \cos\left(\frac{\pi}{2} t\right)$$

17.5 The frequency response of an allpass filter is defined as follows.

$$H(j\omega) = \begin{cases} j, & \omega < 0 \\ -j, & \omega > 0 \end{cases}$$

Determine the output signal $y(t)$ given the following input.

$$x(t) = \cos(t)$$

17.6 Given an ideal filter with frequency response

$$H(j\omega) = j\omega$$

determine the output $y(t)$ given the following input.

$$x(t) = \cos(t)$$

17.7 Obtain the output $y(t)$ of an ideal lowpass filter with frequency response

$$H(j\omega) = \begin{cases} 1, & |\omega| < 5 \\ 0, & \text{else} \end{cases}$$

to the triangle wave input $x(t)$ shown here.

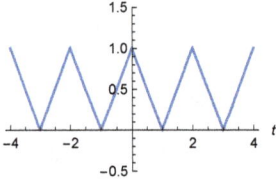

17.8 Obtain the output $y(t)$ of an ideal highpass filter with frequency response

$$H(j\omega) = \begin{cases} 1, & |\omega| > 1 \\ 0, & \text{else} \end{cases}$$

to the triangle wave input $x(t)$ shown here.

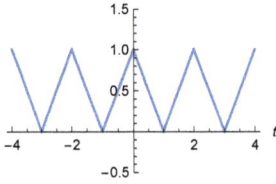

Fourier Analysis
(Discrete)

18 | Discrete-Time Fourier Series

As was the case in continuous time, the discrete-time Fourier series is a representation of a signal as a superposition of complex exponentials. However, in contrast with continuous time, the discrete-time Fourier series is a finite-length superposition and therefore can be easily evaluated numerically.

Major steps in the development of discrete-time techniques in general and in the use of the tools of discrete-time Fourier analysis in particular were first undertaken in the 1940s and 1950s. In the mid-1960s, an algorithm, now known as the fast Fourier transform (FFT), was developed that substantially accelerated the calculation of the Fourier coefficients of a finite-length sequence, thus paving the way for fast processing of digital signals on a computer.

Discrete-Time Exponential Sequences

A Fourier series is a way to represent an arbitrary periodic sequence as a sum of scaled, harmonically related complex exponentials. Two complex exponential sequences are said to be harmonically related if their frequencies are integer multiples of the same fundamental frequency.

This describes a family of discrete-time harmonically related complex exponential sequences with period N and fundamental frequency $\omega_1 = \frac{2\pi}{N}$ radians/second

$$W_N^{kn} = e^{-j\left(\frac{2\pi}{N}\right)kn}$$

with $n, k = 0, 1, \ldots, N - 1$.

This enumerates the exponential sequences of length $N = 4$:

```
In[·]:= N = 4; W = Table[ e^(-i (2π/N) k n), {k, 0, N - 1}, {n, 0, N - 1}]
Out[·]= {{1, 1, 1, 1}, {1, -i, -1, i}, {1, -1, 1, -1}, {1, i, -1, -i}}
```

This shows the real and imaginary parts of the sequences:

In[•]:=**GraphicsRow [** [··· ✛] **]**

Out[•]=

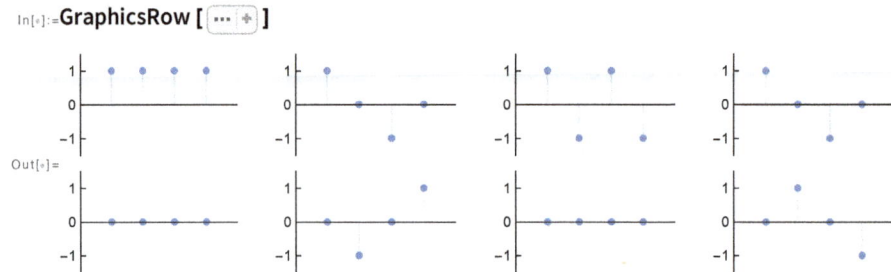

The fundamental frequency is $\frac{\pi}{2}$ and the four harmonically related frequencies are:

In[•]:=**Table [** $\dfrac{2\,\pi}{N}$ **k, {k, 0, 3}]**

Out[•]= $\left\{0, \dfrac{\pi}{2}, \pi, \dfrac{3\,\pi}{2}\right\}$

Definition

The complex Fourier series is a representation of a periodic sequence of period N in terms of a linear combination of N harmonically related complex exponential sequences. The discrete-time complex Fourier series is defined by two formulas commonly called synthesis and analysis.

The synthesis formula is as follows

$$x[n] = \sum_{k=0}^{N-1} c_k\, e^{j\frac{2\pi}{N}kn}, \qquad\qquad n = 0,\ 1,\ ...,\ N-1$$

The coefficients c_k are known as the Fourier series coefficients of the signal $x[n]$ and are generally complex. The quantity $\frac{2\pi}{N}$ is called the fundamental frequency (in radians/second). The quantity $\omega_k = \frac{2\pi}{N} k$ is its kth harmonic.

The analysis formula is as follows

$$c_k = \frac{1}{N} \sum_{n=0}^{N-1} x[n] e^{-j\frac{2\pi}{N}kn}, \qquad\qquad k = 0,\ 1,\ ...,\ N-1$$

The synthesis and analysis formulas are both finite-length summations and can be easily calculated numerically.

Example 1

Obtain the Fourier series coefficients of a discrete-time periodic square wave of period $N = 4$ as shown:

In[·]:=**DiscretePlot [SquareWave [{0, 1}, $\frac{n}{4}$], ⋯ +]**

Out[·]=

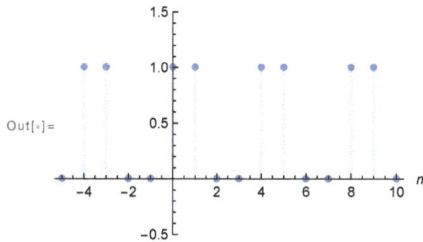

Solution

Substituting the period $N = 4$ and the values of $x[n]$ into the Fourier series analysis formula and simplifying yields the following formula for the Fourier coefficients:

In[·]:=**c [k_] := $\frac{1}{4}$ Sum [$e^{-i \frac{\pi}{2} k n}$, { n, 0, 1 }];**

c [k]

Out[·]= $\frac{1}{4} \left(1 + e^{-\frac{1}{2} i k \pi} \right)$

Evaluating for $0 \le k \le 3$ gives:

In[·]:=**Table [c [k], { k, 0, 3 }]**

Out[·]= $\left\{ \frac{1}{2}, \frac{1}{4} - \frac{i}{4}, 0, \frac{1}{4} + \frac{i}{4} \right\}$

Periodicity and Conjugate Symmetry

There are strong similarities between properties of discrete-time and continuous-time Fourier series. However, a very important distinguishing feature of the discrete-time Fourier series is the following periodicity of the Fourier coefficients. Fourier series coefficients c_k of a discrete-time periodic sequence $x[n]$ with period N are also periodic in frequency with period N

$$c_k = c_{k+N}$$

To derive this property, substitute $k + N$ for k in the analysis formula

$$c_{k+N} = \frac{1}{N} \sum_{n=0}^{N-1} x[n] e^{-j \frac{2\pi}{N} (k+N)n}$$

Simplification of the exponential term leads to

$$= \frac{1}{N} \sum_{n=0}^{N-1} x[n] e^{-j\frac{2\pi}{N}kn} e^{-j\frac{2\pi}{N}Nn}$$

$$= \frac{1}{N} \sum_{n=0}^{N-1} x[n] e^{-j\frac{2\pi}{N}kn} e^{-j2\pi n}$$

Now, since $e^{-j2\pi n} = 1$ for all n, you get

$$= \frac{1}{N} \sum_{n=0}^{N-1} x[n] e^{-j\frac{2\pi}{N}kn}$$

$$= c_k$$

The periodicity of the Fourier coefficients can be readily observed by evaluating and plotting the magnitudes of the Fourier coefficients over successive periods of the index k. The following shows one period of length 4 of the Fourier coefficients $|c_k|$ from Example 1 (in red), on the extended interval $-8 \le k \le 8$:

In[·]:=**DiscretePlot [Abs [c [k]] , ⋯ +]**

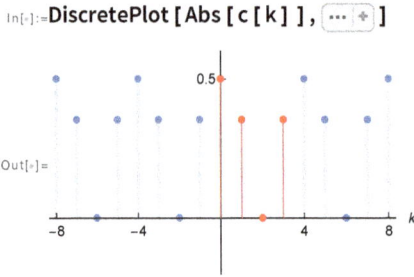

Out[·]=

The discrete-time Fourier series coefficients of a real periodic sequence are also conjugate symmetric

$$c_k = c_{-k}^*$$

However, due to the periodic nature of the coefficients, the conjugate symmetry property additionally manifests itself in the following form

$$c_k = c_{N-k}^*$$

This verifies both forms of the property using the Fourier series coefficients from Example 1:

In[·]:=**Table [c [k] == Conjugate [c [−k]] , { k, 0, 3 }]**

Out[·]=**{ True, True, True, True }**

In[·]:=**Table [c [k] == Conjugate [c [4 − k]] , { k, 0, 3 }]**

Out[·]=**{ True, True, True, True }**

Fourier Series Expansion of a Cosine

In analogy with the continuous-time Fourier series, it is of interest to obtain the Fourier series coefficients of a periodic sinusoidal sequence. For example, consider the following cosine sequence of period $N = 8$

$$x[n] = \cos\left(\tfrac{2\pi}{8}\, 3\,n\right)$$

This shows the sequence:

In[◦]:= **x[n_] := Cos[$\dfrac{\pi}{4}$ 3n]**

    DiscretePlot[x[n], ⋯ ✦]

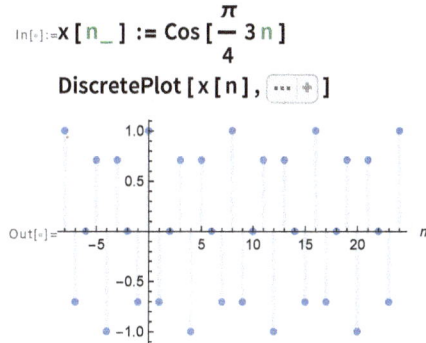

Substitution into the analysis formula and evaluation gives the following formula for the Fourier series coefficients of the cosine sequence:

In[◦]:= **c[k_] := $\dfrac{1}{8}$ Sum[x[n] $e^{-i\frac{\pi}{4}kn}$, {n, 0, 7}];**

    c[k]

Out[◦]= $\dfrac{1}{8}\left(1 - \dfrac{e^{-\frac{1}{4}i k\pi}}{\sqrt{2}} + \dfrac{e^{-\frac{3}{4}i k\pi}}{\sqrt{2}} - e^{-i k\pi} + \dfrac{e^{-\frac{5}{4}i k\pi}}{\sqrt{2}} - \dfrac{e^{-\frac{7}{4}i k\pi}}{\sqrt{2}}\right)$

This returns the Fourier series coefficients:

In[◦]:= **Table[c[k], {k, 0, 7}] // Simplify**

Out[◦]= $\left\{0, 0, 0, \dfrac{1}{2}, 0, \dfrac{1}{2}, 0, 0\right\}$

In analogy with the continuous-time Fourier series, a periodic sine or cosine sequence is represented by a pair of nonzero Fourier series coefficients. The result can be easily generalized and demonstrated. For example, consider the following cosine sequence

$$x[n] = \cos\left(\tfrac{2\pi}{32}\, k\,n\right), \quad n = 0, 1, \ldots, 31$$

Now vary the frequency of the cosine sequence and show the magnitudes of the Fourier series coefficients:

In[•]:=**Manipulate [** ⬚ ▪ **]**

Out[•]=

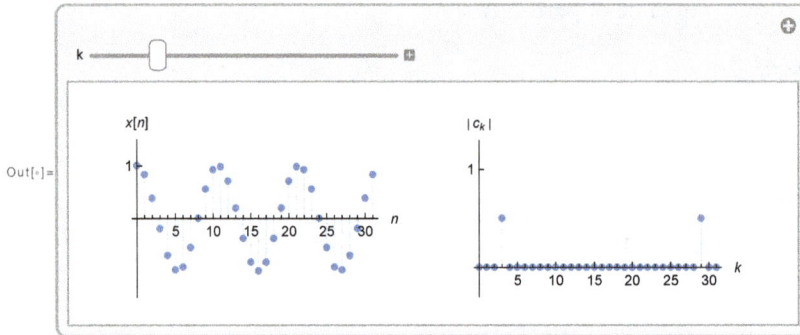

Step-by-step

Express the given sequence using Euler's identity

$$x[n] = \frac{1}{2} \left(e^{j\frac{\pi}{4} 3n} + e^{-j\frac{\pi}{4} 3n} \right)$$

Substitution into the Fourier series analysis formula gives

$$c_k = \frac{1}{8} \sum_{n=0}^{7} \frac{1}{2} \left(e^{j\frac{\pi}{4} 3n} + e^{-j\frac{\pi}{4} 3n} \right) e^{-j\frac{\pi}{4} kn}$$

$$= \frac{1}{16} \sum_{n=0}^{7} e^{-j\frac{\pi}{4}(k-3)n} + \frac{1}{2} \sum_{n=0}^{7} e^{-j\frac{\pi}{4}(k+3)n}$$

Making use of the identity

$$\sum_{n=0}^{N-1} e^{-j\frac{2\pi}{N}(k-l)n} = \begin{cases} N, & \text{for } k = l \\ 0, & \text{otherwise} \end{cases}$$

gives the following result

$$c_k = \begin{cases} \frac{1}{2}, & \text{for } k = 3 \\ \frac{1}{2}, & \text{for } k = -3 \\ 0, & \text{else} \end{cases}$$

Equivalently, due to the conjugate symmetry property

$$c_k = \begin{cases} \frac{1}{2}, & \text{for } k = 3 \\ \frac{1}{2}, & \text{for } k = 5 \\ 0, & \text{else} \end{cases}$$

Example 2

Obtain and plot the Fourier series coefficients for the following periodic sequence with period $N = 15$:

In[•]:=**DiscretePlot [SawtoothWave [$\frac{n}{15}$] , $\boxed{\cdots +}$]**

Out[•]=

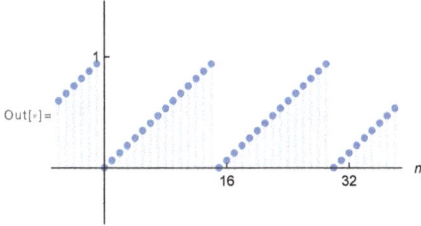

Solution

Substituting into the Fourier series analysis formula results in the following Fourier series coefficients:

In[•]:=**c [k_] := $\frac{1}{15}$ Sum [SawtoothWave [n / 15] $e^{-i \frac{2\pi}{15} k n}$, { n, 0, 14 }] ;**

This evaluates and plots the magnitudes of the Fourier coefficients:

In[•]:=**DiscretePlot [Abs [c [k]] , $\boxed{\cdots +}$]**

Out[•]=

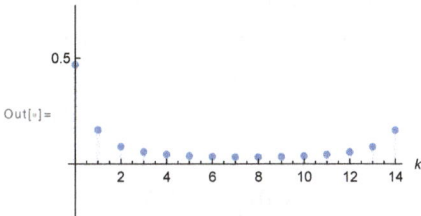

Synthesis

Given a set of N Fourier series coefficients c_k of a sequence $x[n]$ with period N, the synthesis formula guarantees perfect reconstruction of the sequence. For example, given the Fourier series coefficients of length $N = 4$ shown in the following, it is easy to determine the time-domain sequence $x[n]$:

In[•]:=**c [0] $= \frac{1}{2}$; c [1] $= \frac{1}{2} \frac{1}{1 + i}$; c [2] = 0 ; c [3] $= \frac{1}{2} \frac{1}{1 - i}$;**

Substituting into the synthesis formula and evaluating returns the time-domain sequence $x[n]$:

In[•]:= $\text{x} [\text{n}\_] := \text{Sum} [\text{c} [\text{k}]\ e^{i\frac{\pi}{2}\text{kn}}, \{\text{k}, 0, 3\}];$
$\text{x}[\text{n}]$

Out[•]= $\frac{1}{2} + \left(\frac{1}{4} - \frac{i}{4}\right) e^{\frac{i n \pi}{2}} + \left(\frac{1}{4} + \frac{i}{4}\right) e^{\frac{3 i n \pi}{2}}$

This shows the periodic sequence:

In[•]:= $\textbf{DiscretePlot} [\text{x}[\text{n}], \boxed{\cdots\ +}]$

Out[•]=

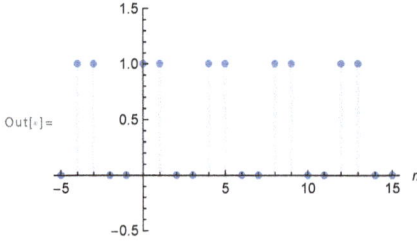

Signal Approximation

The discrete-time Fourier series is a finite summation; however, it is still of interest to consider the issue of signal reconstruction from an incomplete set of Fourier coefficients. The following $(2K+1)$-length $(0 \le K \le (N-1)/2)$ evaluation of the synthesis formula results in an approximation to the original sequence

$$x_K[n] = \frac{1}{N} \sum_{k=-K}^{K} c_k e^{j\frac{2\pi}{N} kn}$$

This shows the synthesis of a discrete-time sawtooth wave with period $N = 15$ from a subset of its Fourier coefficients:

In[•]:= $\textbf{DynamicModule} [\boxed{\cdots\ +}_\blacktriangle]$

Out[•]=

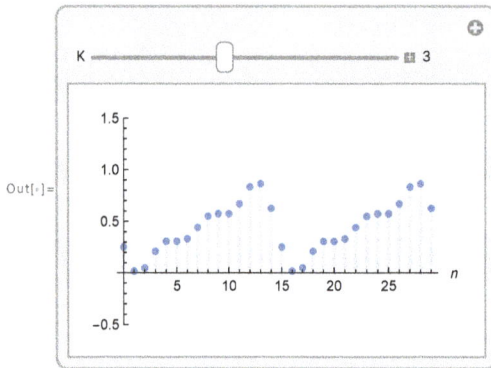

Perfect reconstruction results from summing over all of the Fourier series coefficients.

Fast Evaluation

It is a well-known fact in digital signal processing that the discrete-time Fourier series coefficients can be calculated using the so-called discrete Fourier transform (DFT). Crucially, it can be evaluated quickly using an FFT. Specifically, given a periodic sequence of period N, the DFT of exactly N samples of the sequence equals the Fourier series coefficients of the sequence up to a scaling factor.

For example, this uses the function Fourier to return the Fourier series coefficients of the square wave from Example 1:

In[•]:=**Fourier [{1, 1, 0, 0}, FourierParameters → { −1, −1}]**

Out[•]= { 0.5 + 0. *i* , 0.25 − 0.25 *i* , 0. + 0. *i* , 0.25 + 0.25 *i* }

The option FourierParameters→{-1,-1} is used to match the function Fourier with the discrete-time Fourier series analysis formula defined earlier. Use the function InverseFourier to perform the inverse operation, namely to calculate the time-domain sequence from a list of Fourier series coefficients:

In[•]:=**InverseFourier [%, FourierParameters → { −1, −1}]**

Out[•]= { 1., 1., 0., 0.}

Example 3

Use the function Fourier to calculate the Fourier series coefficients of the following periodic sequence

$$x[n] = \cos\left(\frac{2\pi}{8} 3 n\right)$$

Solution

The given sequence has a period of $N = 8$. Obtain a list of samples that represents one period of the sequence by evaluating the sequence $x[n]$ at $n = 0, 1, ..., 7$:

In[•]:=**x = N [Table [Cos [$\frac{2\pi}{8}$ 3 n] , {n, 0, 7}]]**

Out[•]= { 1., −0.707107, 0., 0.707107, −1., 0.707107, 0., −0.707107 }

Calculate the discrete-time Fourier series coefficients of the cosine sequence $x[n]$ using the function Fourier:

In[•]:=**Fourier [x, FourierParameters → { −1, −1}]**

Out[•]= { 0., 0., 0., 0.5, 0., 0.5, 0., 0.}

Sunspot Activity

The approximate periodicity of sunspot data is a well-known phenomenon (wikipedia.org/wiki/Sunspot). Here is the average yearly sunspot activity from

1700 to 2012, a total of 313 years of measurements (data source: SIDC—Solar Influences Data Analysis Center, sidc.be/SILSO/datafiles):

In[•]:= **data =** {···} + ;
ListPlot [data, ··· + **]**

Out[•]=

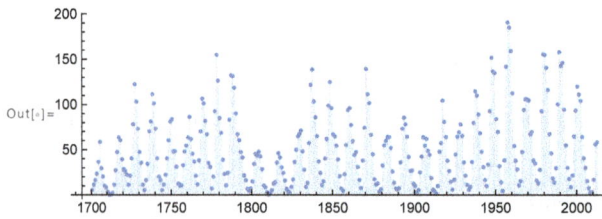

This tests the idea by computing the Fourier series coefficients of the sequence and shows the Fourier series coefficient magnitudes:

In[•]:= **ListPlot [** ··· + **]**

Out[•]=

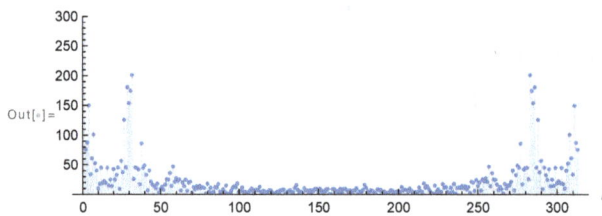

The presence of two dominant peaks resembles the Fourier series coefficients of a sine or cosine sequence. The locations of the peaks are approximately $k = 29$ and $k = 284$, indicating a sunspot frequency of $f = \frac{29}{313}$ inverse years:

In[•]:= **ListPlot [** ··· + **]**

Out[•]=

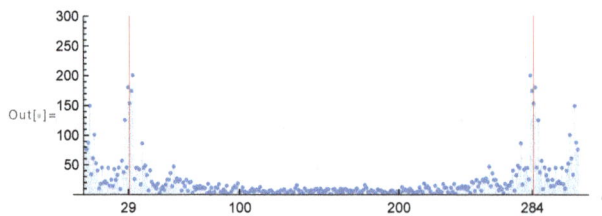

This gives a period of $T = 313/29 \approx 10.79$ years, or 11 years, as frequently given in popular literature.

Summary

The discrete-time Fourier series was presented

$$x[n] = \sum_{k=0}^{N-1} c_k e^{j\frac{2\pi}{N}kn}, \qquad n = 0, 1, ..., N-1$$

$$c_k = \frac{1}{N}\sum_{n=0}^{N-1} x[n] e^{-j\frac{2\pi}{N}kn}, \qquad k = 0, 1, ..., N-1$$

Examples of the Fourier series decompositions of several periodic and quasiperiodic sequences were shown

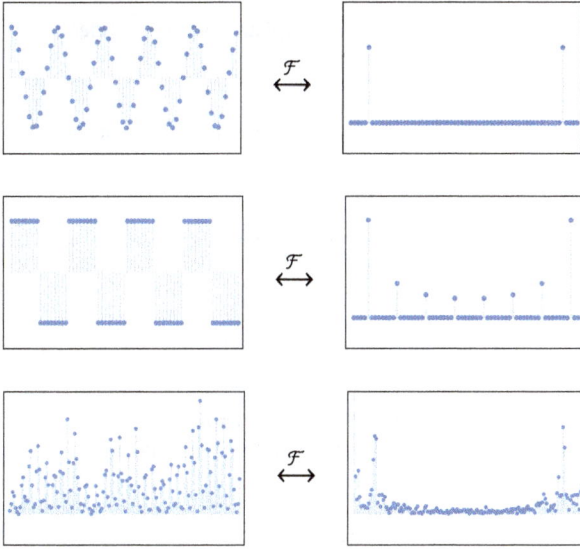

Exercises

Download the solutions manual at wolfr.am/eTextbook-SSSP

18.1 Obtain the discrete-time Fourier series coefficients of the following periodic sequence.

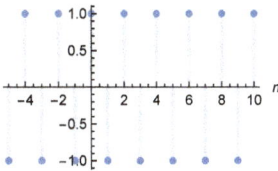

18.2 Obtain the discrete-time Fourier series coefficients of the following periodic sequence.

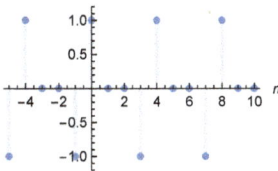

18.3 Obtain the discrete-time Fourier series coefficients of the following periodic sequence.

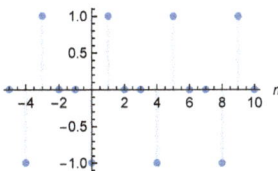

18.4 Determine the Fourier series coefficients of the sequence $x[n]$ in Exercise 3 using the function Fourier.

18.5 Determine the sequence $x[n]$ with period $N = 2$ given the following Fourier series coefficients.

$c_0 = 1, c_1 = 1$

18.6 Determine the sequence $x[n]$ with period $N = 4$ given the following Fourier series coefficients.

$c_0 = 0, c_1 = \frac{1}{2j}, c_2 = 0, c_3 = -\frac{1}{2j}$

18.7 Three Fourier series coefficients of a periodic, real-valued sequence $x[n]$ with period $N = 4$ are known to be

$c_0 = 1, c_2 = -1$ and $c_3 = j$

Obtain the sample value $x[1]$.

18.8 Given the Fourier coefficients $c[k]$ of a sawtooth sequence of period $N = 16$, plot the periodic sequence resulting from a partial Fourier series synthesis using only the three lowest-order Fourier coefficients.

$$c[k\_] := \frac{1}{16} \text{Sum} [\text{SawtoothWave} [n / 16] \, e^{-I \frac{\pi}{8} k n}, \{n, 0, 15\}]$$

19 | Discrete-Time Fourier Transform

The discrete-time Fourier transform (DTFT) is the discrete-time counterpart of the continuous-time Fourier transform (CTFT). It plays the same role in the discrete-time domain as the CTFT does in the continuous-time domain by providing insight into the spectral content of signals and the frequency response of linear shift-invariant (LSI) systems.

Definition and Existence

The DTFT $X(e^{j\omega})$ of a sequence $x[n]$ is defined by the following sum (analysis formula)

$$X(e^{j\omega}) = \sum_{n=-\infty}^{\infty} x[n]\, e^{-j\omega n}$$

In general, the Fourier transform $X(e^{j\omega})$ is a complex function of frequency ω. Thus it may be written

$$X(e^{j\omega}) = |X(e^{j\omega})|\, e^{j\theta(\omega)}$$

where the quantity $|X(e^{j\omega})|$ is called the magnitude function (also called magnitude spectrum) and the quantity $\theta(\omega)$ is called the phase function (phase spectrum). The phase function is typically restricted to the values $-\pi \leq \theta(\omega) \leq \pi$.

The DTFT is an infinite series that may or may not converge. A sufficient condition for the existence of the Fourier transform is that the sequence $x[n]$ needs to be absolutely summable, namely

$$\sum_{n=-\infty}^{\infty} |x[n]| < \infty$$

This guarantees the existence of the Fourier transform $X(e^{j\omega})$ as it bounds the magnitude of the Fourier transform

$$|X(e^{j\omega})| = \left|\sum_{n=-\infty}^{\infty} x[n]\, e^{-j\omega n}\right| \leq \sum_{n=-\infty}^{\infty} |x[n]|\, |e^{-j\omega n}| \leq \sum_{n=-\infty}^{\infty} |x[n]| < \infty$$

The sequence $x[n]$ can be computed from its DTFT $X(e^{j\omega})$ using the following Fourier integral

$$x[n] = \frac{1}{2\pi} \int_{-\pi}^{\pi} X(e^{j\omega}) e^{j\omega n} \, d\omega$$

This formula is commonly known as the synthesis formula, or, alternatively, the inverse DTFT.

The DTFT is periodic with a period of 2π as shown here

$$X(e^{j(\omega+2\pi)}) = \sum_{n=-\infty}^{\infty} x[n] \, e^{-j(\omega+2\pi)n}$$

$$= \sum_{n=-\infty}^{\infty} x[n] \, e^{-j\omega n} \, e^{-j2\pi n}$$

$$= \sum_{n=-\infty}^{\infty} x[n] \, e^{-j\omega n}(1)$$

$$= X(e^{j\omega})$$

The frequency interval $-\pi \le \omega \le \pi$ (or $0 \le \omega \le 2\pi$) is known as the fundamental interval.

Example 1

Obtain the DTFT of the finite-length sequence

$$x[n] = \delta[n+1] + \delta[n] + \delta[n-1]$$

This displays the sequence:

In[•]:= **DiscretePlot [$\delta_{n+1} + \delta_n + \delta_{n-1}$, $\boxed{\cdots \; \updownarrow}$]**

Out[•]=

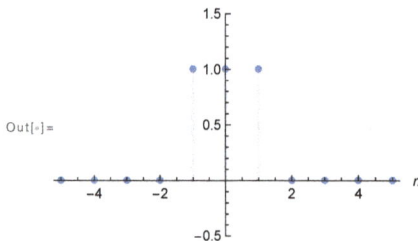

Solution

The sequence is finite length and finite valued, so the DTFT exists. Direct evaluation of the DTFT using the function FourierSequenceTransform gives the following result:

In[•]:= **FourierSequenceTransform [$\delta_{n+1} + \delta_n + \delta_{n-1}$, n, ω] // Simplify // ExpToTrig**

Out[•]= $1 + 2 \cos[\omega]$

Step-by-step

Substituting sequence $x[n]$ into the definition gives

$$X(e^{j\omega}) = \sum_{n=-\infty}^{\infty} x[n]\, e^{-j\omega n}$$

$$= \sum_{n=-1}^{1} (1)\, e^{-j\omega n}$$

which yields the following result

$$= e^{j\omega} + 1 + e^{-j\omega} = 1 + 2\cos(\omega)$$

Example 2

Determine the DTFT of the exponential sequence

$$x[n] = r^n\, u[n], \qquad |r| < 1$$

Solution

First, this confirms that the given sequence is absolutely summable and therefore the Fourier transform exists:

In[•]:=**Sum [r^n UnitStep [n] , { n, $-\infty$, ∞ } , GenerateConditions $\rightarrow$ True]**

Out[•]=$\dfrac{1}{1-r}$ if Abs [r] < 1

Evaluation of the DTFT returns the following result:

In[•]:=**FourierSequenceTransform [r^n UnitStep [n] , n, ω]**

Out[•]=$\dfrac{e^{i\,\omega}}{e^{i\,\omega} - r}$

Step-by-step

Substitute the sequence $x[n]$ into the definition

$$X(e^{j\omega}) = \sum_{n=-\infty}^{\infty} x[n]\, e^{-j\omega n} = \sum_{n=0}^{\infty} r^n\, e^{-j\omega n}$$

Rewrite the summand as α^n, with $\alpha = r\, e^{-j\omega}$

$$= \sum_{n=0}^{\infty} \left(r e^{-j\omega} \right)^n$$

Use the well-known sum formula $\sum_{n=0}^{\infty} \alpha^n = \dfrac{1}{1-\alpha}$ to arrive at the following result

$$= \dfrac{1}{1-re^{-j\omega}}, \qquad |r| < 1$$

Visualizing the DTFT

There are a number of common techniques for plotting and visualizing the spectrum of a signal. For example, consider the DTFT of the sequence in Example 2 with $r = 2/3$:

In[•]:= $X[\omega\_] := \dfrac{1}{1 - \frac{2}{3} e^{-i\omega}}$;

Frequently, the magnitude (sometimes magnitude squared), the phase, or both are of interest. Sometimes it may be of interest to view the real and imaginary parts of the spectrum. Furthermore, due to the periodicity of the Fourier transform, it is common to plot the spectra on the fundamental interval only, either $0 \le \omega \le 2\pi$ or $-\pi \le \omega \le \pi$.

This shows the magnitude, phase, and real and imaginary parts of the DTFT function for the two different choices of the fundamental interval:

In[•]:= **Manipulate [⋯ ✦]**

Out[•]=

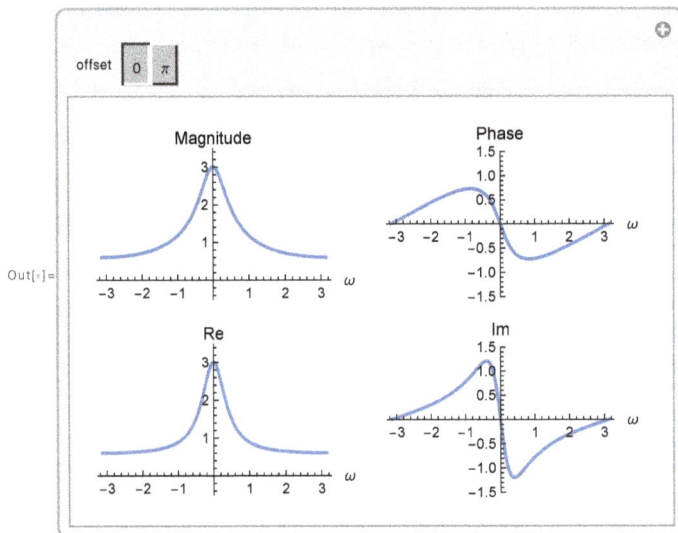

This shows the magnitude of the DTFT on an extended domain, revealing the 2π periodicity:

In[•]:= **Plot [Abs [X [ω]], ⋯ ✦]**

Out[•]=

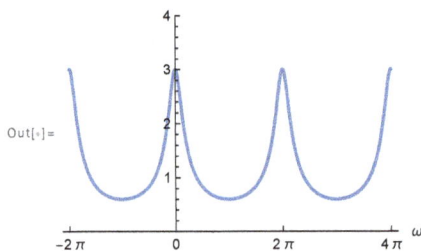

For real signals, the magnitude has even symmetry, so it is sufficient to plot $|X(e^{j\omega})|$ on the interval $0 \le \omega \le \pi$:

In[∘]:=**Plot [Abs [X [ω]] , ⋯ +]**

Out[∘]=

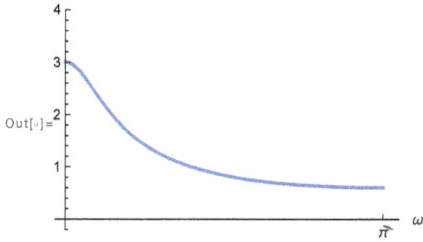

Finally, it is common practice to scale the magnitude logarithmically and to use linear scaling on the frequency axis:

In[∘]:=**Plot [20 Log10 [Abs [$\dfrac{X[\omega]}{X[0]}$]] , ⋯ +]**

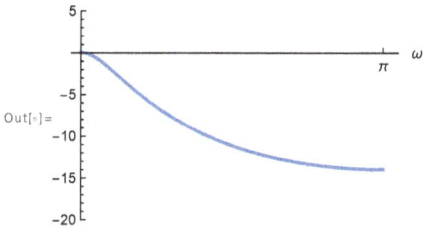

Out[∘]=

Example 3

Obtain the inverse Fourier transform of the following function of frequency

$$X(e^{j\omega}) = \begin{cases} 1, & -\dfrac{\pi}{3} + 2\pi m \le \omega \le \dfrac{\pi}{3} + 2\pi m \\ 0, & \text{else} \end{cases}$$

where m is an integer. This shows the magnitude spectrum on the fundamental half interval $0 \le \omega \le \pi$:

In[∘]:=**Plot [UnitBox [$\dfrac{\omega}{\dfrac{2\pi}{3}}$] , ⋯ +]**

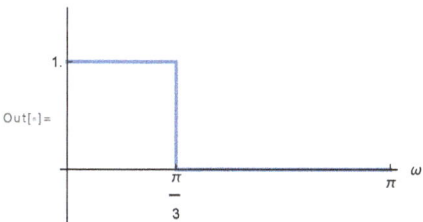

Out[∘]=

Solution

Substituting the function into the inverse DTFT returns:

In[•]:=**InverseFourierSequenceTransform [UnitBox [$\dfrac{3}{2\pi}\,\omega$] , ω, n]**

Out[•]=$\dfrac{\text{Sin}\left[\frac{n\pi}{3}\right]}{n\pi}$

Here is a plot of $x[n]$:

In[•]:=**DiscretePlot [$\dfrac{1}{3}$ Sinc [$\dfrac{\pi}{3}$ n] , $\boxed{\cdots\;+}$]**

Out[•]=

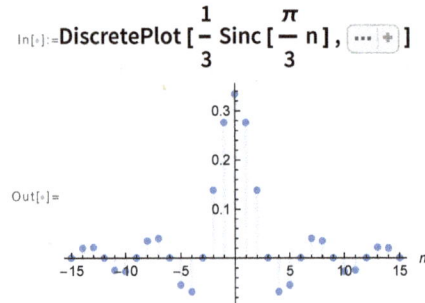

Step-by-step

Directly from the definition of the inverse discrete Fourier transform (DFT), the derivation proceeds as follows

$$x[n] = \frac{1}{2\pi} \int_{-\frac{\pi}{3}}^{\frac{\pi}{3}} e^{j\omega n}\, d\omega$$

$$= \frac{1}{2\pi}\,\frac{1}{jn}\, e^{j\omega n}\, \Big|_{-\frac{\pi}{3}}^{\frac{\pi}{3}}$$

$$= \frac{1}{2\pi}\,\frac{1}{jn}\left(e^{j\frac{\pi}{3}n} - e^{-j\frac{\pi}{3}n} \right)$$

$$= \frac{\sin\!\left(n\frac{\pi}{3}\right)}{n\pi}$$

The Fourier Transform of Periodic Sequences

Periodic sequences do not satisfy the DTFT existence condition. For example:

In[•]:=**Sum [Abs [Cos [$\dfrac{\pi}{2}$ n]] , {n, $-\infty$, ∞}]**

⋯ Sum : Sum does not converge.

Out[•]=$\displaystyle\sum_{n=-\infty}^{\infty} \text{Abs}\left[\text{Cos}\left[\dfrac{n\pi}{2}\right]\right]$

However, periodic sequences do have Fourier transforms, but they must be obtained indirectly using the Fourier series and are formulated in terms of the

Dirac delta function. To derive the Fourier transform representation of periodic sequences, proceed as follows.

Obtain the inverse DTFT of the following periodic impulse train

$$X(e^{j\omega}) = 2\pi \sum_{m=-\infty}^{\infty} \delta(\omega - \omega_0 + 2\pi m)$$

Here is a plot of the function:

In[•]:=**Graphics [** ⋯ **+** **]**

Out[•]=

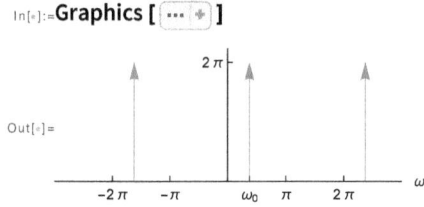

The inverse DTFT gives:

In[•]:=**InverseFourierSequenceTransform [2 π DiracDelta [** ω **–** $\omega 0$ **] ,** ω**, n]**

Out[•]=$e^{i \, n \, \omega 0}$

This establishes the following relation between a complex exponential sequence in time and a periodic impulse train in the frequency domain

$$e^{j\omega_0 n} \overset{\mathcal{F}}{\longleftrightarrow} 2\pi \sum_{m=-\infty}^{\infty} \delta(\omega - \omega_0 + 2\pi m)$$

This important result allows you to obtain the Fourier transform of any periodic sequence. Recall that a periodic sequence $x[n]$ with period N has the following Fourier series representation

$$x[n] = \sum_{k=0}^{N-1} c_k \, e^{j\frac{2\pi}{N} kn}$$

Therefore, the Fourier transform of the periodic sequence $x[n]$ must be of the following form

$$X(e^{j\omega}) = 2\pi \sum_{m=-\infty}^{\infty} \left(\sum_{k=0}^{N-1} c_k \, \delta\left(\omega - \frac{2\pi}{N} k + 2\pi m\right) \right)$$

On the fundamental interval $0 \le \omega \le 2\pi$, this formula simplifies to the following

$$X(e^{j\omega}) = 2\pi \sum_{k=0}^{N-1} c_k \, \delta\left(\omega - \frac{2\pi}{N} k\right)$$

Thus the Fourier transform of a periodic sequence is a sum of scaled and shifted unit impulses, repeating periodically every 2π. Note the similarity with the Fourier transform of periodic continuous-time signals.

Example 4

Obtain the DTFT of the following periodic signal

$$x[n] = \cos\left(\frac{\pi}{2}\, n\right)$$

Solution

The sequence $x[n]$ has period $N = 4$. The Fourier series coefficients are $c_1 = c_3 = \frac{1}{2}$, and you can immediately write the Fourier transform as

$$X(e^{j\omega}) = 2\pi \sum_{m=-\infty}^{\infty} \left(c_1\, \delta\left(\omega - \frac{\pi}{2} + 2\pi m\right) + c_3\, \delta\left(\omega - \frac{3\pi}{2} + 2\pi m\right)\right)$$

$$= \pi \sum_{m=-\infty}^{\infty} \left(\delta\left(\omega - \frac{\pi}{2} + 2\pi m\right) + \delta\left(\omega - \frac{3\pi}{2} + 2\pi m\right)\right)$$

This shows the result on the fundamental interval $0 \le \omega \le 2\pi$:

In[ ]:= **Graphics [⋯ ✦]**

Out[ ]=

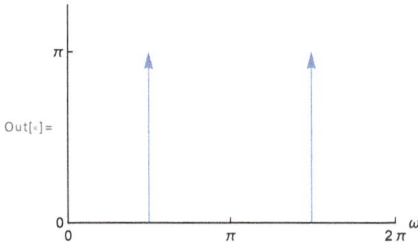

Example 5

Obtain and plot the Fourier transform of the following sawtooth wave:

In[ ]:= **DiscretePlot [SawtoothWave [n / 16], ⋯ ✦]**

Out[ ]=

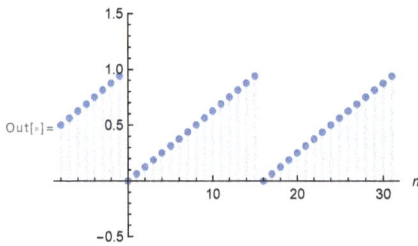

Solution

Recall from the earlier discussion of the discrete-time Fourier series that the Fourier coefficients of the sawtooth wave with period $N = 16$ can be calculated as follows:

In[·]:=$c[k\_] := \frac{1}{16}$ Sum [SawtoothWave [n / 16] $e^{-i \frac{2\pi}{16} k n}$, {n, 0, 15}];

  c[k] // Simplify // Expand

Out[·]=$\frac{1}{256} e^{-\frac{1}{8} i k\pi} + \frac{1}{128} e^{-\frac{1}{4} i k\pi} + \frac{3}{256} e^{-\frac{3}{8} i k\pi} + \frac{1}{64} e^{-\frac{1}{2} i k\pi} + \frac{5}{256} e^{-\frac{5}{8} i k\pi} +$

$\frac{3}{128} e^{-\frac{3}{4} i k\pi} + \frac{7}{256} e^{-\frac{7}{8} i k\pi} + \frac{1}{32} e^{-i k\pi} + \frac{9}{256} e^{-\frac{9}{8} i k\pi} + \frac{5}{128} e^{-\frac{5}{4} i k\pi} +$

$\frac{11}{256} e^{-\frac{11}{8} i k\pi} + \frac{3}{64} e^{-\frac{3}{2} i k\pi} + \frac{13}{256} e^{-\frac{13}{8} i k\pi} + \frac{7}{128} e^{-\frac{7}{4} i k\pi} + \frac{15}{256} e^{-\frac{15}{8} i k\pi}$

Evaluating for $k = 0, 1, \ldots, 15$, one gets the following values:

In[·]:=**Table [c[k], {k, 0, 15}] // N**

Out[·]= { 0.46875, −0.03125 + 0.157104 i, −0.03125 + 0.0754442 i, −0.03125 + 0.0467689 i,
    −0.03125 + 0.03125 i, −0.03125 + 0.0208806 i, −0.03125 + 0.0129442 i,
    −0.03125 + 0.00621601 i, −0.03125, −0.03125 − 0.00621601 i,
    −0.03125 − 0.0129442 i, −0.03125 − 0.0208806 i, −0.03125 − 0.03125 i,
    −0.03125 − 0.0467689 i, −0.03125 − 0.0754442 i, −0.03125 − 0.157104 i }

The Fourier transform is

$$X(e^{j\omega}) = 2\pi \sum_{m=-\infty}^{\infty} \left(\sum_{k=0}^{15} c_k \, \delta\left(\omega - \frac{2\pi}{16} k + 2\pi m\right) \right)$$

This shows the result using the fundamental interval $0 \le \omega \le 2\pi$:

In[·]:=**Graphics [⋯ ✦]**

Out[·]=
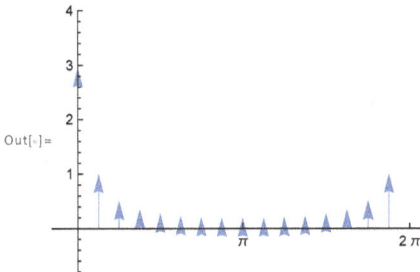

Summary

The DTFT was presented.

Several DTFT pairs were obtained

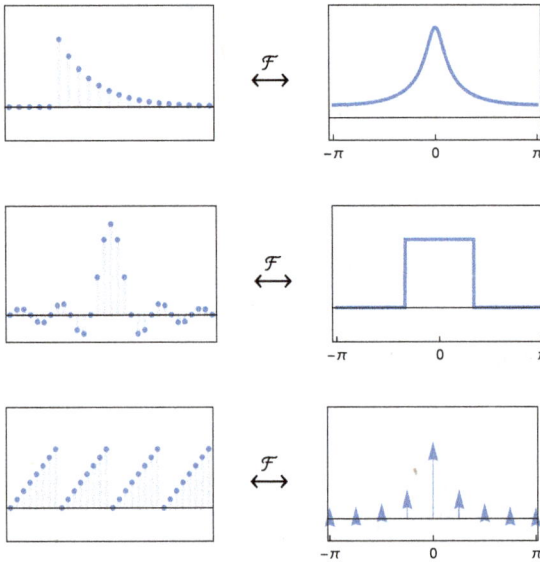

The DTFT was shown to have a periodicity of 2π.

Exercises

Download the solutions manual at wolfr.am/eTextbook-SSSP

19.1 Obtain the general formulas for the following two values of the DTFT of a sequence $x[n]$: $X(e^{j0})$ and $X(e^{j\pi})$.

19.2 Show that the sequence $x[n] = r^n u[n]$ with $|r| < 1$ is absolutely summable.

19.3 Determine the DTFT of the two-sided sequence $x[n] = r^{|n|}$, $|r| < 1$.

19.4 Determine the DTFT of the following finite-length sequence.

$$x[n] = \begin{cases} 1/5, & 0 \le n \le 4 \\ 0, & \text{else} \end{cases}$$

19.5 Determine the inverse DTFT of the following Fourier transform.

$$X(e^{j\omega}) = \cos(3\omega)$$

19.6 Obtain the DTFT of the following periodic sequence.

$$x[n] = (-1)^n$$

20 | Discrete-Time Fourier Transform Theorems

As was the case with the continuous-time Fourier transform (CTFT) discussed earlier, it is useful to be familiar with properties of the discrete-time Fourier transform (DTFT) and with several theorems as they help in understanding how certain operations in time or frequency relate. A few of the most important theorems are:

- Linearity
- Time shift
- Convolution in time
- Parseval's relation

Relevant DTFT properties were discussed earlier.

Linearity

Given the transform pairs $x[n] \overset{\mathcal{F}}{\longleftrightarrow} X(e^{j\omega})$ and $y[n] \overset{\mathcal{F}}{\longleftrightarrow} Y(e^{j\omega})$, the DTFT of a superposition of sequences $x[n]$ and $y[n]$ is

$$ax[n] + b\,y[n] \overset{\mathcal{F}}{\longleftrightarrow} aX(e^{j\omega}) + bY(e^{j\omega})$$

Example 1

Given the following two sequences, use linearity to obtain the DTFT of the difference $x[n] - y[n]$:

```
In[•]:= x [ n_ ] := (4/5)^n UnitStep [ n ] ;

       y [ n_ ] := (1/3)^n UnitStep [ n ] ;
```

Solution

According to the linearity property, the DTFT of $x[n] - y[n]$ is equal to the difference of the Fourier transforms of the two sequences.

The result is:

In[•]:=**FourierSequenceTransform [x [n], n, ω] −**
    FourierSequenceTransform [y [n], n, ω] / / Simplify

$$\text{Out[•]=}\frac{7\,e^{i\,\omega}}{4 - 17\,e^{i\,\omega} + 15\,e^{2\,i\,\omega}}$$

The result can be confirmed by direct evaluation of the difference sequence:

In[•]:=**FourierSequenceTransform [x [n] − y [n], n, ω]**

$$\text{Out[•]=}\frac{7\,e^{i\,\omega}}{4 - 17\,e^{i\,\omega} + 15\,e^{2\,i\,\omega}}$$

Time Shift

Given the transform pair $x[n] \overset{\mathcal{F}}{\longleftrightarrow} X(e^{j\omega})$, the Fourier transform of a time-shifted sequence is

$$x[n - n_0] \overset{\mathcal{F}}{\longleftrightarrow} e^{-j\omega n_0}\, X(e^{j\omega})$$

Proof

In order to prove this property, substitute the shifted sequence into the analysis formula

$$Y(e^{j\omega}) = \sum_{n=-\infty}^{\infty} y[n]e^{-j\omega n}$$

$$= \sum_{n=-\infty}^{\infty} x[n - n_0]\, e^{-j\omega n}$$

Now use the substitution $m = n - n_0$

$$= \sum_{m=-\infty}^{\infty} x[m]e^{-j\omega(m+n_0)}$$

$$= e^{-j\omega n_0} \sum_{m=-\infty}^{\infty} x[m]e^{-j\omega m}$$

Note that the remaining sum is the Fourier transform of the sequence $x[m]$

$$= e^{-j\omega n_0}\, X(e^{j\omega})$$

This concludes the proof.

Observe that the magnitude of the Fourier transform stays unchanged as a sequence is shifted; it is only the phase that is affected.

Example 2

Let $X(e^{j\omega})$ denote the DTFT of the sequence $x[n]$ shown in the following:

$\text{In[}\cdot\text{]:=}\textbf{DiscretePlot} \left[\dfrac{1}{4}\,\delta_n + \dfrac{1}{2}\,\delta_{n-1} + \dfrac{3}{4}\,\delta_{n-2} + \delta_{n-3}, \boxed{\cdots \; +} \; \right]$

$\text{Out[}\cdot\text{]=}$

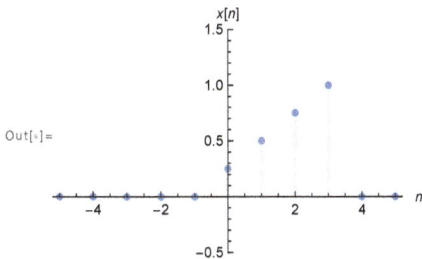

Express the DTFT of the sequence $y[n]$ shown here in terms of $X(e^{j\omega})$. Do not evaluate $X(e^{j\omega})$

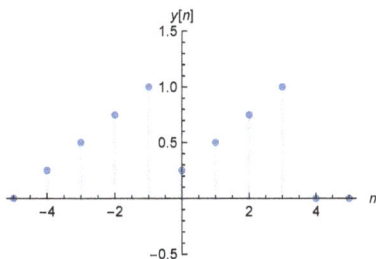

Solution

Note that $y[n] = x[n] + x[n+4]$, so linearity and the time shift theorem give the following result

$$Y(e^{j\omega}) = X(e^{j\omega}) + e^{j4\omega}X(e^{j\omega})$$

Time Convolution

If $x[n]$, $h[n]$, and $y[n]$ are three sequences such that

$$y[n] = x[n] * h[n]$$

where $*$ denotes convolution, then

$$Y(e^{j\omega}) = X(e^{j\omega}) \cdot H(e^{j\omega})$$

where $X(e^{j\omega})$, $H(e^{j\omega})$, and $Y(e^{j\omega})$ are the DTFTs of $x[n]$, $h[n]$, and $y[n]$, respectively.

This maps the convolution of two sequences to multiplication of their Fourier transforms. This greatly assists in the analysis of signals and systems, as the effect of multiplication is easier to understand than convolution.

Proof

The convolution sum is

$$y[n] = \sum_{k=-\infty}^{\infty} h[k]\, x[n-k]$$

The Fourier transform is

$$Y(e^{j\omega}) = \sum_{n=-\infty}^{\infty} \left(\sum_{k=-\infty}^{\infty} h[k]x[n-k] \right) e^{-j\omega n}$$

Substituting $m = n - k$

$$Y(e^{j\omega}) = \sum_{m=-\infty}^{\infty} \sum_{k=-\infty}^{\infty} h[k]x[m]e^{-j\omega(m+k)}$$

$$= \sum_{k=-\infty}^{\infty} h[k]\left(\sum_{m=-\infty}^{\infty} x[m]e^{-j\omega m} \right) e^{-j\omega k}$$

$$= \sum_{k=-\infty}^{\infty} h[k]\left(X(e^{j\omega}) \right) e^{-j\omega k}$$

$$= X(e^{j\omega}) \sum_{k=-\infty}^{\infty} h[k] e^{-j\omega k}$$

$$= X(e^{j\omega}) \cdot H(e^{j\omega})$$

Example 3

Verify the DTFT convolution theorem, given the following sequences:

In[•]:= x [n_] := $\left(\dfrac{1}{2}\right)^n$ UnitStep [n];

y [n_] := $\left(\dfrac{2}{3}\right)^n$ UnitStep [n];

Solution

Convolution gives:

In[•]:= DiscreteConvolve [x [k], y [k], k, n]

Out[•]= $\begin{cases} 6^{-n}\left(-3^{1+n} + 4^{1+n}\right) & n \geq 0 \\ 0 & \text{True} \end{cases}$

The Fourier transform of the result is:

In[•]:= FourierSequenceTransform [%, n, ω]

Out[•]= $\dfrac{6\, e^{2 i \omega}}{2 - 7\, e^{i \omega} + 6\, e^{2 i \omega}}$

Now the product of the Fourier transforms of the two sequences is:

In[•]:=**FourierSequenceTransform [x [n] , n, ω]**
    FourierSequenceTransform [y [n] , n, ω] / / Simplify

Out[•]=$\dfrac{6\,e^{2\,i\,\omega}}{2 - 7\,e^{i\,\omega} + 6\,e^{2\,i\,\omega}}$

This verifies the convolution theorem.

Parseval's Relation

If sequence $x[n]$ and Fourier transform $X(e^{j\omega})$ are a Fourier transform pair

$$x[n] \stackrel{\mathcal{F}}{\longleftrightarrow} X(e^{j\omega})$$

then

$$\sum_{n=-\infty}^{\infty} |x[n]|^2 = \frac{1}{2\pi} \int_{2\pi} |X(e^{j\omega})|^2 \, d\omega$$

This relation states that the total energy of the signal $x[n]$ can be determined by integrating the power spectrum $|X(e^{j\omega})|^2$ over a 2π frequency interval.

Example 4

Verify Parseval's relation for the sequence:

In[•]:=**x [n_] := $\dfrac{1}{3}$ (δ_{n+1} + δ_n + δ_{n-1})**

Solution

Evaluate the energy using the time-domain definition of the sequence:

In[•]:=**Sum [Abs [x [n]]^2, { n, −1, 1 }]**

Out[•]=$\dfrac{1}{3}$

The Fourier transform of this sequence is:

In[•]:=**FourierSequenceTransform [x [n] , n, ω] / / ExpToTrig / / Simplify**

Out[•]=$\dfrac{1}{3}$ (1 + 2 Cos [ω])

Evaluating the energy using Parseval's relation gives:

$$\text{In[·]:=} \frac{1}{2\pi} \text{Integrate} \left[\left(\frac{1}{3} \left(1 + 2 \cos [\omega] \right) \right)^2, \{\omega, -\pi, \pi\} \right]$$

$$\text{Out[·]=} \frac{1}{3}$$

This verifies Parseval's relation.

Summary

The following important Fourier transform theorems were presented:

- Linearity
- Time shift
- Time convolution
- Parseval's relation

Examples showing applications of the properties and theorems in solving several elementary signal processing problems were given.

Exercises

Download the solutions manual at wolfr.am/eTextbook-SSSP

20.1 The Fourier transform of a sequence $x[n]$ is $X(e^{j\omega})$. Determine the Fourier transform of the following sequence.

$$y[n] = \frac{1}{3} (x[n] + x[n-1] + x[n-2])$$

20.2 Let $X(e^{j\omega})$ denote the DTFT of the sequence $x[n]$. Determine the DTFT of the sequence $y[n] = x[-n]$.

20.3 Obtain the DTFT of the sequence $x[n] = \left(\frac{2}{3} \right)^{-n} u[-n]$ by direct evaluation and by using the result of Exercise 2.

20.4 Convolve the following two sequences using the convolution theorem.

$$x[n] = \delta[n] + 2\,\delta[n-1] + 2\,\delta[n-2] - \delta[n-3]$$

$$h[n] = \delta[n] - \delta[n-1]$$

20.5 The Fourier transform magnitude $\left|X(e^{j\omega})\right|$ of the sequence $x[n] = \frac{1}{3}\left(\delta_n + \delta_{n-1} + \delta_{n-2}\right)$ is shown here.

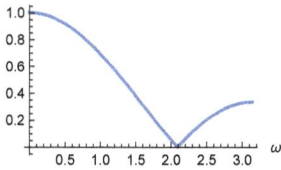

Obtain the Fourier transform of the sequence $y[n] = (-1)^n\, x[n]$ and plot the magnitude $\left|Y(e^{j\omega})\right|$. How does it compare to the magnitude of the sequence $x[n]$?

21 | Discrete-Time Filters

Filters are widely used in electronics and telecommunication, including in radio, television, audio recording, radar, control systems, music synthesis, image processing, and computer graphics. In discrete-time signal processing, a filter is an algorithm, a numerical computation on a computer, a micro-controller, or an embedded system.

The earlier discussion of Fourier domain analysis of signals and linear shift-invariant (LSI) systems laid the foundation for a deeper discussion of digital filters, their types, and the effect they have on signals passing through them.

Filtering in Time and Frequency

The previously discussed discrete-time Fourier transform (DTFT) convolution theorem leads to one of the more important results in the study of signal processing and LSI systems, namely that the application of a filter to a signal is effectively a multiplication in the frequency domain of the Fourier transforms of the signal and the filter's unit sample response.

As derived earlier, the response $y[n]$ of an LSI system with impulse response $h[n]$ to an input $x[n]$ is given by the following convolution sum

$$y[n] = \sum_{k=-\infty}^{\infty} h[k]\, x[n-k]$$

Now, according to the Fourier transform convolution theorem, there is the following equivalent relation between Fourier transforms of the three signals

$$Y\!\left(e^{j\omega}\right) = H\!\left(e^{j\omega}\right) \cdot X\!\left(e^{j\omega}\right)$$

The function $H\!\left(e^{j\omega}\right)$ is known as the filter's frequency response and it is the Fourier transform of a filter's unit sample response $h[n]$. The unit sample response $h[n]$ and the frequency response $H\!\left(e^{j\omega}\right)$ are therefore a Fourier transform pair.

Ideal Filters

Ideal filters allow for distortion-free transmission for a certain range of frequencies while simultaneously suppressing the signal's remaining frequencies. In a distortion-free system, the output must be a delayed and scaled copy of the input or zero

$$y[n] = A\,x[n - n_0]$$

In the frequency domain, the input and output are related as follows

$$Y(e^{j\omega}) = A e^{-j\omega n_0} X(e^{j\omega}) = H(e^{j\omega}) X(e^{j\omega})$$

Therefore the frequency response of the ideal filter is

$$H(e^{j\omega}) = A e^{-j\omega n_0}$$

This gives a constant magnitude and linear phase as a function of frequency

$$|H(e^{j\omega})| = A, \qquad \angle H(e^{j\omega}) = -\omega n_0$$

This shows the frequency response of an ideal filter with $A = 1$ and $n_0 = 1$:

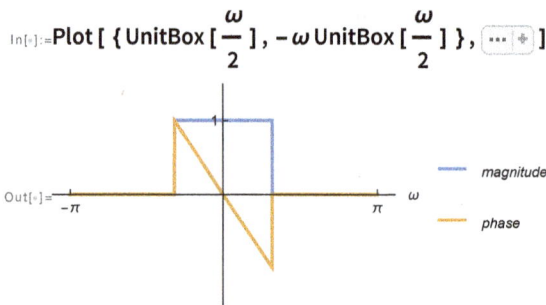

Ideal Filter Types

The following four magnitude responses exemplify the four most common types of frequency-selective ideal filters

The frequency interval over which the gain is nonzero is called the passband, while the range of frequencies over which the gain is zero is called the stopband. The frequency where a passband ends and a stopband begins is typically called the cutoff frequency. A filter that passes all frequencies is called an allpass filter. Examples of allpass filters include

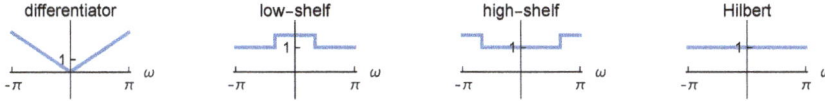

A differentiating filter approximates a continuous-time derivative, low-shelf and high-shelf filters are used to selectively attenuate (or boost) low or high signal frequencies, and a Hilbert filter has the effect of altering the phase of a sequence while leaving the magnitude unchanged.

The Unit Sample Response of an Ideal Lowpass Filter

The following defines an ideal zero-phase (i.e. $\angle H(e^{j\omega}) = 0$) lowpass filter with cutoff frequency $\omega_c = \frac{\pi}{3}$ on the frequency range $-\pi \leq \omega \leq \pi$

$$H(e^{j\omega}) = \begin{cases} 1, & 0 < |\omega| \leq \frac{\pi}{3} \\ 0, & \frac{\pi}{3} < |\omega| \leq \pi \end{cases}$$

Here is a plot of the magnitude response:

In[·]:=**Plot [UnitBox [** $\dfrac{3\,\omega}{2\,\pi}$ **] ,** [··· +] **]**

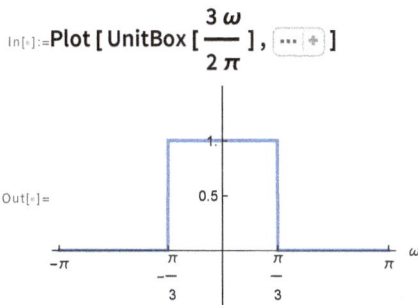

Out[·]=

The unit sample response of the given ideal zero-phase lowpass filter is obtained by taking the inverse DTFT of its frequency response function $H(e^{j\omega})$:

In[·]:=**InverseFourierSequenceTransform [UnitBox [3** $\dfrac{\omega}{2\,\pi}$ **] , ω, n]**

Out[·]= $\dfrac{\operatorname{Sin}\left[\frac{n\pi}{3}\right]}{n\,\pi}$

Here is a plot of the unit sample response:

In[•]:=**DiscretePlot** $\left[\frac{1}{3}\text{ Sinc}\left[\frac{\pi}{3}\text{ n}\right], \cdots + \right]$

Out[•]=

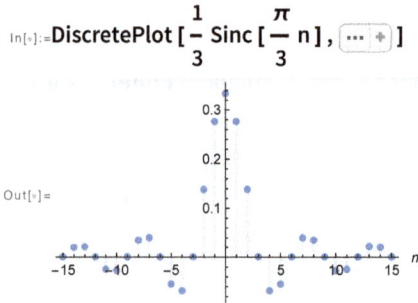

Note that the frequency response function is real and that the impulse response has even symmetry. Importantly, also note that the impulse response is non-causal and of infinite duration.

Step-by-step

The inverse DTFT gives the unit sample response

$$h[n] = \frac{1}{2\pi} \int_{-\pi}^{\pi} H(e^{j\omega}) e^{j\omega n} \, d\omega$$

The impulse response of an ideal zero-phase lowpass filter with cutoff frequency ω_c is

$$h[n] = \frac{1}{2\pi} \int_{-\omega_c}^{\omega_c} e^{j\omega n} \, d\omega$$

$$= \frac{1}{2\pi} \frac{1}{jn} e^{j\omega n}\Big|_{-\omega_c}^{\omega_c}$$

$$= \frac{1}{2\pi} \left(\frac{1}{jn} e^{j\omega_c n} - \frac{1}{-jn} e^{-j\omega_c n} \right)$$

$$= \frac{\sin(\omega_c n)}{n\pi}$$

$$= \frac{\omega_c}{\pi} \text{ sinc}(\omega_c n)$$

The Unit Sample Response of a Differentiator

The following defines an ideal differentiating filter, or simply differentiator, on the frequency range $-\pi \le \omega \le \pi$

$$H(e^{j\omega}) = j\omega$$

Here is a plot of the magnitude response:

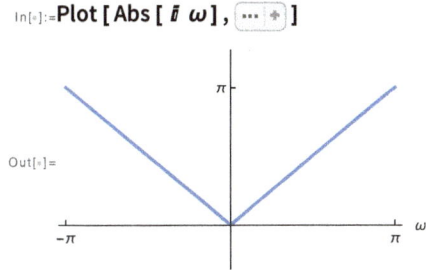

In[•]:=**Plot [Abs [$\tilde{h}$ ω] , $\boxed{\cdots\ \ +}$]**

Out[•]=

The unit sample response of the filter is obtained by taking the inverse DTFT of its frequency response function $H(e^{j\omega})$:

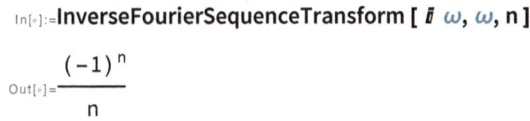

In[•]:=**InverseFourierSequenceTransform [$\tilde{h}$ ω, ω, n]**

Out[•]=$\dfrac{(-1)^n}{n}$

At $n = 0$, the unit sample response reduces to:

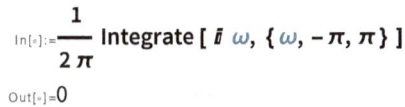

In[•]:=$\dfrac{1}{2\pi}$ **Integrate [$\tilde{h}$ ω, { ω, $-\pi$, π }]**

Out[•]=0

Here is a plot of the unit sample response:

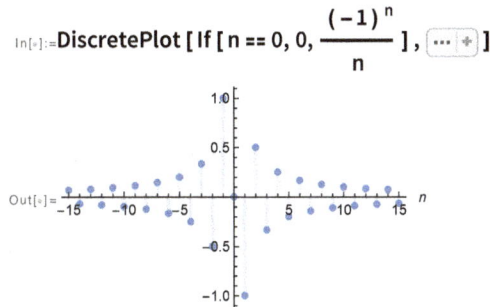

In[•]:=**DiscretePlot [If [n == 0, 0, $\dfrac{(-1)^n}{n}$] , $\boxed{\cdots\ \ +}$]**

Out[•]=

Note that the impulse response is non-causal and of infinite duration.

Step-by-step

The inverse DTFT gives the unit sample response

$$h[n] = \frac{1}{2\pi} \int_{-\pi}^{\pi} H(e^{j\omega}) e^{j\omega n} \, d\omega$$

$$= \frac{j}{2\pi} \int_{-\pi}^{\pi} \omega e^{j\omega n} \, d\omega$$

integrating by parts with $u = \omega$, $du = d\omega$, $dv = e^{j\omega n}\, d\omega$, and $v = \frac{1}{jn}\, e^{j\omega n}$, you get

$$= \frac{j}{2\pi}\frac{1}{jn}\,\omega e^{j\omega n}\,|_{-\pi}^{\pi} - \frac{j}{2\pi}\frac{1}{jn}\int_{-\pi}^{\pi} e^{j\omega n}\, d\omega$$

$$= \frac{j}{2\pi}\frac{1}{jn}\left(\pi e^{j\pi n} + \pi e^{-j\pi n}\right) - \frac{j}{2\pi}\frac{1}{jn}\frac{1}{jn}\, e^{j\omega n}\,|_{-\pi}^{\pi}$$

$$= \frac{1}{n}\cos(\pi n) - \frac{j}{2\pi}\frac{1}{jn}\frac{1}{jn}\left(e^{j\pi n} - e^{-j\pi n}\right)$$

$$= \frac{1}{n}\cos(\pi n) - \frac{1}{\pi n^2}\sin(\pi n)$$

Finally, for integer values of n, the formula reduces to

$$h[n] = \frac{(-1)^n}{n}$$

Frequency Response of FIR Filters

To derive the frequency response of a finite impulse response (FIR) filter, begin with the following input-output relation

$$y[n] = \sum_{k=\mathcal{N}_1}^{\mathcal{N}_2-1} h[k]\cdot x[n-k], \qquad \mathcal{N}_1 < \mathcal{N}_2$$

Without loss of generality, setting $\mathcal{N}_1 = 0$ and $\mathcal{N}_2 = \mathcal{N}$ gives the following more familiar form, that of a finite-length convolution sum

$$y[n] = \sum_{k=0}^{N-1} h[k]\cdot x[n-k]$$

Applying the DTFT and making use of the time shift theorem results in

$$Y(e^{j\omega}) = \sum_{k=0}^{N-1} h[k]e^{-j\omega k}X(e^{j\omega})$$

where $Y(e^{j\omega})$ and $X(e^{j\omega})$ are the Fourier transforms of the output and the input sequences, respectively.

The frequency response of the system is

$$H(e^{j\omega}) = \sum_{k=0}^{N-1} h[k]\, e^{-j\omega k}$$

$$= h[0] + h[1]e^{-j\omega} + h[2]e^{-j\omega 2} + \ldots + h[\mathcal{N}-1]e^{-j\omega(\mathcal{N}-1)}$$

Therefore, the frequency response of any FIR system is a polynomial in $e^{-j\omega}$.

Example 1

Obtain the frequency response of the following moving-average system

$$y[n] = \frac{1}{3}\left(x[n] + x[n-1] + x[n-2]\right)$$

Solution

The filter's unit sample response is given by

$$h[n] = \frac{1}{3} \left(\delta[n] + \delta[n-1] + \delta[n-2] \right)$$

Directly from the definition of the frequency response of an LSI system comes the following result:

In[•]:= **FourierSequenceTransform** $\left[\frac{1}{3} \left(\boldsymbol{\delta}_n + \boldsymbol{\delta}_{n-1} + \boldsymbol{\delta}_{n-2} \right), \text{n}, \boldsymbol{\omega} \right]$ **// Expand**

Out[•]= $\dfrac{1}{3} + \dfrac{e^{-i\,\omega}}{3} + \dfrac{1}{3}\,e^{-2\,i\,\omega}$

This shows the frequency response:

In[•]:= **GraphicsRow** [⋯ +]

Out[•]=

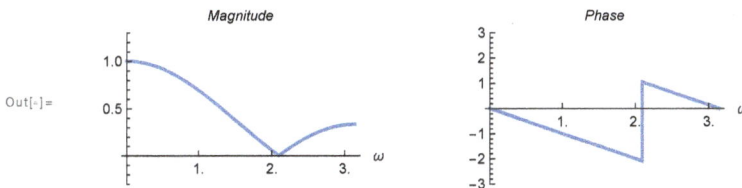

Step-by-step

Apply the Fourier transform and its time shift theorem to the non-recursive difference equation

$$\mathcal{F}\{y[n]\} = \mathcal{F}\left\{ \frac{1}{3} \left(x[n] + x[n-1] + x[n-2] \right) \right\}$$

$$Y(e^{j\omega}) = \frac{1}{3} \left(X(e^{j\omega}) + e^{-j\omega} X(e^{j\omega}) + e^{-2\,j\omega} X(e^{j\omega}) \right)$$

The frequency response is given by the ratio $Y(e^{j\omega}) / X(e^{j\omega})$

$$H(e^{j\omega}) = \frac{Y(e^{j\omega})}{X(e^{j\omega})} = \frac{1}{3} \left(1 + e^{-j\omega} + e^{-2\,j\omega} \right)$$

Frequency Response of IIR Filters

Infinite impulse response (IIR) filters are described by linear constant coefficient difference equations. The frequency response of such systems may be obtained directly from the difference equation as shown next.

Consider a causal LSI system characterized by the following difference equation

$$\sum_{k=0}^{N} a_k\, y[n-k] = \sum_{k=0}^{M} b_k\, x[n-k]$$

Using the time-shift property of the DTFT, the frequency response is obtained as follows

$$\mathcal{F}\left\{ \sum_{k=0}^{N} a_k \, y[n-k] \right\} = \mathcal{F}\left\{ \sum_{k=0}^{M} b_k \, x[n-k] \right\}$$

$$\mathcal{F}\left\{a_0 \, y[n]\right\} + \mathcal{F}\left\{a_1 \, y[n-1]\right\} + \dots + \mathcal{F}\left\{a_N \, y[n-N]\right\} =$$
$$\mathcal{F}\left\{b_0 \, x[n]\right\} + \mathcal{F}\left\{b_1 \, x[n-1]\right\} + \dots + \mathcal{F}\left\{b_M \, x[n-M]\right\}$$

$$a_0 \, Y(e^{j\omega}) + a_1 \, e^{-j\omega} Y(e^{j\omega}) + \dots + a_N e^{-jN\omega} Y(e^{j\omega}) =$$
$$b_0 \, X(e^{j\omega}) + b_1 \, e^{-j\omega} X(e^{j\omega}) + \dots + b_M \, e^{-jM\omega} X(e^{j\omega})$$

Solving for the ratio of $Y(e^{j\omega})$ over $X(e^{j\omega})$ returns the following result

$$H(e^{j\omega}) = \frac{Y(e^{j\omega})}{X(e^{j\omega})} = \frac{b_0 + b_1 \, e^{-j\omega} + \dots + b_M \, e^{-jM\omega}}{a_0 + a_1 e^{-j\omega} + \dots + a_N e^{-jN\omega}}$$

Therefore, the frequency response of an IIR system is a rational polynomial in terms of powers of $e^{-j\omega}$.

Example 2

Determine the frequency response of a system defined by the following difference equation

$$y[n] - \frac{1}{2} \, y[n-R] = x[n]$$

Solution

Applying the Fourier transform and using the time shift theorem gives

$$\mathcal{F}\left\{y[n]\right\} - \mathcal{F}\left\{\frac{1}{2} \, y[n-R]\right\} = \mathcal{F}\left\{x[n]\right\}$$

$$Y(e^{j\omega}) - \frac{1}{2} e^{-j\omega R} \, Y(e^{j\omega}) = X(e^{j\omega})$$

$$Y(e^{j\omega}) \left(1 - \frac{1}{2} e^{-j\omega R}\right) = X(e^{j\omega})$$

$$H(e^{j\omega}) = \frac{Y(e^{j\omega})}{X(e^{j\omega})} = \frac{1}{1 - \frac{1}{2} e^{-j\omega R}}$$

This shows the magnitude response for $2 \leq R \leq 15$:

In[•]:=**Manipulate [** ⋯ ◆ **]**

Out[•]=

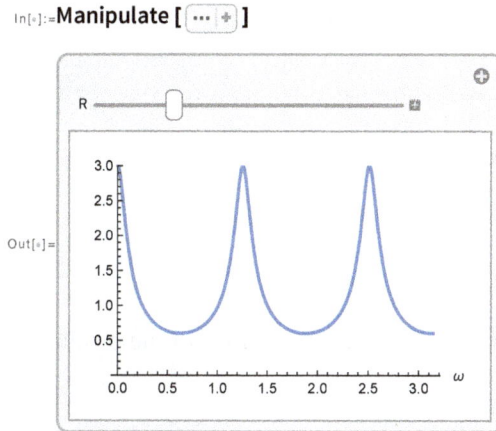

Due to the shape of its magnitude response, this system is commonly called a comb filter.

Sinusoidal Steady-State Response of LSI Systems

An important property of LSI systems is that for a certain type of an input signal, called an eigenfunction, the output signal is a scaled and shifted version of the input signal. The complex exponential $e^{j\omega n}$ is one such eigenfunction of LSI systems.

Recall that the output of an LSI system to an input $x[n]$, knowing its unit sample response $h[n]$, is given by a convolution sum

$$y[n] = \sum_{k=-\infty}^{\infty} h[k] \cdot x[n-k]$$

Now, if $x[n] = e^{j\omega n}$ for $-\infty < n < \infty$, then the output is

$$y[n] = \sum_{k=-\infty}^{\infty} h[k] \cdot e^{j\omega(n-k)}$$

$$= \left(\sum_{k=-\infty}^{\infty} h[k] e^{-j\omega k} \right) e^{j\omega n}$$

$$= H\!\left(e^{j\omega}\right) e^{j\omega n}$$

where the following notation was used

$$H\!\left(e^{j\omega}\right) = \sum_{k=-\infty}^{\infty} h[k] e^{-j\omega k}$$

In conclusion, the output of an LSI system to an exponential input of frequency ω is also an exponential sequence of the same frequency multiplied by a complex constant $H(e^{j\omega})$ (when evaluated at a specific frequency ω).

This is explored in greater detail in the following examples.

Example 3

An LSI discrete-time system has the following frequency response

$$H(e^{j\omega}) = \frac{1}{1 - \frac{1}{2}e^{-j\omega}}$$

Obtain the response to the following input

$$x[n] = \cos\left(\frac{\pi}{2}\,n\right)$$

Solution

By the convolution theorem, the response $y[n]$ is the inverse DTFT of the product $Y(e^{j\omega}) = H(e^{j\omega})X(e^{j\omega})$.

Direct application of the theorem gives the following result:

In[•]:=**InverseFourierSequenceTransform [**

$$(\frac{1}{1 - \frac{1}{2}\,e^{-i\,\omega}})\ \textbf{FourierSequenceTransform [Cos [}\frac{\pi}{2}\,\textbf{n] , n , }\omega\textbf{] , }\omega\textbf{, n]}$$

Out[•]=$\frac{2}{5}\left(2\cos\left[\frac{n\pi}{2}\right] + \sin\left[\frac{n\pi}{2}\right]\right)$

This shows the input $x[n]$ and the output $y[n]$:

In[•]:=**GraphicsRow [{···} ◆]**

Out[•]=

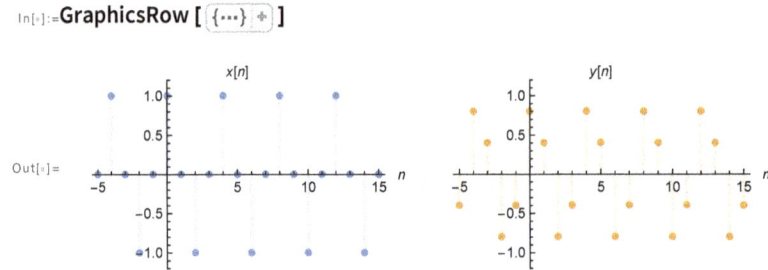

Step-by-step

LSI systems have the property that a response to a complex exponential is itself a complex exponential. It is convenient, therefore, to express the given input using Euler's identity

$$x[n] = \cos\left(\frac{\pi}{2}\,n\right) = \frac{1}{2}\left(e^{j\frac{\pi}{2}n} + e^{-j\frac{\pi}{2}n}\right)$$

Now, the output is guaranteed to be a sum of two scaled complex exponentials as shown here

$$y[n] = \frac{1}{2}\,H(e^{j\omega})_{\omega\to\frac{\pi}{2}}\,e^{j\frac{\pi}{2}n} + \frac{1}{2}\,H(e^{j\omega})_{\omega\to-\frac{\pi}{2}}\,e^{-j\frac{\pi}{2}n}$$

Evaluation of the frequency response $H(e^{j\omega})$ at the frequencies of $\pm \frac{\pi}{2}$ gives

$$= \frac{1}{2} \frac{1}{1-\frac{1}{2} e^{-j\frac{\pi}{2}}} e^{j\frac{\pi}{2} n} + \frac{1}{2} \frac{1}{1-\frac{1}{2} e^{j\frac{\pi}{2}}} e^{-j\frac{\pi}{2} n}$$

or the somewhat simpler form

$$= \frac{1}{2} \frac{1}{1+\frac{1}{2} j} e^{j\frac{\pi}{2} n} + \frac{1}{2} \frac{1}{1-\frac{1}{2} j} e^{-j\frac{\pi}{2} n}$$

It can be shown that further algebraic simplification leads to

$$= \frac{2}{5} \left(2 \cos\left(\frac{\pi}{2} n\right) + \sin\left(\frac{\pi}{2} n\right) \right)$$

Example 4

An LSI discrete-time system known as the Hilbert filter has the following frequency response

$$H(e^{j\omega}) = \begin{cases} j & -\pi \le \omega \le 0 \\ -j, & 0 \le \omega \le \pi \end{cases}$$

Obtain the response to the following input

$$x[n] = \cos\left(\frac{\pi}{2} n\right)$$

Solution

By the convolution theorem, the response $y[n]$ is the inverse DTFT of frequency domain product $Y(e^{j\omega}) = H(e^{j\omega}) X(e^{j\omega})$.

Direct application of the theorem gives the following result:

```
In[•]:= H [ ω_ ] := - i Sign [ ω ];
       InverseFourierSequenceTransform [

           H [ ω ] FourierSequenceTransform [ Cos [ π/2 n ] , n , ω ] , ω , n ]  / / FullSimplify
```

$$\text{Out[•]=} \mathsf{Sin}\left[\frac{n\pi}{2}\right]$$

This shows the input $x[n]$ and the output $y[n]$:

```
In[•]:= GraphicsRow [ {•••} + ]
```

Out[•]=

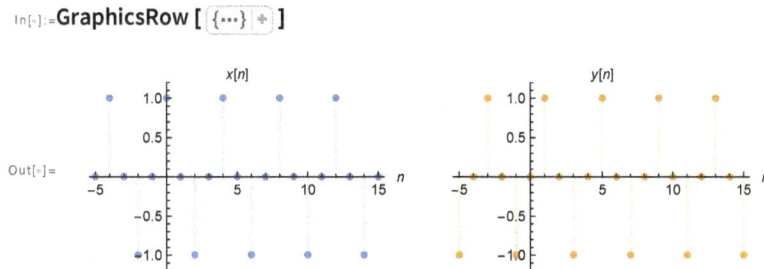

Step-by-step

Following the solution method used in Example 3, express the given input using Euler's relation

$$x[n] = \cos\left(\frac{\pi}{2} n\right) = \frac{1}{2}\left(e^{j\frac{\pi}{2} n} + e^{-j\frac{\pi}{2} n}\right)$$

Now the output is guaranteed to be a sum of two scaled complex exponentials as shown here

$$y[n] = \frac{1}{2} H\left(e^{j\omega}\right)_{\omega \to \frac{\pi}{2}} e^{j\frac{\pi}{2} n} + \frac{1}{2} H\left(e^{j\omega}\right)_{\omega \to -\frac{\pi}{2}} e^{-j\frac{\pi}{2} n}$$

Evaluation of the frequency response at the frequencies of $\pm\frac{\pi}{2}$ gives

$$= \frac{1}{2}(-j)e^{j\frac{\pi}{2} n} + \frac{1}{2} j e^{-j\frac{\pi}{2} n}$$

or again using Euler's relation

$$= \frac{1}{2} j\left(-2 j \sin\left(\frac{\pi}{2} n\right)\right)$$

$$= \sin\left(\frac{\pi}{2} n\right)$$

Summary

The frequency response of an LSI system is the DTFT of its unit sample response $h[n]$

$$h[n] \overset{\mathcal{F}}{\longleftrightarrow} H\left(e^{j\omega}\right)$$

The frequency response of an FIR system is a polynomial in $e^{-j\omega}$

$$H\left(e^{j\omega}\right) = h[0] + h[1]e^{-j\omega} + h[2]e^{-j\omega 2} + ... + h[N-1]e^{-j\omega(N-1)}$$

The frequency response of an IIR system is a rational polynomial in terms of powers of $e^{-j\omega}$

$$H\left(e^{j\omega}\right) = \frac{b_0 + b_1 e^{-j\omega} + ... + b_M e^{-jM\omega}}{a_0 + a_1 e^{-j\omega} + ... + a_N e^{-jN\omega}}$$

The magnitude responses of four common ideal filters are

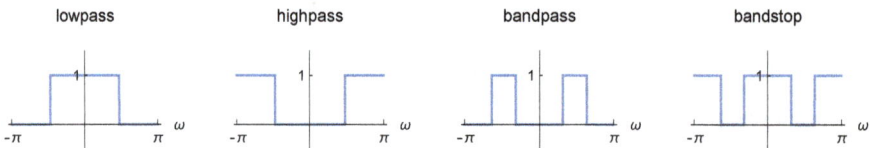

Exercises

Download the solutions manual at wolfr.am/eTextbook-SSSP

21.1 Obtain the frequency response of an LSI system with the following unit sample response.

$h[n] = \delta_n - \delta_{n-1}$

21.2 Obtain the frequency response of an LSI system with the following unit sample response.

$h[n] = \delta_{n+1} - \delta_{n-1}$

21.3 Obtain the unit sample response of the following ideal highpass filter.

$$H(e^{j\omega}) = \begin{cases} 1, & -\pi \le \omega \le -\frac{\pi}{2} \\ 0, & |\omega| < \frac{\pi}{2} \\ 1, & \frac{\pi}{2} \le \omega \le \pi \end{cases}$$

21.4 Determine the frequency response of a system defined by the following difference equation.

$y[n] + \frac{1}{2} y[n-1] = \frac{1}{2} x[n]$

21.5 Given an ideal filter with frequency response

$H(e^{j\omega}) = j\omega, \quad -\pi \le \omega \le \pi$

determine the output $y[n]$ given the input

$x[n] = \cos\left(\frac{\pi}{2} n\right)$

21.6 Obtain the output $y[n]$ of an ideal zero-phase lowpass filter with frequency response

$$H(e^{j\omega}) = \begin{cases} 1, & |\omega| < 1 \\ 0, & \text{else} \end{cases}$$

to the sawtooth sequence $x[n]$ shown here.

DiscretePlot [SawtoothWave [n / 8], … +]

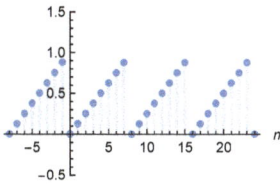

Laplace Transform

22 | Laplace Transform

The Laplace transform plays an important role in the analysis and design of linear time-invariant (LTI) signal processing systems. Some of the common applications of the Laplace transform include:

- Transforming differential equations into algebraic equations

$$y''(t) + \sqrt{2}\ y'(t) + y(t) = x(t) \implies Y(s) = \frac{1}{s^2 + \sqrt{2}\ s + 1}\ X(s)$$

- Easily incorporating initial conditions and impulsive signals
- Reducing electrical networks to simultaneous algebraic equations

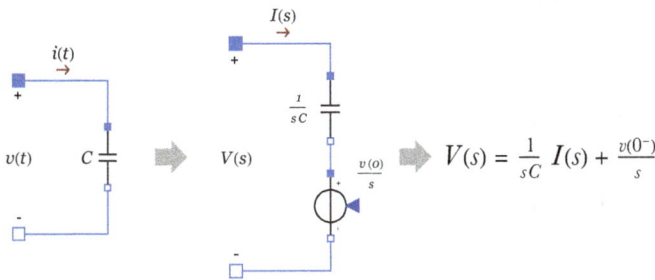

$$V(s) = \frac{1}{sC}\ I(s) + \frac{v(0^-)}{s}$$

Definition

The Laplace transform, also known as the bilateral or two-sided Laplace transform, is defined

$$X(s) = \int_{-\infty}^{\infty} x(t) e^{-st}\, dt$$

where s is a complex variable. The Laplace transform is a generalization of the continuous-time Fourier transform (CTFT). Letting $s = j\omega$, the Laplace transform integral reduces to the CTFT of the signal $x(t)$

$$X(j\omega) = \int_{-\infty}^{\infty} x(t)e^{-j\omega t}\,dt$$

By letting $s = \sigma + j\omega$, the Laplace integral becomes

$$X(\sigma + j\omega) = \int_{-\infty}^{\infty} x(t)e^{-\sigma t}e^{-j\omega t}\,dt$$

which can be interpreted as the CTFT of the modified signal $x(t)\,e^{-\sigma t}$. It immediately follows from the properties of the CTFT that the Laplace integral converges if $x(t)\,e^{-\sigma t}$ is absolutely integrable

$$\int_{-\infty}^{\infty} |x(t)\,e^{-\sigma t}|\,dt < \infty$$

Therefore, the Laplace transform exists for all functions $x(t)$ that do not diverge faster than an exponential function. The range of values of σ for which the Laplace integral converges determines the so-called region of convergence (ROC) of the transform.

Example 1

Obtain the Laplace transform of the unit step function.

Solution

The BilateralLaplaceTransform function returns the Laplace transform and the condition under which this result is valid, namely the ROC:

In[•]:=**BilateralLaplaceTransform [UnitStep [t] , t, s]**

Out[•]= $\dfrac{1}{s}$ if $\mathrm{Re[s]} > 0$

Step-by-step

Substitute the unit step into the Laplace transform and evaluate the integral

$$X(s) = \int_{-\infty}^{\infty} u(t)\,e^{-st}\,dt = \int_{0}^{\infty} e^{-st}\,dt = -\frac{1}{s}\,e^{-st}\,\big|_{0}^{\infty} = -\frac{1}{s}\left(\lim_{t\to\infty} e^{-st} - 1\right)$$

Now, note that $s = \sigma + j\omega$ is complex, so $e^{-st} = e^{-(\sigma+j\omega)t} = e^{-\sigma t}\cdot e^{-j\omega t}$ and

$$\lim_{t\to\infty} e^{-st} = \lim_{t\to\infty} e^{-\sigma t}e^{-j\omega t} \to \begin{cases} 0, & \sigma = \mathrm{Re}(s) > 0 \\ \infty, & \sigma = \mathrm{Re}(s) < 0 \end{cases}$$

Therefore

$$X(s) = -\frac{1}{s}\,(0 - 1) = \frac{1}{s}, \qquad \mathrm{Re}(s) > 0$$

This gives the first Laplace transform pair

$$u(t) \overset{\mathcal{L}}{\longleftrightarrow} \frac{1}{s}, \qquad \mathrm{Re}(s) > 0$$

Visualizing the Laplace Transform

The Laplace transform of the unit step signal is defined

$$X(s) = \frac{1}{s}, \qquad \mathrm{Re}(s) > 0$$

Since s is a complex variable, namely $s = \sigma + j\omega$, you get

$$X(s)|_{s \to \sigma + j\omega} = \frac{1}{s} \Big|_{s \to \sigma + j\omega} = \frac{1}{\sigma + j\omega}, \sigma > 0$$

so the magnitude is

$$|X(s)| = \frac{1}{\sqrt{\sigma^2 + \omega^2}}, \qquad \sigma > 0$$

This plots the magnitude of the Laplace transform of a unit step signal:

In[•]:= **Plot3D [Abs [** $\dfrac{1}{(\sigma + \textbf{\textit{i}}\ \omega)}$ **] ,** ⋯ **+]**

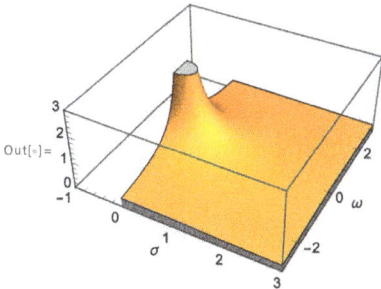

This shows the phase of the Laplace transform

$$\angle X(s) = \angle \frac{1}{\sigma + j\omega} = \angle \frac{\sigma - j\omega}{\sigma^2 + \omega^2} = \arctan\left(-\frac{\omega}{\sigma}\right)$$

Here is a plot of this function:

In[•]:= **Plot3D [Arg [** $\dfrac{1}{(\sigma + \textbf{\textit{i}}\ \omega)}$ **] ,** ⋯ **+]**

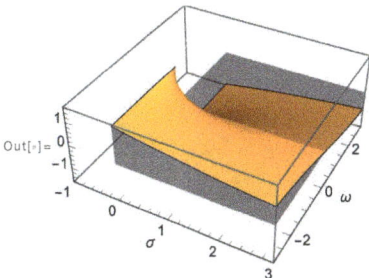

Example 2

Determine the Laplace transform $X(s)$ and the ROC given the following signal

$$x(t) = e^{-at} u(t)$$

Solution

Directly from the definition:

In[•]:=**BilateralLaplaceTransform [e^{-at} UnitStep [t] , t, s]**

Out[•]= $\dfrac{1}{a+s}$ if   Re [a + s] > 0

This shows the magnitude of the transform and its ROC for $a = 1$:

In[•]:=**GraphicsRow [⋯ +]**

Out[•]=

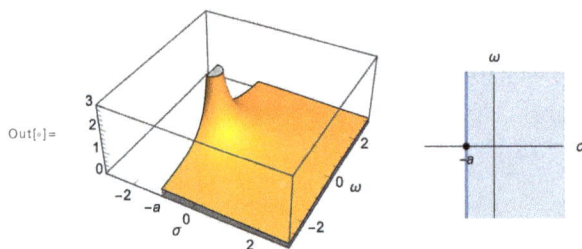

The Laplace transform pair is

$$e^{-at} u(t) \overset{\mathcal{L}}{\longleftrightarrow} \frac{1}{s+a}, \qquad \text{Re}(s + a) > 0$$

Example 3

Determine the Laplace transform of the anti-causal signal $x(t) = -e^{-at} u(-t)$.

Solution

Directly from the definition:

In[•]:=**BilateralLaplaceTransform [$-e^{-at}$ UnitStep [-t] , t, s]**

Out[•]= $\dfrac{1}{a+s}$ if   Re [a + s] < 0

This shows the magnitude of the Laplace transform and the ROC of the signal $x(t)$ for $a = 1$:

In[•]:=**GraphicsRow [** ⋯ + **]**

Out[•]=

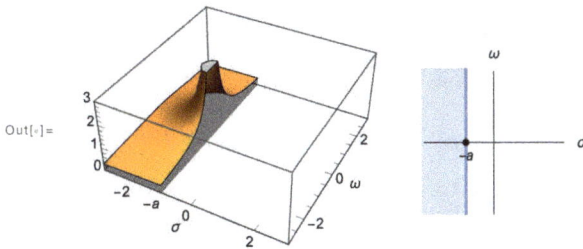

The transform pair is

$$-e^{-at}\, u(-t) \overset{\mathcal{L}}{\longleftrightarrow} \frac{1}{s+a}, \qquad \text{Re}(s+a) < 0$$

ROC—Select Properties

Examples 2 and 3 showed that the two signals $e^{-at}\, u(t)$ and $-e^{-at}\, u(-t)$ have the same Laplace transform expressions but differ in their ROC specification. Therefore, one concludes that both the Laplace transform function and its ROC are necessary to uniquely associate a signal with its Laplace transform.

Finite-duration signals that are absolutely integrable have an ROC that covers the entire s-plane.

ROCs are always vertical half planes or stripes bounded by the roots of the denominator of the Laplace transform. Specifically, left- or right-sided signals have ROCs that are half planes, while two-sided signals have ROCs that are vertical strips.

Here is an example of a two-sided signal, its Laplace transform, and the ROC

$$-e^{t}\, u(-t) + e^{-2t}\, u(t) \overset{\mathcal{L}}{\longleftrightarrow} \frac{2\,s+1}{(s-1)\,(s+2)}, \qquad -2 < \text{Re}(s) < 1$$

This shows the signal and the ROC

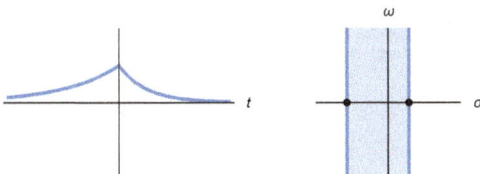

Square integrable signals lead to Laplace transforms with ROCs that include the imaginary axis. Here are three square integrable signals and their ROCs

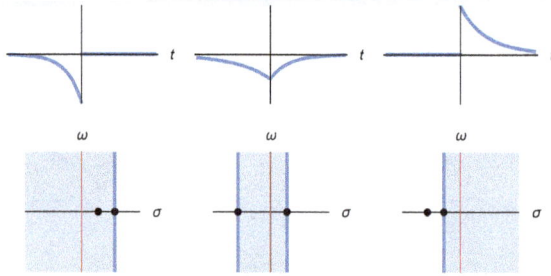

Conversely, if the ROC does not include the imaginary axes, the corresponding time signal must be unbounded.

Fourier Transform from Laplace Transform

As stated earlier, the bilateral Laplace transform is a generalization of the CTFT. Starting with the Laplace transform integral

$$X(s) = \int_{-\infty}^{\infty} x(t)\, e^{-st}\, dt$$

and letting $s = j\omega$ reduces the transform to the CTFT

$$X(j\omega) = \int_{-\infty}^{\infty} x(t)\, e^{-j\omega t}\, dt$$

As long as the imaginary axis lies in the ROC of $X(s)$, the Fourier transform can be obtained by evaluating $X(s)$ for all values of s such that $s = j\omega$.

For example, given the following Laplace transform (with an ROC such that $\text{Re}(s) > -1$):

In[•]:= **X[s_] :=** $\dfrac{1}{s+1}$

The Fourier transform is:

In[•]:= **X[$i\,\omega$]**

Out[•]= $\dfrac{1}{1 + i\,\omega}$

This shows the magnitude of the Fourier transform (in red) superimposed on the magnitude of the Laplace transform:

In[·]:=**Show [{···} +]**

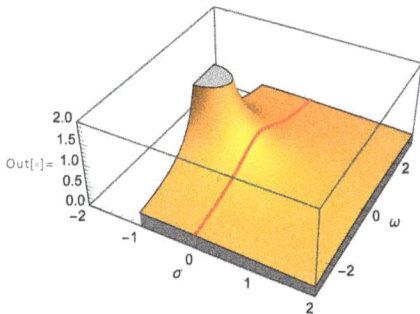

Laplace Transform as a Rational Polynomial

The Laplace transform takes the form of a ratio of two polynomials whenever $x(t)$ is a linear combination of real or complex exponentials or when modeling a continuous-time LTI system represented by a linear constant coefficient differential equation

$$X(s) = \frac{\left(b_0 + b_1\, s + b_2\, s^2 + \ldots + b_M\, s^M\right)}{\left(a_0 + a_1\, s + a_2\, s^2 + \ldots + a_N\, s^N\right)}$$

$X(s)$ is called a (strictly) proper rational if $a_N \neq 0$ and the order of the numerator polynomial M is less than the order of the denominator polynomial N $(M < N)$.

An improper rational function $(M \geq N)$ can always be written as a sum of a polynomial and a proper rational function

$$X(s) = c_0 + c_1\, s + \ldots + c_{M-N}\, s^{(M-N)} + X_p(s)$$

where $X_p(s)$ is a proper rational function. The roots of the numerator polynomial are known as zeros and the roots of the denominator are called poles. A proper rational Laplace transform can be written explicitly in terms of the poles and zeros by using a factored form

$$X(s) = \frac{b_M\, \prod_{k=1}^{M} (s + z_k)}{a_N\, \prod_{k=1}^{N} (s + p_k)} = K\, \frac{\prod_{k=1}^{M} (s + z_k)}{\prod_{k=1}^{N} (s + p_k)}$$

The constant $K = b_M / a_N$ is called the scale factor.

Laplace Transform—Poles and Zeros

Here is a rational Laplace transform:

In[•]:= $X [s\_] := \dfrac{20 \ (s + 3)}{(s + 2) \ (s^2 + 2 s + 5)}$;

These are the zeros:

In[•]:= **Roots [Numerator [X [s]] == 0, s]**

Out[•]= $s == -3$

Here are the poles:

In[•]:= **Roots [Denominator [X [s]] == 0, s]**

Out[•]= $s == -2 \ | \ | \ s == -1 - 2 \ i \ | \ | \ s == -1 + 2 \ i$

A common visualization of the Laplace transform is simply a plot of the location of the poles (■) and zeros (■) of the function:

In[•]:= **poles = Solve [Denominator [X [s]] == 0, s] ;**
    zeros = Solve [Numerator [X [s]] == 0, s] ;
    ComplexListPlot [⋯ +]

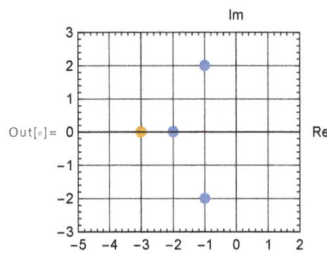

Here is a surface plot of $|X(s)|$:

In[•]:= **Plot3D [⋯ +]**

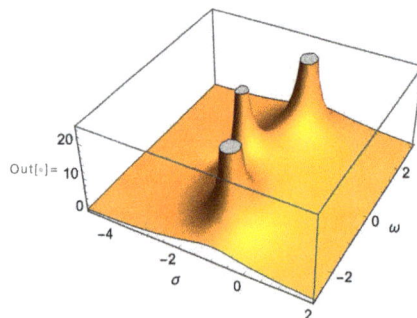

Summary

In this chapter, the Laplace transform, an integral transform of central importance in the study of continuous-time signals and LTI systems, was introduced.

Discussion of the Laplace transform of continuous-time signals included existence, convergence, and uniqueness.

Several examples of evaluating the transform for select continuous-time signals were shown as well as useful graphical representations associated with the Laplace transform, such as the ROC, poles and zeros, and plots of the transform magnitude

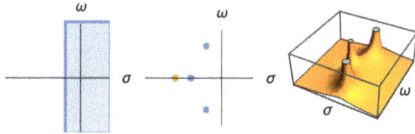

Exercises

Download the solutions manual at wolfr.am/eTextbook-SSSP

22.1 Obtain the Laplace transform of the unit impulse signal $x(t) = \delta(t)$.

22.2 Determine the Laplace transform of the following signal.

$x(t) = tu(t)$

22.3 Find the Laplace transform and the ROC for the following signal.

$x(t) = e^{-|t|}$

22.4 Obtain the Laplace transform of the following complex exponential signal.

$x(t) = e^{-j\omega_0 t}\, u(t)$

22.5 Obtain the Laplace transform of the following signal.

$x(t) = \cos(\omega_0 t)\, u(t)$.

22.6 Plot the magnitude and phase of the following Laplace transform.

$X(s) = \dfrac{1}{1 + 2s + 2s^2 + s^3}$

22.7 Obtain and plot the Fourier transform of a causal signal given by the following Laplace transform.

$X(s) = \dfrac{1}{1 + 2s + 2s^2 + s^3}$

22.8 Obtain and plot the poles and zeros of the following Laplace transform.

$X(s) = \dfrac{-2.09971 - 1.09971s^2}{2.09971 + 2.37261s + 2.4402s^2 + s^3}$

23 | Inverse Laplace Transform

Formally, the inverse Laplace transform is defined as the following complex line integral

$$x(t) = \frac{1}{2\pi j} \int_{\sigma-j\infty}^{\sigma+j\infty} X(s)\, e^{st}\, ds$$

However, as discussed earlier, linear time-invariant (LTI) systems lead to transfer functions in the form of ratio of polynomials. The general form of a rational Laplace transform $X(s)$ is

$$X(s) = \frac{\left(b_0 + b_1\, s + b_2\, s^2 + \ldots + b_M\, s^M\right)}{\left(a_0 + a_1\, s + a_2 s^2 + \ldots + a_N\, s^N\right)}$$

For such Laplace transforms, there is a simpler method for accomplishing the inversion—the method of partial fraction expansion (also called partial fraction decomposition). The goal of partial fraction expansion is to express a rational Laplace transform in terms of superposition of simple terms, with each term corresponding to one of the roots of the denominator polynomial. For each term, the inverse transforms are readily available in tables of transform pairs. In what follows, the cases of distinct and repeated roots are presented.

The details of calculating the inverse transform are presented in spite of the fact that they can be easily obtained using Wolfram Language for the simple reason that an understanding and some basic mastery of the method of partial fractions is typically required of any engineering, mathematics, or physics student.

Distinct Roots

In the case of N distinct poles p_k, the transform $X(s)$ may be expanded into a linear combination of first-order terms as follows

$$X(s) = \frac{A_1}{s + p_1} + \frac{A_2}{s + p_2} + \ldots + \frac{A_N}{s + p_N}$$

with each constant A_k known as the residue of pole p_k, given by

$$A_k = \left. \left((s + p_k)\, X(s) \right) \right|_{s = -p_k}$$

The inverse Laplace transform of each term is obtained from the following transform pairs

$$e^{-pt}\, u(t) \overset{\mathcal{L}}{\longleftrightarrow} \frac{1}{s+p}, \qquad \mathrm{Re}(s) > -p$$

$$-e^{-pt}\, u(-t) \overset{\mathcal{L}}{\longleftrightarrow} \frac{1}{s+p}, \quad \mathrm{Re}(s) < -p$$

Now, assuming that $\mathrm{Re}(s + p_k) > 0$ for $k = 1, 2, \ldots, N$, you get the following as the inverse Laplace transform of $X(s)$

$$x(t) = \left(A_1\, e^{-p_1 t} + A_2\, e^{-p_2 t} + \ldots + A_N\, e^{-p_N t} \right) u(t)$$

Complex roots will appear in complex conjugate pairs.

Partial Fractions for Distinct Roots

The purpose of this example is to demonstrate the method of partial fractions for the case of distinct roots.

Given the following Laplace transform, use the method of partial fractions to express the function as a sum of first-order terms:

$$\text{In[•]:=} \mathsf{X[s\_] :=} \ \frac{(s + 5)}{(s + 1)\ (s^2 + 2\,s + 5)};$$

The three roots of the Laplace transform denominator are:

$$\text{In[•]:=} \mathsf{Solve[\ (s + 1)\ (s^2 + 2\,s + 5) == 0,\, s]}$$

$$\text{Out[•]=} \{\{s \to -1\},\, \{s \to -1 - 2\,i\},\, \{s \to -1 + 2\,i\}\}$$

The transform $X(s)$ may be expanded into the following linear combination of first-order terms

$$X(s) = \frac{A_1}{s + 1} + \frac{A_2}{s + 1 + 2\,j} + \frac{A_3}{s + 1 - 2\,j}$$

Each of the constants A_k, known as the residue of pole p_k, can be calculated as follows:

$$\text{In[•]:=} \mathsf{Limit[\ (s + 1)\ X[s],\, s \to -1]}$$

$$\text{Out[•]=} 1$$

$$\text{In[•]:=} \mathsf{Limit[\ (s + 1 + 2\,i)\ X[s],\, s \to -1 - 2\,i]}$$

$$\text{Out[•]=} -\frac{1}{2} + \frac{i}{4}$$

In[•]:=**Limit [(s + 1 − 2 _i_) X [s] , s → −1 + 2 _i_]**

Out[•]=$-\dfrac{1}{2} - \dfrac{i}{4}$

The partial fraction form of $X(s)$ is

$$X(s) = \dfrac{1}{s+1} + \left(-\dfrac{1}{2} + \dfrac{j}{4}\right) \dfrac{1}{s+1+2j} + \left(-\dfrac{1}{2} - \dfrac{j}{4}\right) \dfrac{1}{s+1-2j}$$

Finally, the calculation of the right-sided signal corresponding to the given Laplace transform proceeds by applying the transform pair $e^{-at}\, u(t) \overset{\mathcal{L}}{\longleftrightarrow} \dfrac{1}{s+a}$ for $\mathrm{Re}(s+a) > 0$ to each term of the expansion.

The inverse form of $X(s)$ is:

In[•]:=**x [t_] = InverseLaplaceTransform [X [s] , s , t] // FullSimplify**

Out[•]=$\dfrac{1}{2}\, e^{-t}\, (2 - 2\,\mathrm{Cos}\,[2\,t] + \mathrm{Sin}\,[2\,t]\,)$

Here is a plot of $x(t)$:

In[•]:=**Plot [x [t] , ⋯ +]**

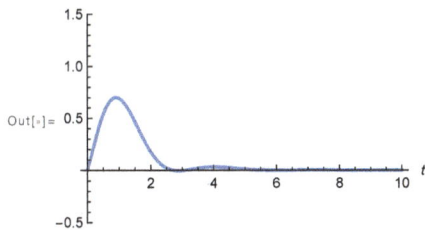

Repeated Roots

Given a transfer function with a root p with multiplicity k, the expansion takes the following form

$$X(s) = \dfrac{A_1}{s+p} + \dfrac{A_2}{(s+p)^2} + \dots + \dfrac{A_k}{(s+p)^k}$$

Each residue A_n for $n = 1, 2, \dots, k$ is given by

$$A_n = \dfrac{1}{(k-n)!}\, \dfrac{d^{k-n}}{ds^{k-n}}\left((s+p)^k\, X(s)\right)\Big|_{s=p}$$

The inverse Laplace transform of each term is obtained from the following transform pairs

$$\frac{t^{n-1}}{(n-1)!}\, e^{-pt}\, u(t) \overset{\mathcal{L}}{\longleftrightarrow} \frac{1}{(s+p)^n}, \qquad \text{Re}(s) > -p$$

$$-\frac{t^{n-1}}{(n-1)!}\, e^{-pt}\, u(-t) \overset{\mathcal{L}}{\longleftrightarrow} \frac{1}{(s+p)^n}, \qquad \text{Re}(s) < -p$$

Now, assuming that $\text{Re}(s + p_k) > 0$ for $k = 1, 2, ..., N$, you get the following as the inverse Laplace transform of $X(s)$

$$x(t) = \left(A_1\, e^{-pt} + A_2\, te^{-pt} + ... + A_k\, \frac{t^{k-1}}{(k-1)!}\, e^{-pt} \right) u(t)$$

Partial Fractions for Repeated Roots

In order to demonstrate the partial fraction expansion method for repeated roots, consider the following Laplace transform:

In[•]:= **X[s_] :=** $\dfrac{4s + 5}{(s + 1)\ (s + 2)^3}$

This returns the poles:

In[•]:= **Solve[(s + 1) (s + 2)^3 == 0, s]**

Out[•]= **{ {s → -2}, {s → -2}, {s → -2}, {s → -1} }**

The expected expansion will take the following form

$$X(s) = \frac{A_{11}}{s + 2} + \frac{A_{12}}{(s + 2)^2} + \frac{A_{13}}{(s + 2)^3} + \frac{A_2}{s + 1}$$

The repeated root residues A_{1m} for $m = 1, 2, 3$ are determined as follows:

In[•]:= **Limit[$\dfrac{1}{2!}$ D[(s + 2)^3 X[s], {s, 2}], s → -2]**

Out[•]= **-1**

In[•]:= **Limit[D[(s + 2)^3 X[s], {s, 1}], s → -2]**

Out[•]= **-1**

In[•]:= **Limit[(s + 2)^3 X[s], s → -2]**

Out[•]= **3**

The residue A_2 for the singular root is:

In[•]:= **Limit[(s + 1) X[s], s → -1]**

Out[•]= **1**

The resulting partial fraction expansion is

$$X(s) = -\frac{1}{s+2} - \frac{1}{(s+2)^2} + \frac{3}{(s+2)^3} + \frac{1}{s+1}$$

Again, it is assumed that the right-sided signal is desired, so directly from the InverseLaplaceTransform, you get:

In[•]:=**x[t_] = InverseLaplaceTransform[X[s],s,t] // FullSimplify**

Out[•]=$\frac{1}{2} e^{-2t} (-2 + 2 e^t + t (-2 + 3t))$

Here is a plot of $x(t)$:

In[•]:=**Plot[x[t], ··· +]**

Out[•]=

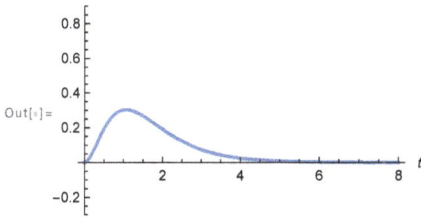

ROC and the Inverse Laplace Transform

The examples given thus far all assumed system causality and, therefore, right-sided signals, requiring that the region of convergence (ROC) spans the right half of the complex plane.

While this may indeed be the most common case encountered in practice, it is important and interesting to consider alternative ROC specifications for a given Laplace transform $X(s)$ and the resulting inverse transforms $x(t)$.

This defines an example Laplace transform:

In[•]:=**X[s_] :=** $\frac{1}{(s+1)(s+3)}$ **;**

The two poles are $p_1 = -1$ and $p_2 = -3$, resulting in three possible ROCs, as shown here:

In[•]:=**GraphicsRow [⋯ ✛]**

Out[•]=

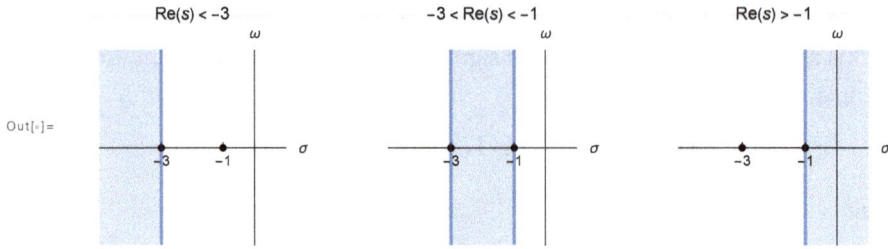

The three examples to follow show how the inverse transform depends on these ROCs.

Example 1

Obtain the inverse Laplace transform, given the following Laplace transform specification

$$X(s) = \frac{1}{(s+1)(s+3)}, \qquad \text{Re}(s) > -1$$

Solution

Substituting the given Laplace transform and the ROC into the inverse Laplace transform function gives:

In[•]:=**InverseBilateralLaplaceTransform [**

ConditionalExpression [$\dfrac{1}{(s+1)\ (s+3)}$, Re [s] > -1], s, t] // Expand

Out[•]=$\begin{cases} \frac{1}{2}\, e^{-3t}\left(-1 + e^{2t}\right) & t \geq 0 \\ 0 & \text{True} \end{cases}$

This shows the signal:

In[•]:=**Plot [$\left(-\dfrac{1}{2}\, e^{-3t} + \dfrac{1}{2}\, e^{-t}\right)$ UnitStep [t], ⋯ ✛]**

Out[•]=

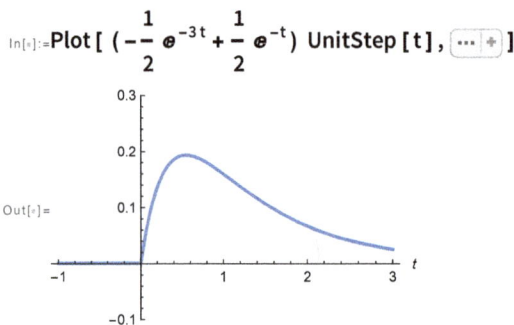

The resulting signal is causal or right sided.

Step-by-step

Partial fraction expansion of $X(s)$

$$X(s) = \frac{1}{(s+1)(s+3)} = \frac{A}{s+1} + \frac{B}{s+3}$$

The values of A and B can be quickly obtained using the method of residues:

In[•]:=**Limit [(s + 1) X[s], s → −1]**

Out[•]=$\frac{1}{2}$

In[•]:=**Limit [(s + 3) X[s], s → −3]**

Out[•]=$-\frac{1}{2}$

This gives the partial expansion as

$$X(s) = \frac{1}{2}\frac{1}{s+1} - \frac{1}{2}\frac{1}{s+3}$$

Each of the two terms can now be inverted using the transform pair

$$e^{-at}\,u(t) \overset{\mathcal{L}}{\longleftrightarrow} \frac{1}{s+a}, \qquad \text{Re}(s) > -a$$

For Re $(s) > -1$ and $a = 1$

$$\frac{1}{2}\frac{1}{s+1} \to \frac{1}{2}e^{-t}\,u(t)$$

For Re$(s) > -1$ and $a = 3$

$$-\frac{1}{2}\frac{1}{s+3} \to -\frac{1}{2}e^{-3t}\,u(t)$$

The signal takes the following form

$$x(t) = \left(\frac{1}{2}e^{-t} - \frac{1}{2}e^{-3t}\right)u(t)$$

Example 2

Obtain the inverse Laplace transform, given the following Laplace transform specification

$$X(s) = \frac{1}{(s+1)(s+3)}, \qquad \text{Re}(s) < -3$$

Solution

Using the same approach as in Example 1 gives:

In[•]:=**InverseBilateralLaplaceTransform [**

$$\text{ConditionalExpression} \left[\frac{1}{(s+1)\ (s+3)}, \text{Re}[s] < -3 \right], s, t \right] \ // \ \text{Expand}$$

Out[•]= $\begin{cases} -\frac{1}{2} \, e^{-3t} \left(-1 + e^{2t} \right) & t < 0 \\ 0 & \text{True} \end{cases}$

This shows the signal:

In[•]:=**Plot [$\left(+\frac{1}{2} \, e^{-3t} - \frac{e^{-t}}{2} \right)$ UnitStep [-t], $\cdots$ +]**

Out[•]=

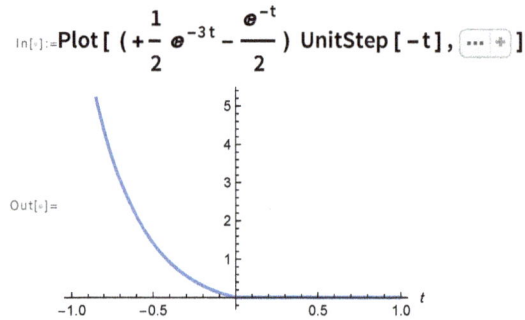

The resulting signal is anti-causal or left sided.

Step-by-step

From Example 1, the partial fraction expansion gives

$$X(s) = \frac{1}{2} \frac{1}{s+1} - \frac{1}{2} \frac{1}{s+3}$$

Each of the two terms can now be inverted using the transform pair

$$-e^{-at} \, u(-t) \overset{\mathcal{L}}{\longleftrightarrow} \frac{1}{s+a}, \quad \text{Re}(s) < -a$$

With an ROC such that $\text{Re}(s) < -3$, this gives

$$\frac{1}{2} \frac{1}{s+1} \rightarrow -\frac{1}{2} \, e^{-t} \, u(-t)$$

$$-\frac{1}{2} \frac{1}{s+3} \rightarrow +\frac{1}{2} \, e^{-3t} \, u(-t)$$

The final result is

$$x(t) = \left(-\frac{1}{2} \, e^{-t} + \frac{1}{2} \, e^{-3t} \right) u(-t)$$

Example 3

Obtain the inverse Laplace transform, given the following Laplace transform specification

$$X(s) = \frac{1}{(s+1)\ (s+3)}, \quad -3 < \text{Re}(s) < -1$$

Solution

Repeating the same approach, this gives the third and final possible inverse Laplace transform:

In[•]:=**InverseBilateralLaplaceTransform [ConditionalExpression [**
$$\frac{1}{(s+1)\ (s+3)}, -3 < \text{Re}[s] < -1], s, t] \ / / \ \textbf{Expand}$$

Out[•]=$\begin{cases} -\frac{1}{2}\,e^{-3t} & t \geq 0 \\ -\frac{e^{-t}}{2} & \text{True} \end{cases}$

This shows the signal:

In[•]:=**Plot [$(\frac{1}{2}\,e^{-3t})$ UnitStep [t] + $(-\frac{e^{-t}}{2})$ UnitStep [-t], ⋯ ✦]**

Out[•]=

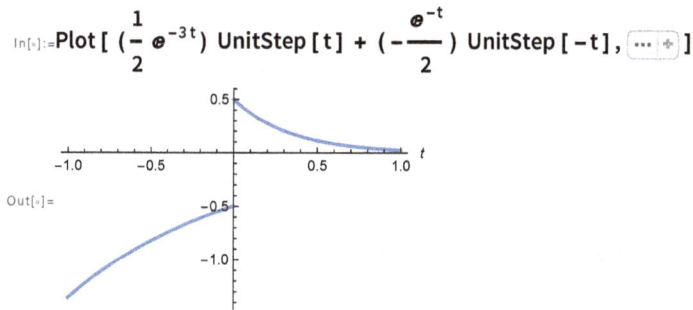

The result is a sum of a right-sided and a left-sided signal.

Step-by-step

Again, from Example 1, the partial fraction expansion gives

$$X(s) = \frac{1}{2}\frac{1}{s+1} - \frac{1}{2}\frac{1}{s+3}$$

With an ROC such that $-3 < \text{Re}(s) < -1$, inversion using the following transform pairs

$$\frac{1}{2}\frac{1}{s+1} \rightarrow -\frac{1}{2}\,e^{-t}\,u(-t), \qquad \text{Re}(s) < -1$$

$$-\frac{1}{2}\frac{1}{s+3} \rightarrow -\frac{1}{2}\,e^{-3t}\,u(t), \qquad \text{Re}(s) > -3$$

gives the following result

$$x(t) = -\frac{1}{2}\,e^{-t}\,u(-t) - \frac{1}{2}\,e^{-3t}\,u(t)$$

Summary

Laplace transform inversion by the method of partial fraction expansion was presented.

Examples of inversions for different ROCs were shown

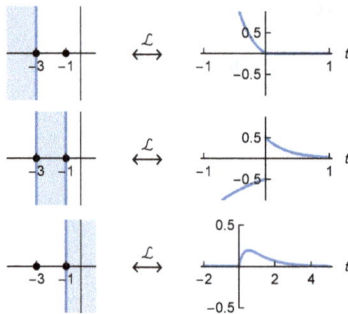

Details describing the evaluation of residues for both distinct and repeated roots were given.

Exercises

Download the solutions manual at wolfr.am/eTextbook-SSSP

23.1 Obtain the inverse Laplace transform.

$$X(s) = \frac{1}{(s+1)(s-1)}, \quad \text{Re}(s) > 1$$

23.2 Obtain the inverse Laplace transform.

$$X(s) = \frac{1}{(s+1)(s-1)}, \quad -1 < \text{Re}(s) < 1$$

23.3 Obtain the inverse Laplace transform.

$$X(s) = \frac{1}{(s+1)(s-1)}, \quad \text{Re}(s) < -1$$

23.4 Obtain the inverse Laplace transform.

$$X(s) = \frac{1}{(s+1)^2(s+3)}, \quad \text{Re}(s) > -1$$

23.5 Obtain the causal inverse Laplace transform.

$$X(s) = \frac{1}{s^2 + \sqrt{2}\,s + 1}$$

24 | Laplace Transform Theorems

Properties and theorems of the transform are useful in deriving Laplace transforms of functions, in finding solutions of integro-differential equations, and in modeling electrical circuits and other linear time-invariant (LTI) systems.

In this chapter, a few of the more important properties and theorems of the Laplace transform are presented. These include:

- Linearity
- Time shifting
- Convolution
- Differentiation in time
- Differentiation in the s-domain

Linearity

Given two functions of time and their Laplace transforms, $x_1(t) \overset{\mathcal{L}}{\longleftrightarrow} X_1(s)$ with the region of convergence (ROC) denoted by R_1 and $x_2(t) \overset{\mathcal{L}}{\longleftrightarrow} X_2(s)$ with the ROC denoted by R_2, a linear superposition of the signals in time has the following Laplace transform

$$ax_1(t) + bx_2(t) \overset{\mathcal{L}}{\longleftrightarrow} aX_1(s) + bX_2(s), \text{ with ROC containing } R_1 \cap R_2$$

Note that the intersection of the two ROCs could be empty, in which case, the signal has no Laplace transform.

Proof

By definition

$$\mathcal{L}\{ax_1(t) + bx_2(t)\} = \int_{-\infty}^{\infty}\{ax_1(t) + bx_2(t)\}e^{-st}\,dt$$

$$= a\int_{-\infty}^{\infty}x_1(t)e^{-st}\,dt + b\int_{-\infty}^{\infty}x_2(t)e^{-st}\,dt$$

$$= aX_1(s) + bX_2(s)$$

Time Shifting

If $x(t)\overset{\mathcal{L}}{\longleftrightarrow}X(s)$ with the ROC denoted by R, then

$$x(t - t_0)\overset{\mathcal{L}}{\longleftrightarrow}e^{-st_0}\,X(s),\text{ with ROC equal to }R$$

The time-shifting property states that delaying a signal by t_0 amounts to multiplying its transform by e^{-st_0}.

Proof

By definition

$$\mathcal{L}\{x(t - t_0)\} = \int_{-\infty}^{\infty}x(t - t_0)e^{-st}\,dt$$

Setting $\tau = t - t_0$

$$= \int_{-\infty}^{\infty}x(\tau)e^{-s(\tau+t_0)}\,d\tau$$

$$= e^{-st_0}\int_{-\infty}^{\infty}x(\tau)e^{-s\tau}\,d\tau$$

$$= e^{-st_0}\,X(s)$$

Example 1

Given the Laplace transform pair $\delta(t)\overset{\mathcal{L}}{\longleftrightarrow}1$, obtain the transform of $x(t) = \delta(t - t_0)$ using the time-shifting property. Confirm your result by direct application of the definition.

Solution

The time-shifting property states that the transform is obtained by multiplying by e^{-st_0}, which immediately gives

$$\mathcal{L}\{\delta(t - t_0)\} = e^{-st_0}$$

Using the definition and the sampling property of the impulse function gives

$$\mathcal{L}\{\delta(t - t_0)\} = \int_{-\infty}^{\infty}\delta(t - t_0)e^{-st}\,d\tau = e^{-st_0}$$

which can be quickly verified as follows:

In[•]:=**BilateralLaplaceTransform [DiracDelta [t – t0] , t, s]**

Out[•]=$e^{-s\,t0}$

Convolution

Given two functions of time and their Laplace transforms, $x_1(t) \overset{\mathcal{L}}{\longleftrightarrow} X_1(s)$ with the ROC denoted by R_1 and $x_2(t) \overset{\mathcal{L}}{\longleftrightarrow} X_2(s)$ with the ROC denoted by R_2, then a convolution of the two signals in time results in multiplication in the s-domain

$$x_1(t) * x_2(t) \overset{\mathcal{L}}{\longleftrightarrow} X_1(s)X_2(s), \text{ with ROC containing } R_1 \cap R_2$$

Proof

Proceed directly by calculating the Laplace transform of the convolution integral

$$\mathcal{L}\{x_1(t) * x_2(t)\} = \mathcal{L}\left\{\int_{-\infty}^{\infty} x_1(\tau)x_2(t-\tau)\,d\tau\right\}$$

$$= \int_{-\infty}^{\infty}\left(\int_{-\infty}^{\infty} x_1(\tau)x_2(t-\tau)\,d\tau\right)e^{-st}\,ds$$

Now by changing the order of integration, you get

$$= \int_{-\infty}^{\infty} x_1(\tau)\left(\int_{-\infty}^{\infty} x_2(t-\tau)e^{-st}\,ds\right)d\tau$$

Applying the shift theorem to the inner integral gives the following result

$$= X_2(s)\int_{-\infty}^{\infty} x_1(\tau)e^{-s\tau}d\tau$$

where $X_2(s) = \int_{-\infty}^{\infty} x_2(t)e^{-st}\,dt$ is the Laplace transform of signal $x_2(t)$. Also, note that the integral in the result is simply the Laplace transform of the signal $x_1(t)$. Therefore, finally

$$= X_1(s)X_2(s)$$

Example 2

Use the time-convolution property of the Laplace transform to determine $y(t) = \left(e^{-at}u(t)\right) * u(t)$.

Solution

From known transform pairs

$$e^{-at}u(t) \overset{\mathcal{L}}{\longleftrightarrow} \frac{1}{s+a}, \qquad \text{Re}(s) > -a$$

$$u(t) \overset{\mathcal{L}}{\longleftrightarrow} \frac{1}{s}, \qquad \text{Re}(s) > 0$$

Next, use the convolution property

$$Y(s) = \frac{1}{s} \cdot \frac{1}{s+a}$$

The inverse transform gives the following well-known result:

In[•]:= **InverseBilateralLaplaceTransform** $\left[-\dfrac{1}{s} \; \dfrac{1}{s+a}, s, t \right]$

Out[•]= $\dfrac{\left(1 - e^{-a\,t}\right) \text{UnitStep}[t]}{a}$

Differentiation in Time

The differentiation-in-time property allows the transformation of constant coefficient differential equations into algebraic equations and therefore provides an alternative method for solving them.

If $x(t) \xleftrightarrow{\mathcal{L}} X(s)$ with the ROC denoted by R, then

$$\frac{dx(t)}{dt} \xleftrightarrow{\mathcal{L}} sX(s), \text{ with ROC containing } R$$

Differentiating twice yields

$$\frac{d^2x(t)}{dt^2} \xleftrightarrow{\mathcal{L}} s^2 X(s)$$

Repeated differentiation results in the transform pair

$$\frac{d^n x(t)}{dt^n} \xleftrightarrow{\mathcal{L}} s^n X(s)$$

Proof

This property follows from differentiating both sides of the inverse Laplace transform integral

$$\frac{dx(t)}{dt} = \frac{d}{dt} \left\{ \frac{1}{2\pi j} \int_{\sigma-j\omega}^{\sigma+j\omega} X(s)\, e^{st} \, ds \right\}$$

$$= \frac{1}{2\pi j} \int_{\sigma-j\omega}^{\sigma+j\omega} X(s) \frac{d}{dt}\left\{ e^{st} \right\} ds$$

$$= \frac{1}{2\pi j} \int_{\sigma-j\omega}^{\sigma+j\omega} sX(s)\, e^{st} \, ds$$

Therefore, the Laplace transform of a derivative of $x(t)$ is the inverse transform of $sX(s)$.

The System Function of an LTI System

Any LTI system can be represented by an Nth-order linear constant coefficient differential equation

$$a_0\, y(t) + a_1\, y^{(1)}(t) + \ldots + a_N\, y^{(N)}(t) = b_0\, x(t) + b_1\, x^{(1)}(t) + \ldots + b_M\, x^{(M)}(t)$$

The Laplace differentiation theorem reduces the differential equation to an algebraic equation

$$a_0\, Y(s) + a_1\, s Y(s) + \ldots + a_N s^N\, Y(s) = b_0\, X(s) + b_1\, s X(s) + \ldots + b_M\, s^M\, X(s)$$

The so-called transfer function of an LTI system is defined

$$H(s) = \frac{Y(s)}{X(s)} = \frac{\left(b_0 + b_1\, s + b_2\, s^2 + \ldots + b_M\, s^M\right)}{\left(a_0 + a_1\, s + a_2\, s^2 + \ldots + a_N\, s^N\right)}$$

Therefore, LTI systems have rational system functions.

The transfer function is a representation of the relationship between the input and output of an LTI system with zero initial conditions. The inverse Laplace transform of the system function is the impulse response of the system

$$H(s) \xrightarrow{\mathcal{L}^{-1}} h(t)$$

Example 3

Obtain the system transfer function and the causal (or right-sided) impulse response of the series RC circuit described by the following differential equation (assume zero initial condition)

$$y'(t) + y(t) = x(t)$$

Solution

Applying the differentiation theorem and substituting the initial condition gives

$$s Y(s) + Y(s) = X(s)$$

Collecting terms and simplifying gives the following transfer function

$$(1 + s)\, Y(s) = X(s)$$

Solving for the ratio of the Laplace transform of the output $Y(s)$ over the input $X(s)$ gives the following transfer function

$$H(s) = \frac{Y(s)}{X(s)} = \frac{1}{1+s}$$

The desired impulse response is obtained by computing the inverse Laplace transform:

In[•]:=**InverseBilateralLaplaceTransform** $\left[\dfrac{1}{1+s}, s, t\right]$

Out[•]=e^{-t} UnitStep $[\,t\,]$

Second-Order Lowpass Filter

Second-order systems are the smallest systems to exhibit behavior generally representative of LTI systems.

In what follows, a system with the following canonical form is considered

$$y''(t) + 2\zeta\omega_n\, y'(t) + \omega_n^2\, y(t) = x(t)$$

where ζ is commonly referred to as the damping ratio and ω_n as the natural frequency.

A system of this form has a transfer function given by

$$H(s) = \frac{1}{s^2 + 2\zeta\omega_n s + \omega_n^2}$$

This shows the poles of the transfer function $H(s)$ and the impulse response $h(t)$ in the top row and the magnitudes of the transfer function $|H(s)|$ and frequency response $|H(j\omega)|$ in the bottom row, respectively, as functions of the damping ratio (in range $0 < \zeta < 1$) and the natural frequency ($0.1 < \omega_n \le 1.$):

In[•]:=**Manipulate** $[\ \cdots\ \boxed{+}\ ]$

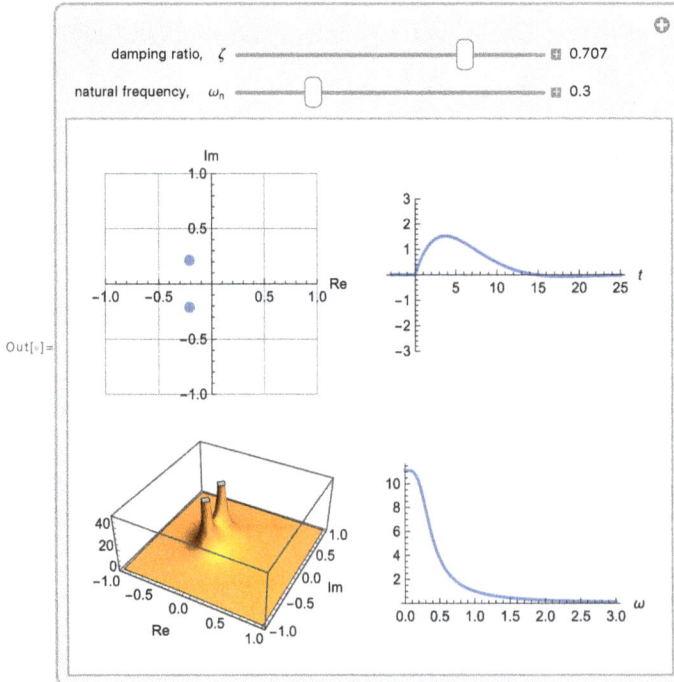

Differentiation in the s-Domain

The differentiation in the s-domain property gives general formulas for the Laplace transform of polynomial expressions. Thus it is useful when solving differential equations with repeated roots, specifically when determining the inverse Laplace transform of a rational function with poles of multiplicity greater than one.

If $x(t) \overset{\mathcal{L}}{\longleftrightarrow} X(s)$ with the ROC denoted by R, then

$$-tx(t) \overset{\mathcal{L}}{\longleftrightarrow} \frac{dX(s)}{ds}, \text{ with ROC containing } R$$

Also

$$t^2 x(t) \overset{\mathcal{L}}{\longleftrightarrow} \frac{d^2 X(s)}{ds^2}, \text{ with ROC containing } R$$

The general expression for an exponent greater than one is

$$(-1)^n \, t^n x(t) \overset{\mathcal{L}}{\longleftrightarrow} \frac{d^n X(s)}{ds^n}, \text{ with ROC containing } R$$

Proof

Differentiating both sides of the Laplace transform integral

$$X(s) = \int_{-\infty}^{\infty} x(t) \, e^{-st} \, dt$$

you get

$$\frac{dX(s)}{ds} = \int_{-\infty}^{\infty} (-t) x(t) \, e^{-st} \, dt$$

Effectively, multiplying a signal $x(t)$ by $-t$ gives a Laplace transform that is the derivative with respect to s of $X(s)$.

The second derivative gives

$$\frac{d^2 X(s)}{ds^2} = \int_{-\infty}^{\infty} (t^2) x(t) \, e^{-st} \, dt$$

Followed by the third derivative

$$\frac{d^3 X(s)}{ds^3} = \int_{-\infty}^{\infty} (-t^3) x(t) \, e^{-st} \, dt$$

Continuing in this manner, you get the following general result

$$\frac{d^n X(s)}{ds^n} = \int_{-\infty}^{\infty} (-1)^n \, t^n x(t) \, e^{-st} \, dt$$

Example 4

Use the differentiation in the s-domain theorem to determine the Laplace transform of the following signal

$$x(t) = t e^{-at} u(t)$$

Solution

Given the transform pair

$$e^{-at} u(t) \overset{\mathcal{L}}{\longleftrightarrow} \frac{1}{s+a}, \qquad \mathrm{Re}(s) > -a$$

it follows from the theorem that

$$t e^{-at} u(t) \overset{\mathcal{L}}{\longleftrightarrow} -\frac{d}{ds}\left(\frac{1}{s+a}\right) = \frac{1}{(s+a)^2}$$

with the same ROC. Continuing in this manner leads to the following general formula

$$\frac{t^{n-1}}{(n-1)!} e^{-at} u(t) \overset{\mathcal{L}}{\longleftrightarrow} \frac{1}{(s+a)^n}, \qquad \mathrm{Re}(s) > -a$$

Summary

Select Laplace transform theorems were discussed.

Time shifting

$$x(t - t_0) \overset{\mathcal{L}}{\longleftrightarrow} e^{-s t_0} X(s), \qquad \text{ROC equal to } R$$

Convolution

$$x_1(t) * x_2(t) \overset{\mathcal{L}}{\longleftrightarrow} X_1(s) X_2(s), \qquad \text{ROC containing } R_1 \cap R_2$$

Differentiation in time

$$\frac{d^n x(t)}{dt^n} \overset{\mathcal{L}}{\longleftrightarrow} s^n X(s), \qquad \text{ROC equal to } R$$

Differentiation in the s-domain

$$(-1)^n t^n x(t) \overset{\mathcal{L}}{\longleftrightarrow} \frac{d^n X(s)}{ds^n}, \qquad \text{ROC equal to } R$$

Several application examples were given.

Exercises

Download the solutions manual at wolfr.am/eTextbook-SSSP

24.1 Given the signals $x(t)$ and $y(t)$ shown here, convolve the two signals using the Laplace transform convolution theorem.

$$x(t) = e^{-t} u(t)$$

$$y(t) = e^{-2t} u(t)$$

24.2 Use the time differentiation theorem to obtain the system transfer function of an LTI system described by the following differential equation.

$$y''(t) + 2 y'(t) + y(t) = x'(t)$$

24.3 Determine the step response of an LTI system described by the following differential equation using the Laplace transform method.

$$y'(t) + y(t) = x'(t)$$

24.4 Determine the impulse response of an LTI system described by the following differential equation using the Laplace transform method.

$$y''(t) + y(t) = x(t)$$

24.5 Use the differentiation in the s-domain theorem to obtain the Laplace transform of the following signal.

$$y(t) = t^2\, e^{-t}\, u(t)$$

24.6 Use the differentiation in the s-domain theorem to obtain the inverse Laplace transform given the following Laplace transform.

$$X(s) = \frac{1}{s^2}, \qquad \text{Re}(s) > 0$$

25 | Unilateral Laplace Transform

In this chapter, the attention turns to an important special case of the Laplace transform known as the unilateral or one-sided Laplace transform defined as follows

$$X(s) = \int_{0^-}^{\infty} x(t)e^{-st}\, dt$$

Since the unilateral transform is defined for causal signals only, the region of convergence (ROC) can be ignored in determining the inverse.

The unilateral Laplace transform is particularly suited for analyzing causal systems specified by linear constant coefficient differential equations with nonzero initial conditions.

Differentiation-in-Time Property

The two transforms differ most substantially in regards to the differentiation property. This takes the unilateral Laplace transform of a derivative of a signal $x(t)$:

In[•]:= **LaplaceTransform [D [x [t] , t] , t , s]**

Out[•]= s LaplaceTransform [x [t] , t , s] − x [0]

The unilateral Laplace transform of the second derivative is:

In[•]:= **LaplaceTransform [D [x [t] , { t , 2 }] , t , s]**

Out[•]= s² LaplaceTransform [x [t] , t , s] − s x [0] − x′ [0]

The general formula for higher-order derivatives takes the following form

$$\mathcal{L}\left\{\frac{d^n}{dt^n}\, x(t)\right\} = s^n X(s) - s^{n-1}\, x(0) - \ldots - s^1 x^{(n-2)}(0) - x^{(n-1)}(0)$$

where $x^{(n)}(0)$ denotes the nth derivative of $x(t)$ evaluated at $t = 0$.

Example 1

Use the unilateral Laplace transform to obtain the step response of a causal linear time-invariant (LTI) system described by the following differential equation and initial condition

$$y'(t) + y(t) = x(t), \qquad y(0) = \alpha$$

Solution

Applying the unilateral Laplace transform to the differential equation gives the following algebraic equation

$$sY(s) - y(0) + Y(s) = X(s)$$

Collecting terms with $Y(s)$ and substituting $X(s) = \frac{1}{s}$ and $y(0) = \alpha$ gives the following result

$$(s + 1)\, Y(s) = \frac{1}{s} + \alpha$$

Solving for $Y(s)$ gives the Laplace transform of the output signal:

In[•]:= $\mathbf{Y[s\_]} := \dfrac{1 + \alpha\, s}{s\,(1 + s)}$

The step response of the filter is given by the inverse Laplace transform:

In[•]:= **InverseLaplaceTransform[Y[s], s, t]**

Out[•]= $1 + e^{-t}\,(-1 + \alpha)$

This shows the unit step response as the value of the initial condition is varied:

In[•]:= **Manipulate[[··· +]]**

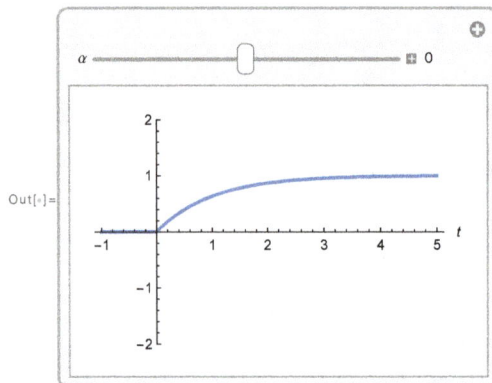

Initial and Final Values

It is sometimes desirable to deduce the so-called initial $(t \to 0^+)$ and final $(t \to \infty)$ values of signal $x(t)$ from knowledge of its Laplace transform $X(s)$.

The initial value theorem states that if $x(t)$ and its derivative $\frac{dx(t)}{dt}$ are both Laplace transformable, then

$$x(0^+) = \lim_{s \to \infty} s X(s)$$

provided the limit on the right-hand side exists.

The final value theorem states that if $x(t)$ and its derivative $\frac{dx(t)}{dt}$ are both Laplace transformable, then

$$x(\infty) = \lim_{s \to 0} s X(s)$$

provided $s X(s)$ has no poles in the right half plane or on the imaginary axis.

Example 2

Determine the initial and final values of $x(t)$ if its Laplace transform $X(s)$ is given by:

In[•]:=**X[s_] :=** $\dfrac{1}{s\,(s^2 + 4s + 3)}$ **;**

Solution

From the initial and final value theorems:

In[•]:=**Limit[s X[s], s → ∞]**

Out[•]=0

In[•]:=**Limit[s X[s], s → 0]**

Out[•]=$\dfrac{1}{3}$

Circuit Analysis—The Transformed Circuit

The differentiation properties of the Laplace transform can be used to transform circuit elements so that network analysis techniques (i.e. nodal or mesh methods) can be used directly in the transform domain.

Resistor

$$v(t) = R\,i(t) \qquad V(s) = R\,I(s) \qquad I(s) = \frac{V(s)}{R}$$

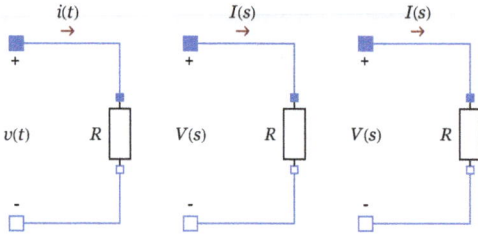

Capacitor

$$i(t) = C\frac{d}{dt}v(t) \qquad V(s) = \frac{1}{sC}I(s) + \frac{1}{s}v(0) \qquad I(s) = s\cdot C\cdot I(s) - C\cdot v(0)$$

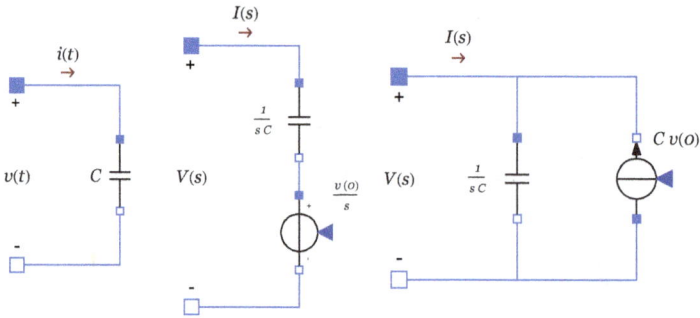

Inductor

$$v(t) = L\frac{d}{dt}i(t) \qquad V(s) = s\cdot L\cdot I(s) - L\cdot i(0) \qquad I(s) = \frac{1}{s\cdot L}I(s) + \frac{1}{s}i(0)$$

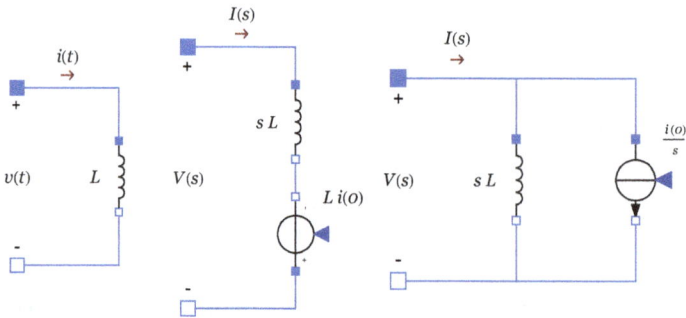

RC Circuit in the Laplace Domain

The method of transforming each of the circuit components in a given electrical circuit into its Laplace transform formulation together with standard circuit analysis techniques can now be used to solve any circuit problem. For example, this shows how to obtain the unit impulse and step responses of the circuit shown here, with $R = 1\ \Omega$ and $C = 1\ F$ and initial condition on the capacitor $y(0) = \alpha$

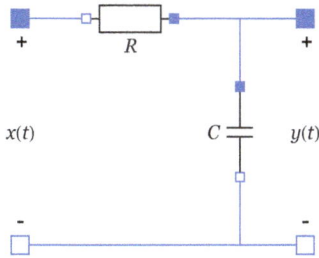

Application of the Laplace transform to the components yields the following circuit configuration

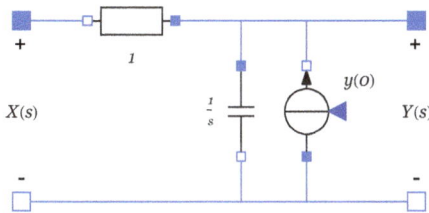

Applying nodal analysis (Kirchoff's current law) results in the following network equation

$$\frac{Y(s) - X(s)}{1} + \frac{Y(s)}{\frac{1}{s}} - y(0) = 0$$

Simplification gives

$$(1 + s)\, Y(s) = X(s) + y(0)$$

With $y(0) = \alpha$, the output in the s-domain is

$$Y(s) = \frac{X(s) + \alpha}{1 + s}$$

The Laplace transform $X(s)$ of a unit impulse input is $X(s) = 1$. The output $Y(s)$ is then

$$Y(s) = \frac{1 + \alpha}{1 + s}$$

and the impulse response is:

In[•]:= InverseLaplaceTransform $\left[\dfrac{1 + \alpha}{1 + s},\, s,\, t \right]$

Out[•]= $e^{-t}\,(1 + \alpha)$

For a unit step input, $X(s) = \frac{1}{s}$ and then the output $y(t)$ is:

In[•]:=**InverseLaplaceTransform** $\left[\dfrac{\frac{1}{s} + \alpha}{1 + s}, s, t\right]$

Out[•]=$1 + e^{-t}\left(-1 + \alpha\right)$

With $\alpha = 0$, you get the well-known step response of an RC circuit with zero initial conditions

$$y(t) = \left(1 - e^{-t}\right)u(t)$$

This plots the impulse and step responses for different values of α:

In[•]:=**Manipulate** $[\ \boxed{\cdots\ +}\ ]$

Out[•]=

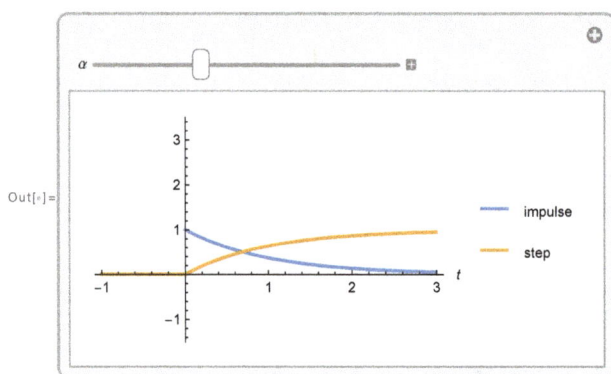

Example 3

Find the step response of the circuit shown using the Laplace transform.

A. Assume zero initial condition

B. Assume the initial voltage across the capacitor is $v_C(0) = -1\,V$

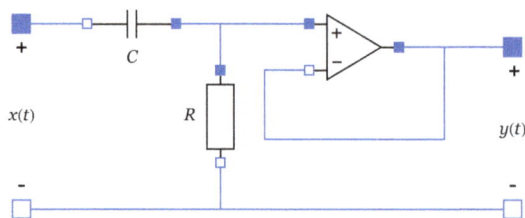

Solution

A. Noting that the voltage at the non-inverting input of the operational amplifier (op-amp) is $V_+ = V_- = Y(s)$, nodal analysis (Kirchoff's current law) in the s-domain gives the following equation

$$\frac{Y(s) - X(s)}{\frac{1}{sC}} + \frac{Y(s)}{R} = 0$$

Simplify

$$\left(\frac{1}{R} + sC\right) Y(s) + sCX(s) = 0$$

Solve for the output voltage $Y(s)$

$$Y(s) = -\frac{sC}{\frac{1}{R} + sC} X(s) = -\frac{sRC}{1 + sRC} X(s)$$

With $R = 1\ \Omega$, $C = 1\ F$, and step input $X(s) = \frac{1}{s}$, the response is

$$Y(s) = -\frac{1}{1 + s}$$

Therefore, the step response is:

In[•]:= **InverseLaplaceTransform** $\left[-\dfrac{1}{1+s}, s, t\right]$

Out[•]= $-e^{-t}$

B. The transformed circuit is

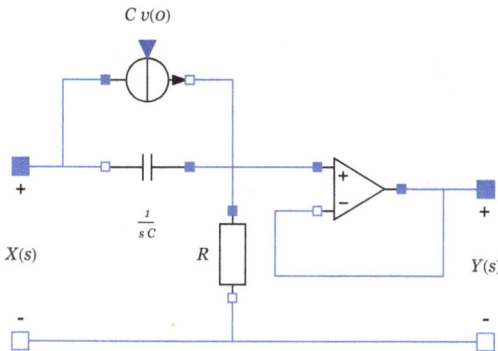

$C\,v(0)$

$X(s)$ $\dfrac{1}{sC}$ R $Y(s)$

The nodal equation at the non-inverting input of the op-amp of the transformed circuit is

$$-Cv_C(0) + \frac{Y(s) - X(s)}{\frac{1}{sC}} + \frac{Y(s)}{R} = 0$$

Reorganization and simplification gives

$$Y(s) = \frac{sRC}{(1+sRC)} X(s) + \frac{RCv_C(0)}{(1+sRC)}$$

Substitution of the values $v_C(0) = -1\ V$, $R = 1\ \Omega$, $C = 1\ F$, and $X(s) = \frac{1}{s}$ results in the following expression for the output

$$Y(s) = \frac{1}{1+s} - \frac{1}{1+s} = 0$$

The step response is identically zero.

Example 4

Obtain the impulse and step responses of the following circuit using the Laplace transform. Assume zero initial conditions and the following component values: $R_1 = R_2 = 1\ \Omega$ and $C_1 = C_2 = 1\ F$

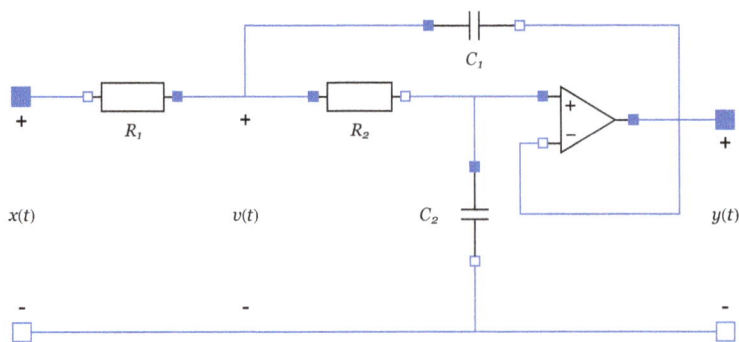

Solution

Nodal analysis in the s-domain at the node labeled $v(t)$ gives

$$\frac{V(s) - X(s)}{1} + \frac{V(s) - Y(s)}{\frac{1}{s}} + \frac{V(s) - Y(s)}{1} = 0$$

Voltage division at the non-inverting input of the op-amp gives the following auxiliary equation

$$Y(s) = \frac{\frac{1}{s}}{1 + \frac{1}{s}} V(s)$$

This gives the following system of two equations with two unknowns ($Y(s)$ and $V(s)$):

```
In[•]:=Clear [X, Y, V];
    eqns = {
        - (1 + s) Y[s] + (2 + s) V[s] == X[s],
        (1 + s) Y[s] - V[s] == 0
    };
```

Solving for the two unknowns returns:

In[•]:=**Solve [eqns, {Y [s] , V [s] }]**

Out[•]=$\left\{\left\{Y[s] \rightarrow \dfrac{X[s]}{(1+s)^2}, V[s] \rightarrow \dfrac{X[s]}{1+s}\right\}\right\}$

For impulse response, set the input $X(s) = 1$, resulting in:

In[•]:=**InverseLaplaceTransform [$\dfrac{1}{(1+s)^2}$, s, t]**

Out[•]=$e^{-t}\,t$

This plots the impulse response:

In[•]:=**Plot [e^{-t} t UnitStep [t] , { t, 0, 10 },**
PlotRange → { 0, 0.5` }, AxesLabel → { t, None }]

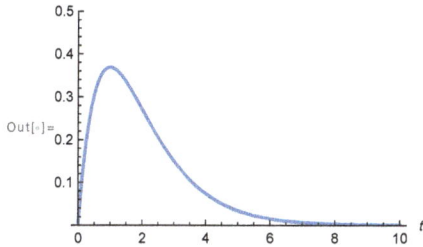

This gives the step response in the time domain:

In[•]:=**InverseLaplaceTransform [$\dfrac{1}{s\,(1+s)^2}$, s, t]**

Out[•]=$e^{-t}\left(-1 + e^t - t\right)$

This shows the step response:

In[•]:=**Plot [e^{-t} (-1 + e^t - t) , { t, 0, 10 }, PlotRange → { 0, 1 }, AxesLabel → { t, None }]**

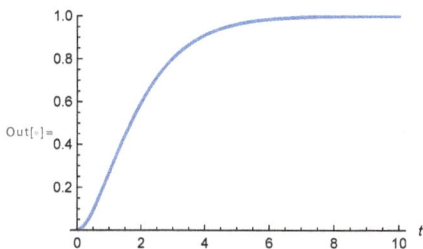

Summary

The unilateral Laplace transform was presented as a special case of the bilateral transform.

The unilateral transform finds particular application in circuit analysis.

Several examples of determining the step or impulse response using the transform method were shown.

Exercises

Download the solutions manual at wolfr.am/eTextbook-SSSP

25.1 Use the unilateral Laplace transform to solve the following initial value problem with $x(t) = \sin(t)$.

$$y'(t) + y(t) = x(t), \qquad y(0) = 1$$

25.2 Use the unilateral Laplace transform to solve the following initial value problem.

$$y''(t) - 5\,y'(t) + 6\,y(t) = 0, \qquad y(0) = 2, y'(0) = 2$$

25.3 Obtain the unit impulse response of the following RC circuit given $R = 1\,\Omega$, $C = 1$ F, and initial condition on the capacitor voltage $y(0) = 1$ V.

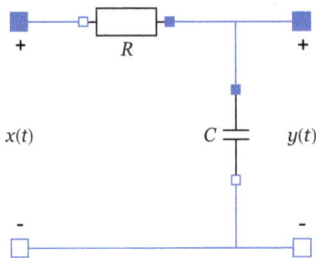

25.4 Given the circuit shown and assuming zero initial conditions, use the method of Laplace component transformations to obtain the system transfer function.

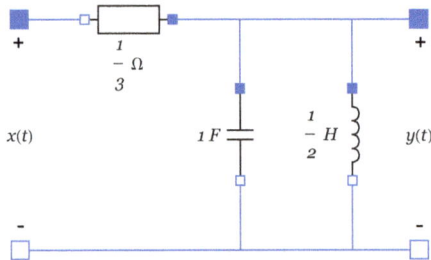

25.5 Find the transfer function for the network shown. Assume zero initial conditions.

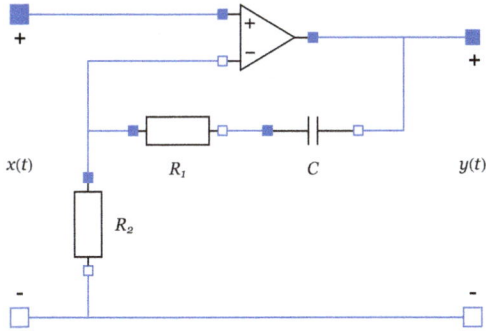

25.6 Use the Laplace transform to determine the step response of the network shown. Assume zero initial conditions.

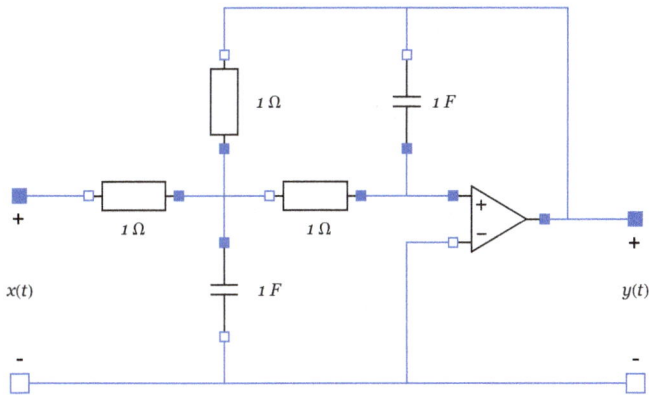

z-Transform

26 | z-Transform

The z-transform plays a similar role in discrete time as the Laplace transform does in continuous time. Discrete-time linear shift-invariant (LSI) systems are commonly defined, analyzed, and designed using their z-transform formulation. It is an important mathematical tool for solving constant coefficient difference equations, easily and conveniently incorporating initial conditions and impulsive input signals.

z-Transform—Definition and Convergence

The z-transform of a discrete-time signal $x[n]$ is defined

$$X(z) = \sum_{n=-\infty}^{\infty} x[n]z^{-n} \tag{1}$$

where z is a complex variable.

Letting $z = re^{j\omega}$, then equation (1) becomes

$$X\left(re^{j\omega}\right) = \sum_{n=-\infty}^{\infty} x[n]r^{-n}\, e^{-j\omega n} \tag{2}$$

which can be interpreted as the discrete-time Fourier transform (DTFT) of the modified sequence $x[n]r^{-n}$. In other words, the z-transform is a generalization of the Fourier transform. It follows from the properties of the DTFT that the sum in equation (2) converges if $x[n]r^{-n}$ is absolutely summable

$$\sum_{n=-\infty}^{\infty} |x[n]r^{-n}| < \infty$$

The z-transform $X(z)$ exists if $x[n]r^{-n}$ is absolutely summable, and the range of values of r for which this happens determines the so-called region of convergence (ROC) of the z-transform.

z-Transform of Finite-Duration Sequences

A finite-length sequence $x[n]$ consisting of a set of sample values $\{x[0], x[1], \ldots x[N-1]\}$ can be represented by the following sum of scaled and shifted unit samples

$$x[n] = \sum_{k=0}^{N-1} x[k]\delta[n-k]$$

Each term in the summation specifies the sample value of the sequence $x[k]$ and the time index $n = k$ at which that value occurs.

The z-transform of the sequence is defined by the formula

$$X(z) = \sum_{n=-\infty}^{\infty} x[n]z^{-n}$$

Substitution of sequence $x[n]$ yields the following

$$= \sum_{n=-\infty}^{\infty} \left(\sum_{k=0}^{N-1} x[k]\delta[n-k] \right) z^{-n}$$

Expansion of the inner sum and simplification lead to the following result

$$= \sum_{n=-\infty}^{\infty} (x[0]\delta[n] + x[1]\delta[n-1] + \ldots + x[N-1]\delta[n-N+1])z^{-n}$$

$$= x[0]z^0 + x[1]z^{-1} + \ldots + x[N-1]z^{-N+1}$$

$$= \sum_{k=0}^{N-1} x[k]z^{-k}$$

Sample values of the sequence $x[n]$ are simply coefficients of a polynomial in powers of z^{-1}.

For example, given the following finite-duration sequence

$$x[n] = \frac{1}{3}\,\delta[n] + \frac{1}{3}\delta[n-1] + \frac{1}{3}\,\delta[n-2]$$

the z-transform is

$$X(z) = \frac{1}{3} + \frac{1}{3}\,z^{-1} + \frac{1}{3}\,z^{-2}$$

Direct evaluation using the BilateralZTransform function confirms this result:

$$\text{In[·]:=}\ \mathbf{X[z\_] = BilateralZTransform}\left[\frac{1}{3}\,(\delta_n + \delta_{n-1} + \delta_{n-2}), n, z\right]$$

$$\text{Out[·]=}\ \frac{1 + z + z^2}{3z^2}$$

Use the function Expand to show that the transform is indeed a polynomial in negative powers of z:

$$\text{In[·]:=}\ \mathbf{Expand[X[z]]}$$

$$\text{Out[·]=}\ \frac{1}{3} + \frac{1}{3z^2} + \frac{1}{3z}$$

This shows the magnitude of the z-transform:

In[•]:=**Plot3D [Abs [X [u + i v]] , $\cdots$ +]**

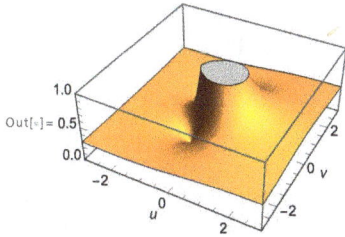

Out[•]=

This shows the phase of the z-transform:

In[•]:=**Plot3D [Arg [X [u + i v]] , $\cdots$ +]**

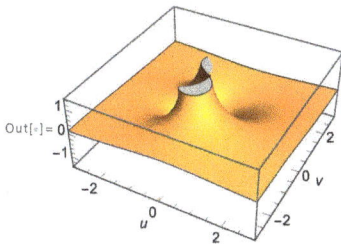

Out[•]=

Relation between the z-Transform and the DTFT

The DTFT $X(e^{j\omega})$ of a sequence $x[n]$, if it exists, may be obtained from the z-transform $X(z)$ by evaluating the z-transform on the unit circle

$$X(e^{j\omega}) = X(z)\big|_{z=e^{j\omega}}$$

For example, given the z-transform $X(z) = \frac{1}{3} \left(1 + z^{-1} + z^{-2}\right)$, the Fourier transform is $X(e^{j\omega}) = \frac{1}{3} \left(1 + e^{-j\omega} + e^{-j2\omega}\right)$.

Move the slider to change the frequency ω in the range $0 \le \omega \le 2\pi$ and observe how the DTFT is traced by traversing the z-transform surface on the unit circle:

In[•]:=**DynamicModule [$\cdots$ +]**

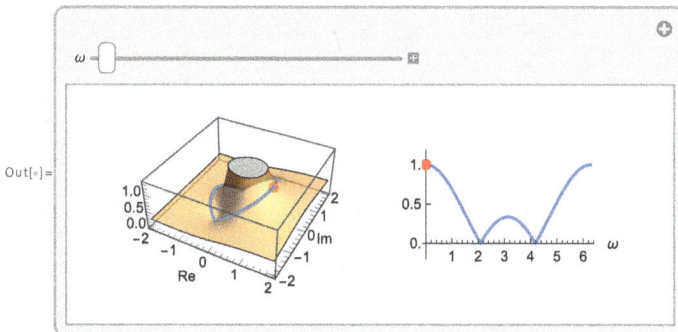

Out[•]=

z-Transform of Infinite-Duration Sequences and the ROC

Infinite-duration sequences may or may not have a z-transform as the defining sum may or may not converge. It is also interesting to note that two different sequences may have the same z-transform and differ only in their ROC. This is shown next.

Example 1

Obtain the z-transform of the following infinite-length sequence

$$x[n] = a^n\, u[n]$$

This shows the sequence with $a = \frac{2}{3}$:

In[•]:= **DiscretePlot [$\left(\dfrac{2}{3}\right)^n$ UnitStep [n] , $\boxed{\cdots\ +}$]**

Out[•]=

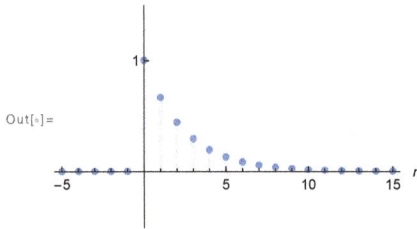

Solution

Direct evaluation using the BilateralZTransform function gives:

In[•]:= **BilateralZTransform [a^n UnitStep [n] , n, z]**

Out[•]= $-\dfrac{z}{a-z}$ if   Abs [a] < Abs [z]

Step-by-step

Proceed as follows

$$X(z) = \sum_{n=-\infty}^{\infty} x[n]\, z^{-n}$$

Substitute $x[n] = a^n\, u[n]$

$$= \sum_{n=-\infty}^{\infty} a^n\, u[n]\, z^{-n}$$

Simplify

$$= \sum_{n=0}^{\infty} \left(a z^{-1}\right)^n$$

The geometric series converges if $\left| a z^{-1} \right| < 1$ and the summation reduces to the following

$$= \frac{1}{1 - a z^{-1}}$$

Or equivalently, in positive powers of z

$$= \frac{z}{z-a}$$

The range of values of z for which the sum $\sum_{n=0}^{\infty} \left(az^{-1}\right)^n$ converges, namely $\left|az^{-1}\right| < 1$ and equivalently $|z| > |a|$. Thus the sequence $x[n]$ has an ROC that is the outside of a circle of radius $|a|$ as shown here:

In[•]:= **RegionPlot [⋯ ✦]**

Out[•]=

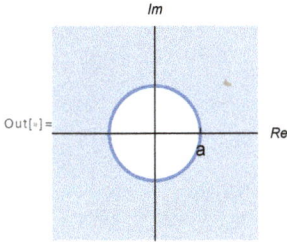

This shows a plot of the magnitude $|X(z)|$ with $a = 1$:

In[•]:= **Plot3D [Abs [$\dfrac{u + i\,v}{u + i\,v - 1}$] , ⋯ ✦]**

Out[•]=

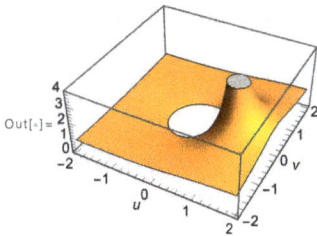

Example 2

Obtain the z-transform of the following left-sided sequence

$$x[n] = -a^n\, u[-n - 1]$$

This shows the sequence with $a = \frac{3}{2}$:

In[•]:= **DiscretePlot [$-\left(\dfrac{3}{2}\right)^n$ UnitStep [$-n - 1$] , ⋯ ✦]**

Out[•]=

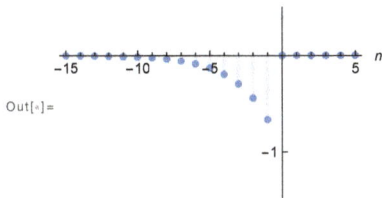

Solution

Direct evaluation using the BilateralZTransform function gives:

In[◦]:=**BilateralZTransform [– a^n UnitStep [– n – 1] ,**
    n, z, Assumptions → Element [a, Reals] && a > 0]

Out[◦]= $-\dfrac{z}{a-z}$ if Abs [z] < a

The ROC is the interior of a circle of radius $|a|$, as shown here:

In[◦]:=**RegionPlot [⋯ +]**

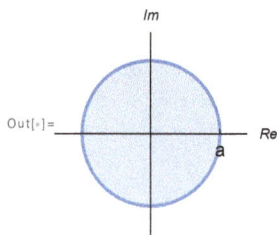

Out[◦]=

Thus, the z-transform expressions in Examples 1 and 2 are the same, but they differ in their ROC. The z-transform expressions are not unique and must always be accompanied by a specification of the ROC.

This shows the magnitude $|X(z)|$ within the ROC only:

In[◦]:=**Plot3D [Abs [$\dfrac{u + \tilde{\imath} \, v}{u + \tilde{\imath} \, v - \frac{3}{2}}$] , ⋯ +]**

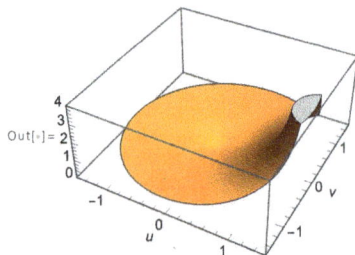

Out[◦]=

Step-by-step

Directly from the definition

$$X(z) = \sum_{n=-\infty}^{\infty} \left(-a^n \, u[-n-1]\right) z^{-n}$$

$$= -\sum_{n=-\infty}^{-1} a^n \, z^{-n}$$

$$= -\sum_{n=1}^{\infty} a^{-n} \, z^{n}$$

$$= -\left(\sum_{n=0}^{\infty} \left(\frac{z}{a}\right)^n - 1\right)$$

$$= 1 - \sum_{n=0}^{\infty} \left(\frac{z}{a}\right)^n$$

Now, for $\left|\frac{z}{a}\right| < 1$, the sum converges, yielding the following result

$$= 1 - \frac{1}{1-\frac{z}{a}}$$

and finally

$$= \frac{1}{1-az^{-1}}$$

$$= \frac{z}{z-a}, \qquad |z| < |a|$$

ROC—Additional Comments

The preceding two examples make it clear that the ROC plays a critical role in determining the properties of a sequence defined by a specific z-transform expression.

The unit circle plays an analogous role in the z-transform as the imaginary axis did in the case of the Laplace transform.

Finite-duration sequences that are absolutely integrable have an ROC that covers the entire z-plane, with the possible exception of $z = 0$ or $z = \infty$.

ROCs are always the interior or exterior of a circle or a ring bounded by the roots of the denominator of the z-transform.

This shows the latter

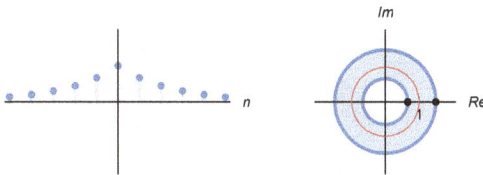

Square integrable sequences lead to z-transforms with ROCs that include the unit circle. Conversely, if the ROC does not include the unit circle, the corresponding sequence must grow without bounds.

Here are three sequences for which the ROC includes the unit circle

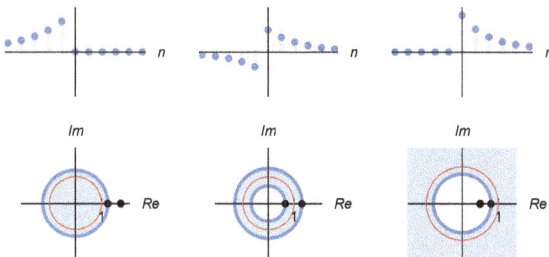

The necessary condition for a causal (i.e. right-sided) and convergent sequence requires all poles to be located inside the unit circle and for the ROC to be the exterior of the largest pole.

Rational z-Transforms

Rational z-transforms, those defined by ratios of two polynomials in z^{-1} (or z), are an important family of z-transforms, namely those representing LSI systems.

The general form of a rational z-transform $X(z)$ in terms of negative powers of z is

$$X(z) = \frac{b_0 + b_1 z^{-1} + \ldots + b_M z^{-M}}{a_0 + a_1 z^{-1} + \ldots a_N z^{-N}} = \frac{\sum_{k=0}^{M} b_k z^{-k}}{\sum_{k=0}^{N} a_k z^{-k}}$$

$X(z)$ is called a proper rational if $a_N \neq 0$ and the order of the numerator polynomial M (in the variable z^{-1}) is less than the order of the denominator polynomial N $(M < N)$.

An improper rational function $(M \geq N)$ can always be written as a sum of a polynomial and a proper rational function by long division in terms of the powers of z^{-1}

$$X(z) = c_0 + c_1 z^{-1} + \ldots + c_{M-N} z^{-(M-N)} + X_p(z)$$

where $X_p(z)$ is a proper rational function.

An equivalent z-transform formulation in terms of positive powers of z can be obtained by factoring out the most negative powers of z in the denominator and numerator

$$X(z) = z^{N-M} \frac{b_0 z^M + b_1 z^{M-1} + \ldots + b_M}{a_0 z^N + a_1 z^{N-1} + \ldots + a_N} = z^{N-M} \frac{\sum_{k=0}^{M} b_k z^{M-k}}{\sum_{k=0}^{N} a_k z^{N-k}}$$

The zeros of a z-transform are the values of z for which $X(z) = 0$.

The poles of a z-transform are the values of z for which $X(z) = \infty$.

$X(z)$ has M finite zeros and N finite poles, and $|N - M|$ zeros if $N > M$ or poles if $N < M$ at the origin. If the poles or zeros at the origin are counted, $X(z)$ has exactly the same number of poles and zeros.

A z-transform can be written explicitly in terms of the poles and zeros by using a factored form

$$X(z) = \frac{b_0}{a_0} z^{N-M} \frac{\prod_{k=1}^{M} (z - z_k)}{\prod_{k=1}^{N} (z - p_k)}$$

Example 3

Obtain the poles and zeros of the following z-transform:

In[•]:=$X[z\_] := \dfrac{1 - z^{-1} + z^{-2}}{1 - \frac{7}{2} z^{-1} + \frac{7}{2} z^{-2} - z^{-3}}$;

Solution

The poles and zeros can now be found as follows:

In[•]:=**poles = SolveValues [Denominator [X [z]] == 0, z] / / Flatten**

Out[•]=$\left\{\dfrac{1}{2}, 1, 2\right\}$

In[•]:=**zeros = SolveValues [Numerator [X [z]] == 0, z] / / ExpToTrig**

Out[•]=$\left\{\dfrac{1}{2} + \dfrac{i\ \sqrt{3}}{2}, \dfrac{1}{2} - \dfrac{i\ \sqrt{3}}{2}\right\}$

This shows the location of the poles and zeros:

In[•]:=**ComplexListPlot [{ poles, zeros },** ⋯ ✚ **]**

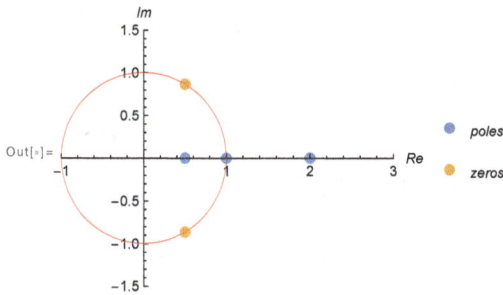

Here is a visualizations of the z-transform as a surface in the complex plane:

In[•]:=**Show [** {⋯} ✚ **]**

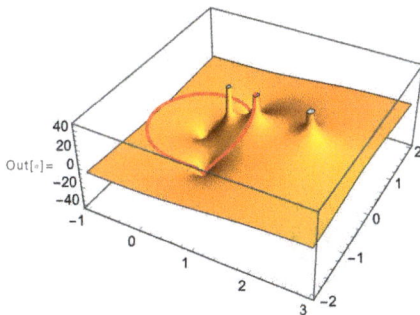

Summary

The z-transform was introduced.

The importance of the ROC in defining a z-transform was discussed.

Examples of obtaining the z-transform of right-sided and left-sided signals were given.

Several different methods of visualizing the z-transform were presented

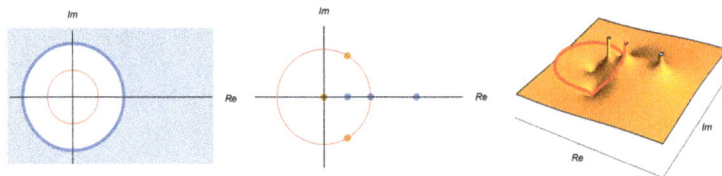

Exercises

Download the solutions manual at wolfr.am/eTextbook-SSSP

26.1 Determine the z-transform and the ROC of the following sequence.

$$x[n] = \delta[n + 1] - 2\,\delta[n] + \delta[n - 1]$$

26.2 Determine the z-transform and the ROC of the unit step sequence $x[n] = u[n]$.

26.3 Determine the z-transform and the ROC of the shifted unit step sequence $x[n] = u[n - 2]$.

26.4 Determine the z-transform and the ROC of the left-sided unit step sequence $x[n] = -u[-n - 1]$.

26.5 Determine the z-transform of the following finite-duration exponential sequence.

$$x[n] = \begin{cases} a^n, & 0 \le n \le M - 1 \\ 0, & \text{else} \end{cases}$$

27 | Inverse z-Transform

Formally, the inverse z-transform is defined as the following contour integral

$$x[n] = \frac{1}{2\pi j} \oint X[z] z^{n-1} dz$$

In the case of discrete-time linear shift-invariant (LSI) systems, inversion by contour integration is unnecessary because such systems invariably lead to rational z-transforms, such as the one shown here, for which there are relatively simple methods for accomplishing the inversion

$$X(z) = \frac{b_0 + b_1 z^{-1} + b_2 z^{-2} + \ldots + b_M z^{-M}}{1 + a_1 z^{-1} + a_2 z^{-2} + \ldots + a_N z^{-N}}$$

The common method for inverting such a z-transform is to use partial fraction decomposition. The goal of partial fraction decomposition is to express a rational z-transform in terms of superposition of simple terms, with inverse transforms readily available in tables of z-transform pairs and therefore by inspection.

Each term of the expansion corresponds to one of the roots of the denominator polynomial. In what follows, the cases of distinct and repeated roots are presented.

Distinct Roots

In the case of N distinct poles p_k, the transform $X(z)$ may be expanded into a linear combination of first-order terms, as follows

$$X(z) = \frac{A_1}{1-p_1 z^{-1}} + \frac{A_2}{1-p_2 z^{-1}} + \ldots + \frac{A_N}{1-p_N z^{-1}}$$

The constants A_i, called the residues, are given by

$$A_i = \left(1 - p_i z^{-1}\right) X(z) \big|_{z=p_i}$$

Then, assuming the region of convergence (ROC) is $|z| > |p_i|$, each term of the partial fraction expansion has an inverse transform of the form

$$A_i(p_i)^n u[n]$$

Therefore, the resulting sequence $x[n]$ is

$$x[n] = A_1(p_1)^n u[n] + A_2(p_2)^n u[n] + \ldots + A_N(p_N)^n u[n]$$

Example 1

Determine the inverse z-transform of the following proper rational function using partial fraction expansion

$$X(z) = \frac{1}{\left(1+z^{-1}\right)\left(1-\frac{1}{2}z^{-1}\right)}, \qquad |z| > \frac{1}{2}$$

Solution

The InverseBilateralZTransform returns:

$$\text{In[•]:=} \quad \mathbf{X[z\_] :=} \frac{1}{\left(1 + z^{-1}\right)\left(1 - \frac{1}{2}z^{-1}\right)};$$

InverseBilateralZTransform [

$$\text{ConditionalExpression}\,[\,X[z]\,,\,\text{Abs}[z] > \frac{1}{2}\,]\,,\,z,\,n\,]\,\,//\,\text{Expand}$$

$$\text{Out[•]=}\begin{cases} \frac{1}{3}\,2^{-n}\left(1 + (-1)^n\,2^{1+n}\right) & n \geq 0 \\ 0 & \text{True} \end{cases}$$

Step-by-step

Express the z-transform in positive powers of z

$$X(z) = \frac{z^2}{(z+1)\left(z-\frac{1}{2}\right)}$$

The advantage of working with positive powers of z stems from the fact that the method is now similar to partial fraction decomposition of rational Laplace transforms.

However, note that the expression in terms of positive powers of z is formally improper. The workaround is to reduce the order of the numerator polynomial by dividing by z and performing the expansion on the reduced rational, as shown here

$$\frac{X(z)}{z} = \frac{z}{z^2 + \frac{1}{2}z - \frac{1}{2}} = \frac{z}{(z+1)\left(z-\frac{1}{2}\right)}$$

Partial fraction decomposition yields

$$\frac{X(z)}{z} = A_1\frac{1}{z+1} + A_2\frac{1}{z-\frac{1}{2}}$$

The values of A_1 and A_2 are:

In[·]:=**Limit [(z + 1)** $\dfrac{\mathsf{X[z]}}{\mathsf{z}}$ **, z → −1]**

Out[·]= $\dfrac{2}{3}$

In[·]:=**Limit [(z − $\dfrac{1}{2}$)** $\dfrac{\mathsf{X[z]}}{\mathsf{z}}$ **, z → $\dfrac{1}{2}$]**

Out[·]= $\dfrac{1}{3}$

This gives

$$X(z) = \frac{2}{3} \frac{z}{z+1} + \frac{1}{3} \frac{z}{z-\frac{1}{2}} = \frac{2}{3} \frac{1}{1+z^{-1}} + \frac{1}{3} \frac{1}{1-\frac{1}{2} z^{-1}}$$

The term-by-term inversion of the partial fraction decomposition of $X(z)$ gives

$$x[n] = \frac{2}{3} (-1)^n u[n] + \frac{1}{3} \left(\frac{1}{2}\right)^n u[n]$$

Repeated Roots

The partial fraction expansion of a z-transform $X(z)$ with a multiple-order pole of order k at $z = p$ takes the following form

$$X(z) = \frac{A_1}{1-p z^{-1}} + \frac{A_2}{(1-p z^{-1})^2} + \dots + \frac{A_k}{(1-p z^{-1})^k}$$

The constants A_i are given by

$$A_i = \frac{1}{(k-i)!} \frac{1}{(-p)^{k-i}} \frac{d^{k-i}}{d(z^{-1})^{k-i}} \left\{(1 - p z^{-1})^k X(z)\right\}\bigg|_{z=p}, \quad i = 1, 2, \ \dots, k$$

Then, assuming the ROC is $|z| > |p|$, each term of the partial fraction expansion has an inverse transform of the form

$$p^n u[n] \overset{z}{\longleftrightarrow} \frac{1}{1-p z^{-1}}$$

$$(n + 1) p^n u[n] \overset{z}{\longleftrightarrow} \frac{1}{(1-p z^{-1})^2}$$

$$\frac{1}{2} (n + 1) (n + 2) p^n u[n] \overset{z}{\longleftrightarrow} \frac{1}{(1-p z^{-1})^3}$$

In general

$$\frac{1}{(k-1)!} (n + 1) (n + 2) \dots (n + k - 1) p^n u[n] \overset{z}{\longleftrightarrow} \frac{1}{(1-p z^{-1})^k}$$

Example 2

Determine the inverse z-transform of the following function using partial fraction expansion

$$X(z) = \frac{1+z^{-1}}{\left(1-\frac{1}{2}z^{-1}\right)^3}, \qquad |z| > \frac{1}{2}$$

Solution

Directly from the InverseBilateralZTransform, you get:

In[•]:=**X[z_] :=** $\dfrac{1+z^{-1}}{\left(1-\frac{1}{2}z^{-1}\right)^3}$;

InverseBilateralZTransform[X[z],z,n]

Out[•]=2^{-1-n} **(1+n) (2+3n) UnitStep[n]**

This shows the first few samples of the sequence:

In[•]:=**Table[2^{-1-n} (1+n) (2+3n) UnitStep[n], {n,0,5}]**

Out[•]=$\left\{1, \dfrac{5}{2}, 3, \dfrac{11}{4}, \dfrac{35}{16}, \dfrac{51}{32}\right\}$

Step-by-step

Using positive powers of z and the reduced transform $X(z)/z$, you get the following partial fraction expansion

$$\frac{X(z)}{z} = \frac{z(z+1)}{\left(z-\frac{1}{2}\right)^3} = \frac{A_1}{z-\frac{1}{2}} + \frac{A_2}{\left(z-\frac{1}{2}\right)^2} + \frac{A_3}{\left(z-\frac{1}{2}\right)^3}$$

The general formula for the coefficients A_i of a kth-order pole is now the same as in the case of the Laplace transform

$$A_i = \frac{1}{(k-i)!} \frac{d^{k-i}}{dz^{k-i}} \left\{ (z-p)^k \frac{X(z)}{z} \right\}\Big|_{z=p}, \qquad i = 1, \, ..., \, k$$

The following returns the value of the A_3 coefficient:

In[•]:=**Limit[$\left(z - \dfrac{1}{2}\right)^3 \dfrac{X[z]}{z}, z \rightarrow \dfrac{1}{2}$]**

Out[•]=$\dfrac{3}{4}$

This gives the A_2 and A_1 coefficients:

In[•]:=**Limit [D [$(z - \frac{1}{2})^3 \frac{X[z]}{z}$, z] , $z \to \frac{1}{2}$]**

Out[•]=2

In[•]:=**Limit [$\frac{1}{2!}$ D [$(z - \frac{1}{2})^3 \frac{X[z]}{z}$, {z, 2}] , $z \to \frac{1}{2}$]**

Out[•]=1

Therefore

$$X(z) = \frac{z}{z - \frac{1}{2}} + 2 \frac{z}{\left(z - \frac{1}{2}\right)^2} + \frac{3}{4} \frac{z}{\left(z - \frac{1}{2}\right)^3}$$

Each of the terms in the decomposition may be inverted by table lookup or evaluated as shown here

In[•]:=**InverseBilateralZTransform [$\frac{z}{z - \frac{1}{2}}$, z, n]**

Out[•]=2^{-n} UnitStep [n]

$$2 \frac{z}{\left(z - \frac{1}{2}\right)^2} \xrightarrow{z^{-1}} 4 \, n \left(\frac{1}{2}\right)^n u[n]$$

In[•]:=**InverseBilateralZTransform [$2 \frac{z}{(z - \frac{1}{2})^2}$, z, n]**

Out[•]=2^{2-n} n UnitStep [n]

$$\frac{3}{4} \frac{z}{\left(z - \frac{1}{2}\right)^3} \xrightarrow{z^{-1}} \frac{3}{4} \, 2 \, n(n-1) \left(\frac{1}{2}\right)^n u[n]$$

In[•]:=**InverseBilateralZTransform [$\frac{3}{4} \frac{z}{(z - \frac{1}{2})^3}$, z, n]**

Out[•]=$3 \, 2^{-1-n}$ (−1 + n) n UnitStep [n]

The resulting time-domain sequence is

$$x[n] = \left(1 + 4 \, n + \frac{3}{2} \, (n - 1) \, n\right) \left(\frac{1}{2}\right)^n u[n]$$

This shows the first few samples of the sequence:

In[•]:=**Table [($1 + 4 \, n + \frac{3}{2}$ (n − 1) n) 2^{-n} UnitStep [n] , {n, 0, 5}]**

Out[•]=$\left\{ 1, \frac{5}{2}, 3, \frac{11}{4}, \frac{35}{16}, \frac{51}{32} \right\}$

Example 3

Given the following z-transform:

$$In[\bullet]:=G\,[\,z\_\,]\,:=\frac{(1+z)^3}{-3+15\,z-25\,z^2+21\,z^3};$$

A. Obtain and plot the poles and zeros.

B. Plot the magnitude of the z-transform $G(z)$.

C. Obtain the causal sequence $g[n]$ with z-transform $G(z)$.

Solution

A. This shows the poles and zeros:

```
In[•]:=zeros = SolveValues [ Numerator [ G [ z ] ] == 0, z]  / / Flatten;
       poles = SolveValues [ Denominator [ G [ z ] ] == 0, z]  / / Flatten;
       ComplexListPlot [ { poles, zeros }, ⋯ ✦ ]
```

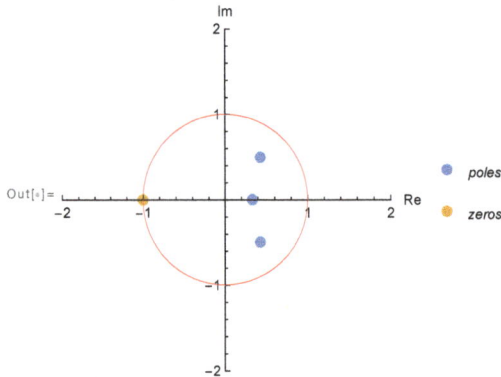

B. This shows the magnitude (in decibels) of the z-transform evaluated on the complex plane:

```
In[•]:=Plot3D [ ⋯ ✦ ]
```

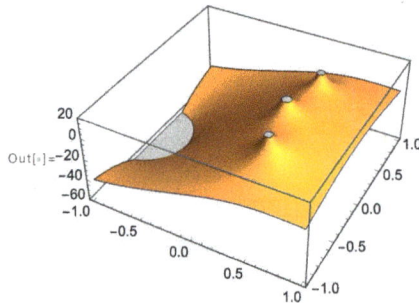

C. The result may be obtained directly from the InverseBilateralZTransform:

In[•]:=**g [n_] = InverseBilateralZTransform [G [z] , z, n]**

$$Out[•]=\frac{1}{21}\left(2\,3^{-n}\left(-14-i\,3^{\frac{1}{2}+n}\left(\frac{1}{7}\left(3-2\,i\,\sqrt{3}\right)\right)^{n}+5\left(\frac{3}{7}\left(3-2\,i\,\sqrt{3}\right)\right)^{n}+\right.$$

$$\left.i\,3^{\frac{1}{2}+n}\left(\frac{1}{7}\left(3+2\,i\,\sqrt{3}\right)\right)^{n}+5\left(\frac{3}{7}\left(3+2\,i\,\sqrt{3}\right)\right)^{n}\right)$$

$$\left(-1+\text{UnitStep}\,[-n]\,\right)+\text{UnitStep}\,[-n]\,\right)\text{UnitStep}\,[n]$$

This shows the sequence:

In[•]:=**DiscretePlot [g [n] , ⋯ +]**

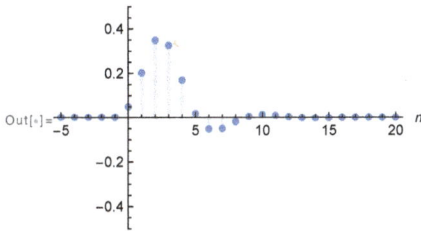

ROC and the Inverse z-Transform

The examples given thus far all assumed system causality and therefore an ROC that spans the exterior of a circle marked by the largest pole. While this may indeed be the most common case encountered in practice, it is important and interesting to consider alternative ROC specifications for a given z-transform $X(z)$ and the resulting sequences $x[n]$.

This defines an example z-transform with two poles:

In[•]:=**X [z_] :=** $\dfrac{1}{(1-\frac{1}{2}\,z^{-1})\,(1-\frac{4}{5}\,z^{-1})}$ **;**

The two poles are $p_1 = \frac{1}{2}$ and $p_2 = \frac{4}{5}$, resulting in three possible ROCs, as shown here

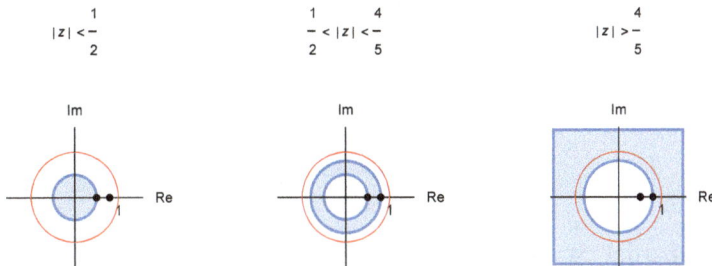

Example 4

Obtain the inverse z-transform given the following specification

$$X(z) = \frac{1}{\left(1-\frac{1}{2}z^{-1}\right)\left(1-\frac{4}{5}z^{-1}\right)}, \quad |z| > \frac{4}{5}$$

Solution

Using the same approach as in Example 1 gives:

In[·]:= **x [n_] = InverseBilateralZTransform [**

ConditionalExpression [X [z] , Abs [z] > $\frac{4}{5}$] , z, n] / / Expand

Out[·]= $\begin{cases} \frac{1}{3}\,10^{-n}\left(2^{3+3n}-5^{1+n}\right) & n \geq 0 \\ 0 & \text{True} \end{cases}$

This shows the resulting sequence:

In[·]:= **DiscretePlot [x [n] , ⋯ ＋]**

Out[·]=

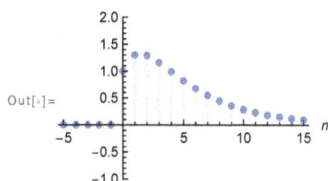

The result is a bounded and causal (or right-sided) sequence.

Step-by-step

Partial fraction expansion of $X(z)$

$$\frac{X(z)}{z} = \frac{z}{\left(z-\frac{1}{2}\right)\left(z-\frac{4}{5}\right)} = \frac{A}{z-\frac{1}{2}} + \frac{B}{z-\frac{4}{5}}$$

The values of A and B can be quickly obtained using the method of residues:

In[·]:= **Limit [(z − $\frac{1}{2}$) $\frac{X[z]}{z}$, z → $\frac{1}{2}$]**

Out[·]= $-\frac{5}{3}$

In[·]:= **Limit [(z − $\frac{4}{5}$) $\frac{X[z]}{z}$, z → $\frac{4}{5}$]**

Out[·]= $\frac{8}{3}$

This gives the partial expansion as

$$X(z) = -\frac{5}{3}\,\frac{z}{z-\frac{1}{2}} + \frac{8}{3}\,\frac{z}{z-\frac{4}{5}}$$

Each of the terms in the decomposition may be inverted by table lookup or evaluated as shown here:

In[•]:=**InverseBilateralZTransform** $\left[-\dfrac{5}{3}\dfrac{z}{z-\frac{1}{2}}, z, n\right]$

Out[•]= $-\dfrac{5}{3}\,2^{-n}\,\text{UnitStep}[n]$

In[•]:=**InverseBilateralZTransform** $\left[\dfrac{8}{3}\dfrac{z}{z-\frac{4}{5}}, z, n\right]$

Out[•]= $\dfrac{1}{3}\,2^{3+2n}\,5^{-n}\,\text{UnitStep}[n]$

The result is the following sequence given the z-transform and ROC

$$x[n] = \left(-\frac{5}{3}\left(\frac{1}{2}\right)^n + \frac{8}{3}\left(\frac{4}{5}\right)^n\right)u[n]$$

Example 5

Obtain the inverse z-transform given the following transform specification

$$X(z) = \frac{1}{\left(1-\frac{1}{2}z^{-1}\right)\left(1-\frac{4}{5}z^{-1}\right)}, \quad |z| < \frac{1}{2}$$

Solution

Substituting the given z-transform and the ROC into the inverse z-transform function gives:

In[•]:=**x[n_] = InverseBilateralZTransform [**

ConditionalExpression [X [z], Abs [z] $< \dfrac{1}{2}$], z, n]

Out[•]= $\begin{cases} \frac{1}{3}\,10^{-n}\left(5^{1+n}-8^{1+n}\right) & n < 0 \\ 0 & \text{True} \end{cases}$

This shows the resulting sequence:

In[•]:=**DiscretePlot [x [n], ⋯ +]**

Out[•]=

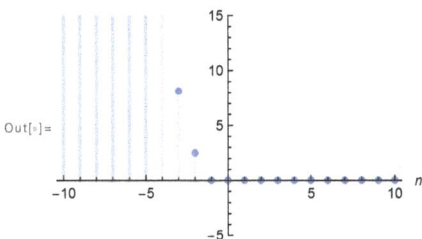

The resulting signal is unbounded and anti-causal (or left sided).

Example 6

Obtain the inverse z-transform given the following specification

$$X(z) = \frac{1}{\left(1-\frac{1}{2}z^{-1}\right)\left(1-\frac{4}{5}z^{-1}\right)}, \quad \frac{1}{2} < |z| < \frac{4}{5}$$

Solution

Using the same approach as in Example 1 gives:

In[•]:= x [n_] = InverseBilateralZTransform [

ConditionalExpression [X [z] , $\frac{1}{2}$ < Abs [z] < $\frac{4}{5}$] , z , n] // Expand

$$\text{Out[•]} = \begin{cases} -\frac{5\,2^{-n}}{3} & n \geq 0 \\ -\frac{1}{3}\,2^{3+2n}\,5^{-n} & \text{True} \end{cases}$$

This shows the resulting sequence:

In[•]:= DiscretePlot [x [n] , ⋯ +]

Out[•] =

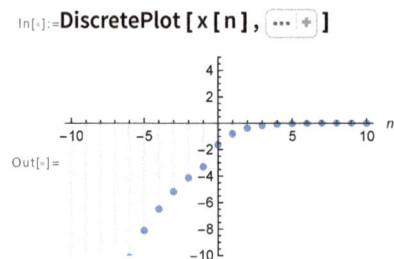

The resulting sequence is two sided and also unbounded.

Summary

The z-transform inversion by method of partial fraction expansion was presented.

Several examples were shown with details describing the evaluation of residues for both distinct and repeated roots.

Examples of inversions for different ROCs were shown

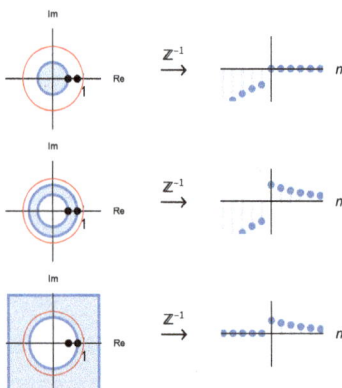

Exercises

Download the solutions manual at wolfr.am/eTextbook-SSSP

27.1 Determine the inverse z-transform of $X(z) = \frac{1}{2} z + 1 + \frac{1}{2} z^{-1} - z^{-3}$.

27.2 Given $X(z)$ and the ROC, determine the inverse z-transform.

$$X(z) = \frac{1+z^{-1}}{1+\frac{1}{4} z^{-2}}, \quad |z| > \frac{1}{2}$$

27.3 Given $X(z)$ and the ROC, determine the inverse z-transform.

$$X(z) = \frac{1+z^{-1}}{1+\frac{1}{4} z^{-2}}, \quad |z| < \frac{1}{2}$$

27.4 Given $X(z)$, determine the causal inverse z-transform.

$$X(z) = \frac{1+2 z^{-1}+z^{-2}}{1-\frac{3}{2} z^{-1}+\frac{1}{2} z^{-2}}$$

27.5 Consider a z-transform $X(z)$ whose pole-zero plot and ROC are as shown.

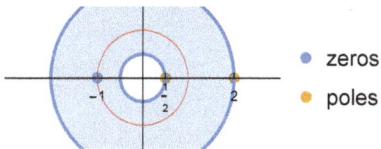

Obtain the inverse z-transform.

28 | z-Transform Theorems

As was the case with other transforms discussed in this book, the z-transform has several important theorems that make it easier to use the transform to validate results, derive properties, and, in general, analyze and design discrete-time systems.

The theorems that are of particular importance are:

- Time shifting
- Time reversal
- Differentiation in the z-domain
- Convolution

Time Shift Theorem

This is arguably the most important of the selected theorems as it allows one to transform a constant coefficient difference equation into an algebraic equation in powers of z, which leads to an alternative method for solving such equations, easily determining the sinusoidal steady-state response, the frequency response, or the transfer function of a linear shift-invariant (LSI) system, and more. The transfer function is the z-transform of the unit sample response of a digital filter and a generalization of the frequency response.

Given the transform pair $x[n] \overset{z}{\longleftrightarrow} X(z)$ with the region of convergence (ROC) denoted by R_x, the z-transform of a time-delayed sequence is

$$x[n - n_0] \overset{z}{\longleftrightarrow} z^{-n_0} X(z), \quad \text{with ROC equal to } R_x$$

Proof

In order to derive this result, start with the z-transform definition

$$Y(z) = \sum_{n=-\infty}^{\infty} y[n]\, z^{-n} = \sum_{n=-\infty}^{\infty} x[n - n_0]\, z^{-n}$$

Substituting $m = n - n_0$ gives

$$= \sum_{m=-\infty}^{\infty} x[m] \, z^{-(m+n_0)}$$

Simplification gives the desired result

$$= z^{-n_0} \left(\sum_{m=-\infty}^{\infty} x[m] \, z^{-m} \right)$$

$$= z^{-n_0} X(z)$$

This completes the proof.

The System Transfer Function of an FIR Filter

Recall that a discrete-time non-recursive LSI system, namely a finite impulse response (FIR) filter, is described by an input-output relation of the form

$$y[n] = \sum_{k=N_1}^{N_2-1} b_k \cdot x[n - k], \qquad N_1 < N_2$$

Without loss of generality, setting $N_1 = 0$ and $N_2 = N$ gives the following simpler form

$$y[n] = \sum_{k=0}^{N-1} b_k \cdot x[n - k]$$

Application of the time shift theorem returns

$$\mathcal{Z}\{y[n]\} = b_0 \, \mathcal{Z}\{x[n]\} + b_1 \, \mathcal{Z}\{x[n - 1]\} + \dots + b_{N-1} \, \mathcal{Z}\{x[n - N + 1]\}$$

resulting in the following equation for the output $Y(z)$

$$Y(z) = b_0 \, X(z) + b_1 \, z^{-1} \, X(z) + \dots + b_{N-1} \, z^{-N+1} \, X(z)$$

$$= \left(b_0 + b_1 \, z^{-1} + \dots + b_{N-1} \, z^{-N+1} \right) X(z)$$

Finally, the system transfer function takes the following form

$$H(z) = \frac{Y(z)}{X(z)} = b_0 + b_1 \, z^{-1} + \dots + b_{N-1} \, z^{-N+1}$$

The transfer function of a non-recursive system is a polynomial in powers of z^{-1}.

Example 1

Obtain the transfer function of the following moving-average filter

$$y[n] = \frac{1}{3} \, x[n] + \frac{1}{3} \, x[n - 1] + \frac{1}{3} \, x[n - 2]$$

Solution

Using the time shift theorem gives

$$Y(z) = \frac{1}{3} \, X(z) + \frac{1}{3} \, z^{-1} \, X(z) + \frac{1}{3} \, z^{-2} \, X(z)$$

This gives

$$Y(z) = \left(\frac{1}{3} + \frac{1}{3} z^{-1} + \frac{1}{3} z^{-2}\right) X(z)$$

Therefore

$$H(z) = \frac{Y(z)}{X(z)} = \frac{1}{3} + \frac{1}{3} z^{-1} + \frac{1}{3} z^{-2}$$

The System Transfer Function of an IIR Filter

Recall that the mathematical representation of an infinite impulse response (IIR) filter takes the form of an Nth-order linear constant coefficient difference equation

$$a_0 \, y[n] + a_1 \, y[n-1] + \ldots + a_N \, y[n-N+1] =$$
$$b_0 \, x[n] + b_1 \, x[n-1] + \ldots + b_M \, x[n-M+1]$$

The difference equation in the z-transform domain

$$a_0 \, \mathcal{Z} \{y[n]\} + a_1 \, \mathcal{Z} \{y[n-1]\} + \ldots + a_N \, \mathcal{Z} \{y[n-N+1]\} =$$
$$b_0 \, \mathcal{Z} \{x[n]\} + b_1 \, \mathcal{Z} \{x[n-1]\} + \ldots + b_M \, \mathcal{Z} \{x[n-M+1]\}$$

Application of the shift theorem results in the following equation

$$a_0 \, Y(z) + a_1 \, z^{-1} \, Y(z) + \ldots + a_{N-1} \, z^{-N+1} \, Y(z) =$$
$$b_0 \, X(z) + b_1 \, z^{-1} \, X(z) + \ldots + b_{M-1} \, z^{-M+1} \, X(z)$$

Solving for the ratio of the $Y(z)/X(z)$ returns the system or transfer function $H(z)$ of the filter

$$H(z) = \frac{Y(z)}{X(z)} = \frac{b_0 + b_1 \, z^{-1} + \ldots + b_M \, z^{-M+1}}{a_0 + a_1 \, z^{-1} + \ldots + a_N \, z^{-N+1}}$$

Note that an LSI system has a rational system function.

Example 2

Obtain the transfer function of the following IIR filter

$$y[n] - \frac{1}{2} \, y[n-1] = x[n]$$

Solution

Using the time shift theorem gives

$$Y(z) - \frac{1}{2} \, z^{-1} \, Y(z) = X(z)$$

This gives

$$Y(z)\left(1 - \frac{1}{2}z^{-1}\right) = X(z)$$

Therefore

$$H(z) = \frac{Y(z)}{X(z)} = \frac{1}{1 - \frac{1}{2}z^{-1}} = \frac{z}{z - \frac{1}{2}}$$

The System Transfer Function and Unit Sample Response

The transfer function is a transform domain representation of the relationship between the input and output of an LTI system with zero initial conditions

$$Y(z) = H(z)\,X(z)$$

Given a unit sample input $x[n] = \delta[n]$ with z-transform $X(z) = 1$, the output reduces to the following

$$Y(z) = H(z)$$

Therefore the unit sample response $h[n]$ of an LTI system and its transfer function $H(z)$ form a z-transform pair

$$h[n] \xleftrightarrow{\;z\;} H(z)$$

Example 3

Obtain the unit sample response of the following IIR filter using the z-transform method

$$y[n] - \frac{1}{2}\,y[n - 1] = x[n]$$

Solution

The transfer function of the given IIR filter (see Example 2) is

$$H(z) = \frac{z}{z - \frac{1}{2}}$$

The unit sample response is a causal sequence so the following returns the desired result:

In[•]:= **InverseBilateralZTransform** $\left[\dfrac{z}{z - \frac{1}{2}}, z, n\right]$

Out[•]= 2^{-n} **UnitStep** [n]

Time Reversal Theorem

Given the transform pair $x[n] \overset{z}{\longleftrightarrow} X(z)$, with the ROC denoted by R_x, the z-transform of a time-reversed sequence is

$$x[-n] \overset{z}{\longleftrightarrow} X\left(\tfrac{1}{z}\right), \text{ with ROC equal to } \tfrac{1}{R_x}$$

Proof

In order to derive this result, start with the defining formula

$$Y(z) = \sum_{n=-\infty}^{\infty} y[n]\, z^{-n} = \sum_{n=-\infty}^{\infty} x[-n]\, z^{-n}$$

Substitute $m = -n$

$$= \sum_{m=\infty}^{-\infty} x[m]\, z^{-(-m)}$$

$$= \sum_{m=-\infty}^{\infty} x[m]\, \left(z^{-1}\right)^{-m}$$

$$= X\left(z^{-1}\right)$$

This completes the proof.

Example 4

Given the transform pair

$$x[n] = 2^n\, u[n] \overset{z}{\longleftrightarrow} X(z) = \frac{1}{1 - 2\, z^{-1}} = \frac{z}{z-2}, \qquad |z| > 2$$

use the time shift and time reversal theorems to obtain the z-transform of the following sequence

$$y[n] = -2^n\, u[-n - 1]$$

Solution

Note that $y[n]$ can be rewritten in the following way

$$y[n] = -2^n\, u[-n - 1]$$

$$= -\left(\tfrac{1}{2}\right)^{-n} u[-n - 1]$$

$$= -\tfrac{1}{2} \left(\tfrac{1}{2}\right)^{-n-1} u[-n - 1]$$

$$= -\tfrac{1}{2}\, x[-(n + 1)]$$

Therefore, application of the time shift and time reversal theorems gives the following result

$$Y(z) = -\frac{1}{2} z X\left(\frac{1}{z}\right)$$

$$= -\frac{1}{2} z \frac{1}{1-2z}$$

$$= \frac{1}{4} \frac{z}{z-\frac{1}{2}}, \qquad \left|\frac{1}{z}\right| > 2$$

Differentiation in the z-Domain

The differentiation theorem is useful in determining the z-transform of sequences scaled by a power of n, or, equivalently, the inverse transform of nth-order poles.

Given $x[n] \overset{z}{\longleftrightarrow} X(z)$ with the ROC denoted by R_x, then

$$nx[n] \overset{z}{\longleftrightarrow} -z\frac{dX(z)}{dz}, \quad \text{with ROC equal to } R_x$$

Proof

In order to derive this result, take the derivative of $X(z)$ with respect to the variable z

$$\frac{dX(z)}{dz} = \frac{d}{dz}\left(\sum_{n=-\infty}^{\infty} x[n]z^{-n}\right)$$

$$= \sum_{n=-\infty}^{\infty} x[n] \frac{d}{dz}(z^{-n})$$

$$= \sum_{n=-\infty}^{\infty} x[n](-n) z^{-n-1}$$

$$= -z^{-1}\sum_{n=-\infty}^{\infty} (nx[n]) z^{-n}$$

Therefore

$$-z\frac{dX(z)}{dz} = \sum_{n=-\infty}^{\infty} (nx[n]) z^{-n}$$

This completes the proof.

Example 5

Given $X(z) = \frac{1}{1-z^{-1}}$, use the differentiation theorem to determine the causal sequence with the following z-transform

$$Y(z) = \frac{z^{-1}}{(1-z^{-1})^2} = \frac{z}{(z-1)^2}$$

Solution

Take the derivative of $X(z)$ with respect to the variable z:

$$\text{In[*]:= } \mathbf{D} \left[\frac{1}{1 - z^{-1}}, z \right] \text{ // Simplify}$$

$$\text{Out[*]= } -\frac{1}{(-1 + z)^2}$$

Multiply by $-z$:

$$\text{In[*]:= } -z \, \mathbf{D} \left[\frac{1}{1 - z^{-1}}, z \right] \text{ // Simplify}$$

$$\text{Out[*]= } \frac{z}{(-1 + z)^2}$$

Observe that this results in the sequence $Y(z)$. Therefore, according to the differentiation theorem, the sequence $y[n]$ is

$$y[n] = nx[n] = nu[n]$$

This verifies the derivation:

$$\text{In[*]:= } \mathbf{BilateralZTransform} \left[\mathbf{n \, UnitStep \, [\, n \,]}, \mathbf{n, z} \right]$$

$$\text{Out[*]= } \boxed{ \frac{z}{(-1 + z)^2} \quad \text{if } \text{Abs}[z] > 1 }$$

Convolution Theorem

Given two sequences $x_1[n]$ and $x_2[n]$ and their respective z-transforms $X_1(z)$ and $X_2(z)$ with the ROCs denoted by R_{x_1} and R_{x_2}, respectively, the z-transform of a convolution of the two sequences in time is equal to the product of the z-transforms of the two sequences

$$x_1[n] * x_2[n] \overset{z}{\longleftrightarrow} X_1(z) \, X_2(z), \qquad \text{ROC contains } R_{x_1} \cap R_{x_2}$$

Proof

To derive this result, proceed as follows

$$Y(z) = \sum_{n=-\infty}^{\infty} y[n] \, z^{-n}$$

$$= \sum_{n=-\infty}^{\infty} \left(\sum_{k=-\infty}^{\infty} x_1[k] \, x_2[n - k] \right) z^{-n}$$

Interchanging the order of summation gives

$$Y(z) = \sum_{k=-\infty}^{\infty} x_1[k] \left(\sum_{n=-\infty}^{\infty} x_2[n - k] \, z^{-n} \right)$$

Substitution of $m = n - k$ and simplification gives

$$Y(z) = \sum_{k=-\infty}^{\infty} x_1[k] \left(\sum_{m=-\infty}^{\infty} x_2[m]\, z^{-(m+k)} \right)$$

$$= \sum_{k=-\infty}^{\infty} x_1[k] \left(\sum_{m=-\infty}^{\infty} x_2[m]\, z^{-m} \right) z^{-k}$$

$$= \left(\sum_{k=-\infty}^{\infty} x_1[k]\, z^{-k} \right) X_2(z)$$

$$= X_1(z)\, X_2(z)$$

The ROC includes the intersection of the regions of convergence of $X_1(z)$ and $X_2(z)$.

This completes the proof.

Example 6

Convolve the sequences $h[n] = \delta[n] - \delta[n-1]$ and
$x[n] = \delta[n] + 2\,\delta[n-2] + 3\,\delta[n-4] + 4\,\delta[n-6]$ using the convolution theorem.

Solution

Making direct use of the theorem:

```
In[·]:=InverseBilateralZTransform [
         BilateralZTransform [δ_n − δ_{n−1}, n, z] BilateralZTransform [
             δ_n + 2 δ_{n−2} + 3 δ_{n−4} + 4 δ_{n−6}, n, z], z, n] / / FullSimplify
```

$$\text{Out[·]} = \begin{cases} -4 & n == 7 \\ -3 & n == 5 \\ -2 & n == 3 \\ -1 & n == 1 \\ 1 & n == 0 \\ 2 & n == 2 \\ 3 & n == 4 \\ 4 & n == 6 \\ 0 & \text{True} \end{cases}$$

Step-by-step

The z-transforms of the sequences $h[n]$ and $x[n]$ are

$$H(z) = 1 - z^{-1}$$

$$X(z) = 1 + 2\,z^{-2} + 3\,z^{-4} + 4\,z^{-6}$$

Multiplying the two polynomials gives

$$Y(z) = H(z)\, X(z) = \left(1 - z^{-1}\right)\left(1 + 2\,z^{-2} + 3\,z^{-4} + 4\,z^{-6}\right)$$

$$= \left(1 + 2\,z^{-2} + 3\,z^{-4} + 4\,z^{-6}\right) - \left(z^{-1} + 2\,z^{-3} + 3\,z^{-5} + 4\,z^{-7}\right)$$

$$= 1 - z^{-1} + 2\,z^{-2} - 2\,z^{-3} + 3\,z^{-4} - 3\,z^{-5} + 4\,z^{-6} - 4\,z^{-7}$$

Taking the inverse transform returns the desired result

$$y[n] = \delta[n] - \delta[n-1] + 2\,\delta[n-2] - 2\,\delta[n-3] + 3\,\delta[n-4] - 3\,\delta[n-5] +$$
$$4\,\delta[n-6] - 3\,\delta[n-7]$$

Summary

Four z-transform theorems of particular importance were presented:

- Time shifting

$$x[n - n_0] \overset{\mathcal{Z}}{\longleftrightarrow} z^{-n_0}\, X(z)$$

- Time reversal

$$x[-n] \overset{\mathcal{Z}}{\longleftrightarrow} X\!\left(\tfrac{1}{z}\right)$$

- Differentiation in the z-domain

$$n\,x[n] \overset{\mathcal{Z}}{\longleftrightarrow} -z\frac{dX(z)}{dz}$$

- Convolution

$$x_1[n] * x_2[n] \overset{\mathcal{Z}}{\longleftrightarrow} X_1(z)\, X_2(z)$$

The system transfer function was defined.

Examples of using the time shift theorem to find the transfer function of FIR and IIR filters were shown.

Exercises

Download the solutions manual at wolfr.am/eTextbook-SSSP

28.1 Determine the z-transform of the sequence $x[n] = \cos(n)u[n]$ using linearity and the transform pair

$$a^n u[n] \overset{\mathcal{Z}}{\longleftrightarrow} \frac{1}{1-az^{-1}}, \qquad |z| > |a|$$

(Hint: use Euler's formula.)

28.2 Determine the convolution of the following two sequences using the convolution theorem.

$$x[n] = \delta[n] - \delta[n-1]$$

$$y[n] = u[n]$$

28.3 Use the time shift and time reversal theorems to determine the z-transform of the following sequence.

$$x[n] = \left(-\tfrac{1}{2}\right)^{|n|}$$

28.4 Determine the z-transform of the sequence $x[n] = n^2 u[n]$ using the z-domain differentiation theorem.

28.5 Consider a z-transform $X(z)$ whose pole-zero plot is as shown.

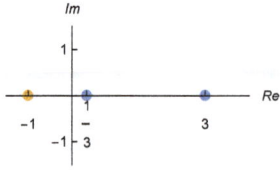

If it is known that the Fourier transform exists, determine the ROC and whether the corresponding sequence is right sided, left sided, or two sided.

28.6 Consider a z-transform $X(z)$ whose pole-zero plot and ROC ($|z| > 3$) are shown.

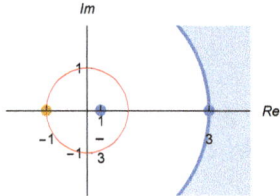

Can the pole-zero plot and the ROC shown represent a sequence that is both stable and causal?

29 | Unilateral z-Transform

In contrast to the bilateral z-transform considered thus far, the unilateral transform is defined as follows

$$X(z) = \sum_{n=0}^{\infty} x[n]\, z^{-n}$$

The unilateral z-transform assumes right-sided sequences, and, therefore, the region of convergence (ROC) is the exterior to a circle defined by the pole farthest away from the origin of the z-plane.

The unilateral z-transform is mainly used in solving systems described by linear constant coefficient difference equations with nonzero initial conditions.

Unilateral z-Transform—Time-Shift Property

The time-shift property for the unilateral z-transform is different from the same property for the bilateral transform.

In order to derive the new property, consider a sequence $x[n]$ with z-transform $X(z)$ and let

$$y[n] = x[n - 1]$$

Then the unilateral transform returns:

In[•]:=**ZTransform [x [n − 1] , n , z]**

Out[•]=$X[-1] + \dfrac{\text{ZTransform}[x[n], n, z]}{z}$

The transform of a two-step delayed sequence $x[n - 2]$ is:

In[•]:=**ZTransform [x [n − 2] , n , z]**

Out[•]=$X[-2] + \dfrac{x[-1]}{z} + \dfrac{\text{ZTransform}[x[n], n, z]}{z^2}$

More generally, for $m > 0$ and

$$y[n] = x[n - m]$$

one gets

$$Y(z) = x[-m] + x[-m + 1] z^{-1} + \ldots + x[-1] z^{-m+1} + z^{-m} X(z)$$

Step-by-step

The derivation of the result for a one-step delay proceeds as follows.

Begin with the transform definition

$$Y(z) = \sum_{n=0}^{\infty} y[n] z^{-n}$$

$$= \sum_{n=0}^{\infty} x[n - 1] z^{-n}$$

With the variable substitution $m = n - 1$, you get

$$Y(z) = \sum_{m=-1}^{\infty} x[m] z^{-(m+1)}$$

Extract the $m = -1$ term from the summation

$$= x[-1] z^0 + \sum_{m=0}^{\infty} x[m] z^{-m-1}$$

$$= x[-1] + z^{-1} \sum_{m=0}^{\infty} x[m] z^{-m}$$

Finally

$$= x[-1] + z^{-1} X(z)$$

Unilateral z-Transform and Initial Value Problems

The time-shift property of the unilateral transform permits the inclusion of initial conditions when transforming difference equations into algebraic equations in the z-domain. It thus serves as the basis for the application of the z-transform to solving difference equations with initial conditions, the so-called initial value problems. Several examples follow.

Example 1

Use the unilateral z-transform to solve the following initial value problem

$$y[n] - y[n - 1] - y[n - 2] = 0, \qquad y[-2] = 0, \; y[-1] = 1$$

Solution

Applying the unilateral z-transform to the difference equation gives

$$\mathcal{Z}\{y[n]\} - \mathcal{Z}\{y[n-1]\} - \mathcal{Z}\{y[n-2]\} = 0$$

$$Y(z) - \left(y[-1] + z^{-1}\, Y(z)\right) - \left(y[-2] + y[-1]\, z^{-1} + z^{-2}\, Y(z)\right) = 0$$

Substituting initial conditions and rearranging, you get

$$\left(1 - z^{-1} - z^{-2}\right) Y(z) = 1 + z^{-1}$$

$$Y(z) = \frac{1+z^{-1}}{1-z^{-1}-z^{-2}}$$

The inverse z-transform returns the following response:

In[•]:= **y [n_] = InverseZTransform [** $\dfrac{1 + z^{-1}}{1 - z^{-1} - z^{-2}}$ **, z, n]**

Out[•]= $\dfrac{2^{-1-n}\left(\left(1 - \sqrt{5}\right)^{n}\left(-3 + \sqrt{5}\right) + \left(1 + \sqrt{5}\right)^{n}\left(3 + \sqrt{5}\right)\right)}{\sqrt{5}}$

The solution gives the famous Fibonacci sequence. Here are the first few values:

In[•]:= **Table [y [n] , { n , -2, 10 }] / / FullSimplify**

Out[•]= { 0, 1, 1, 2, 3, 5, 8, 13, 21, 34, 55, 89, 144 }

Step-by-step

The z-transform in positive powers of z is:

In[•]:= **Y [z_] :=** $\dfrac{z^2 + z}{z^2 - z - 1}$ **;**

The denominator roots are:

In[•]:= **Roots [$z^2 - z - 1 == 0$, z]**

Out[•]= z == $\dfrac{1}{2}\left(1 - \sqrt{5}\right)$ | | z == $\dfrac{1}{2}\left(1 + \sqrt{5}\right)$

Partial fraction decomposition yields

$$\frac{Y(z)}{z} = A_1\,\frac{1}{z - \frac{1}{2}\left(1 - \sqrt{5}\right)} + A_2\,\frac{1}{z - \frac{1}{2}\left(1 + \sqrt{5}\right)}$$

A_1 residue:

In[•]:= **Limit [(z -** $\dfrac{1}{2}$ **(1 -** $\sqrt{5}$ **))** $\dfrac{Y[z]}{z}$ **, z →** $\dfrac{1}{2}$ **(1 -** $\sqrt{5}$ **)] / / Simplify**

Out[•]= $\dfrac{1}{10}\left(5 - 3\,\sqrt{5}\right)$

A_2 residue:

In[•]:=**Limit** [$(z - \frac{1}{2} (1 + \sqrt{5}))$ $\dfrac{Y[z]}{z}$, $z \to \frac{1}{2} (1 + \sqrt{5})$] **//** **Simplify**

Out[•]=$\dfrac{1}{10} \left(5 + 3 \sqrt{5}\right)$

Finally

$$Y(z) = \frac{1}{10} \left(5 - 3 \sqrt{5}\right) \frac{z}{z - \frac{1}{2}(1 - \sqrt{5})} + \frac{1}{10} \left(5 + 3 \sqrt{5}\right) \frac{z}{z - \frac{1}{2}(1 + \sqrt{5})}$$

And the inverse transform is

$$y[n] = \frac{1}{10} \left(5 - 3 \sqrt{5}\right) \left(\frac{1}{2} \left(1 - \sqrt{5}\right)\right)^n u[n] + \frac{1}{10} \left(5 + 3 \sqrt{5}\right) \left(\frac{1}{2} \left(1 + \sqrt{5}\right)\right)^n u[n]$$

Example 2

Obtain the output of a system defined by the difference equation

$$y[n] - \frac{1}{2} y[n - 1] = x[n]$$

with input $x[n] = \cos\left(\frac{\pi}{2} n\right) u[n]$ and initial condition $y[-1] = 1$.

Solution

Applying the unilateral z-transform and solving for $Y(z)$ gives

$$\mathcal{Z}\{y[n]\} - \mathcal{Z}\left\{\frac{1}{2} y[n - 1]\right\} = \mathcal{Z}\{x[n]\}$$

$$Y(z) - \frac{1}{2} \left(y[-1] + z^{-1} Y(z)\right) = \frac{1}{1+z^{-2}}$$

$$\left(1 - z^{-1}\right) Y(z) = \frac{1}{1+z^{-2}} + \frac{1}{2}$$

$$Y(z) = \frac{3+z^{-2}}{2 \left(1-z^{-1}\right)\left(1+z^{-2}\right)}$$

The z-transform in positive powers of z

$$Y(z) = \frac{3 z^3 + z}{2 (z-1)(z^2+1)}$$

The inverse z-transform returns the following sequence:

In[•]:=**InverseZTransform** [$\dfrac{z + 3 z^3}{2 \ (z - 1) \ (z^2 + 1)}$, z, n, $\boxed{\cdots \to \cdots \ \ast}$] **//** **Expand**

Out[•]=$1 + \left(\dfrac{1}{4} + \dfrac{i}{4}\right) i^{-n} + \left(\dfrac{1}{4} - \dfrac{i}{4}\right) (-1)^n \, i^{-n}$

This shows the input and the output:

In[•]:= **DiscretePlot [{ Cos [** $\dfrac{\pi n}{2}$ **] , 1 + (** $\dfrac{1}{4}$ + $\dfrac{i}{4}$ **) (** $-i$ **)** ^{n} **+ (** $\dfrac{1}{4}$ $-$ $\dfrac{i}{4}$ **)** i^n **},** ⌈ ⋯ ✦ ⌉ **]**

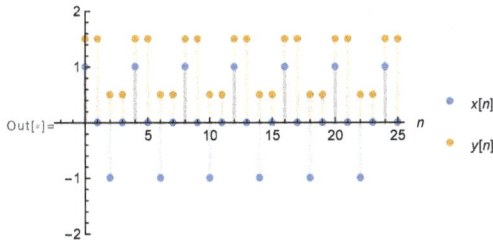

Out[•]=

Step-by-step

The z-transform in positive powers of z is:

In[•]:= **Y [z_] :=** $\dfrac{3 z^3 + z}{2 (z - 1) (z^2 + 1)}$

Partial fraction decomposition yields

$$\frac{Y(z)}{z} = A_1 \frac{1}{z-1} + A_2 \frac{1}{z-j} + A_3 \frac{1}{z+j}$$

The residues:

In[•]:= **Limit [(z - 1)** $\dfrac{Y[z]}{z}$ **, z → 1]**

Out[•]= 1

In[•]:= **Limit [(z -** i **)** $\dfrac{Y[z]}{z}$ **, z →** i **]**

Out[•]= $\dfrac{1}{4} - \dfrac{i}{4}$

In[•]:= **Limit [(z +** i **)** $\dfrac{Y[z]}{z}$ **, z → -** i **]**

Out[•]= $\dfrac{1}{4} + \dfrac{i}{4}$

This gives

$$Y(z) = \frac{z}{z-1} + \left(\frac{1}{4} - \frac{j}{4}\right) \frac{z}{z-j} + \left(\frac{1}{4} + \frac{j}{4}\right) \frac{z}{z+j}$$

And the inverse transform is

$$y[n] = u[n] + \left(\frac{1}{4} - \frac{j}{4}\right) (j)^n u[n] + \left(\frac{1}{4} + \frac{j}{4}\right) (-j)^n u[n]$$

$$= u[n] + \frac{1}{2} \cos\left(\frac{\pi}{2} n\right) + \frac{1}{2} \sin\left(\frac{\pi}{2} n\right)$$

Example 3

Given a linear time-invariant (LTI) system defined by the following difference equation and initial condition

$$y[n] - \frac{1}{2}\, y[n-1] = x[n] - \frac{1}{2}\, x[n-1], \quad y[-1] = 1$$

determine the zero-input and zero-state (with unit step input, $x[n] = u[n]$) responses by using the unilateral z-transform.

Solution

Application of the unilateral z-transform to the difference equation gives

$$\mathcal{Z}\{y[n]\} - \mathcal{Z}\left\{\tfrac{1}{2}\, y[n-1]\right\} = \mathcal{Z}\{x[n]\} - \mathcal{Z}\left\{\tfrac{1}{2}\, x[n-1]\right\}$$

$$Y(z) - \frac{1}{2}\left(y[-1] + z^{-1}\, Y(z)\right) = X(z) - \frac{1}{2}\left(x[-1] + z^{-1}\, X(z)\right)$$

$$\left(1 - \frac{1}{2}\, z^{-1}\right) Y(z) - \frac{1}{2} = \left(1 - \frac{1}{2}\, z^{-1}\right) X(z) - \frac{1}{2}\, x[-1]$$

$$Y(z) = \frac{1}{2}\, y[-1]\, \frac{1}{1-\frac{1}{2}\, z^{-1}} - \frac{1}{2}\, x[-1]\, \frac{1}{1-\frac{1}{2}\, z^{-1}} + X(z)$$

The zero-input response (ZIR) is obtained by setting $X(z) = 0$, $x[-1] = 0$, and $y[-1] = 1$

$$Y_{\text{ZIR}}(z) = \frac{1}{2}\, \frac{1}{1-\frac{1}{2}\, z^{-1}}$$

The inverse z-transform gives the following ZIR:

In[•]:= **yzir [n_]** = **InverseZTransform [** $\dfrac{z}{2\, z - 1}$ **, z, n]**

Out[•]= 2^{-1-n}

The zero-state response (ZSR) is obtained by setting $X(z) = \frac{1}{1-z^{-1}}$, $x[-1] = 0$ and $y[-1] = 0$

$$Y_{\text{ZSR}}(z) = \frac{1}{2}\, \frac{1}{1-\frac{1}{2}\, z^{-1}} + \frac{1}{1-z^{-1}}$$

The inverse z-transform gives the following ZSR:

In[•]:= **yzsr [n_]** = **InverseZTransform [** $\dfrac{z}{2\, z - 1}$ **+** $\dfrac{z}{z - 1}$ **, z, n]**

Out[•]= $1 + 2^{-1-n}$

Summary

The unilateral z-transform was presented as a special case of the bilateral transform.

The unilateral transform finds particular application in solving difference equations.

Several examples of solving difference equations with initial conditions using the z-transform method were shown.

Exercises

Download the solutions manual at wolfr.am/eTextbook-SSSP

29.1 Use the unilateral z-transform to obtain the unit sample response of the system $y[n] - y[n - 1] = x[n]$, with initial condition $y[-1] = 1$.

29.2 Use the unilateral z-transform to obtain the unit step response of the system $y[n] - y[n - 1] = x[n]$, with initial condition $y[-1] = 1$.

29.3 Use the unilateral z-transform to obtain the unit sample response of the system $y[n] - y[n - 2] = x[n]$, with initial conditions $y[-1] = 1$ and $y[-2] = -1$.

29.4 Use the unilateral z-transform to obtain the ZIR of the system $y[n] - y[n - 1] = x[n]$, with initial condition $y[-1] = 1$.

29.5 Use the unilateral z-transform to obtain the ZSR of the system $y[n] - y[n - 1] = \delta[n]$, with initial condition $y[-1] = 1$.

29.6 Use the unilateral z-transform to obtain the unit step response of the system $y[n] - y[n - 1] + \frac{1}{2} y[n - 2] = x[n]$, with initial conditions $y[-1] = 1$ and $y[-2] = 0$.

Sampling and Filter Design

30 | Sampling

Sampling, as presented here, is an operation that leads to a representation of a continuous-time signal by a discrete-time signal. Consider the following signal $x(t)$ and a discrete-time sequence obtained using uniform sampling

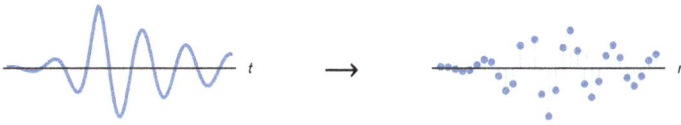

The most common form of sampling is known as uniform sampling, meaning that the samples of the discrete-time signal are uniformly spaced in time or space. The spatial distance between samples is known as the sampling interval or sampling period and its inverse is known as the sampling frequency or sampling rate.

Sampling Theorem

The sampling theorem (commonly called the Shannon or Nyquist–Shannon sampling theorem) is a fundamental result in signal processing.

It gives the conditions under which a sequence of samples uniformly distributed in time fully captures all the information in a band-limited continuous-time signal. The theorem states:

Let $x(t)$ be a band-limited signal with $X(j\omega) = 0$ for $|\omega| > \omega_{MAX}$. Then $x(t)$ is uniquely determined by its samples $x(kT)$, with $k = 0, \pm 1, \pm 2, \ldots$, if and only if it is sampled using the following sampling rate: $\omega_s > 2\,\omega_{max}$. The sampling period is then $T = \frac{2\pi}{\omega_s}$. Given these samples, $x(t)$ can be reconstructed exactly.

The sampling rate that is equal to twice the highest frequency in a continuous-time signal is known as the Nyquist rate.

Example 1

Determine the sampling rate and the sampling period for the continuous-time signal $x(t) = \cos(2\pi t)$.

Solution

Note that the signal $x(t)$ is band limited with maximum frequency $\omega_{max} = 2\pi$. It therefore satisfies the necessary condition of the sampling theorem. The sampling theorem states that the sampling frequency ω_s must be strictly greater than twice the signal's maximum frequency, which gives the following result

$$\omega_s > 4\pi$$

which then gives the following value for the sampling period

$$T = \frac{2\pi}{\omega_s} < \frac{1}{2}$$

For example, using a sampling period of $T = \frac{1}{6}$ on the interval $0 \le t \le 1$ gives the following sequence of samples:

In[•]:= **Table [Cos [2 π t] , { t , 0 , 1 , 1 / 6 }]**

Out[•]= $\left\{ 1, \dfrac{1}{2}, -\dfrac{1}{2}, -1, -\dfrac{1}{2}, \dfrac{1}{2}, 1 \right\}$

This shows the result:

In[•]:= **Show [{•••} +]**

Out[•]=

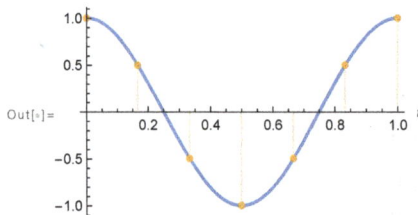

Sampling Theorem (Cont.)

To better understand the sampling frequency condition, it is necessary to obtain the continuous-time Fourier transform (CTFT) of the sampled signal. The derivation proceeds as follows.

Consider a signal $x(t)$ that is band limited to ω_{MAX} radians/second. Sampling $x(t)$ at a rate of ω_s can be accomplished by multiplying $x(t)$ by an infinite impulse train

$$\delta_T(t) = \sum_{k=-\infty}^{\infty} \delta(t - kT)$$

The impulse train consists of unit impulses repeating every T seconds:

In[•]:=**Graphics [** ⋯ + **]**

Out[•]=

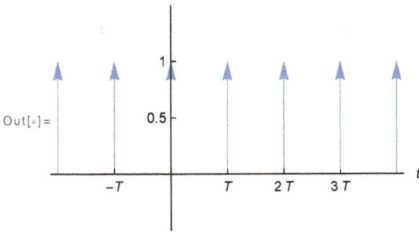

The resulting sampled signal $x_\delta(t)$ is also an impulse train

$$x_\delta(t) = x(t)\, \delta_T(t)$$

$$= x(t) \sum_{k=-\infty}^{\infty} \delta(t - kT)$$

$$= \sum_{k=-\infty}^{\infty} x(kT)\, \delta(t - kT)$$

This shows the amplitude-modulated impulse train $x_\delta(t)$:

In[•]:=**Show [** {⋯} + **]**

Out[•]=

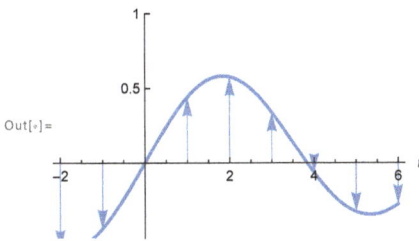

The Fourier transform of the signal $x_\delta(t)$ may now be obtained by making use of the Fourier transform time multiplication theorem (the symbol * denotes convolution)

$$X_\delta(j\omega) = \frac{1}{2\pi} \mathcal{F}\{x(t)\} * \mathcal{F}\{x_\delta(t)\}$$

$$= \frac{1}{2\pi} X(j\omega) * \left(2\pi \sum_{k=-\infty}^{\infty} \frac{1}{T} \delta\left(\omega - k\frac{2\pi}{T}\right)\right)$$

$$= \frac{1}{T} \sum_{k=-\infty}^{\infty} X(j(\omega - k\omega_s))$$

This expands the sum for a few values of index k

$$X_\delta(j\omega) = \frac{1}{T} (\dots + X(j(\omega + \omega_s)) + X(j\omega) + X(j(\omega - \omega_s)) + X(j(\omega - 2\omega_s)) + \dots)$$

In conclusion, the spectrum of a sampled signal is a superposition of shifted (and scaled) copies of the spectrum of the original continuous-time signal.

Example 2

Sample the signal $x(t) = \frac{1}{2\pi} \text{sinc}\left(\frac{t}{2}\right)^2$, with Fourier transform $X(j\omega) = \Delta(\omega)$, over the following range of sampling frequencies $1 \leq \omega_s \leq 3$ and observe the spectrum of the sampled signal.

Solution

This shows the continuous-time signal $x(t)$ (left) and its Fourier transform (right):

In[•]:=**GraphicsRow [⋯ +]**

Out[•]=

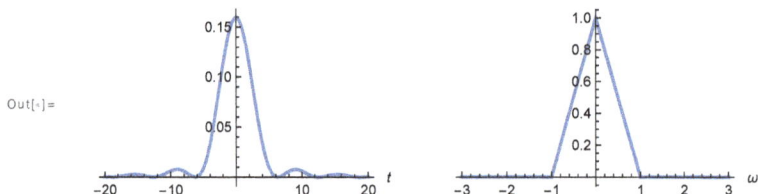

The following shows the sampled signal $x(kT)$ and its Fourier transform. With the sampling frequency set to $\omega_s = 2\omega_{max}$, the so-called Nyquist rate or critical sampling frequency, the Fourier transform forms a contiguous spectrum:

In[•]:=**Manipulate [⋯ +]**

Out[•]=

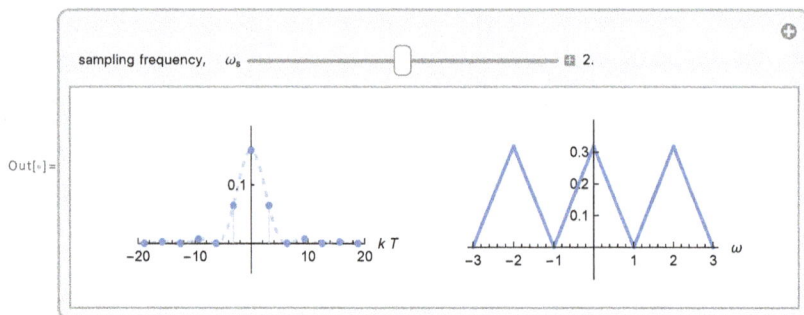

As the sampling frequency is increased, or, equivalently, the sampling period decreased, copies of $X(j\omega)$ move further apart from each other. At sampling frequencies below the Nyquist rate, the neighboring copies of $X(j\omega)$ begin to overlap, leading to the phenomenon known as aliasing.

Aliasing

To explore the aliasing phenomenon in more detail, the cosine signal $x(t) = \cos(t)$ is sampled at two different sampling frequencies, one above the Nyquist rate and one below.

Recall that the Fourier transform of a cosine function is a pair of impulses

$$\cos(\omega_0 t) \longleftrightarrow \pi(\delta(\omega + \omega_0) + \delta(\omega - \omega_0))$$

This shows the signal $x(t)$ and its Fourier transform $X(j\omega)$ with $\omega_0 = 1$:

In[•]:= **GraphicsRow [** ⋯ ✦ **]**

Out[•]=

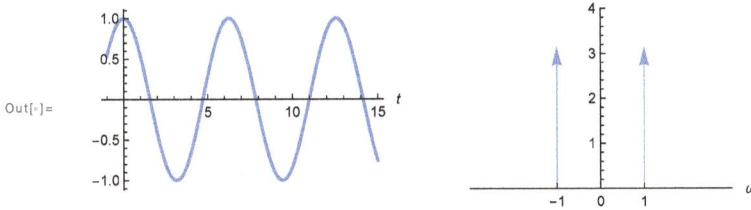

The general formula for the frequency spectrum of a cosine function with fundamental frequency ω_0 sampled at a rate of ω_s radians/second is

$$\cos\left(\omega_0 k \frac{2\pi}{\omega_s}\right) \longleftrightarrow \frac{\omega_s}{2} \sum_{k=-\infty}^{\infty} (\delta(\omega + \omega_0 - k\omega_s) + \delta(\omega - \omega_0 - k\omega_s))$$

Substituting a fundamental frequency of $\omega_0 = 1$ radians/second and a sampling rate of $\omega_s = 3$ radians/second gives the following Fourier transform

$$X(j\omega) = \frac{3}{2} \sum_{k=-\infty}^{\infty} (\delta(\omega + 1 - 3\,k) + \delta(\omega - 1 - 3\,k))$$

This expands the sum for a few values of index k

$$= \frac{3}{2} (\,\dots + \delta(\omega + 4) + \delta(\omega + 2) + \delta(\omega + 1) + \delta(\omega - 1) + \delta(\omega - 2) + \delta(\omega - 4) + \dots)$$

This shows the result of sampling the signal $x(t) = \cos(t)$ with a sampling frequency of $\omega_s = 3$ radians/second:

In[•]:= **GraphicsRow [** ⋯ ✦ **]**

Out[•]=

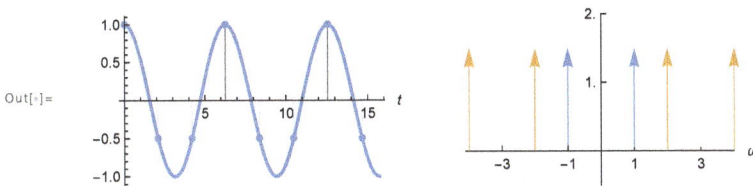

Next, this gives the Fourier spectrum of the sampled signal at the sampling rate of $\omega_s = \frac{3}{2}$ radians/second

$$X(j\omega) = \frac{3}{4} \sum_{k=-\infty}^{\infty} \left(\delta\left(\omega + 1 - \frac{3}{2}\,k\right) + \delta\left(\omega - 1 - \frac{3}{2}\,k\right)\right)$$

This expands the sum for a few values of index k

$$= \frac{3}{4} \left(\,\dots + \delta\left(\omega + \frac{5}{2}\right) + \delta(\omega + 1) + \delta\left(\omega + \frac{1}{2}\right) + \delta\left(\omega - \frac{1}{2}\right) + \delta(\omega - 1) + \delta\left(\omega - \frac{5}{2}\right) + \dots\right)$$

As the sampling frequency ω_s falls below the Nyquist rate, frequencies in the sampled signal may masquerade as lower frequencies than in the original.

For example, the original frequency ω may now manifest itself as frequency $\omega_s - \omega < \omega$. This is now referred to as an alias, and the frequency $\omega_s - \omega$ is called the apparent frequency.

In this example, the aliases are the frequencies at $\omega = \pm\frac{1}{2}$.

This shows the result of sampling the signal $x(t) = \cos(t)$ with a sampling frequency of $\omega_s = \frac{3}{2}$ radians/second:

In[ ]:=**GraphicsRow [⟨ ⋯ + ⟩]**

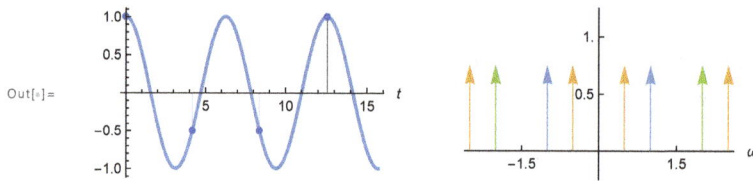

Out[ ]=

Listening to Aliasing

Aliasing can be demonstrated audibly by sampling a simple sinusoidal signal using different sampling rates.

This returns a one-second clip of a sine function of frequency $f = 1209$ Hz, one of the seven frequencies used in dual-tone multi-frequency (DTMF) signals for phone dialing operations, sampled at the standard rate of $f_s = 8000$ samples per second:

```
In[ ]:=sr = 8000;
       a1 = Audio [ Table [ Sin [ 2 1209. Pi / sr n ] + RandomReal [ 0.1 ] ,
             { n, 0, sr / 2 – 1 } ] , SampleRate → sr ]
```

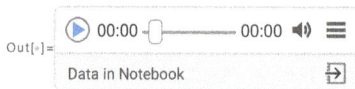

Out[ ]=

This shows the spectrum of the audio signal a1:

In[ ]:=**Periodogram [a1, ⟨ ⋯ → ⋯ + ⟩]**

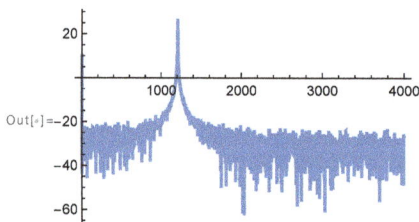

Out[ ]=

Now sample the signal with a sampling rate of 2000 samples/second and listen to the tone:

```
In[•]:=sr = 2000;
    a2 = Audio [ Table [ Sin [ 2 1209. Pi / sr n] + RandomReal [ 0.1] ,
        {n, 0, sr / 2 – 1} ] , SampleRate → sr ]
```

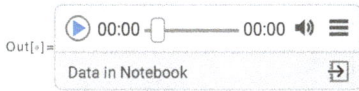

Out[•]=
```
▶ 00:00 ─○──────── 00:00 ◀) ≡
Data in Notebook                  ⇥
```

Does it sound different from the original signal?

Viewing the spectrum shows that the apparent frequency of the sampled signal is now different from $f = 1209$ Hz:

```
In[•]:=Periodogram [ a2, ⋯ → ⋯ ⊕ ]
```

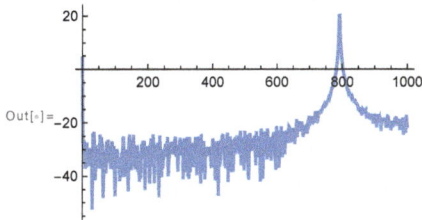

Note that the aliased frequency now manifests itself as the following apparent frequency:

```
In[•]:=2000 – 1209
```

Out[•]=791

Example 3

Consider the case of a signal that is not band limited. Obtain the result of sampling $x(t) = e^{-t} u(t)$ using a sampling period of T. Plot the resulting Fourier spectrum.

Solution

As derived earlier, the spectrum of the signal $x(t)$ is

$$x(t) = e^{-t} u(t) \longleftrightarrow X(j\omega) = \frac{1}{1 + j\omega}$$

This shows the signal $x(t)$ and its magnitude spectrum $|X(j\omega)|$:

In[•]:=**GraphicsRow [⋯ +]**

Out[•]=

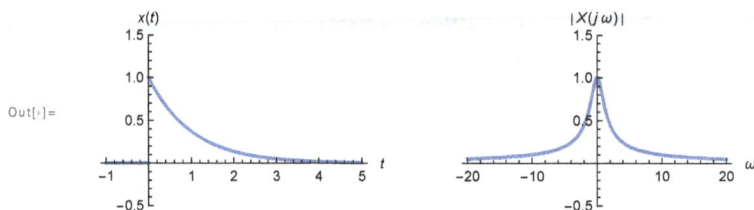

The sampled signal is

$$x(kT) = e^{-kT} u(kT)$$

The spectrum of the impulse sampled signal is a superposition of shifted copies of $X(j\omega)$. Therefore

$$X_\delta(j\omega) = \frac{1}{T} \sum_{k=-\infty}^{\infty} X\left(j\left(\omega - k \frac{2\pi}{T}\right)\right)$$

Since the Fourier transform of the decaying exponential is not band limited, superposition will result in aliasing and distortion. This is demonstrated here:

In[•]:=**DynamicModule [⋯ +]**

Out[•]=

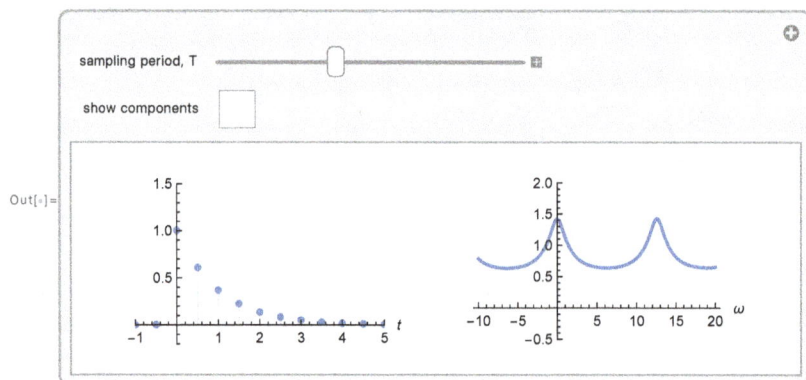

What commonly happens when sampling non-band–limited signals is that the signal is passed through a lowpass filter (anti-aliasing) to suppress frequencies beyond $\omega_s / 2$ prior to sampling to minimize the inevitable distortion arising from any of the aliased frequencies.

Interpolation

Interpolation is the operation of fitting a continuous signal to a set of sample values. It is commonly used to reconstruct either exactly or approximately a signal from its samples.

Ideal interpolation is the perfect recovery of the original continuous-time signal from its samples if and only if the conditions of the sampling theorem were satisfied.

This is accomplished by passing the sampled signal $X_\delta(j\omega)$ through an ideal lowpass filter $S(j\omega)$

$$X(j\omega) = S(j\omega) \cdot X_\delta(j\omega)$$

The ideal lowpass filter has a cutoff of $\omega_c = \frac{\omega_s}{2} = \frac{\pi}{T}$, where ω_s is the sampling frequency and T is the sampling period

$$S(j\omega) = \begin{cases} 1, & |\omega| < \omega_c \\ 0, & \text{else} \end{cases}$$

The ideal lowpass filter is an ideal interpolator in the sense that it reconstructs the original signal at all points on the real domain exactly.

Ideal Interpolation

The impulse response of the ideal interpolator is the sinc function; therefore, ideal interpolation is a convolution of the sampled signal with a sinc function (* denotes convolution)

$$x(t) = \left(\sum_{k=-\infty}^{\infty} x(kT)\, \delta(t - kT) \right) * \mathrm{sinc}\left(\frac{\pi}{T} t \right)$$

which simplifies to a superposition of scaled and shifted sinc functions

$$x(t) = \sum_{k=-\infty}^{\infty} x(kT)\, \mathrm{sinc}\left(\frac{\pi}{T}(t - kT) \right)$$

For example, given the following samples

$$x(kT) = \begin{cases} 1, & k = 0 \\ \frac{1}{2}, & k = 1 \\ -1, & k = 2 \\ 0, & \text{otherwise} \end{cases}$$

the resulting signal, with $T = 1$, is

$$x(t) = \mathrm{sinc}(\pi t) + \left(\frac{1}{2} \right) \mathrm{sinc}(\pi(t - 1)) + (-1)\mathrm{sinc}(\pi(t - 2))$$

The three samples give rise to the following three scaled and shifted sinc signals:

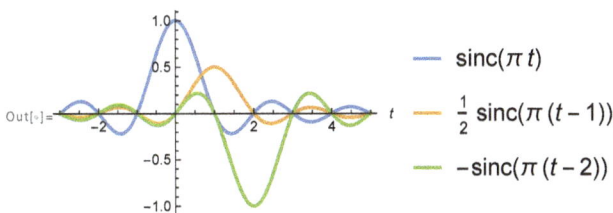

Their superposition gives the original continuous-time signal:

In[•]:=**Plot [Sinc [π t] + $\dfrac{1}{2}$ Sinc [π (t – 1)] – Sinc [π (t – 2)],** ⋯ **+]**

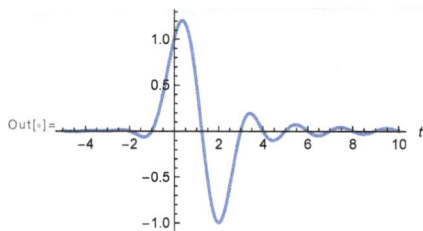

Out[•]=

Example 4

Obtain the continuous-time signal $x(t)$ given the following impulse sampled data values and a sampling period of $T = 1$

$$x(kT) = \begin{cases} -1, & k = 0 \\ 2, & k = 1 \\ 3, & k = 2 \\ 3, & k = 3 \\ 1, & k = 4 \\ 0, & \text{otherwise} \end{cases}$$

Solution

This defines the sample values:

In[•]:=**v = { –1, 2, 3, 3, 1};**

Ideal interpolation gives the following continuous-time function $x(t)$:

In[•]:=**x [t_] = Sum [v〚k〛 Sinc [π (t – k + 1)], {k, 5}]**

Out[•]=Sinc [π (–4 + t)] + 3 Sinc [π (–3 + t)] +
  3 Sinc [π (–2 + t)] + 2 Sinc [π (–1 + t)] – Sinc [π t]

Here is a plot of the result:

In[•]:=**Plot [x [t],** ⋯ **+]**

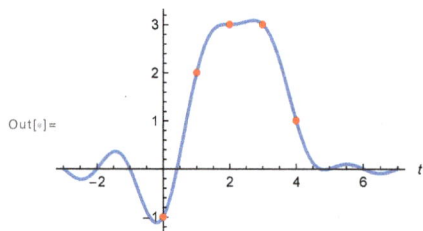

Out[•]=

Other Interpolation Methods

The ideal interpolating function cannot be used in practice because of its infinite support.

All practical interpolating functions (commonly called kernels) have finite support. Here are some typical examples

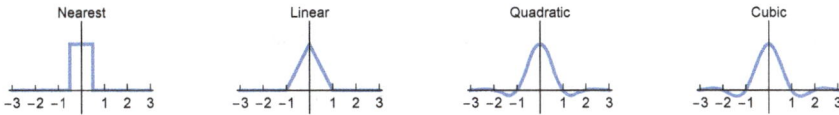

Interpolation with kernels, such as the ones shown, is based on the same formulation as in the case of ideal sampling with a particular kernel function, denoted here as $\phi(t)$, replacing the infinite-duration sinc function

$$x(t) = \sum_{k=1}^{n} x(kT)\,\phi(t-k)$$

The function $\phi(t)$ is an interpolating kernel with local support and the following important property

$$\phi(k) = \begin{cases} 1, & k = 0 \\ 0, & k = \pm 1, \pm 2, \pm 3, \ \ldots \end{cases}$$

Frequently, the interpolating kernel is normalized to have unity area (with r denoting the radius of support)

$$\int_{-r}^{r} \phi(t)\,dt = 1$$

This shows the result of interpolating the example sequence with the interpolating kernels shown:

In[•]:=**DynamicModule [⋯ ✦]**

Out[•]=
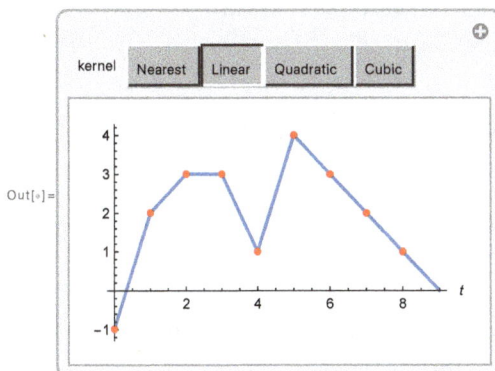

Summary

In this chapter, the complementary operations of sampling and interpolation were presented.

Sampling is used to convert continuous-time signals into sequences suitable for discrete-time processing.

Shannon's sampling theorem was presented and examples of sampling selected signals were shown.

The related concept of aliasing was discussed and its effects were demonstrated with a couple of examples.

Exercises

Download the solutions manual at wolfr.am/eTextbook-SSSP

30.1 A band-limited signal with bandwidth $B = 1000$ Hz is to be sampled. Determine the Nyquist rate (in Hz).

30.2 A band-limited signal with bandwidth $B = 10$ Hz is to be sampled. Determine a sampling period that exceeds the requirements of the sampling theorem.

30.3 Sample the signal $x(t) = \sin(2\pi t)$ at the Nyquist rate.

30.4 Determine the Nyquist rate for the following signal.

$x(t) = 1 + \cos(\pi t) + \cos(6\pi t)$

30.5 Determine the Nyquist rate for the following signal.

$x(t) = (1 + \cos(2\pi t))^2$

30.6 If ω_N is the Nyquist sampling rate for signal $x(t)$, determine the Nyquist rate for the following signal.

$y(t) = \frac{d}{dt} x(t)$

30.7 A band-limited signal $x(t)$ has a Fourier spectrum $X(j\omega)$ defined as follows.

$$X(j\omega) = \begin{cases} 1 - |\omega|, & |\omega| < 1 \\ 0, & \text{else} \end{cases}$$

Plot the frequency spectrum of the sampled signal for the following three sampling rates.

A. $\omega_s = 5$

B. $\omega_s = 2$

C. $\omega_s = 3 / 2$

30.8 Find the apparent frequency of a cosine signal with a frequency of $f_0 = 16$ Hz if the sampling rate is 20 samples per second, $f_s = 20$ Hz.

30.9 The spectrum of a signal $x(t)$ with maximum frequency f_{MAX} = 30 Hz is shown here.

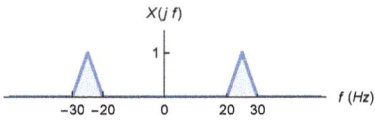

Show the spectrum of the signal sampled at a rate of 60 Hz.

30.10 The spectrum of a signal $x(t)$ with maximum frequency f_{max} = 30 Hz is shown here.

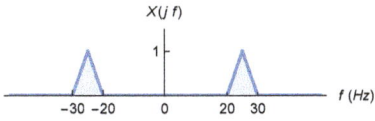

Show the spectrum of the signal sampled at a rate of 20 Hz. Does the sampling result in aliasing?

31 | FIR Filter Design

A popular method of designing finite impulse response (FIR) filters with linear phase suitable for many signal processing applications is the so-called window method. The method requires two steps:

■ Given a desired ideal filter specification in the frequency domain, compute the impulse response by way of the inverse discrete-time Fourier transform (DTFT).

■ Truncate or reshape the infinite impulse response (IIR) by means of an appropriate window sequence.

Ideal Lowpass Filter

The goal is to design a lowpass filter with a cutoff frequency of ω_c. Here is the definition of a so-called zero-phase ideal lowpass filter

$$H_{\text{ideal}}\!\left(e^{j\omega}\right) = \begin{cases} 1, & |\omega| \le \omega_c \\ 0, & \text{else} \end{cases}, \qquad -\pi \le \omega \le \pi$$

This shows the magnitude spectrum of the lowpass filter:

In[◦]:= **Plot [UnitBox [$\dfrac{\omega}{2}$] , $\boxed{\cdots\ +}$]**

Out[◦]=

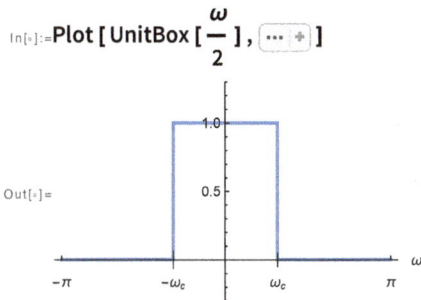

Recall that the unit sample response is the inverse DTFT of $H_{\text{ideal}}\!\left(e^{j\omega}\right)$

$$h_{\text{ideal}}[n] = \frac{1}{2\pi} \int_{-\omega_c}^{\omega_c} e^{j\omega n}\, d\omega$$

$$= \frac{1}{2\pi} \frac{1}{jn} \left(e^{j\omega_c n} - e^{-j\omega_c n} \right)$$

$$= \frac{\sin(\omega_c n)}{n\pi}$$

$$= \frac{\omega_c}{\pi} \operatorname{sinc}(\omega_c n)$$

This shows a short segment of the impulse response for $\omega_c = \frac{\pi}{3}$:

In[·]:= **DiscretePlot** $\left[\frac{1}{3} \text{ Sinc}\left[\frac{\pi n}{3}\right], \boxed{\cdots +}\right]$

Out[·]=

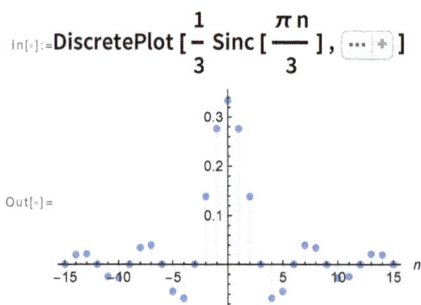

The unit sample response is infinite and non-causal, and thus cannot be used to realize a practical filter.

Lowpass FIR Filter

An approximation of the ideal frequency response can be obtained by simply truncating the infinite unit sample response. For example, an FIR filter of length $2\mathcal{N} + 1$ approximating the ideal lowpass filter can be obtained by using the following truncation

$$h[n] = \begin{cases} h_{\text{ideal}}[n], & -\mathcal{N} \leq n \leq \mathcal{N} \\ 0, & \text{otherwise} \end{cases}$$

This shows the impulse response of an FIR filter of length 17 ($\mathcal{N} = 8$):

In[·]:= **h = Table** $\left[\frac{1}{3} \text{ Sinc}\left[n \frac{\pi}{3}\right] // \text{ N}, \{n, -8, 8\}\right]$;

ListPlot $\left[\text{h}, \boxed{\cdots +}\right]$

Out[·]=

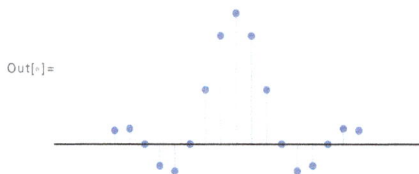

The frequency response $H(e^{j\omega})$ of the FIR filter is

$$H(e^{j\omega}) = \sum_{n=-\mathcal{N}}^{\mathcal{N}} h[n] e^{j\omega n}$$

$$= \frac{1}{3} \sum_{n=-\mathcal{N}}^{\mathcal{N}} \operatorname{sinc}\left(\frac{\pi}{3} n\right) e^{j\omega n}$$

This shows the magnitude response $\left|H(e^{j\omega})\right|$ of the FIR filter and compares it with the ideal filter:

In[ ]:= **H [ω_] = ListFourierSequenceTransform [h, ω] ;**

  Plot [{ UnitStep [$\dfrac{\pi}{3}$ – ω] , Abs [H [ω]] } , ⋯ ➕]

Out[ ]=

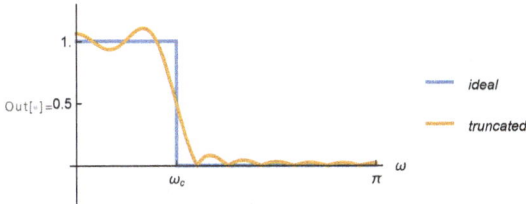

Rectangular Window Sequence

Truncation, as just described, is effectively a multiplication by a finite-length constant sequence $w[n]$ of unit height

$$h[n] = h_{\text{ideal}}[n]w[n]$$

The sequence $w[n]$ used here is commonly known as a rectangular or Dirichlet window

$$w[n] = \begin{cases} 1, & -\mathcal{N} \le n \le \mathcal{N} \\ 0, & \text{else} \end{cases}$$

The DTFT of the rectangular window is

$$W(e^{j\omega}) = \sum_{n=-\mathcal{N}}^{\mathcal{N}} e^{j\omega n} = \frac{-e^{-j\mathcal{N}\omega}+e^{j(\mathcal{N}+1)\omega}}{-1+e^{j\omega}}$$

This shows the magnitude $\left|W(e^{j\omega})\right|$ for $\mathcal{N} = 8$, revealing the familiar sinc function shape:

In[ ]:= **Plot [Abs [$\dfrac{-e^{(-i\,8)\,\omega}+e^{(i\,9)\,\omega}}{17\,(-1+e^{i\,\omega})}$] , ⋯ ➕]**

Out[ ]=

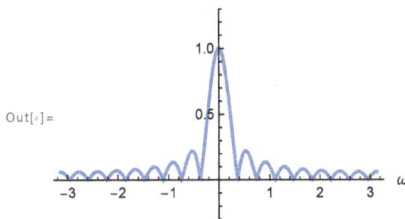

It follows from the DTFT modulation theorem that the Fourier transform of $h[n]$ is a convolution of the desired ideal frequency response $H_{\text{ideal}}(e^{j\omega})$ with $W(e^{j\omega})$

$$H_w(e^{j\omega}) = \frac{1}{2\pi} \int_{-\pi}^{\pi} H_{\text{ideal}}(e^{j\theta}) W(e^{j(\omega-\theta)})\, d\theta$$

Therefore, all FIR filters obtained using truncation, or, equivalently, by applying the rectangular window, will exhibit the characteristic sinc function ripples in their magnitude spectrum.

Magnitude Spectrum of Windowed FIR Filters

The following demonstration shows the frequency response of a lowpass FIR filter truncated using a rectangular window as the length of the window is varied:

In[•]:=**Manipulate [$\left[\begin{array}{c|c} \cdots & + \end{array}\right]$]**

Out[•]=

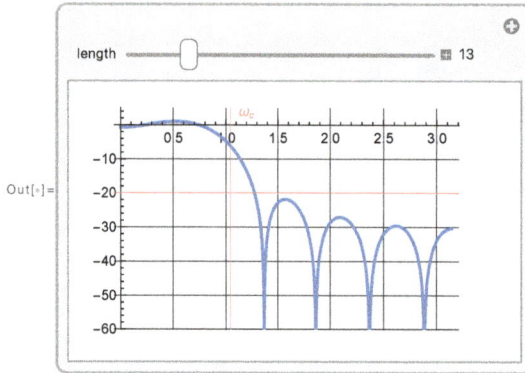

There are two important features of the frequency response to note. First, the height of the stopband sidelobe nearest to the cutoff frequency stays approximately constant at about −20 dB, so it is independent of the length of the filter. Second, the width of the transition region narrows as the length of the filter is increased, so it is dependent on the length of the filter.

Example 1

A shelving equalizer is a piecewise constant allpass filter typically defined over two frequency intervals. Such equalizers are commonly used to amplify audio signals over a selected range of frequencies while leaving the remaining frequencies unchanged.

For example, this defines a so-called low-shelf equalizer that amplifies low signal frequencies

$$H\!\left(e^{j\omega}\right) = \begin{cases} 2 & |\omega| < \frac{\pi}{3} \\ 1, & \text{else} \end{cases}$$

Obtain a length-23 FIR filter that approximates the desired low-shelf equalizer.

Solution

This defines the frequency response function:

In[•]:=**H [ω_] := Piecewise [{ {2, Abs [ω] ≤ π / 3}, {1, π / 3 < Abs [ω] < π} }];**

This returns the unit sample response of the prototype filter:

In[•]:=**InverseFourierSequenceTransform [H [ω] , ω, n]**

Out[•]=$-\dfrac{i\ (-1)^{n}\left(-1+e^{\frac{2\,i\,n\pi}{3}}\right)\left(1+e^{\frac{2\,i\,n\pi}{3}}\right)^{2}}{2\,n\,\pi}$

This gives the value of the impulse response at $n = 0$:

In[•]:=**Limit [%, n $\rightarrow$ 0]**

Out[•]=$\dfrac{4}{3}$

This returns the truncated unit sample response:

In[•]:=**h = Table [If [n == 0, $\dfrac{4}{3}$, $-\dfrac{i\ (-1)^{n}\ (-1+e^{\frac{2\,i\,n\pi}{3}})\ (1+e^{\frac{2\,i\,n\pi}{3}})^{2}}{2\,n\,\pi}$],**
  { n, -11, 11 }] // N // Chop

Out[•]={ -0.0250604, -0.0275664, 0, 0.0344581, 0.0393806, 0, -0.0551329, -0.0689161,
  0, 0.137832, 0.275664, 1.33333, 0.275664, 0.137832, 0, -0.0689161,
  -0.0551329, 0, 0.0393806, 0.0344581, 0, -0.0275664, -0.0250604}

The DTFT of the FIR filter is:

In[•]:=**dtft = ListFourierSequenceTransform [h, ω]**

Out[•]=$-0.0250604 - 0.0275664\ e^{-i\,\omega} + 0.0344581\ e^{-3\,i\,\omega} + 0.0393806\ e^{-4\,i\,\omega} -$
  $0.0551329\ e^{-6\,i\,\omega} - 0.0689161\ e^{-7\,i\,\omega} + 0.137832\ e^{-9\,i\,\omega} +$
  $0.275664\ e^{-10\,i\,\omega} + 1.33333\ e^{-11\,i\,\omega} + 0.275664\ e^{-12\,i\,\omega} + 0.137832\ e^{-13\,i\,\omega} -$
  $0.0689161\ e^{-15\,i\,\omega} - 0.0551329\ e^{-16\,i\,\omega} + 0.0393806\ e^{-18\,i\,\omega} +$
  $0.0344581\ e^{-19\,i\,\omega} - 0.0275664\ e^{-21\,i\,\omega} - 0.0250604\ e^{-22\,i\,\omega}$

The magnitude spectra of the FIR filter and the ideal filter are shown here:

In[•]:=**Plot [Evaluate [{ Abs [H [ω]] , Abs [dtft] }], ⋯ +]**

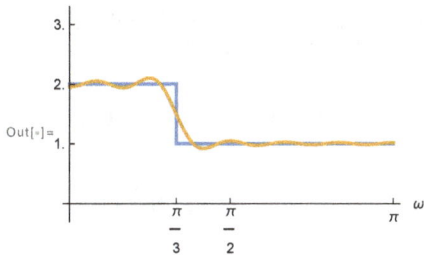

Out[•]=

Common Window Sequences

The stopband attenuation limit of 20 dB achievable with a rectangular window is inadequate in many application areas. For this reason, numerous alternative window sequences have been defined, all of which provide greater attenuation at the cost of wider transition bands.

The following four are the best known and most widely used:

- Bartlett $\qquad w[n] = 1 - \frac{|n|}{\mathcal{N}}$ $\qquad\qquad\qquad\qquad -\mathcal{N} \leq n \leq \mathcal{N}$

- Hann $\qquad\quad w[n] = \frac{1}{2}\left(1 + \cos\left(\frac{2\pi n}{2\mathcal{N}}\right)\right)$ $\qquad\qquad -\mathcal{N} \leq n \leq \mathcal{N}$

- Hamming $\quad w[n] = \frac{25}{46} + \frac{21}{46}\cos\left(\frac{2\pi n}{2\mathcal{N}}\right)$ $\qquad\quad -\mathcal{N} \leq n \leq \mathcal{N}$

- Blackman $\quad w[n] = \frac{21}{50} + \frac{25}{50}\cos\left(\frac{2\pi n}{2\mathcal{N}}\right) + \frac{4}{50}\cos\left(\frac{4\pi n}{2\mathcal{N}}\right)$ $\quad -\mathcal{N} \leq n \leq \mathcal{N}$

This shows the five common window sequences and their magnitude spectra:

In[·]:= **DynamicModule [⋯ + ⚠]**

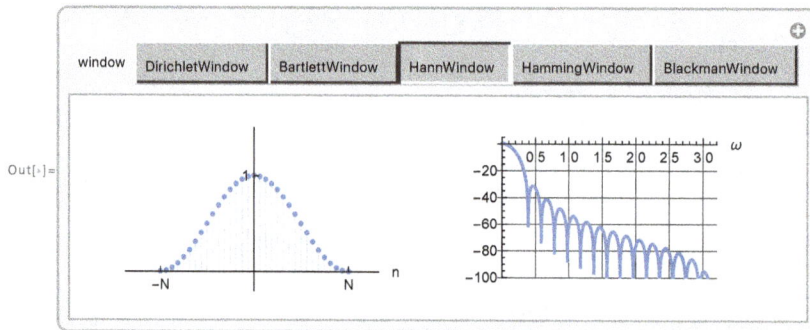

Improved Lowpass FIR Filter

Consider again the FIR lowpass filter with cutoff frequency $\omega_c = \frac{\pi}{3}$ designed earlier by means of a rectangular window of length 17 ($2\mathcal{N} + 1$, with $\mathcal{N} = 8$):

In[·]:= **h = Table [$\frac{1}{3}$ Sinc [n $\frac{\pi}{3}$], {n, -8, 8}] // N // Chop**

Out[·]= { 0.0344581, 0.0393806, 0, -0.0551329, -0.0689161, 0, 0.137832, 0.275664, 0.333333,
0.275664, 0.137832, 0, -0.0689161, -0.0551329, 0, 0.0393806, 0.0344581 }

It is now of interest to replace the rectangular window with a Hamming window and compare the frequency responses of the two filters.

This returns a Hamming window sequence of the same length as the FIR filter:

In[·]:= **w = Array [HammingWindow, Length [h], { -0.5, 0.5 }]**

Out[·]= { 0.0869565, 0.121707, 0.220669, 0.368775, 0.543478,
0.718182, 0.866288, 0.965249, 1., 0.965249, 0.866288,
0.718182, 0.543478, 0.368775, 0.220669, 0.121707, 0.0869565 }

This gives a new FIR filter with attenuation determined by a Hamming window:

In[•]:=**w h**

Out[•]= { 0.00299635, 0.00479291, 0., −0.0203316, −0.0374544,
    0., 0.119402, 0.266085, 0.333333, 0.266085, 0.119402, 0.,
    −0.0374544, −0.0203316, 0., 0.00479291, 0.00299635 }

The DTFTs of the truncated and windowed FIR filters are:

In[•]:=**H [ω_] = ListFourierSequenceTransform [h, ω] ;**
    HW [ω_] = ListFourierSequenceTransform [w h, ω] ;

The resulting magnitude spectra of sequences **h** and **w h** are shown in the following:

In[•]:=**Plot [{ 20 Log10 [Abs [H [ω]]] , 20 Log10 [Abs [HW [ω]]] } , ⋯ ✛]**

Out[•]=

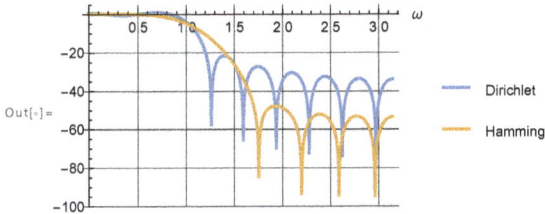

The Hamming window substantially improves stopband attenuation but doubles the transition width of the filter. If needed, the transition width of the new filter may be reduced by increasing the length of the filter. For example, to equal the bandwidth of a filter windowed by a rectangular window of length $2N + 1$, a Hamming window of length $4N + 1$ should be used, thereby almost doubling the length of the filter.

This returns the coefficients of an FIR filter of length 33:

In[•]:=**hnew = Table [$\frac{1}{3}$ Sinc [n $\frac{\pi}{3.}$] , {n, −16, 16}] // Chop**

Out[•]= { −0.017229, 0, 0.0196903, 0.021205, 0, −0.0250604, −0.0275664, 0, 0.0344581,
    0.0393806, 0, −0.0551329, −0.0689161, 0, 0.137832, 0.275664, 0.333333,
    0.275664, 0.137832, 0, −0.0689161, −0.0551329, 0, 0.0393806, 0.0344581,
    0, −0.0275664, −0.0250604, 0, 0.021205, 0.0196903, 0, −0.017229 }

This returns a Hamming window of the same length:

In[•]:=**wnew = Array [HammingWindow, Length [hnew] , { −0.5, 0.5 }]**

Out[•]= { 0.0869565, 0.0957285, 0.121707, 0.163894, 0.220669, 0.289848,
    0.368775, 0.454415, 0.543478, 0.632541, 0.718182, 0.797108, 0.866288,
    0.923062, 0.965249, 0.991228, 1., 0.991228, 0.965249, 0.923062,
    0.866288, 0.797108, 0.718182, 0.632541, 0.543478, 0.454415, 0.368775,
    0.289848, 0.220669, 0.163894, 0.121707, 0.0957285, 0.0869565 }

The DTFTs of the truncated and windowed FIR filters are:

In[•]:=**Hnew [ω_] = ListFourierSequenceTransform [hnew, ω] ;**
    HWnew [ω_] = ListFourierSequenceTransform [wnew hnew, ω] ;

This compares the magnitude spectra of the truncated and windowed FIR filters:

In[•]:=**Plot [{ 20 Log10 [Abs [Hnew [ω]]] , 20 Log10 [Abs [HWnew [ω]]] } , ⋯ +]**

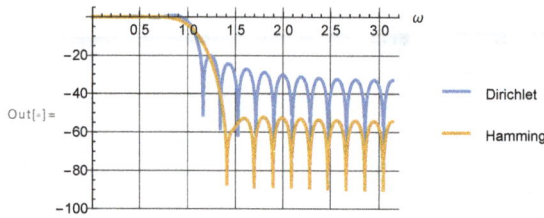

Out[•]=

Example 2

In this example, the goal is to filter an audio clip of a piano key in such a way that all the low frequencies up to and including the fundamental are retained and all the higher harmonics are substantially attenuated.

Here is a clip of the sound of a piano key:

In[•]:=**key =**

This shows the magnitude spectrum of the audio signal:

In[•]:=**Periodogram [key]**

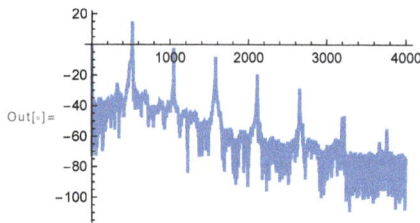

Out[•]=

Solution

Here is a close-up of the fundamental and its first harmonic:

In[•]:=**Periodogram [key, PlotRange → { { 400, 1200 } , Automatic }]**

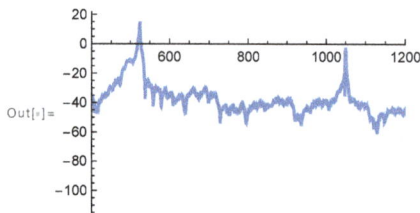

Out[•]=

The desired FIR filter needs to meet the following criteria:

- A cutoff frequency of f_c = 800 Hz, roughly midway between the two frequencies of interest

- The width of the transition band should not exceed Δf = 500 Hz

- Attenuation in the range of the popular Hamming window (approximately A = 54 dB)

As demonstrated earlier, the length of the filter is directly dependent on the width of the transition band and the desired attenuation. A commonly used formula for the length of a lowpass/highpass filter in terms of the values of Δf and A is

$$L = \left\lceil \frac{A-7.95}{14.36} \frac{f_s}{\Delta f} + 1 \right\rceil$$

with f_s denoting the sampling frequency and the symbol $\lceil . \rceil$ the ceiling operator.

This returns an estimate of the length of the FIR filter:

In[•]:= **L = Ceiling [** $\dfrac{54 - 7.95}{14.36}$ $\dfrac{8000}{500}$ **+ 1]**

Out[•]= **53**

This returns the filter coefficients of a lowpass FIR filter of length L with normalized cutoff frequency (in radians/second) and smoothed by a Hamming window:

In[•]:= **h = LeastSquaresFilterKernel [{ "Lowpass", 2 π $\dfrac{800}{8000}$ }, L] ;**

w = Array [HammingWindow, L, { –0.5, 0.5 }] ;
fir = w h;

This evaluates the normalized DTFT of the filter fir:

In[•]:= **H [ω_] = ListFourierSequenceTransform [** $\dfrac{fir}{Total [fir]}$ **, ω] ;**

This plots the magnitude spectrum of the FIR filter:

In[•]:= **Plot [20 Log10 [Abs [H [ω]]], ⋯ +]**

Out[•]=

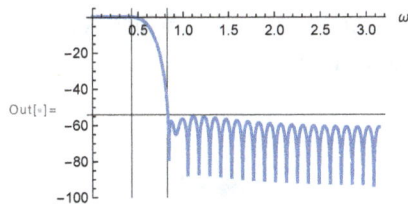

The designed filter can now be applied to the audio signal by means of a convolution. Here, for convenience, the LowpassFilter function is used. Note that the cutoff frequency is given as $2\,\pi\,f_c$ since frequency normalization with respect to the signal's sampling rate is done inside of LowpassFilter:

In[•]:=**res = LowpassFilter [key, 2 π 800, L]**

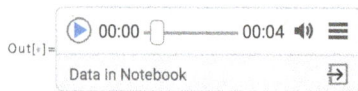

Out[•]=

> ▶ 00:00 ─○─────── 00:04 ◀») ☰
>
> Data in Notebook   ⤵

This compares the magnitude spectra of the two audio clips:

In[•]:=**Periodogram [{ key, res }, ⋯ ✦]**

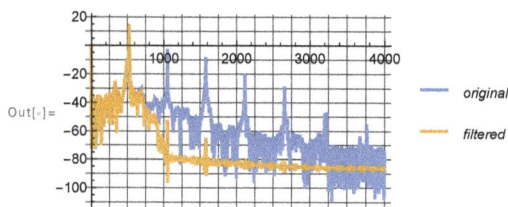

Out[•]=

Adjustable Windows—Kaiser

The window method of FIR filter design can be improved by using adjustable window sequences, the shape of which can be determined directly from the desired stopband attenuation and width of the transition region. One of the most commonly used adjustable window sequences is the so-called Kaiser window.

The discrete-time Kaiser window is defined

$$w[n] = \begin{cases} \dfrac{I_0\left(\alpha\,\sqrt{1.-\left(\frac{n}{N}\right)^2}\right)}{I_0(\alpha)}, & -\mathcal{N} \le n \le \mathcal{N} \\ 0, & \text{else} \end{cases}$$

where I_0 is the zeroth-order modified Bessel function of the first kind and α is an arbitrary, non-negative real number that determines the shape of the window and a tradeoff between mainlobe width and sidelobe level (i.e. attenuation), which is a central decision in FIR filter design using the window method.

This shows the Kaiser window and its magnitude spectrum as a function of the shape parameter α:

In[•]:=**DynamicModule [** ⋯ ⊕ ▲**]**

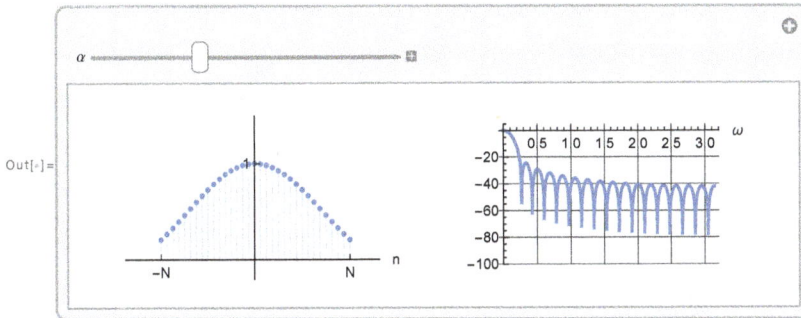

Kaiser Window Parameters

The two window parameters, length L and shape α, are computable from filter specifications. The parameter α controls the stopband attenuation of the FIR filter. Its value given a desired attenuation in decibels was developed by Kaiser (1974)

$$\alpha = \begin{cases} 0.1102\,(A - 8.7), & A > 50 \\ 0.5842\,(A - 21)^{0.4} + 0.07886\,(A - 21), & 21 \le A \le 50 \\ 0, & A < 21 \end{cases}$$

where $A = -20\log_{10}(\delta)$ and δ is a gain value.

The filter's length is computed using the following formula

$$L = \begin{cases} \frac{A-7.95}{2.285\,\Delta\omega} + 1, & A > 21 \\ \frac{5.79}{\Delta\omega} + 1, & A \le 21 \end{cases}$$

where $\Delta\omega = |\omega_p - \omega_s|$ is the normalized transition bandwidth (in radians/second).

Example 3

Calculate the Kaiser window for a desired ripple of $A = 80$ dB and a transition width of $\Delta\omega = 0.2\,\pi$.

Solution

This implements the shape parameter:

```
In[•]:=α [A_] := 0.1102 (A − 8.7)  /; A ≥ 50;
       α [A_] := 0.5842 (A − 21) 0.4 + 0.07886 (A − 21)  /; 21 < A < 50;
       α [A_] := 0. /; A ≤ 21;
```

The shape parameter is:

In[•]:=α [80]

Out[•]=7.85726

This implements the length formula:

In[•]:=Clear [L] ;

$$L [A\_, w\_] := \frac{A - 7.95}{2.285 \, w} + 1 \; / \; ; A > 21$$

$$L [A\_, w\_] := \frac{5.79}{w} - 1 \; / \; ; A \leq 21$$

This calculates the length:

In[•]:=L [80, 0.2 π]

Out[•]=51.1843

This returns an odd-length Kaiser window of length 53:

In[•]:= (w = Array [KaiserWindow [#, α [80]] &,

Ceiling [L [80, 0.2 π]] + 1, { $-\frac{1}{2}, \frac{1}{2}$ }] / / N) / / Short

Out[•]={ 0.00267262, «51», 0.00267262 }

This shows the Kaiser window:

In[•]:=ListPlot [w, ⋯ +]

Out[•]=

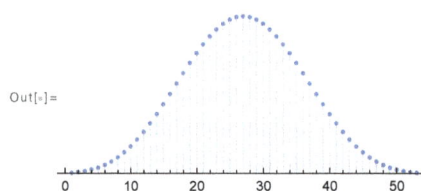

This shows the magnitude of the DTFT of the Kaiser window:

In[•]:=W [ω_] = ListFourierSequenceTransform [$\frac{w}{\text{Total} [w]}$, ω] ;

Plot [20 Log10 [Abs [W [ω]]], ⋯ +]

Out[•]=

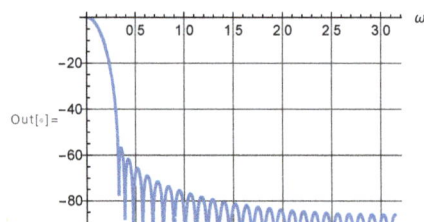

This truncates the unit sample response of an ideal lowpass filter with cutoff frequency $\omega_c = \frac{\pi}{3}$:

In[•]:=**h = Table [$\frac{1}{3}$ Sinc [n $\frac{\pi}{3}$] ,**

        { n , −Floor [Length [w] / 2] , Floor [Length [w] / 2] }] / / N;

The product of the Kaiser window **w** with truncated unit sample response **h** gives the desired FIR filter:

In[•]:=**fir = w h;**

A plot of the magnitude response of the resulting filter shows that it is close to meeting the desired specification:

In[•]:=**H [ω_] = ListFourierSequenceTransform [$\dfrac{\text{fir}}{\text{Total [fir]}}$, ω] ;**

    Plot [20 Log10 [Abs [H [ω]]] , ⋯ +]

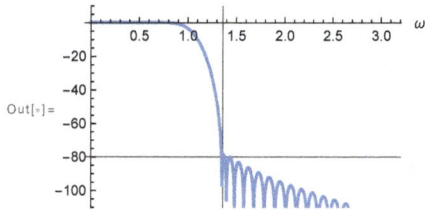

Summary

The window method of FIR filter design was presented.

The method begins with an ideal frequency response prototype of the desired filter.

The inverse DTFT is then used to obtain the impulse response of the ideal filter.

The method continues with the selection of an appropriate fixed or adjustable window that meets the desired attenuation requirements.

Exercises

Download the solutions manual at wolfr.am/eTextbook-SSSP

31.1 Obtain and plot the frequency response of the following FIR filter.

    h = {1, 1, 1, 1, 1} / 5.;

31.2 Obtain and plot the frequency response of the following FIR filter.

    h = {1, 1, 1, 1, 1, 1, 1, 1, 1, 1, 1, 1, 1, 1, 1} / 15.;

31.3 Use a decibel scale to plot the magnitude responses of the filters in Exercises 1 and 2 and compare the magnitudes of the first stopband sidelobes. Does the magnitude change appreciably with filter length?

31.4 Use the method of truncation to obtain a length $L = 3$ FIR filter given the following unit sample response of the ideal filter.

$$h_d[n] = \begin{cases} 0, & n = 0 \\ \frac{(-1)^n}{n}, & n \neq 0 \end{cases}, \qquad -\infty < n < \infty \text{ and } n \in \text{integers}$$

31.5 It is occasionally necessary to create an even-length FIR filter. This typically can be done by evaluating the unit sample response midway between the integers, as shown here.

$L = 6;$

Table $[\, \text{h}\,[\,\text{n}\,]\,,\, \{\,\text{n}, -\dfrac{L-1}{2}, \dfrac{L-1}{2}\,\}\,]$

$$\left\{ h\left[-\frac{5}{2}\right], h\left[-\frac{3}{2}\right], h\left[-\frac{1}{2}\right], h\left[\frac{1}{2}\right], h\left[\frac{3}{2}\right], h\left[\frac{5}{2}\right] \right\}$$

Given the unit sample response $h[n] = \frac{1}{3}\,\text{sinc}\!\left(\frac{\pi}{3}n\right)$, obtain the length $L = 16$ FIR filter and plot its magnitude response.

31.6 The unit sample response of a bandpass filter is defined

$$h_d[n] = \frac{\omega_2}{\pi}\,\text{sinc}(\omega_2 n) - \frac{\omega_1}{\pi}\,\text{sinc}(\omega_1 n)$$

Use the method of truncation to obtain an odd-length ($L = 25$) FIR bandpass filter with $\omega_1 = 0.75$ and $\omega_2 = 1.25$.

31.7 The Hann window is defined

$$w[n] = \frac{1}{2}\left(1 + \cos\!\left(\frac{2\pi n}{2N}\right)\right), \qquad -N \leq n \leq N$$

Obtain the length $L = 25$ ($N = 12$) Hann window and apply it to the FIR filter obtained in Exercise 6. Plot the magnitude responses of the two filters using a decibel scale.

31.8 Determine the Kaiser window shape parameter for a stopband attenuation of $A = 40$ dB.

31.9 Determine the length of a Kaiser window given a stopband attenuation of $A = 40$ dB and a transition width of $\Delta\omega = 0.3\pi$.

31.10 Use the results of Exercises 8 and 9 to obtain an odd-length Kaiser window for an attenuation of $A = 40$ dB and a transition width of $\Delta\omega = 0.3\pi$.

31.11 Use the Kaiser window obtained in Exercise 10 to create a lowpass FIR filter with cutoff frequency $\omega_c = \frac{\pi}{2}$. Plot the filter's magnitude response using the decibel scale.

32 | Butterworth Filter

The design of infinite impulse response (IIR) digital filters is commonly based on a transformation of an analog prototype filter into the desired digital filter. This chapter provides a brief introduction to or a review of analog filters, specifically the Butterworth filter.

Analog filter design usually begins with a specification of the filter's desired frequency response. The filter specification is application dependent and typically requires the determination of the desired passband and stopband frequency ranges and the gains or attenuations in each of the bands. The specification is then used to compute the transfer function of the desired filter, with the specific set of calculations dependent on the filter family selected. The following four classic filters are commonly used: Butterworth, Chebyshev 1, Chebyshev 2, and elliptic.

This shows the typical lowpass squared magnitude response functions of the four filter families

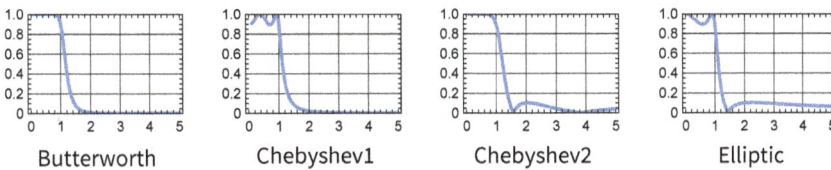

| Butterworth | Chebyshev1 | Chebyshev2 | Elliptic |

The remainder of the chapter is devoted to the popular and widely used Butterworth family of filters.

Frequency Response

Butterworth filters have a smooth magnitude response that decreases or increases monotonically at a rate that can be adjusted to fit most applications.

The magnitude squared response of a lowpass Butterworth filter is given by the following formula

$$|H(j\omega)|^2 = \frac{1}{1+\left(\frac{\omega}{\omega_c}\right)^{2n}}$$

The frequency ω_c is commonly called the cutoff frequency. It is the frequency at which the magnitude spectrum $|H(j\omega_c)| = \frac{1}{\sqrt{2}}$, or, equivalently, $-20\log_{10}|H(j\omega_c)| \approx 3$ dB. The parameter n, known as the filter order, determines the width of the transition region.

This shows $|H(j\omega)|$ for several values of parameter n:

In[•]:= **Plot [** ⬚ **···** ⬚ **+** ⬚ **]**

Out[•]=

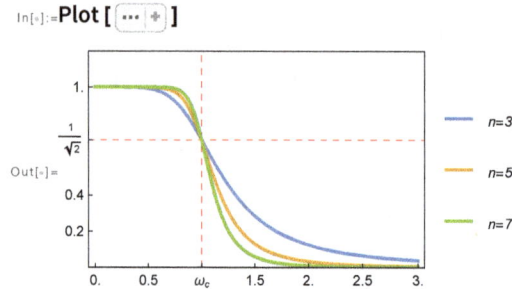

Butterworth filters are a good choice for many filter design needs.

Butterworth Filter Design Procedure

The typical filter specification gives the corner passband and stopband frequencies, ω_p and ω_s, respectively, and the attenuations (gains) in each of the two bands, a_p and a_s, as shown here

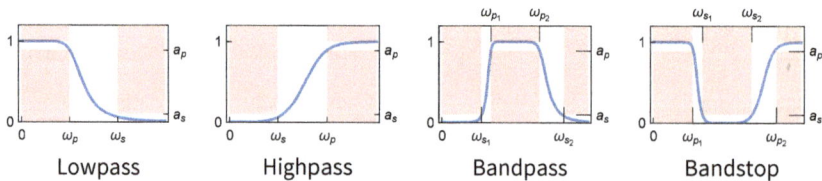

Lowpass   Highpass   Bandpass   Bandstop

For example, consider a lowpass filter with passband and stopband edge frequencies at $f_p = 500$ Hz and $f_s = 1500$ Hz, respectively.

This gives the two frequencies in radians/second:

In[•]:= **{ ωp = 2 π 500, ωs = 2 π 1500 }**

Out[•]= **{ 1000 π, 3000 π }**

Also, assume that the desired passband and stopband gains are $g_p \geq 0.9$ and $g_s \leq 0.1$. These gain values, also known as attenuations, are commonly specified as positive decibel values:

In[•]:= **{ ap = − 20 Log10 [0.9] , as = − 20 Log10 [0.1] }**

Out[•]= **{ 0.91515, 20. }**

The ButterworthFilterModel function returns the desired transfer function:

In[•]:=**tf = ButterworthFilterModel [{ "Lowpass", { ωp, ωs }, { ap, as } } , s] / /
         TransferFunctionExpand / / Chop**

Out[•]=$\left(\dfrac{6.40199 \times 10^{10}}{6.40199 \times 10^{10} + 3.20066 \times 10^{7}\, s + 8000.83\, s^2 + s^3} \right)^{\mathcal{T}}$

This shows the frequency response:

In[•]:=**BodePlot [tf, ⋯ +]**

Out[•]=

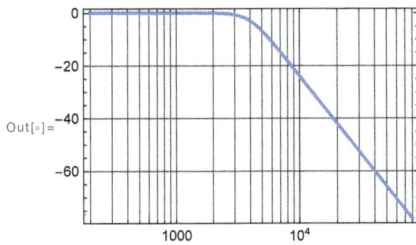

Butterworth Transfer Function

The filter specification permits the calculation of the filter order n

$$n = \frac{1}{2} \log_{10}\!\left(\frac{g_p^{-2}-1}{g_s^{-2}-1} \right) \Big/ \log_{10}\!\left(\frac{\omega_p}{\omega_s} \right)$$

Given the value of n, the stopband gain g_s, and edge frequency ω_s, the following formula gives the cutoff frequency

$$\omega_c = \frac{\omega_s}{\left(g_s^{-2}-1\right)^{\frac{1}{2n}}}$$

Finally, given the filter order n and the cutoff frequency ω_c, the lowpass Butterworth filter transfer function is given by the following formula

$$H(s) \;=\; \frac{\omega_c{}^{n}}{(s-s_0)\,(s-s_1)\,\ldots\,(s-s_{n-1})} \;=\; \frac{\omega_c{}^{n}}{\prod_{k=0}^{n-1}(s-s_k)}$$

where the poles of $H(s)$ are uniformly distributed on a semicircle of radius ω_c in the left-half s-plane.

The poles of $H(s)$ are given by

$$s_k = \omega_c e^{j\frac{\pi}{2n}(2k+n-1)}, \quad k = 1, 2, \ldots, n$$

The denominator of $H(s)$ is known as the Butterworth polynomial of order n.

The system transfer functions of lowpass Butterworth filters of orders $n = 1, 2, \ldots, 5$ (with $\omega_c = 1$) are:

In[•]:=**Table [ButterworthFilterModel [{n, 1.}, s] // TransferFunctionExpand //
        Chop, {n, 5}] // Column**

$$\left(\frac{1.}{1.+s}\right)^{\mathcal{T}}$$

$$\left(\frac{1.}{1.+1.41421\,s+s^2}\right)^{\mathcal{T}}$$

Out[•]=$\left(\frac{1.}{1.+2.\,s+2.\,s^2+s^3}\right)^{\mathcal{T}}$

$$\left(\frac{1.}{1.+2.61313\,s+3.41421\,s^2+2.61313\,s^3+s^4}\right)^{\mathcal{T}}$$

$$\left(\frac{1.}{1.+3.23607\,s+5.23607\,s^2+5.23607\,s^3+3.23607\,s^4+s^5}\right)^{\mathcal{T}}$$

This shows the locations of the poles of Butterworth filters of orders $1 \leq n \leq 5$ (with $\omega_c = 1$):

In[•]:=**GraphicsRow [Table[•••] +]**

Out[•]=
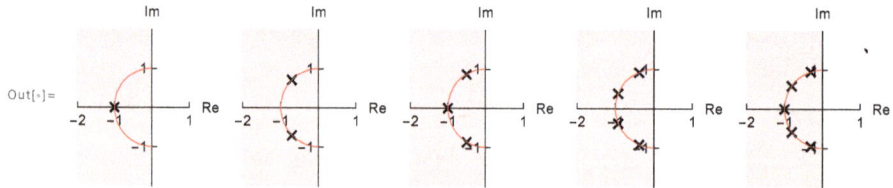

Example 1

Calculate the Butterworth filter poles for $n = 3$ assuming a cutoff frequency of $\omega_c = 1$. Obtain the Butterworth transfer function and plot the magnitude and phase response of the filter.

Solution

The three poles are:

In[•]:=**TransferFunctionPoles [ButterworthFilterModel [{ 3, 1. }, s]]**

Out[•]=$\{\ \{\ \{\ -1.,\ -0.5 - 0.866025\ i\ ,\ -0.5 + 0.866025\ i\ \}\ \}\ \}$

The transfer function is:

In[•]:=**tf = TransferFunctionExpand [ButterworthFilterModel [{ 3, 1. }, s]] / / Chop**

Out[•]=$\left(\dfrac{1.}{1. + 2.\,s + 2.\,s^2 + s^3} \right)^{\tau}$

The magnitude and phase spectra, respectively, are shown here:

In[•]:=**GraphicsRow [BodePlot [tf, ⋯ ✦]]**

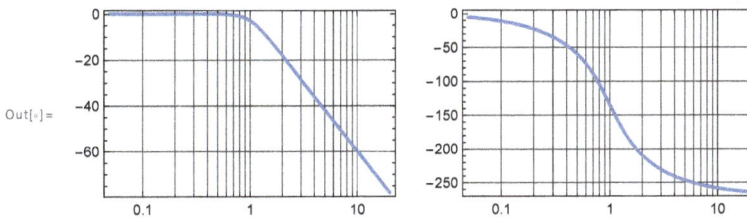

Out[•]=

Step-by-step

For $n = 3$ and $\omega_c = 1$, the three Butterworth poles are

$$s_k = e^{j\left(\frac{\pi}{2n}\,(2k-1)+\frac{\pi}{2}\right)}, \quad k = 1, 2, 3$$

This gives

$$s_1 = e^{j\left(\frac{\pi}{6}+\frac{\pi}{2}\right)} = e^{j\frac{2}{3}\pi} = -\frac{1}{2} + \frac{i\sqrt{3}}{2}$$

$$s_2 = e^{j\left(\frac{\pi}{6}\,3+\frac{\pi}{2}\right)} = e^{j\pi} = -1$$

$$s_3 = e^{j\left(\frac{\pi}{6}\,5+\frac{\pi}{2}\right)} = e^{j\frac{4}{3}\pi} = e^{-j\frac{2}{3}\pi} = -\frac{1}{2} - \frac{i\sqrt{3}}{2}$$

This gives the Butterworth polynomial of order $n = 3$:

In[•]:=**Expand [(s + 1) $\left(s + \dfrac{1}{2} - \dfrac{i\,\sqrt{3}}{2}\right)$ $\left(s + \dfrac{1}{2} + \dfrac{i\,\sqrt{3}}{2}\right)$]**

Out[•]=$1 + 2\,s + 2\,s^2 + s^3$

The Butterworth transfer function is:

In[•]:=**H [s_] := $\dfrac{1}{1 + 2\,s + 2\,s^2 + s^3}$**

The resulting frequency response is:

In[•]:= **GraphicsRow [** ⋯ + **]**

Out[•]=

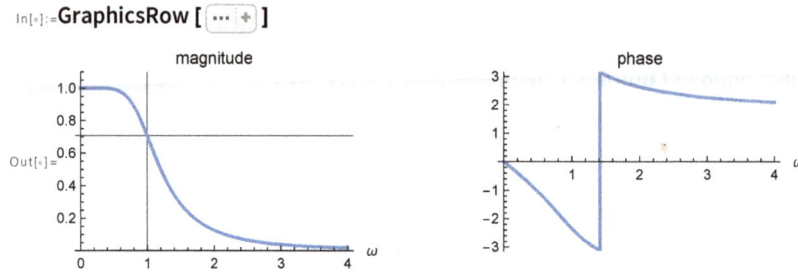

Frequency Transformations

Given a normalized lowpass filter $H_{\mathrm{LP}}(s)$ with cutoff frequency $\omega_c = 1$, the following frequency transformations can be used to obtain filters of type lowpass, highpass, bandpass, and bandstop:

- Lowpass $s \to \dfrac{s}{\omega_c}$

- Highpass $s \to \dfrac{\omega_c}{s}$

- Bandpass $s \to \dfrac{s^2 + \omega_0{}^2}{s\,\omega_\Delta}$, where $\omega_\Delta = \omega_{c_2} - \omega_{c_1}$ and $\omega_0 = \sqrt{\omega_{c_1}\,\omega_{c_2}}$

- Bandstop $s \to \dfrac{s\,\omega_\Delta}{s^2 + \omega_0{}^2}$, where $\omega_\Delta = \omega_{c_2} - \omega_{c_1}$ and $\omega_0 = \sqrt{\omega_{c_1}\,\omega_{c_2}}$

Frequencies ω_c, ω_{c_1}, and ω_{c_2} are the desired cutoff frequencies in the transformed lowpass, highpass, bandpass, and bandstop filters and ω_Δ is the width of the passband and stopband in the bandpass and bandstop filters, respectively.

This shows four transformations of a normalized lowpass Butterworth filter of order $n = 2$:

In[•]:= **Grid [Transpose [{ {** "s → s", "s → $\dfrac{s}{2}$", "s → $\dfrac{2}{s}$", "s → $\dfrac{s^2 + 3}{2\,s}$", "s → $\dfrac{2\,s}{s^2 + 3}$" **}**,

      tfs = Chop [TransferFunctionExpand [#]] & /@

         { tf = ButterworthFilterModel [{ 2, 1 }, s],

            TransferFunctionTransform [$\dfrac{\#}{2}$ &, tf],

            TransferFunctionTransform [$\dfrac{2}{\#}$ &, tf],

            TransferFunctionTransform [$\dfrac{\#^2 + 3}{2\,\#}$ &, tf],

            TransferFunctionTransform [$\dfrac{2\,\#}{\#^2 + 3}$ &, tf] } }]]

$$s \to s \qquad \left(\frac{1}{1+ \sqrt{2}\, s+s^2} \right)^{\mathcal{T}}$$

$$s \to \frac{s}{2} \qquad \left(\frac{4}{4+2\, \sqrt{2}\, s+s^2} \right)^{\mathcal{T}}$$

Out[•]= $\quad s \to \frac{2}{s} \qquad \left(\frac{2\,s^2}{8+4\, \sqrt{2}\, s+2\,s^2} \right)^{\mathcal{T}}$

$$s \to \frac{s^2+3}{2\,s} \quad \left(\frac{4\,s^2}{9+6\, \sqrt{2}\, s+10\,s^2+2\, \sqrt{2}\, s^3+s^4} \right)^{\mathcal{T}}$$

$$s \to \frac{2\,s}{s^2+3} \quad \left(\frac{18+12\,s^2+2\,s^4}{18+12\, \sqrt{2}\, s+20\,s^2+4\, \sqrt{2}\, s^3+2\,s^4} \right)^{\mathcal{T}}$$

This shows the frequency responses of all the filters:

In[•]:= **BodePlot [tfs, ⋯ ⊞]**

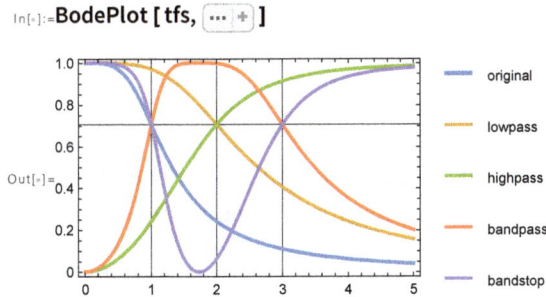

Example 2

Given the following normalized lowpass Butterworth filter

$$H(s) = \frac{1}{1+2s+2s^2+s^3}$$

obtain the transfer function of a highpass filter with cutoff frequency $\Omega_c = 2$ radians/second.

Solution

The transfer function:

In[•]:= **H [s_] :=** $\dfrac{1}{1 + 2\,s + 2\,s^2 + s^3}$

The transformation calls for the substitution $s \to 2/s$:

In[•]:= **H [2 / s] / / Simplify**

Out[•]= $\dfrac{s^3}{8 + 8\,s + 4\,s^2 + s^3}$

This shows the lowpass and highpass Butterworth filters:

In[∘]:=**BodePlot [{ TransferFunctionModel [H [s] , s] ,**

$$\text{TransferFunctionModel [H [} \frac{2}{s} \text{] , s] } , \cdots \boxed{+} \text{]}$$

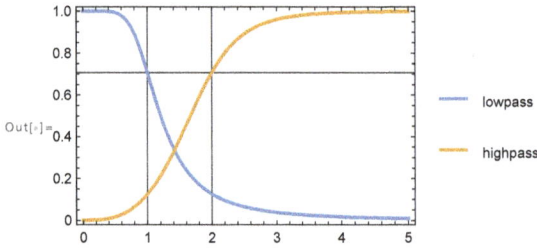

Circuit Configuration

Given a desired transfer function, the immediate next steps include selecting the appropriate circuit configuration and calculating the circuit component values.

The analog circuit designer has a whole array of choices available to implement the desired transfer function.

For example, the following Sallen–Key lowpass unity gain configuration is a good choice for implementing any second-order section of a lowpass transfer function

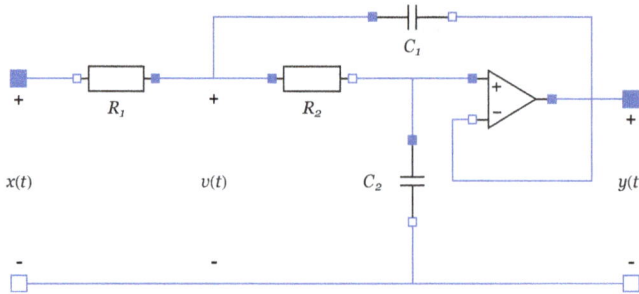

Standard circuit analysis of the shown network results in the following transfer function

$$H(s) = \frac{1}{1+(C_2 R_1 + C_2 R_2)s + C_1 C_2 R_1 R_2 s^2}$$

Circuit Components

The Sallen–Key circuit will be used to realize a lowpass Butterworth filter of order $n = 2$ and cutoff frequency $\omega_c = 1000$ radians/second (or approximately 159 Hz):

In[·]:=**ButterworthFilterModel [{2, 1000 }, s] // TransferFunctionExpand**

Out[·]=$\left(\dfrac{1\,000\,000}{1\,000\,000 + 1000\,\sqrt{2}\,s + s^2} \right)^{\tau}$

This matches the transfer function of the unity gain Sallen–Key circuit with the transfer function of a lowpass Butterworth filter

$$\frac{1}{1+(C_1 R_1+C_1 R_2)s+C_1 C_2 R_1 R_2 s^2} = \frac{1}{1+10^{-3}\,\sqrt{2}\,s+10^{-6}\,s^2}$$

Equating the denominator polynomials gives two equations with four unknowns

$$(C_2 R_1 + C_2 R_2) = \frac{\sqrt{2}}{1000}$$

$$C_1 C_2 R_1 R_2 = \frac{1}{1\,000\,000}$$

To determine the component values, suitable values for two of the unknown components need to be selected followed by a solution of the system of equations for the remaining two.

With the following values for the two capacitors, $C_1 = 0.1\ \mu F$ and $C_2 = 0.047\ \mu F$ (it can be shown that in order to get real resistor values the capacitors must be such that $C_1 \geq 2\,C_2$), the resistor values are:

In[·]:=**sol = Quiet@Solve [{C$_2$ (R$_1$ + R$_2$) == $\sqrt{2}$ / 1000., C$_1$ C$_2$ R$_1$ R$_2$ == 1. 10^{-6},**
        C$_1$ == 0.1 10^{-6}, C$_2$ == 0.047 10^{-6}}, {C$_1$, C$_2$, R$_1$, R$_2$}] // First

Out[·]=$\{C_1 \to 1. \times 10^{-7}, C_2 \to 4.7 \times 10^{-8}, R_1 \to 11\,359.6, R_2 \to 18\,730.\}$

Using standard resistor values, such that $R_1 = 10\ K\Omega$ and $R_2 = 20\ K\Omega$, gives the following transfer function:

In[·]:=**tf = TransferFunctionModel [$\dfrac{1.}{(1. + 1.41\ 10^{-3}\,s + 9.4\ 10^{-7}\,s^2)}$, s];**

This shows the frequency response of the filter:

In[·]:=**BodePlot [tf, ⋯ +]**

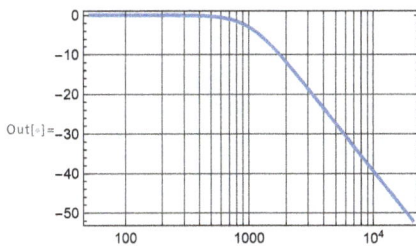

Furthermore, the function OutputResponse can be used to obtain the sinusoidal response, again confirming the 3 dB attenuation of the output $y(t)$ with respect to the input $x(t)$:

In[•]:=**res = OutputResponse [tf, Sin [1000. t] UnitStep [t], { t, 0., 0.05 }];**
       Plot [{ Sin [1000. t] UnitStep [t], res }, ··· +]

Out[•]=

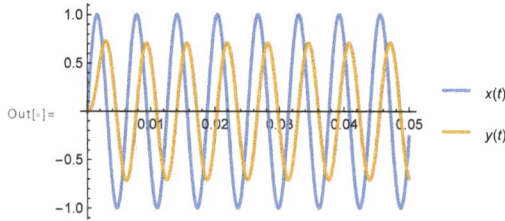

Simulate, Build, and Test

Once the circuit architecture has been selected and the component values calculated, it is common to perform simulation tests prior to building the circuit. For example, this loads a circuit model of the Butterworth filter created in Wolfram System Modeler and displays the circuit diagram:

In[•]:=**model = ImportString [sallenKeyLowpass + , "MO"];**
       model [{ "Diagram", Frame → False, ImageSize → 300 }]

Out[•]=

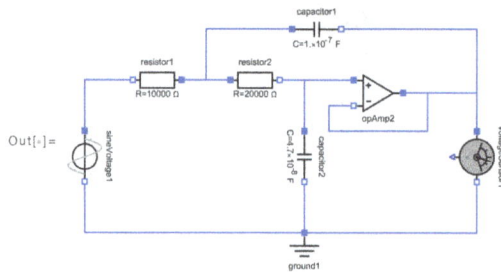

Conveniently, thanks to the tight integration between Mathematica and System Modeler, the model can be simulated and the results plotted immediately:

In[•]:=**SystemModelPlot [model, ··· +]**

Out[•]=

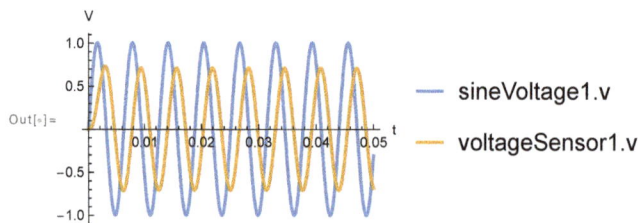

Even better, model parameters can be modified and the model resimulated. For example, the following increases the frequency of the sinusoidal source voltage to 300 Hz. As expected, this further diminishes the amplitude of the output signal:

```
In[·]:=SystemModelPlot [ model, { "sineVoltage1.v", "voltageSensor1.v" },
        0.05, <| "ParameterValues" → { "sineVoltage1.freqHz" → 300 } |>,
        PlotLegends → Automatic ]
```

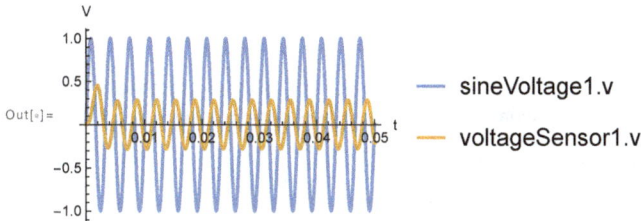

A physical circuit realization completes the design, verification, and implementation process

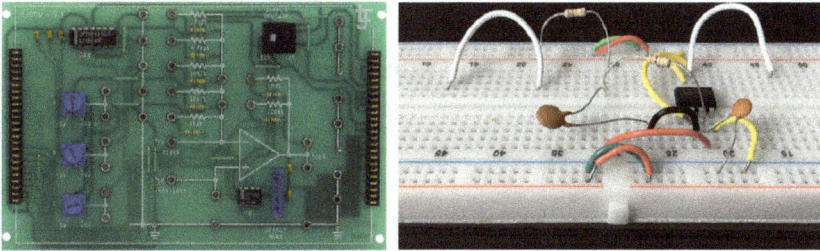

Finally, the physical circuit can be tested using standard laboratory techniques and instrumentation.

Summary

The Butterworth filter, a popular and widely used analog filter, was presented.

Formulas for its magnitude squared response and transfer function were given. For $n = 3$ and $\omega_c = 1$, you get

$$| H(j\omega) |^2 = \frac{1}{1+\omega^6}, \qquad H(s) = \frac{1}{1+2s+2s^2+s^3}$$

The magnitude response of this Butterworth filter is

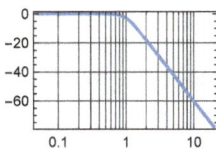

The poles of a lowpass Butterworth filter were shown to lie on a semicircle in the complex plane

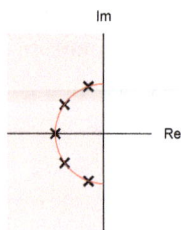

A procedure for determining the circuit components, namely the resistor and capacitor values, for a unity-gain Sallen–Key implementation of a lowpass Butterworth filter of order $n = 2$ was described.

The Butterworth filter was built and simulated in System Modeler.

Exercises

Download the solutions manual at wolfr.am/eTextbook-SSSP

32.1 Plot the magnitude response of a lowpass Butterworth filter of order $n = 3$ with a cutoff frequency of $f_c = 3$ Hz.

32.2 Determine the transfer function of a lowpass Butterworth filter of order $n = 1$ with cutoff frequency $\omega_c = 1$.

32.3 Determine the transfer function of a highpass Butterworth filter of order $n = 1$ with cutoff frequency $\omega_c = 1$.

32.4 Determine the transfer function of a bandpass Butterworth filter with center frequency $\omega = 1$, quality factor $Q = 1$, and $n = 1$.

32.5 Determine the values of n and ω_c for a lowpass Butterworth filter with the following specification.

spec = { { ωp = 2 π 500., ωs = 2 π 1500.}, { gp = 0.95, gs = 0.01} };

32.6 Determine the poles of a lowpass Butterworth filter given $n = 6$ and $\omega_c = 10$. Calculate the magnitudes of all the poles.

32.7 Given the following Butterworth transfer function

tf = ButterworthFilterModel [{3, 1}, s]

$$\left(\frac{1}{(1 + s)\left(\frac{1}{2} - \frac{i\sqrt{3}}{2} + s\right)\left(\frac{1}{2} + \frac{i\sqrt{3}}{2} + s\right)} \right)^{\boxed{\tau}}$$

use frequency transformations to obtain both a lowpass and a highpass filter with cutoff frequency $\omega_c = 10$ radians/second.

33 | IIR Filter Design

Digital infinite impulse response (IIR) filters are typically designed by transforming a continuous-time filter into a discrete-time filter. The transformation most commonly used is the so-called bilinear transformation, also known as Tustin's method. Given a stable and causal analog filter, the transformation returns a stable and causal digital filter while also preserving the order of the filter.

Bilinear Transformation

The bilinear transformation is the following mapping of the s-plane to the z-plane

$$s = \frac{2}{T}\left(\frac{1-z^{-1}}{1+z^{-1}}\right)$$

where T is the sampling period. This transformation maps the imaginary axis in the s-plane to the unit circle in the z-plane

$$j\Omega = \frac{2}{T}\left(\frac{1-e^{-j\omega}}{1+e^{-j\omega}}\right)$$

where Ω and ω denote analog and digital frequencies, respectively. The bilinear transformation also leads to the following nonlinear mapping between the analog and digital frequencies

$$j\Omega = \frac{2}{T}\,\frac{e^{-j\frac{\omega}{2}}\left(e^{j\frac{\omega}{2}}-e^{-j\frac{\omega}{2}}\right)}{e^{-j\frac{\omega}{2}}\left(e^{j\frac{\omega}{2}}+e^{-j\frac{\omega}{2}}\right)}$$

$$j\Omega = \frac{2}{T}\,\frac{2j\sin\left(\frac{\omega}{2}\right)}{2\cos\left(\frac{\omega}{2}\right)}$$

Finally

$$\Omega = \frac{2}{T}\tan\left(\frac{\omega}{2}\right)$$

This relation is also known as the pre-warping transformation and is an essential step in any IIR filter design based on an analog prototype.

The reverse mapping is

$$\omega = 2\arctan\left(\frac{\Omega T}{2}\right)$$

This shows the pre-warping transformation:

In[◦]:=**Plot [2 Tan [ω / 2] , ⋯ ✦]**

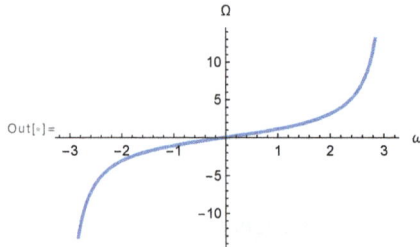

The bilinear transformation guarantees that stable analog filters become stable digital filters. This means that the left-half s-plane must map to the interior of the unit circle in the z-plane and that the imaginary axis $s = j\Omega$ maps to the unit circle $z = e^{j\omega}$.

The following demonstrates this property:

In[◦]:=**DynamicModule [⋯ ✦]**

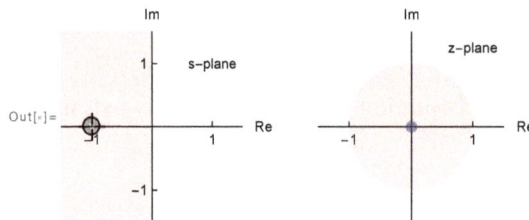

This shows frequencies uniformly distributed on the imaginary axis in the s-plane mapped onto the unit circle in the z-plane:

In[◦]:=**T = 1; Ω = Range [0, 10, 1 / 5] ;**
ComplexListPlot [Exp [i 2 ArcTan [Ω T / 2]] , ⋯ ✦]

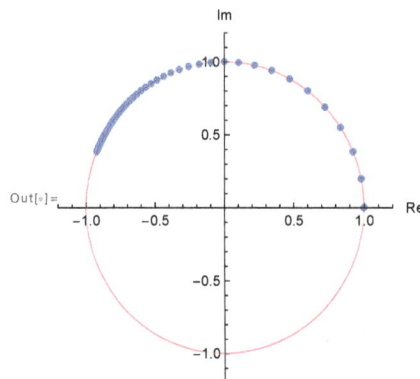

Example 1

The transfer function of an analog filter is given as

$$H(s) \; = \; \frac{1}{s+1}$$

Obtain the corresponding discrete-time filter $G(z)$ using the bilinear transformation with $T = 1$.

Solution

This returns the discrete-time filter:

In[•]:=**T = 1;**

$$\left(\frac{1}{s+1} \; /. \; s \to \frac{2}{T} \left(\frac{1-z^{-1}}{1+z^{-1}}\right)\right) \; / / \; \text{Simplify}$$

Out[•]=$\dfrac{1+z}{-1+3\,z}$

As shown, the bilinear transformation preserves the order of the filter.

Equivalently, this uses the function ToDiscreteTimeModel:

In[•]:=**ToDiscreteTimeModel [TransferFunctionModel [$\dfrac{1}{s+1}$, s] , T, z]**

Out[•]=$\left(\dfrac{1+z}{-1+3\,z}\right)_{1}^{\mathcal{T}}$

This compares the magnitude responses of the two filters, continuous time and discrete time, left to right, respectively highlighting a select number of corresponding frequency-magnitude pairs in the two frequency domains:

In[•]:=**GraphicsRow [⋯ ✦]**

Out[•]=

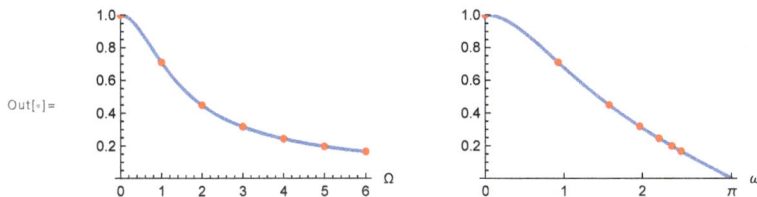

In[•]:=**Clear [Ω] ;**

Example 2

Given a linear time-invariant (LTI) system defined by the following differential equation

$$2\,y''(t) + 2\,y'(t) + y(t) = x(t)$$

use the bilinear transformation to obtain the difference equation model of the corresponding discrete-time system. Assume zero initial conditions.

Solution

Obtain the system transfer function by applying the Laplace transform to the differential equation

$$\mathcal{L}\{2\,y''(t)\} + 2\,\mathcal{L}\{y'(t)\} + \mathcal{L}\{y(t)\} = \mathcal{L}\{x(t)\}$$

$$2\,s^2\,Y(s) + 2\,s\,Y(s) + Y(s) = X(s)$$

$$\left(2\,s^2 + 2\,s + 1\right) Y(s) = X(s)$$

$$H(s) = \frac{Y(s)}{X(s)} = \frac{1}{2\,s^2 + 2\,s + 1}$$

The transfer function of the continuous-time system is:

In[ ]:= **tf = TransferFunctionModel [** $\dfrac{1}{2\,s^2 + 2\,s + 1}$ **, s]**

Out[ ]= $\left(\dfrac{1}{1 + 2\,s + 2\,s^2}\right)^{\!\mathcal{T}}$

This shows the magnitude response of the given system:

In[ ]:= **BodePlot [tf, ⋯ +]**

Out[ ]=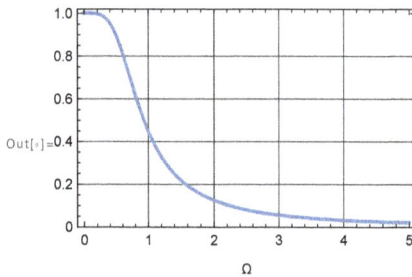

The bilinear transformation returns the following transfer function:

In[ ]:= **dtf = ToDiscreteTimeModel [tf, 1, z]**

Out[ ]= $\left(\dfrac{(1+z)^2}{5 - 14\,z + 13\,z^2}\right)^{\!\mathcal{T}}_{\!1}$

This shows the magnitude response of the discrete-time system:

In[•]:=**BodePlot [dtf, ⋯ ✛]**

Out[•]=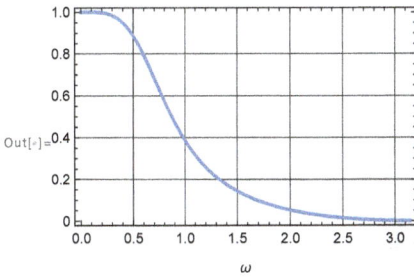

The coefficients of the transfer function imply the following difference equation

$$13\ y[n] - 14\ y[n-1] + 5\ y[n-2] = x[n] + 2\ x[n-1] + x[n-2]$$

This shows the unit sample response:

In[•]:=**sol =**
RecurrenceTable [{ 13 y [n] − 14 y [n − 1] + 5 y [n − 2] == δ_n + 2 δ_{n-1} + δ_{n-2},
y [−1] == 0, y [−2] == 0 }, y [n], { n, 0, 15 }] / / N

Out[•]= { 0.0769231, 0.236686, 0.30223, 0.234446, 0.136237, 0.0565458,
0.00849652, −0.0125983, −0.0168353, −0.0132848, −0.00783161,
−0.0033245, −0.000568071, 0.000666885, 0.000936672, 0.00075223 }

In[•]:=**ListPlot [sol, ⋯ ✛]**

Out[•]=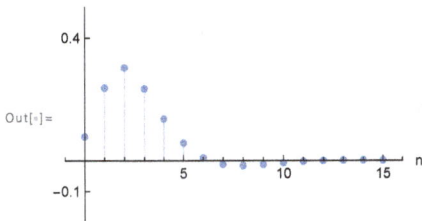

IIR Filter Design Method

The IIR design method begins with a desired magnitude response specification for the digital filter, which prescribes its cutoff frequencies and attenuations. As the first step, the pre-warping transformation

$$\Omega = \frac{2}{T}\ \tan\left(\frac{\omega}{2}\right)$$

is used to determine the corresponding frequencies of the analog filter prototype. Given a specification for the analog filter, traditional analog design methods are employed to determine its transfer function $H_a(s)$.

Once the transfer function is known, the bilinear transformation is used to map the analog filter to the desired digital filter $H_d(z)$

$$H_d(z) = H_a(s)\big|_{s \to \frac{2}{T}\left(\frac{1-z^{-1}}{1+z^{-1}}\right)}$$

A simple example follows.

Example 3

Obtain a second-order IIR lowpass Butterworth filter with cutoff frequency $\omega_c = \pi/3$.

Solution

The design of the IIR filter proceeds as follows.

First, pre-warp the discrete-time frequency using the bilinear transformation to obtain the corresponding analog frequency ($T = 1$):

In[•]:= **T = 1;**

$$\omega_c = \frac{\pi}{3};$$

$$\Omega_c = \frac{2.}{T}\,\text{Tan}\,[\,\frac{\omega_c}{2}\,]$$

Out[•]=1.1547

Second, compute the analog Butterworth transfer function:

In[•]:= **tf = ButterworthFilterModel [{ 2, Ω_c } , s] // TransferFunctionExpand // Chop**

Out[•]=$\left(\dfrac{1.33333}{1.33333 + 1.63299\,s + s^2}\right)^{\mathcal{T}}$

This shows the magnitude response of the analog filter:

In[•]:= **BodePlot [tf, ⋯ ➕]**

Out[•]=

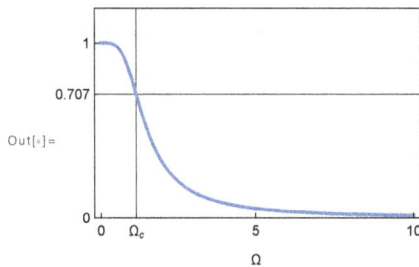

Third, use the bilinear transformation to obtain the transfer function of the digital filter:

In[ ]:= **dtf = ToDiscreteTimeModel [tf, T, z] / / Chop**

Out[ ]=
$$\left(\frac{1.33333 \ (1. + z)^2}{2.06735 - 5.33333 \ z + 8.59932 \ z^2} \right)^{\boxed{\mathcal{T}}}_1$$

This shows the magnitude response of the digital filter:

In[ ]:= **BodePlot [dtf, $\cdots$ $+$]**

Out[ ]=

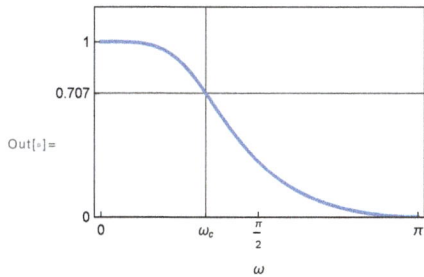

Summary

A common IIR filter design method based on the bilinear transformation was presented

$$s = \frac{2}{T} \left(\frac{1-z^{-1}}{1+z^{-1}} \right)$$

The transformation maps a stable and causal analog filter into a stable and causal discrete-time filter of the same order

$$\left(\frac{1}{1+s} \right)^{\boxed{\mathcal{T}}} \longrightarrow \left(\frac{1+z}{-1+3\,z} \right)^{\boxed{\mathcal{T}}}_1$$

The design of a discrete-time Butterworth filter was described.

Exercises

Download the solutions manual at wolfr.am/eTextbook-SSSP

33.1 Use the bilinear transformation to convert an analog filter given by the following transfer function to an IIR filter.

$$H(s) = \frac{s}{1+s}$$

33.2 Use the bilinear transformation to convert the following analog Butterworth filter to an IIR filter.

tf = ButterworthFilterModel [{3, 1}, s] / / TransferFunctionExpand

$$\left(\frac{1}{1 + 2\,s + 2\,s^2 + s^3} \right)^{\boxed{\mathcal{T}}}$$

33.3 A discrete-time transfer function model of an IIR filter is given.

$$\text{dtf} = \left(\frac{1 + z}{-1 + 3z} \right)_1^{\boxed{\tau}} ;$$

Determine the difference equation model of the filter.

33.4 Determine the unit sample response of the system defined in Exercise 3.

33.5 Obtain a discrete-time lowpass Butterworth filter of order $n = 3$ with a cutoff frequency of $\omega_c = 0.5$. The sampling period is $T = 1$.

33.6 Use the function RecurrenceFilter to apply the lowpass Butterworth filter obtained in Exercise 5 to the image shown here.

img =  ;

Sample Exam

Sample Exam

This sample exam is representative of an end-of-semester final exam in a typical signals and systems course in a four-year undergraduate electrical engineering program accredited by the Accreditation Board for Engineering and Technology (ABET).

Problem 1

Given the following two signals

$$x(t) = u(t), \qquad h(t) = \begin{cases} 1, & -1 \le t \le 0 \\ -1, & 0 < t \le 1 \end{cases}$$

shown here

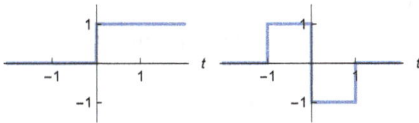

A. Determine the energy of signals $x(t)$ and $h(t)$.

B. Convolve the two signals.

Problem 2

A. Determine the general solution for the step response of a linear time-invariant (LTI) system modeled by the following difference equation and initial conditions.

$$y[n] - \frac{1}{4} y[n-2] = \frac{3}{4} x[n], \qquad y[-1] = 0, \ y[-2] = 1$$

B. Use recursion to obtain the step response for $n = 0, 1, 2$. Compare with the result obtained in (A). Do the two results match?

Problem 3

The periodic signal

$$x(t) = \sin(t)$$

is filtered by a filter with the following frequency response

$$H(j\omega) = \begin{cases} j, & \omega < 0 \\ -j, & \omega > 0 \end{cases}$$

A. Obtain $X(j\omega)$, the Fourier transform of $x(t)$.

B. Plot $|X(j\omega)|$.

C. Plot magnitude $|H(j\omega)|$ and phase $\angle H(j\omega)$.

D. Determine the output signal $y(t)$.

Problem 4

Given a filter defined by the following second-order differential equation

$$y''(t) + y(t) = x(t), \quad y(0) = 0, \ y'(0) = 0$$

A. Determine the filter's impulse response by directly solving the differential equation.

B. Obtain the filter's transfer function $H(s)$.

C. Obtain the filter's poles and zeros and plot them.

D. Obtain the filter's frequency response $H(j\omega)$.

E. Determine the impulse response using the Laplace transform method.

Problem 5

A. Plot the magnitude spectrum $|X(j\omega)|$ of the following continuous-time periodic signal $x(t)$.

$$x(t) = \cos(t) + \frac{1}{2} \cos(3\,t)$$

B. Plot the magnitude spectrum of the signal sampled with sampling frequency $\omega_s = 7$ radians/second. Determine the apparent frequencies of the sampled signal.

C. Plot the magnitude spectrum of the signal sampled with sampling frequency $\omega_s = 5$ radians/second. Determine the apparent frequencies of the sampled signal.

WolframMedia
The Publishing Unit of the Wolfram Group

Join our mailing list for
the latest updates:
wolfr.am/WM-Updates-SignalsMJ

By Stephen Wolfram

> **Predicting the Eclipse:
> A Multimillennium Tale of Computation**

> **The Second Law: Resolving the Mystery of the
> Second Law of Thermodynamics**

> **What Is ChatGPT Doing ...
> and Why Does It Work?**

> **Metamathematics: Foundations
> & Physicalization**

> **Twenty Years of A New Kind of Science**

> **Combinators: A Centennial View**

> **A Project to Find the Fundamental
> Theory of Physics**

> **Adventures of a Computational Explorer**

> **An Elementary Introduction
> to the Wolfram Language**

> **Idea Makers: Personal Perspectives
> on the Lives & Ideas of Some Notable People**

> **A New Kind of Science**

By Other Authors

> **Introduction to Calculus:
> A Computational Approach**
> *John Clark and Devendra Kapadia*

> **Query: Getting Information from Data
> with the Wolfram Language**
> *Seth J. Chandler*

> **Introduction to Machine Learning**
> *Etienne Bernard*

> **A Field Theory of Games: Introduction to
> Decision Process Engineering, Volume 1**
> *Gerald H. Thomas*

> **A Field Theory of Games: Introduction to
> Decision Process Engineering, Volume 2**
> *Gerald H. Thomas*

> **Wolfram Summer School Research Reports 2023**
> *edited by Mohammad Bahrami*

> **The Math(s) Fix:
> An Education Blueprint for the AI Age**
> *Conrad Wolfram*

> **Hands-on Start to Wolfram|Alpha
> Notebook Edition**
> *Cliff Hastings and Kelvin Mischo*

> **Hands-on Start to Wolfram Mathematica
> and Programming with the Wolfram Language**
> *Cliff Hastings, Kelvin Mischo and Michael Morrison*

> **Introduction to Statistics
> with the Wolfram Language**
> *Juan H. Klopper*

> **A Numerical Approach to Real Algebraic
> Curves with the Wolfram Language**
> *Barry H. Dayton*